Hearing Maskanda

Hearing Maskanda

Musical Epistemologies in South Africa

Barbara Titus

BLOOMSBURY ACADEMIC
NEW YORK • LONDON • OXFORD • NEW DELHI • SYDNEY

BLOOMSBURY ACADEMIC
Bloomsbury Publishing Inc
1385 Broadway, New York, NY 10018, USA
50 Bedford Square, London, WC1B 3DP, UK
29 Earlsfort Terrace, Dublin 2, Ireland

BLOOMSBURY, BLOOMSBURY ACADEMIC and the Diana logo
are trademarks of Bloomsbury Publishing Plc

First published in the United States of America 2022
This paperback edition published 2023

Copyright © Barbara Titus, 2022

Cover design: Louise Dugdale
Cover image: Busi Mhlongo holding her *undondolo* (walking stick)
during performance. (Photo by Leon Morris/Redferns/Getty Images)

All rights reserved. No part of this publication may be reproduced or
transmitted in any form or by any means, electronic or mechanical, including
photocopying, recording, or any information storage or retrieval system,
without prior permission in writing from the publishers.

Bloomsbury Publishing Inc does not have any control over, or responsibility for,
any third-party websites referred to or in this book. All internet addresses given in
this book were correct at the time of going to press. The author and publisher
regret any inconvenience caused if addresses have changed or sites have
ceased to exist, but can accept no responsibility for any such changes.

Library of Congress Cataloging-in-Publication Data
Names: Titus, Barbara, 1973- author.
Title: Hearing maskanda : musical epistemologies in South Africa / Barbara Titus.
Description: New York : Bloomsbury Academic, 2021. |
Includes bibliographical references and index. |
Identifiers: LCCN 2021024049 (print) | LCCN 2021024050 (ebook) |
ISBN 9781501377761 (hardback) |
ISBN 9781501377808 (paperback) | ISBN 9781501377778 (epub) |
ISBN 9781501377785 (pdf) | ISBN 9781501377792
Subjects: LCSH: Maskanda–History and criticism. |
Popular music–South Africa–History and criticism. | Zulu (African people)–Music–History and criticism. |
Popular music–Social aspects–South Africa.
Classification: LCC ML3503.S6 T57 2021 (print) | LCC ML3503.S6 (ebook) |
DDC 781.630968–dc23
LC record available at https://lccn.loc.gov/2021024049
LC ebook record available at https://lccn.loc.gov/2021024050

ISBN:	HB:	978-1-5013-7776-1
	PB:	978-1-5013-7780-8
	ePDF:	978-1-5013-7778-5
	eBook:	978-1-5013-7777-8

Typeset by Integra Software Services Pvt. Ltd.

To find out more about our authors and books visit www.bloomsbury.com
and sign up for our newsletters.

To S'kho and Khoni, and the whole Miya family

Contents

List of Figures	viii
Preface	xiii
Introduction: Foregrounding Aural Experiences	1
Part I Maskanda in Colonial, Apartheid and Post-Apartheid South Africa	
1 Maskanda's Colonial, Apartheid and Post-Apartheid Presence	27
2 Foregroundings of Maskanda's Styles and Substyles	47
Part II Maskanda as a Discourse of Power in Post-Apartheid South Africa	
3 Ground Level: The Kushikisha Imbokodo Festival in Durban	69
4 Middle Level: The MTN Onkweni Royal Cultural Festival in Ulundi	91
5 Up Level: Shiyani Ngcobo's Tour through the Netherlands	115
Part III Hearing Maskanda	
6 Knowing Zuluness Aurally	137
7 At Home in the World	163
8 Sharing Aural Space	185
Conclusion: Maskanda Epistemology	203
Appendix: Song Lyrics and Translations	213
References	227
Index	242

Figures

1.1 David Jenkins (a.k.a. Qadasi) (left) with his friend and mentor Maqhinga Radebe, 2015. Photograph by Amy Jenkins. Reproduced with kind permission — 28

1.2 'Sab' Inganono'. Lyrics transcribed and translated by Ignatia Madalane and Elias Nxumalo with kind permission from David Jenkins — 30

1.3 'Sab' Inganono', Jenkins and Band (2011: 00'18"–00'25" and 2013 Pt 1: 01'41"–01'49"). Main melody and harmonic progression in g-mixolydian or d-dorian. Transcribed with kind permission from David Jenkins — 39

1.4 'Sab' Inganono', Jenkins and Band (2013 Pt 2: 00'03"–00'19"). Heterophonic texture and interaction between lead voice, backing chorus and instruments. Transcribed with kind permission from David Jenkins — 40

2.1 Map indicating Tugela River, Mandeni, Msinga, Bergville, Colenso, Mapumulo, Ndwedwe, Durban, Umkomazi, Mpondo, Pietermaritzburg and Johannesburg — 53

2.2 'Sevelina'. Texture and interaction between lead voice and guitar parts (S. Ngcobo 2008a). Transcribed with kind permission from heir Shiyani Ngcobo — 62

2.3 'Izinyembezi'. Voice, lower and upper guitar parts showing the alternation between f-sharp and f, and the insertion of e in the pentatonic scale as well as the presentation of motives A, A', A" and B (S. Ngcobo 2008b). Transcribed with kind permission from heir Shiyani Ngcobo — 63

3.1 S'kho Miya instructs the members of her Abagqugquzeli Band during rehearsal at the Stable Theatre, Warwick Triangle, Durban, 3 October 2008 — 76

3.2 Khoni Miya performs at the Kushikisha Imbokodo Festival — 79

3.3 S'kho Miya performs at the Kushikisha Imbokodo Festival and reappropriates the *ibhodlo*. Photograph by Mageshen Naidoo (S. Miya 2009b: 00'20"ff, 2009c) — 82

3.4a S'kho Miya's Abagqugquzeli/Khombisile Band at the Kushikisha Imbokodo Festival (S. Miya 2009a). Dancers from left to right: S'kho Miya (lead), Bonisiwe Phungula, Dolly Ndlovu, Nontobeko Mtshare, Pinky Mabaso, Barbara 'Nompilo' Titus. — 83

3.4b	The Abagqugquzeli/Khombisile Band prepares for performance at the Kushikisha Imbokodo Festival (S. Miya 2009a). Photographs by Mageshen Naidoo	84
3.5	Barbara Titus and S'kho Miya (right front corner) at Vibe FM, 19 September 2009. Photograph by Selby Ngcobo	87
3.6	DAC Mission Statement at the Kushikisha Imbokodo Festival	88
4.1	S'kho Miya in performance costume at Selby Ngcobo's car during the MORC Festival	96
4.2a–b	S'kho Miya and her Abagqugquzeli Band on stage at the MORC Festival	98–99
4.3	S'kho Miya and Selby Ngcobo after performance at the MORC Festival	100
4.4a–d	Album covers of maskanda releases during, and in the early years after, apartheid	102–103
4.5	S'kho Miya and her Abagqugquzeli band in *umbaselwa* dress. From left to right: Mqapheli Hadebe (1st guitar), S'kho Miya (lead vocals), Mtolo (keyboard), Somnyama Ndabandaba (2nd guitar), Wiseman Chiyi (bass). Khayalethu Mkhize (drums) sits in front of the band in the shade	108
4.6	S'kho Miya teaching the choreography of the song 'Sithi Khuzani' to Barbara Titus, Stable Theatre rehearsal room, Warwick Triangle, Durban. Photograph by Nhlanhla 'Ntshokovane' Shinga (S. Miya 2008b)	110
4.7	'Sithi Khuzani'. Placing of the dance steps in relation to bass and guitar parts (S. Miya 2008b). Transcribed with kind permission from S'kho Miya	111
4.8	'Ya Khulum' Ingoma'. Notation in $\frac{6}{8}$, $\frac{3}{4}$ and $\frac{4}{4}$ metres (Umkomazi Dance Group n.d.)	112
5.1	Advertising material for Shiyani Ngcobo's performance at RASA, Utrecht, the Netherlands	123
5.2	Shiyani Ngcobo and Band in *ubeshu* dress prior to their performance at RASA, Utrecht, 4 June 2010. From left to right: Zwelakhe Mnguni a.k.a. Khetelo (concertina), Njabulo Shabalala (djembe), Marieke Pieters (tour manager), Joseph Bhekizizwe Chiliza (bass), Maureen Bongekile Ngwabe (vocals and dance), Shiyani Ngcobo (lead vocals, guitar)	124
5.3	Lebombo support act consisting of Niels Brouwer (guitar), Phola Mamba (vocals, guitar, mbira) and Sean Bergin (flute, saxophone) at RASA, Utrecht, 4 June 2010	125
5.4	'Asinankomo'. Lyrics transcribed and translated by Ignatia Madalane and Elias Nxumalo (S. Ngcobo 2010d), with kind permission from heir Shiyani Ngcobo	129
5.5	'Asinankomo'. Pentatonic scale derived from two fundamentals. Transcribed with kind permission from heir Shiyani Ngcobo	130

Figures

5.6 'Asinankomo'. Main guitar and bass parts (S. Ngcobo 2010d). Transcribed with kind permission from heir Shiyani Ngcobo 130

6.1 'Inkunzi Emnyama'. Lyrics transcribed and translated by Ignatia Madalane and Bongani Mkhonza (B. Nkwanyana 2014), with kind permission from Bongani Nkwanyana 142

6.2 'Molomolo Mama'. Voice, bow and guitar in the first verse (Mrs Nkwanyana 2009a: 02'00"). Transcribed with kind permission from heir Mrs Nkwanyana 145

6.3 'Inkunzi Emnyama'. Motive A and B (B. Nkwanyana 2014: 00'20"–00'33"). Transcribed with kind permission from Bongani Nkwanyana 146

6.4 'Inkunzi Emnyama'. Motive C (B. Nkwanyana 2014: 01'25"–01'30"). Transcribed with kind permission from Bongani Nkwanyana 147

6.5 'Mthembu kaMthele'. Fundamental E-flat, audible harmonic partials, peak resonances and resulting scale. Transcribed with kind permission from heir Mrs Nkwanyana 150

6.6 'Mthembu kaMthele'. Starting motive sounding through harmonic partials (Mrs Nkwanyana 2009b). Transcribed with kind permission from heir Mrs Nkwanyana 151

6.7 'Mthembu kaMthele'. Starting motive being brought back to a core of 1st/4th (e-flat) and 3rd (b-flat) harmonic partials (with bends to adjacent tones) (Mrs Nkwanyana 2009b). Transcribed with kind permission from heir Mrs Nkwanyana 152

6.8 'Inkunzi Emnyama'. 'Chorus' communications with the ancestor world as an exorcization of the evil competitor (B. Nkwanyana 2014: 02'51"–03'25"). Transcribed with kind permission from Bongani Nkwanyana 153

6.9 'Inkunzi Emnyama'. Motive A" with extension and 'chorus' response (B. Nkwanyana 2014: 02'22"–02'50"), preceding the 'chorus' communication with the ancestor world represented in Figure 6.8. Transcribed with kind permission from Bongani Nkwanyana 153

6.10 'Inkunzi Emnyama'. Intro with horn section and bass (B. Nkwanyana 2009a: 00'00"–00'14"). Transcribed with kind permission from Bongani Nkwanyana 156

6.11 'Inkunzi Emnyama'. Lead voice, guitar and bass in $\frac{6}{8}$ and $\frac{4}{4}$ metre. (B. Nkwanyana 2009a: 00'14"–00'37"). Transcribed with kind permission from Bongani Nkwanyana 157

6.12 'Inkunzi Emnyama'. Transition from Motive C to Motive A" in bass, with involvement of backing chorus and lead voice (B. Nkwanyana

	2009a: 01'30"–01'40"). Transcribed with kind permission from Bongani Nkwanyana	158
6.13	'Wentandane Zobaba'. Multipart rendering in 'rural style' (J. Nkwanyana 2009a: 00'40"). Transcribed with kind permission from heir Josefa Nkwanyana	160
7.1	Marvin Gaye's riff for 'Sexual Healing' (1982) and Shwi noMtekhala's riff for 'Ngafa' (2003). Reproduced with kind permission from Titus 2016a	164
7.2	S'kho Miya's *izibongo* from her album *Ungcayi Lweqhikiza* (S. Miya 2010a: 02'20"), transcribed and translated by Elias Nxumalo and Ignatia Madalane, with kind permission from S'kho Miya	169
7.3	'DJ Gogo'. Lyrics, transcribed and translated by Ignatia Madalane (Majozi 2008)	174–175
7.4	'DJ Gogo'. Bass guitar introduction (Majozi 2008: 00'01"–00'08")	178
7.5	'DJ Gogo'. Twelve-bar blues scheme with changes and *isihlabo* motive (Majozi 2008: 00'13"–00'40")	179
8.1	'Sithi Khuzani'. Melodic shape of the lead voice (S. Miya 2010a: 00'28"–00'36"). Transcribed with kind permission from S'kho Miya	191
8.2	'Sithi Khuzani'. Bass riff (S. Miya 2008b). Transcribed with kind permission from S'kho Miya	191
8.3	'Sithi Khuzani'. Guitar motives suggesting an alternation between two adjacent tones with chromatic additions (S. Miya 2008b). Transcribed with kind permission from S'kho Miya	192
8.4a	'Sithi Khuzani'. Reservoir of motives employed by Guitar 2 in texturing the song (S. Miya 2008b, 2010a). Transcribed with kind permission from S'kho Miya	194
8.4b	'Sithi Khuzani'. Reservoir of motives employed by Guitar 1 in texturing the song (S. Miya 2008b, 2010a). Transcribed with kind permission from S'kho Miya	195
8.5	'Sithi Khuzani'. Ways in which guitarists set their material against lead singer's verse, enabling a heterophonic texture. Transcribed with kind permission from S'kho Miya	196–197
8.6	Jamming in isiZulu style during the break of the Abagqugquzeli rehearsal, Stable Theatre, Durban, 16 September 2008. Guitar picking in $\frac{6}{8}$ metre with alternating E-flat and D-flat tonal orientations, with drumbeats and bass line (Abagqugquzeli 2008: 00'00"–05'20"). Transcribed with kind permission from S'kho Miya	198

8.7 Mbube riff for a jam during the break of the Abagqugquzeli rehearsal, 16 September 2008 (Abagqugquzeli 2008: 06'20"–09'19"). Transcribed with kind permission from S'kho Miya 199

8.8 Marabi riff for a jam during the break of the Abagqugquzeli rehearsal, 16 September 2008 (Abagqugquzeli 2008: 09'34"–11'30"). Transcribed with kind permission from S'kho Miya 200

Preface

This book presents sedimented layers of understanding maskanda music in South Africa. The book's main concern is epistemology: it outlines ways in which people make sense of their world. The roles of sound, music and listening in these practices of sense making can inform us about dynamics of knowledge formation and transmission in a highly unequal world. My motivations for writing the book are intricately entwined with these dynamics. I outline these motivations here in order to introduce myself as a privileged, centralized, but certainly not single author of this book. This (self-centred) introduction in turn serves to culturally and epistemically position myself vis-à-vis the experiences that I documented and construed in this book. Through the book's publication in print, these experiences acquire the status of academic knowledge about maskanda.

These sedimented layers indicate my perennially changing in/ability to tap into maskanda practice and maskanda discourse, into theories about (musical) epistemology and intersectionality, and into histories of colonial, apartheid and post-apartheid South Africa. They also point at the changing worldwide societal engagements with these discourses, theories and histories. In 2007, when I started my fieldwork research, #RhodesMustFall and #BlackLivesMatter were largely unheard of and their agendas remained unseen. In 2021, when this book approaches its manifestation in print, these agendas have radically transformed the perspectives towards the research I carried out during these fourteen years. Mainly due to these shifts, I might not embark on the endeavour now that I embarked on in 2007: setting sail from the Netherlands to South Africa, a country I had never been to and knew little about, in order to research music of the Zulu people.

There is ample literature and non-academic discourse pertaining to the macroscopic conditions that set the terms for the ways in which all maskanda participants were able to interact with each other. These macroscopic conditions include South Africa's apartheid past, Europe's colonial past and present and the continued worldwide extraction of capital from natural resources and (human) bodies. The sounding dimensions of these conditions are increasingly acknowledged and theorized (Ochoa 2016; Radano and Olaniyan 2016; Sykes and Steingo 2019). The white and epistemic privileges I enjoyed during my research are grounded in these macroscopic conditions and impacted on my microscopic analyses. Acknowledging these privileges was an eye-opener and an ear-opener for me then – now it seems an obvious thing to do. Nevertheless, it is imperative that the process of my growing awareness of the unsustainability of these conditions shines through this book. This process surfaces in the various sediments of understandings that I try to articulate, and in the book's critical tone towards the research practices I employ. This criticism is mainly levelled at myself. It forms part of the autoethnographic dimension of the book.

My ascribed and assumed identity as a white female academic from Europe with a PhD in nineteenth-century German music aesthetics was a fundamental parameter for what and how I could learn about a musical genre that many South Africans perceive as black, traditional, body-orientated and virile. It took me a while and some courage to admit that my initial fascination for maskanda was an intellectual rather than an aural one. It satisfied an emotional need for intellectual expansion by engaging with musics that existed at the margins of my cultural horizon and which I hence experienced as exotic. Some more engagement with, and reflection on, my intellectual and emotional propensities is necessary in order to explicate what Tomie Hahn calls 'the embodied knowledge' that I have brought and still bring into the project and that is a resource within the research (Hahn 2007: 10). Julia Byl observes that '[e]thnographers know the interpretative riches their experiences offer' (2014: 4). Yet, there were immense differences and striking similarities in the experiences of the various participants in maskanda practice, including myself. These differences and similarities constitute the material of this book. They indicate that there is an analytical space that needs to be traversed between my embodied knowledge or sensual orientation and the field data I collected (Hahn 2007: 20). In her groundbreaking study of Japanese dance, Hahn discusses this embodied knowledge in the context of her dancing body. In this book, I would like to discuss it in the context of my musicking body (Small 1998: 9) that hears, gazes, sings, dances, analyses, theorizes, asserts, controls and doubts in her capacity as participant-observer-researcher.

My initial fascination for maskanda was embedded in a broader interest I cherished for South Africa generally. I had never been to South Africa when I started googling maskanda musicians (*maskandi*) Zibakwakhe Johnston Mnyandu a.k.a. Phuzekhemisi and Shiyani Ngcobo in 2007. However, I had heard a lot about it through the many South African exiles living in the Netherlands, and via Dutch media extensively covering the Struggle against apartheid in the 1980s. (I happened to know more about this than some of my white South African friends from the same generation.)

During my visits to South Africa, between 2007 and 2019, I increasingly felt that this explicit siding of Dutch media, government and institutions with the aims of the anti-apartheid Struggle in the 1970s and 1980s may have been a form of compensation or even atonement for the Dutch colonial past. The word apartheid, after all, is derived from Dutch. Dutch colonial intervention from 1652 onwards had enabled the organizational and ideological infrastructure of apartheid. On more than one occasion did I discuss with my South African friends from all kinds of backgrounds the remarkable similarities between the Dutch societal structure of 'verzuiling' and the South African apartheid doctrine of 'separate development'. The Dutch verzuiling (pillarization) pertains to the habit and societal norm that all those belonging to a denomination (Protestant, Catholic, socialist, liberal) socially assemble around their own 'zuil' or pillar, having their own (government-funded) schools, universities, unions, political parties, recreational spaces, broadcasting corporations, newspapers, artist representatives/stars and sometimes even neighbourhoods. There was a crucial difference with the apartheid imposition of 'separate development' in that all Dutch pillars were equal to the law and received equal government funding in the Netherlands

– an aspect that the architects of apartheid chose to ignore. Yet, the kinship between these societal structures as well as the age-old cultural, linguistic and familial ties between Dutch and Afrikaner people put the explicit Dutch anti-apartheid rhetoric of the 1970s and 1980s that I was exposed to as a child and a teenager in an interesting light.

Both the Dutch colonial past and the cultural, and notably linguistic, familiarity I experienced between myself and my Afrikaans colleagues and friends fuelled my interest in South Africa, even if my research subject only dealt in passing with expressions of Afrikaans culture. My choice, instead, to research a South African performance practice that was generally presented as having emerged from a situation of displacement and deprivation may have been a personal echo of this Dutch tendency for atonement. This choice also exemplified my position of privilege as a member of the nation that used to colonize Southern Africa. In material, epistemic and socio-cultural respects, I have been enabled to choose whatever I like, and I decided to choose a music, language, custom, culture and socio-economic position that I experienced as different from mine in any way I could imagine.

This tension of privilege in, and atonement for, a colonial condition also has a personal dimension. My unwillingness to keep researching the history of ideas that continues to construe a notion of European 'high art' music – a notion with which I had exclusively engaged myself up to my doctorate – was partly informed by my childhood outside Europe, namely in one of those other major former colonies of the Dutch: Indonesia. My father grew up on a milk farm near Surabaya and had never set foot in the Netherlands before his seventeenth birthday. By that time, he was no longer able to settle permanently in that grey and cold little country by the North Sea, and he managed to get himself a university lectureship in human geography that necessitated him to be in Java at least three months each year for research and teaching at the Universitas Gadjah Mada in Yogyakarta. He always brought his family along, and hence I lived in Yogya for three months per year in the first twelve years of my life, which were periods I intensely kept longing for when I was not there.

Gradually, I got entangled in the fibres of South Africa's traumatized societal fabric. I sensed in my very own daily life the unfairness, the inequalities as well as the perfidious combination of sky-high hopes and a loss of trust among those whom I befriended and loved. Only then did I realize that my upbringing in Indonesia in the 1980s had in many ways been very similar to the upbringing of many white kids in South Africa during that same period. Obviously, Indonesia was not an apartheid state, even though it was a totalitarian state. It was politically independent from the Netherlands. My parents were development workers and human rights activists and they had always told me and my brother that we were guests in this country without any special entitlements. Yet, we had a whole army of personnel – gardeners, maids, cooks, cleaners, drivers and guards whom we then called 'servants' – and the economic and white privilege we enjoyed translated into everything we were able to do and did, covering the whole spectrum from indulgence to charity.

With this background, there were many much more obvious choices for me to make than researching maskanda music. I was in a position to delve into musicking practices on one of the many islands of the Indonesian archipelago, or in South African Afrikaner communities, or Cape Malay communities. In all of them I could have moved around more easily than in a Zulu community, both culturally and linguistically. Yet, I had this drive and the opportunity to further expand my horizon, to search for difference, newness, to access unknown territory – very much like David Livingstone. However, as my explorations progressed, I also felt an increasing urge to demonstrate (if not prove) that a musical practice that had always been representative for those who are socially marginalized, badly educated, economically deprived and intellectually disadvantaged in fact enjoyed and facilitated high social status, intricate education and intellectual depth as well as economic advancement. The longer I worked with and befriended maskandi, the more I caught myself subliminally downplaying their strength, charitizing their poverty and misconceiving their aesthetics, poetics and profound intricacies of knowledge acquisition and transmission. Each time I caught myself in such prejudices, I became more convinced that I needed to actively resist those prejudices, by interrogating and decentring my own indigenous epistemologies. Gradually, this motivation replaced my motivation for horizon expansion. It became a(n equally privileged) horizon expansion in a completely different direction, a space I had never imagined to dwell in, because it enabled me (another privilege) to explore and develop more relational modes of knowing, and thus regard my academic practice as a social practice. Decentring and undermining the alleged coherence and self-sufficiency of my own epistemologies is, hence, a key concern of this book that I will further explain in the Introduction.

As I stated earlier, I am by no means the single author of this book, and I have tried to acknowledge the agency of all those whose insights and skills I have engaged with. Since the start of the project, which took much longer than I had envisaged, three maskanda musickers, without whom I could not have written this book, have passed on: Shiyani Ngcobo (1956–2011), Josefa Nkwanyana (1952–2012) and Selby Ngcobo. Although I feel their continued presence as *amadlozi* (shades), especially but certainly not solely in this book, I am sad they could not witness the emergence of this book in print, entailing my admiration for their craftsmanship and knowledge that will hopefully surface in the chapters that follow.

Johnny Clegg, a seminal protagonist in my narrative, passed away in 2019. The untimely passing of Busi Mhlongo (1947–2010) prevented me from sufficiently accrediting her electrifying musical energy that I witnessed at a couple of her maskanda performances in Durban. For this reason, her mighty *undondolo* (walking stick) features on the cover of this book. Mhlongo was not only a performer but also an *isangoma* (traditional healer). In these capacities, she continues to be a prime keeper and developer of Zulu epistemology. The *undondolo* enables the *isangoma* to walk with *amadlozi* – those who have gone before us and continue to walk with us (Madalane 2021b).

Fortunately, there are also many living people who need separate mentioning for supporting me in the progress and completion of this project. First and foremost, I want to thank Ignatia Madalane. She helped as an interlocutor from Zulu to English during some of my interviews (Ntuli 2009), transcribed and translated many song lyrics and recordings of conversations for me and explained the cultural reference and significance of musical and poetic symbols to me. Moreover, she made me feel welcome and loved in Mzansi through her friendship and continuous encouragement in personal matters in my life. Thank you, Mkhulu Mngomezulu! I'd also like to thank interpreters Elias Nxumalo, Bongani Mkhonza and Concord Nkabinde for their help with the lyrics of the songs I address in this book, as well as Nandi Khumalo and my Zulu language teacher Thokozani Khuzwayo for their simultaneous interpretation of my interviews with Joe Nkwanyana (2009b) and Shiyani Ngcobo (2008f). Without the help of Lichaba Nthethe, Nhlanhla Ngwekazi and Nomcebo Ngema, I would not have been able to speak to so many musicians.

My field research was enabled by funding from the Research Institute for History and Culture (OGC) of Utrecht University in the Netherlands where I was employed before I accepted an associate professorship at the University of Amsterdam in 2013. Before I received the funding in 2008, my interest in maskanda had already been awakened. I had been playing with the idea of researching it for some time, but I hesitated because of my background as a historical musicologist without any fieldwork experience, and because of my limited familiarity with South African music and society, as outlined above. A decisive turning point in my ponderings was constituted by several encounters with Kofi Agawu who visited the Netherlands as Music Theorist in Residence of the Dutch-Flemish Society for Music Theory (VvM). He outlined the reasons why my reservations about embarking on this project were ill-founded and I would like to thank him for the encouragement that his argument constituted for me.

During my longer fieldwork research visits to South Africa in 2008 and 2009, I was affiliated as a guest researcher and lecturer at the School of Music of the University of KwaZulu-Natal (UKZN) in Durban, and I would like to thank the then Head of School, Emily Akuno, for the kind invitation. The School's wonderful academic and social environment offered me platforms to share my findings and to receive feedback from colleagues who had been moving around in this field for much of their (academic) lives. Many of them also helped me out with practical advice concerning places to go and people to talk to. Without them, I would not have been able to get where I got. I would like to thank in particular my friend and colleague Kathryn Olsen, who had been researching maskanda for many years by the time I jumped on the scene, and generously shared her findings, her insights and her contacts with me. I also want to mention the continuous support of Sazi Dlamini whose brain I was allowed to pick about many of the intricacies not only of maskanda practice but also of the many musicking practices with which maskanda converses and interacts and that – thanks to Dlamini – will be outlined in this book in detail. I also thank maskandi Bongani Nkwanyana and David Jenkins as well as *Moribo* anchorman Nhlanhla Ngwekazi for their patient answering of all the questions I fired at them by email in the final stages of writing.

Conversations with and feedback from Nishlyn Ramanna, Neil Gonsalves, Christopher Ballantine, Patricia Opondo and Mageshen Naidoo also decisively helped me shape my thoughts about the complexities and sensitivities of making music in (post-)apartheid South Africa. In this capacity many of them became my friends rather than colleagues, and I want to thank them for their warm-heartedness and trust in me. They also made me teach at UKZN and interact with South African students from a variety of backgrounds. As many of my readers know, students teach their teachers in ways we can never teach them. So, my students, too, in South Africa and the Netherlands, deserve mentioning as subjects who helped me, because they shaped my thinking about many of the issues that are addressed in this book. One of them, Vuma Levin, I would like to thank in particular for his courage and generosity to think not only with me but also against me. I have learned a lot from this.

My conversations with academics with and without academic degrees reached beyond UKZN to my colleagues from the South African Society for Research in Music (SASRIM) and from other South African universities. Recurring discussions with Christine Lucia, Michael Blake, Rob Allingham, Brett Pyper, Sylvia Bruinders, Stephanus Muller and Marie Jorritsma were particularly rewarding. Outside UKZN, too, many of my colleagues became my friends. Nishlyn Ramanna, Lindelwa Dalamba, Sazi Dlamini, Xolani Nxumalo, Grant Olwage and, again, Ignatia Madalane require special mentions, because they were there for me in sometimes difficult personal circumstances, and they have decisively impacted on how I was able to think about and sense South Africa's rich, overwhelming and also traumatized societal fabric of which musicking practices form such an important part. In this context, I would also like to thank Louise Torr and Jon Rash as well as Angus Muir for their friendship and their warm hospitality.

The transferral of these experiences to academic prose, too, encompassed a range of acts and decisions that I have not and could not have made on my own. Christopher Ballantine's and Ronald Radano's sustained encouragement have been crucial in my envisaging of a book in the first place. Whereas Ignatia Madalane has transcribed the larger part of my field recordings, the interview transcription work of Jeroen Gevers, too, has contributed immensely to my ability to make sense of my research material. Paul Bocken spent many afternoons processing my scribbled music notation in the music notation software programme Sibelius, which brought to light a range of further interesting disjunctions between maskanda aurality and the affordances of eurogenic staff notation.

With Stéphanie Helfferich I spent long (and sometimes sunny) afternoons writing, which was always a pleasure to do together rather than alone, even if we wrote our own stories. Jochem van der Heide helped me manage my musical source material that occupies a central position in the articulation of my approach. I thank Eggo Müller for his feedback on the Introduction of this book as well as David Coplan for his feedback on the book's structure. I also thank meLê yamomo for being such a dear, sharp-witted friend and colleague, notably but certainly not exclusively regarding colonial, postcolonial and decolonial stances of thought. From the very start, my thinking about knowledge formation through music and sound has developed in fruitful interaction with that of Birgit Abels, and I am grateful for our many inspiring thought exchanges during the last one-and-a-half decades, often with a glass of milk within reach.

I have deliberately listed oral (including musical) and written sources together in the reference list. Moreover, I refer to musical sources in a similarly singular manner (through exact timings) as to written sources (through page numbers). In this way, I intend to attribute equal epistemic status to all these enunciations, which is crucial to my engagement with musical epistemologies. Moreover, this enables me to show in the reference list how various participants in maskanda practice have various modes of knowledge inscription at their disposal for transmitting and disseminating their understanding of maskanda. This multimodality provides an insightful indication of their agencies and (sometimes multiple) subject positions in the field. All their releases – whether in personal communication with me, in academic prose or in musical performance on my field recordings, on studio-produced albums or the internet – are enunciations in a Bhabhaesque sense of the word. They acquire their cultural authority through their release. In this capacity they also represent a time lag between event and enunciation that I will further explore and theorize in the Introduction of this book. For the same reason, I consistently reference my fellow participants in maskanda practice with their family names, even if I was, and still am, quite close to some of them. I intend to treat the information I received from them in the same way as the information I obtained from written sources which are conventionally referenced with author surnames.

All interviews took place in English, unless otherwise stated in the reference list, which, obviously, enhances the fraughtness of the (musical) knowing and understanding that I pretend to describe, since for both me and many other participants in maskanda discourse English is a second, third or fourth language. Moreover, many maskandi have been denied access to education in English during the apartheid years which made communication in English much harder for them than for me. Still, despite weekly language lessons during my fieldwork visits, my Zulu language skills have remained less proficient than the English language skills of many of my colleagues, due to the relatively short periods of time that I spent in South Africa.

In line with my deliberate employment of eurogenic staff notation for the transmission of my hearings of maskanda (see Introduction), I employ anglicized orthography of Zulu concepts in specific cases, in order to align my argument with comparable scholarly literature. Thus, I refer to 'maskanda' instead of the orthographically more correct 'umaskandi' (Pooley 2016: 7), and to more than one 'igama' (statement) as 'igamas' rather than 'amagama'. However, I refer to 'amahubo' as the plural of 'ihubo' (hymn), since traditional hymns are generally regarded as a unified repertoire with normative cultural status in Zulu discourse. Along the same lines of reasoning I refer to 'amadlozi' as the plural of 'idlozi' for the ancestor/shade world. I retain prefixes for Zulu noun stems ('ubeshu' rather than 'beshu', 'umuntu' rather than 'ntu'). When referring to languages ('isiZulu', 'isiXhosa'), I do not use the Zulu prefix isi-. However, I do use this prefix in the indication of maskanda styles ('isiZulu', 'isiBhaca') in order to distinguish them from their linguistic equivalents (see Chapter 2). Evidently, this distinction undermines the close association of musical and linguistic modes of expression articulated in the use of this prefix in Zulu discourse. With my anglicized reference to the genre 'maskanda' I also undermine its close association with its purveyor (plural and singular) 'maskandi', both called 'umaskandi' in Zulu language.

All photographs have been taken by me, unless otherwise stated. They are being published with the kind permission of those being portrayed or their heirs. Transcriptions of music are my own. These transcriptions as well as the transcriptions and translations of song lyrics are published with the kind permission of almost all of the music's creators or their heirs. In a few cases it was impossible to obtain explicit permission from the musicians after repeated attempts to contact them. In those cases I have assumed they don't object to the publication of my notated representation of their music and poetry.

This book is about knowledge, about searching and acquiring a temporarily positioned resonance between a self and the world through sound, gestures, performances, prose and many more modes of expression and inscription. Reading the Preface should suffice to recognize that this resonance is relational and social. The remainder of this book serves to demonstrate how this relationality works in what can be articulated as music and research and friendship. The close intersection of these three occupations, made meaningful by humans and living creatures anywhere in the world, was taught to me most pervasively and most poignantly by S'kho and Khoni Miya – sisters, musicians, friends, teachers – for reasons that will become clear in the following chapters. Therefore, I dedicate this book to them, to their musicianship, creativity and persistence, and to our friendship.

Utrecht, April 2021

For the presentation of musical examples and audio files, see this book's website: bloomsbury.pub/hearing-maskanda

Introduction: Foregrounding Aural Experiences

In July 2009, I had lunch with jazz bassist Concord Nkabinde in Wilson's Wharf, a trendy assemblage of markets, outdoor performance venues and restaurants situated between the yacht mole and the sugar factory in Durban's harbour. Concord was a friend of a friend, with a profound knowledge of Zulu culture and the South African music industry and with a mindboggling social and professional network. 'So, why have you come to South Africa to study maskanda?' he asked, and I struggled in formulating a coherent answer to his question. While I heard myself talking, I wondered why it was so difficult to explain this, despite the fact I had been asked this question so many times before. Frustrated and embarrassed with my recurring inability to articulate my motivations and intentions, I sensed and transmitted the alienation that was always part of my participation in maskanda practices.

My search for motivations and intentions and my feelings of alienation introduce the issues in this book extremely well. They touch on the book's prime concern with musical epistemology – how people know music, and how we make sense of the world with our ears (see also Abels 2016: 11). My search and my doubts also shed light on the epistemic regime I was – and still am – part of: an academic practice carried out from a safe position of privilege with years of government-funded training in handling very specific analytical, conceptual and theoretical devices within a global community of selected peers. This regime demands singular articulation and explication in the form of concepts. Even if it pretends to be able to harbour doubt, this conceptual singularity remains ill-suited to transmit and appreciate undecidability, ambivalence or equivocality – sensations that overwhelmed me when I talked to Nkabinde.

Some of these sensations I was able to conceptualize in hindsight, often with the help of reviewers and readers of my academic work including the manuscript of this book. For one, I was acutely aware, but unable to admit, that many ways in which maskandi themselves understand their aural experiences (through performance, aesthetic and critical judgement, or other modes of expression) remained unarticulated in my observations and reports, because I was unable to sense these experiences and account for them. I also sensed viscerally but subconsciously the inevitable epistemic gaps between what I thought maskanda musickers told me, demonstrated to me and taught me on the one hand, and what that meant to them on the other. This results in the fact that the book's predominant content – the aural experiences of maskanda musickers – is partial, incomplete and often fraught.

Yet, as I will demonstrate, this fraughtness can be employed productively. It can shed light on colonial modes of hearing and listening as well as on the ways in which the (academic) study of music is indebted to such modes of hearing. This academic self-search is urgently needed in light of larger social and ecological concerns pertaining to the un/sustainability of current conventions of interaction, representation and exchange of (all forms of) capital (Viveiros de Castro 2013; Graeber 2015). Several sound and music researchers have taken up these concerns during the last decade (Agnew 2008; Bloechl 2008; Ochoa 2014; Ochoa 2016; Radano and Olaniyan 2016; Impey 2018; Mundy 2018; Sykes and Steingo 2019; Hoffmann 2020). This has resulted in systematic academic attention for the ways in which coloniality can be heard and listened to: in presences and absences in sound and written archives, in acts of speech and performance, and in the opportunities for (groups of) people to raise their voices musically and discursively.

Literature about music and performance as modes of knowing reaches further back into the twentieth century (Feld 1981, 1982; Seeger 1987). Literature on the specifically aural (rather than oral) dimensions of knowing per se is expanding (Erlmann 2004; Clarke 2005; Ochoa 2014; Feld 2015; Abels 2016). This includes literature that decentres those modes of inscription employed and privileged in academic acts of knowledge acquisition about music and performance, such as conceptual thought and writing (Fabian 1990; Monson 1996; Hahn 2007; Turino 2008). It also encompasses publications addressing the history of such epistemic privilege that brought epistemic riches to some and nothing less than epistemicide to others (Bloechl 2008; Chikowero 2015). This history inevitably raises questions about technologies of inscription of knowledge: imagery, speech, writing, performance, etc.; and the material on which they inscribe: memories, (human) bodies, paper, hard drives, songs, sound carriers, internet pages or optical lenses (Barz [1997] 2008; Clayton 2001; Sterne 2003; Erlmann 2010; Abels 2012).

This book intends to contribute to these research interests by foregrounding maskanda's epistemic and epistemological implications and complexities, and by taking the reader along experientially in an act of (academic) knowledge formation through this book. This means that I will strategically halt my written argument at specific points and reflect on the ways I came to know maskanda, and how these ways distort, boost, invade or bridge understandings between participants in maskanda practice, including myself. In this way, I explicate and account for the workings and the limitations of the modes of knowledge inscription I am using.

Engagement with sonic and aural knowledge poses larger questions about what knowledge is or could be and on which 'ongoing cumulative and interactive processes of participation and reflection' (Feld 2015: 13–14) it relies. I will reference the recent literature that engages with these questions throughout this book, but I have been particularly inspired by the starting points that Ingrid Monson laid down more than twenty years ago in her groundbreaking study of jazz improvisation and interaction. Many of the issues she raised then are being developed in current literature: the aesthetics of social interaction (1996: 8), the dialogical, multi-voiced and inconsistent riches of knowing (86–8) and the tension between (aural) experience and text (3). Like her, I intend to foreground those moments 'of community' in which 'musical sounds, people and their musical and cultural histories' simultaneously interact (Monson 1996: 2). Monson describes knowledge as a way of sharing, the living out of a pact of mutual understanding between musicians, audiences and their predecessors that culminates in a shared set of skills (2). Her attention for 'vernacular perspectives' and 'insider knowledge' (7) that necessarily accompanies her approach covers a number of key issues of music research of the past forty years. Since the groundbreaking work on (musical) epistemologies by Hugo Zemp (1978), Steven Feld (1981, 1982), James Clifford (1988) and George Marcus (Clifford and Marcus 1986), implications of 'the arrogance of claiming to "represent" or "speak for" persons other than oneself' (Monson 1996: 6) have been painstakingly identified by generations of scholars, while they also point at the impossibility of ridding oneself of that arrogance.

With all his open enthusiasm for my interest in maskanda, Nkabinde emphasized how important it is that those whom I work with know what I want to do with their contribution and collaboration. 'I am so curious', he said, 'what the impact of your work will be on how maskanda musicians think about themselves and about their music' (2009). The more I was able to value his plea for reciprocity, the more I wondered whether written prose substantiating an academic research question is the best way to facilitate such reciprocity. Moreover, one could wonder whether it is even the most insightful way to share knowledge about maskanda with those who have never heard (of) it. Yet, I never seriously considered alternative modes of knowledge inscription, such as a documentary film or the organization of a global tour of maskanda performances. This is partly because the production of prose possesses more academic status than a film or a concert tour (a situation that I will interrogate on several instances in this book), but more decisively this is because I feel safe and relatively confident in the domain of written prose. The longer I worked on the project, the more I sensed that this issue of safety and confidence in my employment of a specific set of epistemic skills (writing, close listening, transcribing and reading) underlies exertions of epistemic power that need to be explicated. I had always known this – it is a trope in almost all ethnographic research I encountered – but only in the mode of *practical identification* (Derrida [1967] 1997: 116 as cited in Scherzinger 2004: 273) could I sense this power and critically engage with it.

Maskanda musickers

In order to foreground this sensation in my written prose, I employ Christopher Small's notion of 'musicking' (1998: 9) as a range of activities, which supplants the singular noun 'music' as an object. The construction of this book is an obvious part of maskanda musicking processes. All those who engage in acts of maskanda musicking I call 'maskanda musickers': musicians, audiences, critics, representatives of the music industry and (broadcast) media, and researchers. By regarding myself as one of those musickers, I am able to address 'moments of community' (Monson 1996: 2) in which I perceived the sharing of sound and cultural sensibility, and to point out gaps, arrests and disjunctions in (musical) experience, understanding and communication among all maskanda musickers, including those between me and my fellow musickers. In identifying such moments of community and alienation, I focus on the ways in which musickers foreground their aural experience. This method constitutes my main research question: how do maskanda musickers foreground their aural experiences? In what ways do we musically and performatively adapt and appropriate sounding and stage material that we encounter in our lives and careers? What words do we use to describe what we hear? How do we use our voices, bodies and musical instruments to signify, evoke, present, produce, interpret and comment on the world in which we live?

I am aware that the assumption of one category (maskanda musickers), encompassing those for whom maskanda is a way of life as well as those – like me – for whom maskanda will never be a way of life, might be considered problematic. Yet, I consciously employ this problem to foreground the epistemic, social and relational difficulties of my intention to delve into the dynamics of (cross-cultural) musical sense making and of presenting this publication as a source of knowledge about maskanda. There was a distinct rift between the kind of knowledge I acquired in South African communities of maskanda peers on the one hand, and the knowledge I acquired writing the book behind European desks on the other. The former remains accessible only in as far as it is 'legible' within the requirements of the latter, and hence remains subaltern to this hegemony. This rift in knowledge formation was symbolized by the often deprived socio-economic position in which many maskanda musickers still find themselves as opposed to the privileged environments in which I can shape my thoughts. I need to account for this privilege by dropping my (aural, epistemic and discursive) guard (see also Kisliuk [1997] 2008: 187). I intend to identify those instances in my research where I was reluctant or unable to hear or understand something, and explicate moments of silence and absence that foreground the hegemonic position of my epistemic tools in global orderings of knowledge. Moreover, I need to identify you as my readership. This book has been produced, edited and made legible to an international readership of academically trained peers through a Northern Hemisphere academic publisher. This readership might not always have prior knowledge of maskanda practice or an *experiential* understanding of many black people's living conditions in South Africa from which this musicking practice is said to have emerged. This implies that I am not writing the book for those who do have this knowledge and experience. As problematic as this is, it also enables me to further observe, dissect and question accepted and/or normative forms of knowledge formation and acquisition that have been, and still are, complicit to exertions of power and control that directly affect the musickers in my project.

For quite some time now, this complicity has been phrased in terms of several binary confrontations: experiential versus bookish knowledge, or precolonial indigenous versus colonial imported knowledge, or reason and resonance (Erlmann 2010). These binaries continue to be poignant in present-day South Africa, for instance through the metaphor of mining 'raw' epistemic material from the Global South that is employed and exploited for the development and refinement of Northern Hemisphere theory

(Buthelezi 2017: 17; Sykes and Steingo 2019). Although all of these qualifications are cases in point for criticizing global orderings of knowledge, they become monoliths in themselves if the subject positions and agencies of those who experience knowledge as experiential, bookish, indigenous, imported, raw or refined are not taken into account. One of the aims of this book is to demonstrate that maskandi as much as academics and fieldworkers mine their musical, cultural and epistemic material (seen as raw by some and acknowledged as refined by others) from many places of the world and make it theirs through their acts of musicking. Obviously, inequalities of power and representation always accompany such acts of appropriation. It is crucial to foreground such inequalities. However, it is also important to look and listen beyond the regimes (such as industries, governments, 'regimes of signs and texts' [Erlmann 1999: 4], academic infrastructures of knowledge formation and dissemination) that presume and thrive on these inequalities. Increasingly, the epistemic agency, authority and also hegemony of maskanda musicking is acknowledged in proliferating published and unpublished literature about maskandi modes of knowing (Hadebe 2000; Pewa 2005; Shandu 2007; Ntombela 2016; Nyezwa 2018; Shumba and Meier-Weitz 2019; Manana 2021).

My engagement with such practices of hearing through academic prose has been inspired by the research of two music researchers. In her book *Aurality* (2014), Ana María Ochoa Gautier searches for 'the traces and excesses of the acoustic' in writings from nineteenth-century Colombia. These traces are imbued in the 'technology of writing' (2014: 7), 'in the nooks and crannies of history, dispersed across several fields and sites of knowledge and sound inscription' (6). For her research into Native American song at the frontiers of early modern music, Olivia Bloechl observes that the sources she consulted were, despite their status as 'European "master narratives," … forged in the crucible of early modern colonialism and slavery and that they never lose this doubled origin – the debt of their belonging both "here" and "there"' (2008: 23).

In many ways I regard my book about maskanda as an ethnographic counterpart of Bloechl's historical 'master narratives' from which future historians may or may not be able to extract 'the traces and excesses of the acoustic'. It is crucial to acknowledge its doubled origin, its debt of its belonging both 'here' and 'there'. While it is impossible to document what I am unable or reluctant to see or hear, it is possible – as Judith Butler (1988: 520), among others, has argued – to critically engage with the selectivity of what I hear and see, to point out instances of aural inconclusiveness and to explicate instances of absence and silence in which one would have expected someone or some enunciation to be there (see also Barz [1997] 2008: 216). What is not being said by maskanda musickers (including me) and why not? Or what is being sanctioned, by whom and why?

Igama

In order to foreground these instances, and at the same time to downplay an *a priori* epistemological difference between my embodied knowledge and that of my fellow maskanda musickers, I intend to explicate these binaries (of the indigenous and the colonial, the Global South and the Global North, the experiential and the bookish) in my own argument rather than work around them, with the aim of demonstrating their complex entanglement. I will employ two powerful modes of knowledge inscription and transmission for this.

Firstly, I introduce in Chapter 1 the Zulu concept of igama. Igama can be translated as 'statement', 'word' or 'name', but decidedly has non-verbal implications too. Many maskandi translated it as a 'message' that can be passed on through a combination of words, gestures, movements, images and sounds. A maskanda song is often called an *igama* rather than *umculo* (music). Musician and university lecturer Sazi Dlamini explained the concept of igama to me, emphasizing the combination of expressive modalities in maskanda that constitute an igama, as well as the expressive prominence of dance in Zulu culture:

> The song itself is called: the *igama*, or a statement. If you ask: 'which igama are you gonna play?', it means: song. Which piece of music? Because igama is a statement. You dance a certain contention, or a certain word. Or a certain … ja: dance a word. Say what you wanna say. To encourage a meaning and argument, you dance! … If you want to say: 'a child that does not get beaten becomes naughty'. That's igama. You find it's become a chorus. [They] [correspond]. You say a few statement[s], and then embellish it with dance.
>
> (Dlamini 2011b)

As Dlamini indicates, dance is, and long has been, inextricably intertwined with verbal and musical expression. Many maskandi have told me that talking to *amadlozi* (ancestors/shades) and gods always occurs through ritual song (B. Nkwanyana 2009b; Nokwe 2009) called *ihubo*. In his monograph about Zulu thought, Ivar-Axel Berglund records that 'when ihubo is sung, the shades are in a very real and intimate manner present' ([1976] 1989: 199). It is, however, inappropriate to address shades with words and sounds only; speaking to shades without *ukugiya* (dance) is considered weak. *Ukugiya* is necessary to awaken the shades and excite them to action before talking with them (236).

Thus, dance is a mode of understanding oneself and one's environment, but it never means something through its bodily gestures only. Musician and anthropologist Jonathan (Johnny) Clegg describes how verbal, musical and gestural movements are dependent on each other in the construction of meaning that reaches beyond referentiality. It could be called a musical form of meaning formation with musicking as a decidedly social form of interaction at the centre of these activities, but it also exceeds the musical as a merely sounding form of social interaction. Beginning dancers are given a dance name 'and you are encouraged to think about the rhythm of the name … That group of thirty or forty men will shout your praise name and you are to manipulate that praise name so as to make it work for you' through dance patterns (Clegg 1984: 67). The purpose of this encouragement of manipulation is the expression and release of social tension. One is supposed to irritate the shouters of the praise name, and '[a]ccording to the standing that you have among the dancers, if you're a good dancer they will accept your irritating them and they'll actually like it' (1984: 67).

In this respect, posing an igama could be compared to Ingrid Monson's musical rendition of Louis Henry Gates Jr's notion of 'signifyin' (Monson 1996: 87) as a speaking style that revolves around word games, the exchange of individual statements with multiple meanings, meant to tease and provoke the addressees and challenge them to deliver a clever response. Many maskandi deliberately confuse their audiences with textual, musical and gestural ambiguities in order to tease or mock them or themselves, often taking on the role of jester or societal critic. In temporal context, the notion of igama converses with existing and competing social or cultural discourses, constructing a relation between past and present that is participatory, interactive and dialogical rather than uni-linear and synchronic. Dance is a crucial mode of communication in this interaction. As Tomie Hahn observes in her study about Japanese dance as 'sensational knowledge', dance can tell us a lot about the complex relations and intersections of human bodies, social bodies and bodies of musical, poetic or religious repertoire that constitute forms of knowing and understanding that encapsulate but also surpass what Thomas Turino calls 'symbolic signification' in the form of language (2008: 13). Moreover, the dancing body is a fleeting presence, an elusive informant to research (Hahn 2007: 6), just like sound, and arouses understanding through kinetic activity and sensual orientation (17).

Maskanda's multimodality of expression – through words, musical idioms, gestures, dance and dress – in the communication of a message or igama foregrounds the multifariousness of knowing at large. The importance of dance in this epistemic practice can tell us more about this multimodality. The centrality of dance in maskanda has a fraught history ripe with colonial impositions and contradictory claims on traditionality. Johnny Clegg relates in detail not only how '[t]he structure of the dance is saying something … about the people who are dancing it' (1984: 65–6), but also how social tensions are being expressed and released through dance, and how one is to understand one's own body as well as one's social position through dance (1982: 13). Clegg draws attention to the intricate intertwining of social and physical bodies, emphasizing that 'the physical experience of the body … sustains a particular view of society' and also that '[t]he social body constrains the way the physical body is perceived' (Mary Douglas [1970] 1996: 69 quoted in Clegg 1982: 13). In her magnificent book about *ingoma* dance, *Dust of the Zulu* (2017), Louise Meintjes addresses these and other intertwinings in great detail. An igama is simultaneously social and material, and is intended to share a time-space with consociates and contemporates, a relational ontology that Steven Feld happens to attribute to the physicality of sound per se in his concept of 'acoustemology' (2015). Therefore, the notion of igama is useful for the many ways in which maskanda musickers foreground their aural experiences.

A second mode of inscription I employ to engage with the embodied knowledge of maskanda musickers (including myself) is my objectification of sound through analysis. Throughout this book, I provide a wide range of close listenings, close transcriptions and close readings of selected maskanda songs as discrete musical entities, but also of the spaces, occasions and instances in which maskanda sounds, such as lessons, rehearsal rooms, YouTube channels, (festival) stages, albums and the studios in which they have been recorded. I regard this eurogenic, deliberately object-driven and formalist approach to be part of the multitude of expressive and inscriptive modes (sound, gesture, conceptual discourse, dress, visuals) that the posing of a maskanda igama invites. Whereas the maskandi igamas are objectified as sources in the reference list of this book, my music analyses, playing a role in transmitting those igamas, are objectified in the figures accompanying the written text of this book.

(Ethno)musicologists advocating an 'interpretative turn' in the humanities in the late twentieth century were understandably sceptical about a primary research focus on sonic structure that serves the establishment of a relatively isolated, self-referential aesthetic meaning of musical entities as objects (McClary [1991] 2002; Tomlinson 1991: 248; Rice 1994; Subotnik 1996; Small 1998). Such focus potentially ignores the social acts that musicking encompasses and from which aesthetic judgements emanate in the first place. My close listenings and close readings of selected maskanda songs as discrete musical entities might unintentionally boost eurogenic epistemologies as self-referential and independent (Bloechl 2008: 23). This imposes the risk of an old-fashioned articulation of my Self against the background of subaltern Others. For whereas my participant-observation in singing, playing and dancing maskanda was undoubtedly reciprocal, the analytical, critical and historiographical exchange of ideas between me and my fellow musickers remained limited and fraught. My analytical accounts (in Part III of this book) are hence much more single-authored and object-driven than my accounts of my musicking encounters with maskanda musickers (in Part II). This structure reiterates binaries between social and formalist research orientations and between musical sensation and conceptual knowledge that I want to surpass in this book.

I argue that it is exactly for this reason that my formalist approach is useful: I intend to regard music analysis as a social, culturally situated and performative practice. In the early twenty-first century, a younger generation of ethnomusicologists highlights the potential benefits of closely engaging with aural experiences, hearing and reading them. They regard the close engagement with sounding structure as a creative and interpretative practice rather than as a transcendental and exclusivist dissection of units into parts (Monson 1996: 3; Agawu 2003: 196–7; Scherzinger 2004: 258; Tenzer 2006: 6; Solis 2012: 548). At the same time, there is an increasing interest within the realm of music cognition in the ways cultural knowledge steers aural experiences and expectations (Sloboda 1985: 242–58; Curtis and Barucha 2009: 365 as quoted in Koenis 2018: 41), something that early comparative musicologists, such as Benjamin Ives Gilman and Carl Stumpf, already acknowledged in the late nineteenth century (Kursell 2017: 3).

Rather than regarding this bias as an obstruction to research, I intend to employ it as a tool to explicate my aural subject position and culturally situate the signifying tools (including staff notation and concepts devised for articulating specific European musics as high art traditions) through which I know music. Thus, rather than distancing myself from it rhetorically, I intend to regard 'the embodied knowledge of the participant-observer-researcher[,] as a resource within the research' (Hahn

2007: 10), which is necessary to explain how I was able and unable to tune in with the ways in which maskanda constitutes a positioned resonance between a self and the world: a mode of knowing. This also enables me to emphasize the hegemony of my subject position, and point out how it can be and is being used to invade or cover up lived experiences and sharings of music worldwide. In order to 'excise layers of European assumptions that might have impeded our understanding of African musical practice' (Agawu 2003: 21), we first must identify and acknowledge those layers and assumptions. Moreover, as Martin Scherzinger observes, close transcription and close reading can be employed as very specific means to identify and articulate instances of structural undecidability (2004: 258), and I would add that these instances of structural undecidability are also culturally situated. As will become clear throughout this book, those instances in which my (analytical and conceptual) tools blatantly fell short in signifying the aural experiences that I took part in are the most fruitful ones in demonstrating the epistemic riches of maskanda epistemology and in decentring eurogenic modes of knowledge inscription.

Maskandafication

In my analyses, I focus on how maskanda musickers 'maskandafy' ideas, statements and musical practices alike by making them accessible *as* maskanda: through performance, composition, aesthetic judgement, sound production, dissemination or critique. These acts of 'maskandafication' as well as my analyses foregrounding these acts are, in the words of Peter Szendy, a 'twofold process of "hearing another person listen"' (Szendy [2001] 2008 as paraphrased by Erlmann 2004: 18). Maskanda is a funnel through which other forms of expression find their exposure: lessons, statements, prayers, outcries and emotions, but also other musical practices: *amahubo* singing, *ugubhu* and *umakhweyana* gourd bow playing, *isitorotoro* mouth harp and *imfilitshi* mouth organ playing, *ukugiya* and *ingoma* dance, *izibongo* spoken self-praise, Anglican and Catholic church song, *boereliedjies* and currently also R&B, hip-hop, gospel and jazz. I regard all acts of maskandafication (including my analyses of maskanda songs in this book) as performative acts as much as acts of academic dissection and interpretation, even though maskanda performance and academic interpretation enjoy unequal status as knowledge. Through my close readings of maskanda performances, maskanda compositions and maskanda receptions, I attempt 'to offer a way for the reader to vicariously "know with the ear" through text' (adapted from Hahn 2007: 8).

Making maskanda out of something – maskandafication – constitutes a continuous sonic and aural (re)organization of space (i.e. home, labour conditions, performance venues) and a (re)assemblage of concepts or genres (i.e. social networks, styles, praising and poetic practices). Yet, acts of maskandafication reach beyond the representationalities of those spaces and concepts, even though they are obvious discursive starting points for all maskanda musickers I talked to. Maskandafication also works through the provocation of intensities, sensations and affects. This provocation takes place in its temporary articulation of genres, styles, traditions, musicking positions as well as its equally temporary constitution of interior subjectivities such as experiences of the body, of movement and of consciousness. Those who maskandafy what they encounter, distance themselves from what they encounter in their observation and then approach it again on their own terms through a variety of expressive modes – speech, sounding structures, dress, performance – as a maskanda song.

For example, a maskanda rendering of a famous R&B bass line – such as Shwi noMtekhala's hit song 'Ngafa' (2003) that revamped Marvin Gaye's 'Sexual Healing' (1982) – encompasses several stages of relating. Shwi noMtekhala encounter Gaye's song, they observe the song's features, they identify and select features (a bass line, a vocal timbre, a groove) and extract these from their environment (the song) which comprises a distantiation, and then they re-approach these features on their own terms by making them sound as maskanda (see Titus 2016a for a detailed analysis of this song). This is an exertion of power. In its modes of operation such an act of maskandafication can be compared to eurogenic academic modes of knowing such as historiography, ethnography and analysis (Titus 2021) because all these academic modes of knowing employ a similar succession of observation, identification, selection, extraction and reconceptualization of features. The only difference is that maskandi do this sonically rather than merely conceptually. Maskandafication is hence a powerful mode of knowledge formation.

With this parallel in mind, I can demonstrate how the maskanda performance of an igama and the ethnographic study or musical analysis of maskanda are folded into each other. They are not intrinsically or *a priori* different modes of knowledge and expression. In their modes of operation, similar negotiations of power take place (Clifford 1988; Rice 1994: 10). This insight helps me relax the binary between music and conceptualization (Monson 1996: 2), between sense making through performance and through reading a 'text' and between hegemonic and subaltern forms of knowledge. Musical performance and verbal explanation constitute different means but equal degrees of detail and precision in foregrounding an aural experience. Still, musical epistemologies as well as African epistemologies are often dubbed 'subaltern': out of the order, illegible, which keeps them trapped in their relationship with the legible, normative, e.g. the hegemonic. Decentring hegemonic modes of knowing starts with no longer describing the non-hegemonic ones as subaltern. There are many potential hegemonies in musical maskanda modes of knowing, which I will outline in detail in this book.

Illustrative for the need to reach beyond binaries of conceptual and musical modes of expression or between hegemonic and subaltern capabilities of knowing is the condition in which maskanda is said to have emerged. The many publications about South African popular musics, such as isicathamiya (Erlmann 1996), marabi (Ballantine [1993] 2012), sefela (Coplan 1994, [1985] 2008b), kiba (James 1999), mbaqanga (Meintjes 2003) and maskanda (Olsen 2014), invariably start with outlining the social and cultural consequences of forced labour migration in South Africa in the late nineteenth and early twentieth centuries, since they still determine to a large extent the lives of many South Africans to date. During the late nineteenth century, the discovery of gold and diamonds in South African soil initiated a colonial demand for cheap labour.

> The black population ... was subjected to a barrage of legislation designed to relegate it to a strictly subordinate role and to exploit its labour potential. In 1911, the Mines and Works Act barred blacks from skilled industrial jobs. In 1913 the Natives' Land Act laid down the principle of territorial segregation .... Africans were prohibited from purchasing or leasing land in white areas; the only areas where they could lawfully acquire land henceforth were in native reserves which then amounted to about 8 per cent of the country .... Some sought refuge in the reserves, though overcrowding there was already becoming a noticeable feature. Others were forced, after selling their livestock and implements, to work as labourers for white farmers. A whole class of prosperous peasant farmers was eventually destroyed .... The Natives' Urban Areas Act of 1923 established the principle that the towns were white areas in which Africans were permitted to reside in segregated 'locations' only as long as they served white needs.
>
> (Meredith 2007: 522–3)

The implications of this social disruption were decisive for the emergence of a variety of music practices. Firstly, the recruitment of miners, farm labourers and urban domestic workers covered an area that included not only present-day South Africa, but also what is now Namibia, Botswana, Zimbabwe, Mozambique and Zambia. Secondly, the migration was predominantly seasonal: while labourers spent the larger part of the year in mine compounds, on farms or in hostels in urban areas, they returned to their villages for a couple of months per year to be with their families in the reserves. Closely connected to the forced labour is the experience of wandering as an experience of displacement and disempowerment. Labourers commuted between their homes and their hostels during the year. This implied, thirdly, that most men were absent from their families for long periods on end and that masculinity became an important trope in the day-to-day communication and cultural expression in mine compounds, on farms and in hostels.

These social transformations exposed labourers to an immense range of cultural and musical impressions, including languages, rituals, belief systems, food, songs, dances, musical instruments, playing techniques and singing techniques, which they brought back home to their villages. Existing practices from workers from various parts of sub-Saharan Africa, the music of British and Afrikaner employers and the music played on new media such as the radio equally informed the syncretic culture that emerged from this urbanization and migration over a period of several decades. Dating the emergence of maskanda is hence an impossible endeavour, just as locating maskanda in a specific city or area is problematic. Maskanda is often described in general terms as a range of street guitar and concertina practices, carried out by individual musicians (*maskandi*) singing about the events and experiences they encounter on their way. Currently, maskanda is played and enjoyed as studio-produced pop music in virtually any public space in KwaZulu-Natal and Johannesburg. While its line-up generally consists of guitar, bass and drums complemented with concertina or violin and a backing chorus/dance group, its twenty-first-century manifestations are as diverse as the twentieth-century ones. There are many maskandas. They occupy a tiny niche in the international world music market as some kind of 'Zulu blues' (eThekwini Online 2005; Wikipedia 2021).

Colonial positions

Many of the authors outlining these social circumstances in these broad terms are aware that such narrative forms of inscription in many ways ignore, even out or write out the extremely disruptive, individual and incompatible experiences that these incessant migratory movements and displacements produced. It is no coincidence that, invariably, the prominent published monographs about the musics that emerged from the conditions of forced labour migration have been written by white authors: those who have never been subjected to the kind of legislation that Meredith describes. My book exemplifies this once more. Meredith's reference to 'the black population', 'blacks', 'Africans' and 'white needs' inadvertently repeats the systematic colonial and later apartheid separation of blacks and whites as distinct monoliths. In academic prose, it proves to be very difficult not to employ and exploit the coherence that such condensed narratives provide. Following postcolonial critiques of the reductive implications of such narratives, various modes of description and theorization have been tried out to allow for less quantifiable experiences and more subjective accounts to surface and to reach beyond the binary dynamic of suppression and submission, or control and resistance.

I employ Small's notion of musicking in order to point out the myriad relationships between various musickers without regarding these musickers as a coherent group of people. Along the same lines, I describe the colonial conditions sketched by Meredith as a space shared by colonizers and colonized with the very aim of articulating their positions and agencies that are in some ways prescribed and reified, but in other ways diversified, changeable and contingent. Literary scholar Homi Bhabha is one of the most infamous authors devising and employing theoretical tools to articulate these positions. According to Bhabha, colonizer and colonized, or dweller and migrant, are subject to very similar experiences and adopt very similar strategies for processing these experiences. Thus, Bhabha argues, they keep each other in their respective colonial positions. Bhabha's theoretical framework enables me to point at the inequalities of power in these environments, but also acknowledges the agency of those participants in the discourse who are often too easily regarded as voiceless and subaltern.

In his 1977 article about 'Zulu town music' based on fieldwork in Durban in 1964, David Rycroft describes the social position of what he calls 'manual workers' in urban areas. He describes them as 'neither strict traditionalists, nor Christians', and observes that they were popularly referred to 'as a distinct class': *abaqhafi* (in the 1920s) and later as *amagxagxa*. 'They seek to emulate Western customs to a certain extent in order to dissociate themselves from the "backwood traditionalists" they have left behind in the country. Yet, lacking education, they do not fit into sophisticated African town life, and consequently occupy the lowest social and economic strata in town society' (1977: 221–2). Clegg, too, mentions the *gxagxa* people as an 'interstitial' social class, 'problematically situated' in between *bhinca* people (skin wearers) and *kholwa* people (believers or Christians). He claims that they mixed the music of *bhinca* and *kholwa* people into a 'mazkande' (Clegg 1981: 2), a 'musician's music' that could not be attributed to anyone, and often remained unacknowledged, unrecognized and unrepresented to people from other social strata of urban society,[1] yet had high social status among labour migrants who considered maskanda a prime validation of tradition.

As discussed on several instances in this book, maskanda was a cultural and epistemic anchor point for those who were forcibly removed from their homes and families and excluded from formal education. Maskanda's oral and aural modes of knowledge inscription were crucial for its status as an alternative to the suppressing and humiliating discourses that were inescapable in apartheid times. Emblematic in this context is the trope of the maskandi as a wandering guitarist positioned *in between* rural and urban experiences that are often constructed as a binary in many maskanda narratives. The Zulu labour migrant is in the know of both urban and rural ways of life, being able to combine and reflect on the knowledge and experiences of multiple realities, but belongs to neither of them, commuting back and forth from designated homelands to temporary places of residence to provisional job occupations.

The interstitial position of the *gxagxa* people, dissociating themselves from one group and aspiring to be accepted by another, substantiates Bhabha's observation that colonial conditions are based on feelings of ambivalence, an opposing pair of instincts, towards communities or individuals that are experienced (and discursively constructed) as Other (Childs and Williams 1997: 124). This ambivalence comes down to a simultaneous fear to become like the Other and a desire to be as the Other. In his description of this ambivalent identification, containing both fear and desire (125), Bhabha relies on Frantz Fanon's description of an enslaved person who wants to be in the position of their master while simultaneously maintaining their anger towards him, and hence wants to be in two identificatory places at once. Bhabha describes this position as double (Self) and split (the Other) (Bhabha 1994b: 52; Childs 1997: 123).

Much of the double-and-split position of the *gxagxa* people can be clarified by centuries of colonial and later apartheid stereotypification of Zulu culture, reducing the experience of being Zulu to the constructed domains of the body, dance, warriordom and rural simplicity in order to domesticate Zulu cultural expression as decidedly and fixatedly Other (Erlmann 1991: 95–111; Meintjes 2017: 2). Precisely these stereotypes currently still have national and global appeal (Meintjes 2003: 225), as I will point out at several instances in this book. Bhabha observes that the colonial stereotype is both a recognition and a denial of difference (Bhabha 1994c: 66) designed to manage the ambivalent urge to identify (with) and to disavow the Other simultaneously. Colonizer and colonized equally employ them. Stereotypes are reductive representations (fixities) of the Other in order to secure the Other's Otherness as known and predictable (Childs and Williams 1997: 125). Often these fixities function as Neo-Freudian fetishes (Bhabha 1994c: 75): both as a metaphor, providing a substitute for the colonial subject,

---

[1] The dis- or rather non-placement of maskandi in the 1960s and 1970s is further illustrated by Rycroft in mentioning that, in sharp contrast to his recordings of 'indigenous Zulu country music', his '"town" material' was 'consistently rejected by a succession of recording companies' (1977: 221n).

and as a metonymy, providing an association with the colonial subject (Childs and Williams 1997: 127).

Mimicry and Third Space

I outline Bhabha's theorizations of feelings of ambivalence and the construction of stereotypes in order to introduce a concept that is crucial to my explanation of maskanda as a mode of knowing, namely its capacity to mimic existing normative musical and cultural practices in such a way that it authorizes as well as questions the cultural status of these practices. The amalgamation of the fear and the desire to be as the Other in a colonial environment underlies this process. Maskanda is often said to refer to deep Zulu culture, encompassing notions of authenticity and cultural normativity, but since it is heard and conceptualized as an urban practice it articulates the distinction between deep Zulu and contemporary urban experiences by hovering in between them. In its discriminatory capacity, maskanda also asks questions about what it means 'to music' (Small 1998: 9) in an urban or rural, traditional or modern, in a Zulu or Boer or Anglican or white or black manner. It simultaneously authorizes, sidesteps and menaces these cultural categories, which accounts for maskanda's huge popularity among Zulu South Africans of older and younger generations at present.

Bhabha describes this threefold – authorizing, discriminating and menacing – form of appropriation as mimicry. Mimicry is a strategy of authority (used by colonizers and the colonized alike) through the creation of a class of interpreters such as missionaries, schoolteachers and civil servants who transmit aspects of the dominant culture to the (colonial) subjects. They are supposed to ensure that the Other learns to behave like you behave, talk like you talk and believe what you believe. Maskandi can be understood to constitute a class of interpreters in the construction of a binary between current and precolonial Zulu culture and senses of belonging, which prioritizes the precolonial imagination as normative and stable. The modes by which this knowledge is inscribed (for instance guitar playing in the transmission of deep Zulu eloquence, or Bible texts and positivist science in European colonial conquest) constitute a kind of discriminatory knowledge through which the difference between colonizer and colonized, or between deep Zulu culture and urban Zulu culture, can be constructed.

Interestingly, the class of interpreters in the liminal space between these two constructed classes determines to a large extent how this discriminatory knowledge is transmitted and adapted, which accounts for the mimicking capacity to articulate a metonymic identity that can be menacing to (colonial or traditional) hegemony. 'The menace of mimicry is its double vision which in disclosing the ambivalence of colonial discourse also disrupts its authority' (Bhabha 1994d: 88). Here, according to Bhabha, can we find the construction and location of culture with agents that possess knowledge from both worlds and belong to neither of them. These agents, often migrants (the *gxagxa* people being an obvious example), have a double vision that exposes the close similarity (but not sameness) between 'the mother culture and its bastards' or 'the self and its doubles' (Bhabha 1994e: 111) as hybrids of each other. Maskandi, cladding allegedly rural and traditional sensibilities in musical formats experienced as urban and modern, derive their cultural authority from this rural–urban or traditional–modern double vision that accounts for maskanda's hybridity as a genre. Mimicry is thus a crucial component of what I have called maskandafication: in making maskanda out of existing musical and expressive practices, maskandi distort and hybridize these practices with maskanda doubles that are 'not-quite' copies.

In early-twenty-first-century post-apartheid South Africa, maskanda musickers still pride themselves on their interstitial position possessing a double vision and a 'double hearing'. Often, they explained maskanda to me in terms of global hip-hop or R&B practices, possibly assuming that this would be music I was already familiar with. Thus, they marked hip-hop and R&B as authoritative knowledge confirming the existing global hegemony of these musics. Yet, they consciously situated and rooted the specific set of musical practices (spoken self-praise, vocal techniques) that constitute the similarities between maskanda and hip-hop or R&B in Africa. These musical practices function as discriminatory knowledge deciding who is entitled to be part of this hegemony and on what terms. Thus, they function as menacing knowledge too, undermining the global hegemony of hip-hop by making it 'legible' in terms of maskanda. Typical for the contingency of such attempts is the fact that I learned more about hip-hop and R&B through these associations than I would have without my maskanda research. In other words: global hip-hop culture and R&B became legible and audible to me through maskanda; I learned (about) them from a maskandi perspective. The maskanda doubles (such as Shwi noMtekhala's 'Ngafa') were points of entry for me to familiarize myself with the mother culture (Marvin Gaye's R&B). This trajectory also featured my familiarization with what my Zulu colleagues explained to me as deep Zulu traditional culture: *amahubo* choral dance song, *umakhweyana* gourd bow playing and *ukugiya* dance.

These multiple and contingent workings of epistemic and cultural exchange prompt Bhabha to conceive of a notion of a Third Space, which he describes as a time lag between event and the instance in which this event acquires cultural authority in the form of an enunciation. Hence, Third Space is a space not only of contingency and potentiality, but also of agency and intervention, which Bhabha summarizes with Jacques Derrida's concept of *différance*, where the attribution of cultural meaning to events is deferred and differentiated simultaneously (1994b: 58–9). The conditions of language as well as the performative, institutional and subconscious implications of an event are not yet determined or fully comprehensive and hence not completely enunciated. Here, Bhabha argues, culture as practice is constructed and, hence, located.

Not only the 'location of culture', but also the processes and acts of locating culture can be conceptualized by means of Bhabha's theoretical starting points. Whereas Bhabha remains deliberately implicit about the tangible manifestations of Third Space, I explore the possibility of regarding maskanda music as a Third Space of enunciation, a location of culture and a practice exemplifying the processes of locating culture through maskandafication. Important parameters in interpreting maskanda as a Third Space of enunciation are its multiplicity of social and epistemological positions in colonial and postcolonial environments as described above, exemplified by the many (sometimes) contradictory ways in which cultural and epistemic status is attributed to it. This is the reason why I focus on the ways in which musickers foreground their aural experiences: these foregroundings provide insight into the process of sonic events becoming cultural enunciations.

Imaginations of home

This process is shaped by spatial, aural and intersubjective dynamics that I outline below. These dynamics, involving acts of dwelling, moving, hearing, seeing and relating, serve as points of orientation throughout this book. They are supposed to provide insight into maskanda musicking practices in colonial, apartheid and post-apartheid environments as formations of knowledge.

Unsurprisingly, notions of home acquired particularly poignant meanings for those exposed to conditions of forced labour migration. Before maskanda became subject to dynamics of public performance and commercial recording, the songs, or rather igamas, were tailored to an ongoing walking pace for the entire duration of a commute from home to work, and they centralized the longing for a lost home (Clegg 1981; Allingham 1990). Thus, maskanda played a crucial role in what the cultural theorist Sara Ahmed and colleagues call the 'continuous act of production and reproduction [of home] that is never fully complete' (Irene Gedalof quoted in Ahmed et al. 2003: 106) – an act that (re)creates 'soils of significance' (Eva Hoffman quoted in Ahmed et al. 2003: 9). Such acts become increasingly theorized in current anthropology and cultural studies, particularly in the context of diaspora and migration studies (see also Titus 2019).

Maskanda's perceived rootedness in a range of earlier musical practices – which I will discuss throughout this book – underlies its authority as a substitute for what Bhabha calls a 'mother culture' that can no longer be retrieved (1994e: 111). Olsen has shown how such performative (re)imaginings and (re)claimings of home were almost instantly appropriated by the apartheid government as an instrument of power to deny people a home, turning enactments of homing into a form of violent domestication:

> Rural life is constructed in maskanda of the apartheid era as a place of stability, comfort, and belonging, and indeed also one of realness or authenticity. And it is through this recourse to a retrospective view of their identity that maskanda musicians contested the identity that they had in the present of their lived experience. Paradoxically, it was this same retrospective view of Zuluness that was appropriated by the apartheid government in its design of an ethnically divided South Africa. The clearly expressed location of these songs, not just as Zulu music, but Zulu music rooted in a rural past, was ripe for use as validation of the notion of a Zulu homeland.
>
> (Olsen 2014: 188)

Yet, the longer I spent time with maskanda musickers, the more I felt maskanda musicking cannot be explained in terms of retrospectivity only, not in apartheid times, and not now.[2] Maskanda was and is a mode of knowing for those who were being kept out of formal education systems, but it is also legible within hegemonic systems of recording and distribution including media broadcasts and music industries. This free-rein in-between status engenders a multitude of processes of becoming liminal or becoming subaltern or becoming normative. Often, these becomings occur simultaneously, with a maskanda guitarist being a nameless non-presence in the world of South African middle classes and a normative validator of tradition in the world of South African labour migrants. Focusing on ways in which maskanda musickers foreground what they hear allows for this multiplicity, liminality and fluidity of subject positions to be heard. Thus, maskanda performance is also an enactment of new forms of belonging. This clarifies why many musickers perceive maskanda as a hybrid musical practice (Titus 2008: 47). Bhabha would call this act of mimicry an articulation of a metonymic identity – a 'not quite' copy of the self as a mother culture – that transforms, and often distorts, normative or established knowledge, practices or skills in unanticipated ways (Bhabha 1994d: 86). Sara Ahmed notes in a similar strain of thought that 'diasporic homes' can 'queer' conventional conceptions of home (Ahmed et al. 2003: 8).

The double vision and double hearing of these acts of home making acquires an additional complexity with the regimes of hearing that shaped and continue to shape South African society. Johnny Clegg explains how maskanda was consistently Othered during the apartheid era:

> [a]partheid taught you [i.e. white middle-class South Africans] not to see, to walk down the street and *not* see a black man, coming up the street, playing the guitar. If you heard the sound, it was a foreign sound. It made no sense to you, it was a garbled, distorted sonic representation of a culture that is dangerous to you.
>
> (Clegg quoted in Coplan 1993a: 321, emphasis in original)

In her monograph about maskanda, Kathryn Olsen points to the consequences of such aural strategies of Othering, telling that, until she started her research,

> the path of my existence and the paths of maskanda musicians had not intersected, except perhaps incidentally, anonymously, or under the weight of the identities assumed and controlled by the apartheid regime. The guitar music that I heard on the streets of the middle-class suburb where I lived as a young child was nameless in my world, just as those who played this music were nameless.
>
> (Olsen 2014: xii)

I have observed with my own ears and eyes that maskanda's perceived non/presence among the South African white middle classes continues up to this day, with a sustained tension between (not) hearing, seeing and naming maskandi, as testified by

---

[2] Deborah James (1999: 187) also observes this in the context of her research into kiba singing and dancing of migrant women from a variety of South African communities in the late 1980s and early 1990s.

Olsen during her youth. When I spoke about my research subject to white Durbanites, it struck me that they had never *heard* (of) maskanda in their entire life, but had nevertheless *seen* black people plucking their guitars on the street. They had simply neither ever paid attention to them, nor wondered what they were playing.

These testimonies from privileged white South Africans (please note the absence of black voices here) powerfully illustrate the observation by Bruce Smith that 'people dwelling in a particular soundscape know the world in fundamentally different ways from people dwelling in another soundscape' (Smith 1999: 47). I would like to complicate this observation by claiming that people who dwell in the very same soundscape also know (and hear) the world in fundamentally different ways (see also Hahn 2007: 21). During the apartheid era, segregated knowings and hearings were imposed consistently as a strategy of divide and rule.³ This imposition led to attitudes and predispositions that continue to feature in colonial situations and interactions, in South Africa and beyond. Firstly, it sustained the tension between (not) hearing, seeing and naming maskandi. Secondly, it facilitated a subconscious articulation of the sonic as a subjective, multifarious and spherical Constitutive Other of the visual as objective, singular and directional (Santiago Castro-Gómez as cited in Ochoa 2014: 13). Thirdly, it propagated a reified distinction between the natural and the cultural, with sound being unreflectively 'given' and music being sophistically 'made'. These predispositions are increasingly acknowledged as eurogenic strategies of control with long colonial histories, Othering the sonic worlds of the colonized as less human or not human at all (Ochoa 2014: 31ff).

Acoustic assemblages

The power of obstructing people to develop (aural) relationships with each other points at the importance of Paul Carter's recognition that 'our speech originates not in a disembodied silence, but in a tumultuous incorporation of the other's voice and that discourse is the process of giving meaning to echoic mimicry' (2004: 50). This recognition prompts him to explore 'the feedback loop between listening and speaking' (55). Veit Erlmann observes that Carter's point of focus 'resonates strongly' with Peter Szendy's engagement with 'a twofold process of hearing another person listen' (Szendy [2001] 2008 paraphrased by Erlmann 2004: 18):

> One area where this seems to be possible, surprisingly, is in musical arrangements. Arrangers, Szendy says, sign their listening into the work of another. Arrangements then are no longer second-class citizens in a world of original musical works, but rather key elements in Szendy's concept of ears that hear each other hear.
> (Erlmann 2004: 18)

---

³ In his book about kwaito and the aesthetics of freedom in South Africa, Gavin Steingo, too, observes that '[t]he apartheid policy of ethnic zoning was not merely spatial; it was also, and at the same time, a distribution of the sensible .... It produced, in other words, a triangular relationship between bodily postures, cognitive affordances, and practices of sense making' (2016: 95).

Ana María Ochoa Gautier succinctly outlines these dialogical understandings of sonic expression and communication in her theorization of a circulating acoustic assemblage:

> [A] theory of sound implies a listener, which in turn imagines a listener and an idea of reception of sound. In the relation between each of these entities – a listening subject, an object that produces sound, and a supposed listener of that sound object – what is produced is an ontology of relationships, an idea of how to think the interaction between entities that produce/hear sounds .... What this implies is the need to explore the richness of a multiplicity of variables among what different peoples consider the given and what they consider the made that come together in the acoustic .... Such an assemblage circulates between different listening entities through different practices of inscription of sound: rituals, writing, acoustic events, and so forth that, in turn, are also heard.
>
> (Ochoa 2014: 22)

The aim of apartheid (cultural) policy was to police and restrict the circulation of acoustic assemblages between listening entities mentioned by Ochoa: maskanda's multiple constellations of imagined or potential listening subjects and sound-producing objects, as well as the fluid ever-changing relationships between them, were singularized through prescribed modes of (sonic) knowledge inscription (picking style playing, pentatonicism, *izibongo* spoken self-praise, *ingoma* dance music, *ubeshu* dress), in order to articulate singular and controllable subject positions (martial bodily excess, rural courtship, Zuluness, African folklore). By preventing certain people from hearing certain others, apartheid – quite literally as a notion of separateness – could perfidiously creep into the nooks and crannies of people's minds and bodies, into their sub/consciousness. Musical performance, arrangement (maskandafication) as well as scholarship, within and outside South Africa, were some of the key modes of exerting control of the circulation of aural relationships between subjects.

My focus on Bhabha's conception of a Third Space of enunciation, Ahmed et al.'s interpretation of home making, Ochoa's theorization of acoustic assemblages that circulate between listening entities, Carter's identification of a feedback loop between listening and speaking and Szendy's engagement with the process of hearing another person listen serve the aim of elucidating how such enunciations, groundings, circulations, feedback loops, arrangements and reifications in maskanda practices operate as knowledge. They all concern the same capacity of confronting and sharing aural experiences, which is an intrinsically epistemic capacity, since it constitutes a temporarily positioned resonance between a self and the world.[4] The presentation of existing (musical) practices, techniques, ideas, norms and statements as maskanda performance (maskandafication) is a predominant mode of sharing aural experiences and hence constitutes the main focus of this book. Through maskandafication,

---

[4] I emphatically do not distinguish between the categories of hearing and listening. Although I acknowledge the various degrees of attentiveness and voluntariness in hearing music, I maintain that the idea of listening is Eurocentric and conceptually limiting, in having emerged from, and being tied to, a specific nineteenth-century European musicking practice.

maskandi present their maskanda performance as a way of life and as a mode of sense making. Through writing this book, I present my readings of maskanda performance (with my own eurogenic analytical tools) as my mode of sense making. I confront these modes of sense making, but I also want to reach beyond the binary they represent by demonstrating how maskandi's musical maskandafication and my conceptual academic analysis intersect and operate along comparable procedures and strategies of sense making.

Nearly agential pressures

Olivia Bloechl foregrounds the dichotomy of knowledge as representative, singular, coherent and unified versus sentience as plural, variable and inconsistent (2008: xiv) by drawing on the insights of Gayatri Spivak, Dipesh Chakrabarty and Homi Bhabha. This dichotomy continues to be employed as a colonial strategy of Othering, coming uncannily close to Santiago Castro-Gómez's observation of difference between the visual and the aural respectively (quoted in Ochoa 2014: 13). I demonstrate how this dichotomy underlay the apartheid attempts to 'know' maskanda, and I point at its alignment with similar articulations of difference during the early period of colonization in the sixteenth to eighteenth centuries that shaped 'the increasingly important fantasy' of Europe's cultural autonomy and superiority (Bloechl 2008: xiv). Bloechl explains how this ideology was an anxious response to the intermingling of peoples and cultures caused by colonial conquest. This intermingling challenged existing politico-cultural identities through the highlighting of 'alternate vectors of identification' and through 'uncomfortable questions regarding relations of likeness and difference' (xiv). She convincingly demonstrates how the consistent and coherent narratives 'about' colonial subjects started to function as imperious codes in themselves, and continue to do so up to this day in the 'absence of a skeptical, transculturally literate, and interventionist approach to colonial sources' that 'as if by default, reinstates "Europe" as the subject and object of the knowledge musicologists produce' (23).

One way of being transculturally literate and interventionist, she suggests, is to observe that colonialism (and apartheid) worked to annihilate the possibility of witnessing to its atrocities (2008: 10). Despite this, and because of this, she asserts, there is knowledge 'subtly active as a nearly agential pressure' that 'does not constitute a discrete ... figure, gesture or style process' (11) in historical sources, and is hence unavailable for music hermeneutical or critical interpretation (20). As such, it cannot be 'read' directly from hegemonic (academic) written discourse: in sources, accounts of cultural memory or histories that present (and are supposed to present) coherent, directive, synchronous, self-sufficient and singular narratives.

I observed that maskanda's epistemological implications have been similarly (made) illegible. They, too, might end up as barely perceivable pressures for those who read the literature about maskanda in three hundred or four hundred years. With my foregrounding of maskanda musickers' aural experiences as modes of knowing, I hope to make them available for hermeneutical and critical interpretation. Yet, the 'discrete figures, gestures or style processes' they might become through my foregrounding also make them subservient to my hermeneutical and critical interpretation as eurogenic modes of knowing.

Whose hearing?

This problem surfaces in all the book's chapters as well as with regard to the primary sources that feature in this book: the maskanda musickers I worked with and talked to. I never consciously chose to select them for information about maskanda and about their musical way of life. They came upon my path through the suggestions by colleagues and friends and my growing personal network that was shaped by those maskandi and maskanda musickers who possessed the agency to access it. I worked and musicked over sustained periods of months with maskandi active in Durban on a local and regional level (the sisters S'kho and Khoni Miya). I talked repeatedly or occasionally with musicians active in the Johannesburg music industry (Nothi Ntuli, Bongani Nkwanyana, iHashi Elimhlophe, Phuzekhemisi, Zuluboy, Madala Kunene). I worked for long periods of time with maskandi with past and current international careers (Shiyani Ngcobo, Qadasi) and talked to others occasionally (Joe Nkwanyana, Tu Nokwe, Johnny Clegg). This makes this monograph about maskanda a partial account in several respects. I predominantly worked with people for whom maskanda is a way of life rather than a successful commercial enterprise, but I was often unable to articulate their aural experiences of maskanda in favour of my own aural experiences of maskanda.

I did carry out research into the commercial aspects of maskanda (see Part II). I talked to commercially successful musicians such as Phuzekhemisi, iHashi Elimhlophe, Bongani Nkwanyana, Bheki Khoza, Madala Kunene and Zuluboy. I discussed the hugely popular music of Shwi noMtekhala (Titus 2016a). I attended performances by maskanda stars, such as Thokozani Langa, Busi Mhlongo and Imithente, and I interviewed record producers and programmers at the centre of the South African music industry (Tshepo Nzimande, Abraham Mija, Lichaba Nthethe, Nhlanhla Ngwekazi). Nevertheless, the maskanda produced for a local market does not take centre stage in my account of maskanda even though such commercially produced maskanda music is enjoyed by a majority of maskanda musickers. This indicates, as one of my peer reviewers emphasized, the multiplicity and diversity of maskanda practice. There are many maskandas, and only some of them are covered in this book.

In Chapter 1, I address the age-old Zulu war song 'Sab' Inganono' in the maskanda rendering of two white Zulu maskandi, Johnny Clegg and David Jenkins. This enables me to introduce maskanda's fraught history of social and racial distinction and inequality, and to demonstrate the topicality of this history more than twenty years after the demise of apartheid. In Chapter 2, I address the multiple ways in which maskanda styles and skills are linked to specific regions through sound, dance, poetry, critical debate and scholarly research. This enables me to point out the disruptive migratory movements maskanda musickers made in colonial and apartheid eras and the multifarious and sometimes contradictory ways in which these movements have acquired meaning. Thus, Chapters 1 and 2 constitute Part I of this book introducing maskanda's presence in multiple times and places.

Part II deals with local, national and international events that provide platforms for maskandi to produce and reproduce home, and (re)ground heritage and knowledge that has been uprooted in centuries of colonial and apartheid rule. In Chapter 3, I carry out a close reading of the vocal appropriation of an *ibhodlo* (roaring) sound by my friend and colleague Khombisile 'S'kho' Miya (b. 1972) at the Kushikisha Imbokodo Festival in Durban in August 2009. At this local women's festival, she consciously imbued this *ibhodlo* with renewed female agency. In Chapter 4, I focus on the polymetric sensation I got from her song 'Sithi Khuzani', which she performed at the national MTN Onkweni Royal Cultural (MORC) Festival in Ulundi in October 2009. This sensation enables me to engage with the intersections of (aural) experiences and assumptions, and notably with ways in which cultural stereotypes that have already been recognized as fetish (Agawu 2003: 82–6) remain operative as metaphoric and metonymic reductions in formations of knowledge about the experience of music and culture. In Chapter 5, I deliver a close reading of Shiyani Ngcobo's song 'Asinankomo' at the Tropentheater in Amsterdam, the Netherlands, in June 2010. My delayed acknowledgement of the epistemic and epistemological depth of this song serves to demonstrate the difficulty, embarrassment and representational inequality that accompanies the acquisition and formation of knowledge about and through musicking in cross-cultural situations.

Whereas Part II of this book focuses on the events and the spaces in which maskanda becomes heard and becomes legible to its audiences, Part III addresses *how* maskanda becomes legible to its audiences. Here, I further develop my assumption that maskanda functions as a Third Space of enunciation. Through their presentation of igamas, maskandi hear other people hear, construe meanings that 'constantly reanimate themselves in a potentially never-ending feedback loop [between hearing and speaking]' (Erlmann 2004: 18–19) and, by moving about in this feedback loop, are able to ground anew existing habits (singing techniques, tonal material), objects (riffs, songs), names (maskandiR&B, skandihop) and histories (of home, segregation and apartheid) *as* maskanda. They maskandafy their experiences through their continuous sonic and aural (re)organization of space and (re)assemblage of concepts. In Chapter 6, I provide a close reading of two versions of Bongani Nkwanyana's song 'Inkunzi Emnyama' by outlining how it draws on performance, poetry and musical techniques of (Zulu) musical practices that are said to predate colonial imposition, such as *umakhweyana* gourd bow and *isitorotoro* mouth harp playing. I discuss Nkwanyana's same song in its album version, released on the commercial market, this time conversing with global jazz and pop idioms. My engagement with the rap song 'DJ Gogo' by hip-hop artist Zuluboy and S'kho Miya's outspokenly feminist spoken self-praise (*izibongo*) in Chapter 7 further substantiates my insight that maskandi (re)process and (re)create global musical idioms and norms within maskanda as conscious acts of appropriation and grounding, rather than as reactive conformations to global musical norms. In Chapter 8, I focus on S'kho Miya's song 'Sithi Khuzani' on stage, in rehearsal and on her album *Ungcayi Lweqhikiza* (2010). I outline the sonic and aural implications of the various spaces (stage, rehearsal room, studio) in which maskanda is supposed to become legible, addressed in Part II, and how the aesthetic appreciation of maskanda's sound is influenced by these spaces that often also have a specific social status.

The social and the formal

Already in the mid-1990s, Ingrid Monson observed a 'non-intersection' between 'interdisciplinary studies of music and identity' on the one hand, and 'close readings of music works and performances' on the other (1996: 3). Nishlyn Ramanna (2016: 9) has outlined how this non-intersection became particularly urgent in South Africa after the demise of apartheid when cultural scholars expressed a keen interest in 'denaturalizing' apartheid categories and discriminations that had been culturally constituted through formalist analyses of articulated musical 'pieces', and through conclusive historicist accounts of these pieces' allegedly inalienable roots and coherent musical developments (Kirby [1934] 1953; Rycroft 1977; Clegg 1981; Ntuli 1990; Davies 1992). Deconstructing the coherence of these narratives became a primary concern of many music studies in the post-apartheid era (Ballantine [1993] 2012; Coplan 2002; Muller 2004; Olsen 2014). Yet, as Ochoa observes:

> [I]n 'denaturalizing' the cultural constructions through which the knowledge of the 'other' has been subordinated in order to recognize and reveal an 'other' knowledge we often leave intact the underlying relation between nature and culture that such knowledge implies. Instead of denaturalizing we often reculturalize by proposing new modes of representation.
>
> (2014: 21)

Maskanda's epistemological implications have remained illegible and unacknowledged because maskanda has ended up at one side of the absolutist separation between the social and the formal. According to Martin Scherzinger (2004: 253), this separation creates a new regime of inclusion and exclusion. By pointing out *what* knowledge maskanda shares, and, more importantly, *how* it shares this knowledge, I intend to interrogate the categories of the social and the formal. I denaturalize their status as self-sufficient signifiers. I also draw attention to the underlying relation between what is considered given (inexhaustible and to be taken for granted) and what is considered made (polished and rare) – a relation exemplified in the one between 'nature' and 'culture' respectively. In my conclusion I explore some options for ways in which we can stop assuming an *a priori* difference (Agawu 2003: 151ff) between maskanda epistemologies and academic epistemologies; operations of knowledge acquisition and formation in my research overlap with maskandafication as a sense making device. These options might help us refrain from expelling maskanda epistemologies (and many others worldwide) to the domain of epistemic Otherness, and prevent us from upholding the fantasy of Europe's epistemic and epistemological self-sufficiency and autonomy. This is my way of being 'transculturally interventionist' (Bloechl 2008: xiv).

This interventionist approach is also inspired by Concord Nkabinde's encouragement that I keep initiating a dialogue with fellow musickers about what it is that I am doing, even if this dialogue does not always materialize. For only in such a dialogue are participants able to 'hear another person listen' and, subsequently, to position themselves in the exchange of experiences, something that apartheid rule has always deliberately obstructed. And only through such a requirement of cultural positioning can my academic account and understanding of maskanda be treated as culturally situated, even though it is being epistemologically privileged. This might open up possibilities for more relational forms of sense making.

Part I

Maskanda in Colonial, Apartheid and Post-Apartheid South Africa

1

Maskanda's Colonial, Apartheid and Post-Apartheid Presence

'Sab' Inganono' (Afraid of the Cannon) is 'an age-old Zulu war song' (Clegg 2009). In the innumerable struggles over land documented in South Africa's history, such as the Battle of the Blood River (1838), the Battle of Isandlwana (1879) and the Bambatha Rebellion (1906), cannons coerced warriors from various camps to fight or flee. The song produces and presents the various attitudes, emotions and states of mind that accompanied these acts: fear, aggression, interrogation of each other's position. At present, the song is most readily available in two recent maskanda renditions, performed by white Zulu maskandi, Jonathan (Johnny) Clegg a.k.a. Sikeyi (1953–2019) and David Jenkins a.k.a. Qadasi (b. 1992). The immediate presence of singing voices and antiphonal backing choruses, virtuosic guitar picking, synchronized regimental *ingoma* dance routines and assertive poetic statements in spoken self-praise summon the circumstances and conditions of maskanda's emergence, dis/placement and transculturation. This song is about itself. For it was (and is) the cannons featuring in this song that managed to impose the controlling ideologies of difference and segregation as well as to enforce the massive labour migration of the late nineteenth and early twentieth centuries that gave rise to maskanda practice. Both this migration and these ideologies unabatedly govern South African cohabitation on many levels in the early twenty-first century. Past and present cannot easily be separated.

White maskandi

Both Clegg and Jenkins immersed themselves fully in Zulu culture from a young age onwards. Clegg recalls his participation in Bhaca dance sessions as a life-changing experience at the age of fifteen (Clegg 2009). He joined the Nala age regiment of the Zulu king Zwelethini as a Shameni dancer and continued to participate in isiShameni and umzansi dance and street guitar song next to his successful career as an internationally acclaimed pop artist until the very end of his life. Several Zulu South Africans stated they learned about their own culture through Johnny Clegg (Ngwekazi 2009; Nkabinde 2009). Jenkins developed a passionate interest in Zulu culture at the

Figure 1.1 David Jenkins (a.k.a. Qadasi) (left) with his friend and mentor Maqhinga Radebe (right), 2015. Photograph by Amy Jenkins. Reproduced with kind permission.

age of nine, initially through the TV series *Shaka Zulu* (Faure 1986).[1] Thus, he began his collection of books, traditional clothing, beadwork and music. He was given a guitar at the age of twelve and taught himself maskanda with maskandi Phuzekhemisi as his musical example (Jenkins 2013a). Both Clegg and Jenkins are fluent in the Zulu language and present themselves as members of the Zulu community in their language, music and clothing (Figure 1.1). The fact that they have grown up in/with the culture they say they represent is often quoted as a reason by musickers (Nkabinde 2009; Ntuli 2009) for taking them seriously as Zulu musicians.

It is highly problematic to start a monograph about a musical practice known as a Zulu way of expression with the igamas of two white Zulu South Africans. The participation of white people in black performance practices that are so closely intertwined with black life experiences during colonial and apartheid eras is profoundly meaningful and carries a range of tensions. It triggers long and consistent histories of white appropriations of black cultural capital, which are and have been present anywhere in the world, but which have been sanctioned and encouraged extensively in South Africa in particular. Nevertheless, I have decided to employ the maskanda performances

---

[1] Several authors point at 'the historical inaccuracies and apartheid politics involved in the making of the film *Shaka Zulu*' (Carton and Draper 2008: 603) based on the TV series from 1986, yet '[e]merging on screen as economic sanctions and cultural boycotts further ostracised South Africa, *Shaka Zulu* garnered praise and audiences – and has seldom been absent from TV screens since' (594).

of Clegg and Jenkins as modes of telling the story of maskanda's emergence in this chapter and to situate them at the start of this book. I state three reasons for doing this.

Firstly, their participation in maskanda practice, although far more long-standing and intensive than mine, unearths similar issues as to my participation, which will be addressed throughout this book. There are inequalities on almost every level of interaction with those maskanda musickers who still experience in their daily lives the circumstances from which maskanda emerged: inequalities in social status, financial remuneration, education, mobility, available means of expression, self-confidence, etc. Inevitably, this leads to acts of white appropriation of black musical and cultural agency, which audibly and visibly surfaces in performance, aesthetic judgements and academic research. These appropriations need to be foregrounded and critically discussed in order to facilitate a dialogue about the dynamics of these processes and an honest acknowledgement of everyone's subject position in performance and conceptual discourses that are so closely intertwined.

Secondly, I intend to resist the representation of maskanda as a parochial Zulu artefact. Although Clegg's and Jenkins's Zuluness is beyond doubt for the Zulu South Africans I talked to, it is important to emphasize that maskanda is no longer only practised and presented as the musical equivalent of an apartheid homeland. 'Sab' Inganono' is a song that invites many ways of hearing it, and allows for associations with many musics from within and from outside Africa that account for maskanda's early and current syncretism. Thus, I emphatically aim to foreground not only Clegg's and Jenkins's aural experiences and the way they use their bodies and voices to present their igama, but also the comments, interpretations and critiques of those maskanda musickers who engage with the igamas of these two 'white Zulus'.

Thirdly, the renderings that Clegg and Jenkins present are in many ways emblematic for the (different) ways in which maskanda is created, experienced and appreciated in present-day South Africa, possibly because they need to assert their Zulu status as white maskandi. In a way, the emblematic character of their renderings says something about their position as relatively privileged maskandi, a privilege that enables them to engage themselves with conserving the genre and with the genre's orientation to musical practices elsewhere in the world.

I discuss four renderings of 'Sab' Inganono', two by David Jenkins – a live performance on stage in Dublin, Ireland from 2013 (Jenkins and Band 2013) and his 2011 release of the song on his album *Child of Africa / Ingane yase Afrika* (Jenkins and Band 2011)[2] – and two by Johnny Clegg. One of them has been released on his DVD *My Favourite Zulu Street Guitar Songs*, set in the famous Mai Mai Market in Johannesburg where many street musicians performed and competed with each other during apartheid times (Clegg and Band 2007: 02'33"). A slightly different non-staged

---

[2] Jenkins's rendering of this song served as a case study for my publication in the volume *Transcultural Music History*, edited by Reinhard Strohm (Titus 2021). In this publication, the transcription of the song, Jenkins's role as a white maskandi and the various subject positions in the song lyrics as outlined in this chapter were employed for the specific aim of articulating the historiographical implications of maskanda music.

[Verse:]
We sab' inganono
[Lead] Ubalekelani?

We sab' ukuduma kwayo
[Lead:] Lashona

Is he / [Hey,] are you afraid of the cannon?
[Why] is he / are you running away? /
Don't run from the gun
He is / You are afraid of its sound
The sun has set / He is dead [terrified]

[Chorus:]
Wathukuthela,
We sab' ukuduma kwayo
Wathukuthela,
We sab' inganono
[Lead:] Ubalekelani?

He / You got angry,
He / You got afraid of its sound
He / You got angry,
He / You got afraid of the cannon
[Why] is he / are you running away? /
Don't run from the gun

[*Izibongo* Clegg 2011:]
Thatha Mfezi
Zibambe Skegi
Vikela Eshobeni
Bayamzonda abantu
bamzondela ngoba uthanda umculo waba ntwana

Take Mfezi
Hold Skegi
Protect Eshobeni
They hate him
because he likes music of children

*** [too rapid to transcribe and translate] ***

[Verse:]
Zafik' ezakithi ukushona kwelanga

Zafik' ezakithi nodumo lwazo

[Lead:] Lashona

We (warriors) are coming in thousands when the sun sets
We (warriors) are coming in thousands with thunderous sound
The sun has set / He is dead [terrified]

[Chorus Clegg 2011:]
We nsizwa ubalekelani?

Hey, why are you running away?

[Chorus Jenkins 2013:]
Shi hom, hom – Shi hom

[War song incantations]

Figure 1.2 'Sab' Inganono'. Lyrics transcribed and translated by Ignatia Madalane and Elias Nxumalo with kind permission from David Jenkins.

version of this rendering is available and widely accessed on YouTube (Clegg 2011). Like all maskandi, Clegg and Jenkins re-'read' and appropriate an existing 'text' that has verbal, musical and performance-based dimensions. By analysing what they do – with my own culturally situated eurogenic tools – I participate in this process of re-reading and appropriation.

Who is talking here? This question inevitably surfaces when white Zulu maskandi articulate the lyrics of an age-old Zulu war song (Figure 1.2). Multiple voices are speaking simultaneously in this song. 'He' is afraid of the cannon and is running away, but 'we' are coming with our warriors in their thousands. These multiple voices represent opposite affective attitudes towards the sound of the cannons with opposite movements: fear (through flight) and aggression (through attack). Whether the protagonist is described as a distant third person ('he') or addressed directly as a second person ('you') remains undecided, since the verb conjugation with prefix u- can refer to both the second and third person singular, and the subject is not articulated, apart from the exclamation *we* that could – but does not have to – be short for *wena* ('you'). There is a multivocality not only in manner of address but also in singular and plural addressees. Translator Ignatia Madalane observed that through 'Sab' Inganono''s distinctiveness as a war cry song, 'the "he" in the song can refer to any man who is afraid of going to war or battle. Therefore, though it is singular, it can refer to anyone or any man' (Madalane 2016b). Both instances of undecidedness are features of the Zulu language at large and are functional to this specific statement, enhancing its immediacy in the here and now (with third and second person being the same) and enhancing its general validity (with individual and general addressees). These instances of undecidedness were substantiated by the various translations I heard for the sentence 'Ubalekelani?'. Madalane observed the confrontational manner of the inquisitive tense: 'Why are you running away?' (2016b). In other sources, this confrontational tone has been incorporated in a stating rather than inquisitive translation: 'Don't run from the gun' (Mchunu 1979).

The 'Sab' Inganono' lyrics refer to the sound rather than the sight of the cannons and the warriors in their thousands, enhancing the immediacy of the statement: 'even if you don't see them, they are here: hear!'. Crucial for the focus on the sound rather than the sight of the battle is the interpretation of the stem '-*duma*' which refers to being noisy as well as being (in)famous, and literally means (to) thunder. Thus, the reference to warriors in their thousands could refer to Zulu armies with thunderous *impi* (warrior) regiments as well as to British or Boer armies with thunderous cannons. Madalane observed that those who flee and those who fight can be understood to belong to the same (Zulu) camp against the British or Boers, 'confronting the coward ... members of the team about their cowardice',[3] or they can be understood to belong to opposing (Zulu) camps, one with cannons (possibly siding with the British or Boers),[4]

---

[3] This is also how Clegg (2007) reads the song.
[4] Clegg (2007) asserts that guns not only were used by British and Boer settlers but were also widely distributed among Zulu (and other Nguni) communities in clan warfare.

and another without (running from the cannons). Deliberate textual obscurities are abundant in Zulu poetry, including maskanda practice. Often the lyrics are directed towards those who have witnessed the expressed event themselves, so that only members of the community will understand what is being said. This further enhances the immediacy of the event 'as if you were/are there'.

Thus, the igama is cast in the lyrics, dance, dress and music simultaneously. This multimodality of the statement illustrates how 'the physical experience of the body … sustains a particular view of society' (Mary Douglas [1970] 1996: 69 quoted in Clegg 1982: 13). This sustenance of 'a particular view of society' acquires a specific urgency in Jenkins and Clegg being 'white Zulus', a subject position that crystalizes from their stage presence in embodiment, dance and dress, but also from the sound composition and the lyrics they identify with. Their performances could be described as acts of Bhabhaesque mimicry. They claim cultural authority by appropriating (partly colonially constructed) Zulu modes of performance and expression (mimicry as strategy of colonial authority), they erect structures of cultural discrimination through this appropriation (mimicry as discriminatory knowledge) and they undermine, respell and queer these authorities and structures at the same time (mimicry as menace to this same colonial authority).

The implications of their performances that confirm or reproduce colonial authority became clear to me only gradually through Ignatia Madalane's explanation of the subject positions in the war song, and how these are complicated by being sung by a white man. By speaking in the Zulu language, the song's protagonist likely converses with Zulu men, and this leaves room for their self-representation 'as the colonizer with his "magical negro" warriors' (Madalane 2016c). The stereotype of the 'magical negro' as a 'lower-class, uneducated, and magical black character who transforms disheveled, uncultured, or broken white characters into competent people' (Hughey 2009: 543) has been prominent in centuries of literary imagination and decades of globally distributed US cinema. '"Magical negro" films thus … empower normalized and hegemonic forms of whiteness, and glorify powerful black characters in so long as they are placed in racially subservient positions' (Hughey 2009: 543). In South Africa, this trope has acquired a compelling historical dimension through the many examples of 'blacks who … revolted against the leader' (Madalane 2016c) and sided with the whites. Clegg mentions the example of the Chunu and the Tembu people absconding from the Zulu state (1981: 3), to be discussed in Chapter 2. All battles with cannons that 'Sab' Inganono' potentially reproduces, ranging from the Battle of the Blood River in 1838 to the Bambatha Rebellion in 1906, feature such allegiances that always thrived on black subservience to a white cause. In this context, Jenkins's performance facilitates a very specific third scenario of the various subject positions in 'Sab' Inganono' outlined earlier by Madalane: 'our [colonial] warriors [with thunderous cannons] come in their thousands, and why are you ["magical negro" belonging to our camp] running away from them?' (Madalane 2016c).

The appearance of Jenkins's band on the Dublin stage can be seen to reinforce the 'magical negro' stereotype. Jenkins's maskandi name Qadasi means 'white person'. This indicates that those who gave him this name – a maskandi's name is always given by fellow musickers – consider his skin colour to be meaningful. The privileges that Jenkins and his ancestors have enjoyed because of this as well as his image on centre stage flanked by black musicians complicate the inclusive message he embodies: we see a white protagonist with subservient black helpers (Jenkins and Band 2013). Clegg's setting on the Mai Mai Market is more diversified: Clegg is not visually centralized and the members of his backing chorus, Bongani Masuku, Sithembiso Makhoba, Bafazana Qoma and Sipho Nxumalo, not only have responsive agency to his lead call, but also take on parts of the *izibongo* self-praise (Clegg and Band 2007: 04'17" – Bafazana Qoma). They are named in the credit titles of the documentary. Yet, in many of the other songs, Clegg is the central protagonist walking through the market, flanked by several black singers and dancers, which has a musical equivalent in lead singer calls and backing-chorus responses. Many extremely profitable musical collaborations (ranging from Paul Simon's *Graceland* in 1986 to Miley Cyrus's 'We Can't Stop' in 2013) continue to thrive on this stage delivery. Clegg and Jenkins may be seen to reinforce the discriminatory knowledge on which these collaborations thrive.[5]

Another issue that begs critical engagement was the fact that Madalane (being a black, Zulu-speaking South African) noted this third scenario, and I (being a white, barely Zulu-speaking European) initially did not. Moreover, I felt reluctance in writing down the problematic implications of Jenkins's and Clegg's stage deliveries. Explicating the conformist potential of their stage deliveries to colonial and apartheid epistemologies went against my intention to present them as musickers that consciously want to reach beyond apartheid and segregation. I was much more inclined to highlight their menacing of colonial gazes: Jenkins's stage presence as a white Zulu and Clegg's walking through the formerly black domain of the Mai Mai Market 'rewrite' the categorical inscriptions that the concept of race fulfilled in apartheid South Africa. Being born in the heartland of the Zulu Kingdom and having learned maskanda guitar from a young age onwards, Jenkins consciously and sensitively articulates himself as a Zulu musician through his relation with his band members (fellow guitarist Maqhinga Radebe is his teacher rather than his helper), his command of the language and his careful use of cultural symbols in dance (*ukugiya*), song (war song incantations) and dress (*umbaselwa* aestheticized mining suits).

Clegg and Jenkins find themselves in social positions that enable them to resist the reduction of their performances to a matter of race. Many maskandi, also those from a post-apartheid generation born in the 1990s, do not enjoy this privilege. They told me about their hunger for new musical stimuli, for exposure to music they haven't heard before (N. Shabalala 2013), for musical collaborations that cross genres, nations and racial, ethnic, gender or age identities (Kunene 2008; Khama 2009). After decades of cultural boycott during the apartheid years, South African musicians and listeners feel hampered in their musical development by being understood as Zulu

---

[5] It is important to note that the visuals of Clegg's recording (2007) were carefully staged for a commercial release, whereas Jenkins's staging (Jenkins and Band 2013) was coincidentally recorded by a member of the audience and shared on YouTube without the involvement or consent of Jenkins and his band members.

musicians playing Zulu music only. As Ignatia Madalane commented (2021a), it will be unthinkable for them to ever get accepted as, for instance, an Afrikaans rock star, even if they perfect their Afrikaans pronunciation and musical expression. Clegg and Jenkins have never been subjected to this constriction to the same extent. They have always been in a position to choose to be Zulu musicians playing Zulu music.

Female and male agencies

Whereas Clegg's presence on stage can be interpreted in many different ways, his presence in written discourses about maskanda is outright hegemonic. Scholars who have researched maskanda's early history and its structural features (N. Davies 1992; Nhlapo 1998; Muller 1999; Olsen 2000; Coplan 2002; Pewa 2005; Collins 2006–7; Titus 2008; Olsen 2014) were more or less forced to build their argument on Clegg's insights, available through various means of publication and dissemination. His work is groundbreaking, because Clegg is so much at home in all modes of expression and signification of maskanda musicking: guitar playing, singing, embodying the state of *ubukunzi* (bullness) including *umgangela* (stick fighting), *izibongo* self-praising, *ukugiya* and *ingoma* dancing. Crucially, he is able to sense his position among kings (*amakhosi*), chiefs and headmen (*izinduna*) in the hierarchical organization of Zulu society. Clegg is, moreover, academically trained as an anthropologist.

There are a couple of aspects in maskanda that illustrate the fact that maskanda discourse is still ultimately retraced to Clegg's musical and social experiences of the genre. The first of these aspects is the dominance of the historiography of maskanda as a male urban musical response to the condition of forced labour migrancy, a culture that – according to Clegg – has been on the wane for decades (Clegg 1981: 4; 2009). Another aspect is the categorization and geographical location of maskanda's substyles. By critically addressing these two aspects in Chapters 1 and 2, I will introduce maskanda as a performance practice and as a knowledge system that intricately intersects with (scholarly) narratives about it.

Clegg states how maskanda developed as an urban practice that signified, transmitted and shaped the image of village life in precolonial times. This aspect of maskanda has become a truism in maskanda research.

> When these migrants left home they were locked in compounds … they started to play on these instruments – the guitar, which they bought from the mine shop – songs to remind them of home, songs which their sweethearts sung … A lot of the songs were drawn from the woman's musical tradition, from the umakhweyana bow … and this took on a dynamic of its own, an autonomy of its own, developing a very masculine tradition in the sense that the metaphor of a stick fight was introduced. As musicians competed in this arena they strove to create new songs, new techniques by which they could win and generate a name around themselves.
>
> (Clegg 1981: 5)

Clegg locates maskanda in urban areas as a decidedly male performance practice. Whereas an increasing number of women maskandi appear on stages, broadcast media and in studios, the fierce maskanda competitions held in hostels in Durban and Johannesburg remain, indeed, almost exclusively male events. Still, as Olsen points out (2014: 142ff), laying the agency of maskanda creation and performance almost exclusively in the hands and minds of men is a simplification of the narrative. Afropop singer and self-declared feminist Khoni Miya (b. 1961) complicates and enriches the historiography of maskanda's emergence as a male response to the experience of labour migrancy. She locates maskanda in both rural and urban environments, and she explains it as an exchange of male and female musical expressions:

> Maskande is something when the women, the ladies are going out, they do the washing by the river. Between the washing and all these things ... they used to sing loud, and start dancing traditional dance over that .... The men, they used to do it when they were going there, looking for the women, in the river, the men were doing it .... So he is going to sing maskanda, playing the concertina, moving, shaking all these things. Then the woman starts loving a theme because they are enjoying it. So the men do the maskande and the women do the maskande. Because it is the thing from rural areas ... Maskanda is right deep from the homelands ... deep homelands.
> (K. Miya 2009a)

Although Clegg, and many maskandi, incorporate the aspect of village courtship into their maskanda narratives, they describe the influence of female practices on migrant workers' music as a one-way adoption,[6] and they describe the musical courtship as a male act. Miya, however, was adamant about the fact that both men and women have always practised maskanda. Nobody knows about this, she argued, because, until recently, women couldn't go to the studio, record their music and make it known. Her account was seconded by record producer Tshepo Nzimande, who has produced albums by female maskanda bands such as Izintombi (Ngobese and Ngobese 2009) and Izingane Zoma. He asserted that female maskanda bands sound different from male bands, exactly for maskanda's (imagined) roots in both urban and rural environments:

> If you listen to the girls, the way they sing ... sometimes it sounds like they're off key ... it is laid back ... girls. Maybe they are doing the washing in the river or they are gossiping about men and all of that, so it's something: you can tell it's different if you know the music.
> (Nzimande 2009)

---

[6] One of maskanda's alleged precursory practices (see Chapter 6), playing the *umakhweyana* gourd bow, is often described as a predominantly female musical practice (Clegg 1981: 2; Davies in Lucia 2005: 208; Olsen 2014: 22). Kirby reports that 'the instrument is played by both sexes, the larger sizes by men, single or married, and the smaller by maidens or newly-married women' ([1934] 1953: 208). Impey reports that the *umakhweyana* was mainly used for the composition of love songs (*amaculo othando*). Since young men were engaged in military service, this was predominantly done by young women (Impey 1983: 2–3).

Nzimande's male chauvinist account is a clear act of gendering space (Ahmed et al. 2003: 4): the countryside is associated with women, and their lives (and reproductive bodies) are supposed to represent the nostalgic peace and quietness of precolonial rural life that became a trope among urban migrant workers. This image is still often evoked in maskanda songs themselves, such as Shwi noMtekhala's song 'Imali' (Xaba and Magubane 2003a). Miya's and Nzimande's account, as well as Shwi noMtekhala's video clip, suggest the existence of a narrative that emphasizes a continuous tradition of female maskanda practice ranging from the banks of rural rivers in the early twentieth century to the performance in Johannesburg studios in the twenty-first, even though they all take different subject positions towards this narrative, and use different modes of inscription for it. As such, maskanda evokes and embodies the experiences that are often cast in terms of abstract social transformation initiated by forced labour, apartheid and globalization. The verbal foregroundings of aural and kinetic experiences ('loud singing', 'traditional dance', 'shaking all these things', 'laid back' and 'off key') as well as the performance-based ones (the use of specific tunings, styles, dance and dress) testify to the capacity to hear one another hear (Szendy in Erlmann 2004: 18), creating a 'feedback loop between listening and speaking' (Carter 2004: 55) ('you can tell it's different if you know the music') that constitutes a circulation of acoustic assemblages in which positions of different listening entities are constantly negotiated 'through different practices of inscription of sound' (Ochoa 2014: 22–3). The position of women in maskanda practice is an insightful case in point to demonstrate the epistemological implications of these foregroundings.

Through these foregroundings – despite their representation of divergent positions and perspectives – maskanda has been constructed as a male practice, with female agency and participation being reduced to a responsive rather than proactive role. To some extent, the disruptive consequences of male labour migration have determined this construction, even though women had demonstrable agency in male–female interaction and courtship. To a larger extent, as Chris Ballantine (2000: 378) and Kathryn Olsen (2014: 147) point out too, the neglect of female agency in narratives about maskanda's history may be due to the instalment of patriarchal discourses generally, which facilitated apartheid ideology at large, and moreover served racial segregation through the reduction of Zulu culture to masculinity and warriordom (Martens 2008). It is one of the aims of this study to expose and, if possible, diversify such cultural and epistemological reductions.

The many ways in which maskanda is experienced at present have been determined to a large extent by the perceived (and regularly described) transformation maskanda is said to have undergone from a social activity into a way of making a living. Clegg describes early maskanda as 'a huge leisure activity' in the hostels 'where you are a flat cleaner but you play guitar, you hang out with other guitarists, and it is purely the pleasure and the fun and the competition amongst guitarists for a name' (Clegg 2009). Clegg observes a shift in the mid-1970s, when, in the wake of the success of legendary maskanda guitarist John Bhengu a.k.a. Phuzushukela (1930–1985), 'you could supplement your income by having a record, and you'd earn royalties'. This implies that the experience of rural nostalgia, described in the Introduction, became commercially viable and, thus, served the aims of apartheid cultural policy. Olsen describes in great detail

> the process through which [Phuzushukela's] music developed into a commercial genre, a process that involves the transition of his music from a solo performance practice to a group performance practice and that embodies or at least coincides with the formulation of maskanda as a genre. This transition produced a significant shift in maskanda aesthetic ideals and in the way it was put to work in society generally.
>
> (Olsen 2014: 30)

Building on research by Gallo producer Rob Allingham, Olsen mentions musical features that emerged from this transition, and, as such, became determinant for maskanda as a genre. Important in this respect is the iconic status that Phuzushukela still enjoys for being the first black guitarist to emerge on the radio and to be recorded. Hence, the exposure of his music is incomparable to that of other maskandi. Guitarists Bongani Nkwanyana and Bheki Khoza recalled that

> he was played on the radio, and everyone was saying: 'yoyoyoyo, this young man of Bhengu is played on the radio! Now he is becoming white.' Because there was no-one … there was no black person on the radio at that time. But the man was singing on the radio! … So when a song played, they'd never forget.
>
> (B. Nkwanyana 2009b)[7]

Thus, Bhengu's decision to play *ukupika* (picking) style rather than *ukuvamba* (strumming) style, his virtuosity and competitiveness in *izibongo* spoken self-praise and his collaboration with Gallo producer Hamilton Nzimande became normative for Zulu street guitar practice as a genre.

> Nzimande had a considerable influence on the production of Bhengu's music for the commercial market. With more modern production techniques, an electrified backing band, backing vocals and his own switch from an acoustic to an electric guitar, his music was set for greater commercial appeal.
>
> (Allingham paraphrased by Olsen 2014: 29)

The band practice required the conception of standardized song formats with clear musical 'signposts' (Coplan 2002: 114; Collins 2006–7: 19), for the musicians to play together. From a walking song or a guitar picking competition that could potentially last for a whole afternoon, maskanda transformed into three-minute songs with standardized musical ingredients that would reference or connote the walking song

---

[7] Olsen dates Bhengu's early (single) recordings from 1956 to 1968 (2014: 29–30). Allingham states that '[a]lthough it is claimed that he recorded in the late 1940s, Bhengu's earliest traceable sides were cut for the Troubadour label in about 1955' (1990).

and hostel competition practices. These standard ingredients still make up most of the commercially produced maskanda songs today and legitimize maskanda's status as traditional music for many Zulu South Africans.

Song formats

A maskanda song typically starts with a rhythmically free guitar or concertina introduction, an *ilado* or *isihlabo*. According to Clegg (1981: 4), the *isihlabo* has always been a crucial aesthetic criterion for the audience to judge the technical brilliance and competitiveness of the maskanda guitarist or concertina player, and he explicitly likens *isihlabo* to *ukugiya* in the ritual of stick fighting (the stem *–hlabo* means 'to stab'). There are many other ways, however, in which the *isihlabo* could be interpreted, for instance as a personal signature or as an introduction comparable to a European prelude: a means of tuning the instrument and introducing fellow musickers to the mode or mood of the piece. The aspect of tuning is very important to maskanda, and the explanation of an *isihlabo* as a personal signature of the maskandi (B. Nkwanyana 2009b; Nzimande 2009) depends to a large extent on the importance of personal tunings (and tunes) of the guitar, to be discussed in Chapter 2. By means of several transcriptions, guitarist Tom Collins identifies 'microcosmic relationships within the izihlabo that impact on the remainder of the song' (2006–7: 4).

In his 2011 release of 'Sab' Inganono', Jenkins almost literally copies Clegg's 2011 *isihlabo* in melodical, rhythmical and timbral respects (Jenkins 2011: 00'00"–00'09") which is interesting since Clegg's *isihlabo* is atypical (Clegg 2011: 00'00"–00'08"). Rather than presenting tonal material and mood of the song in quickly descending, unmetred, rhythmically free lines in order to 'make the guitar speak Zulu' (Khoza 2009), Clegg presents (in an emblematically eurogenic preluding manner) the first half of the song's main motive in metre, rhythm and melody. Sipho Mchunu, by contrast, whose subject position in the 'Sab' Inganono' renderings will be discussed later on, plays the *isihlabo* of his performance in an emblematically maskandi manner: quick, rhythmically free and repeatedly descending in melodic shape (Mchunu 1979: 00'28"–00'35"). Although Jenkins usually employs an *isihlabo* as his own signature, here he seems to want to pay tribute to Clegg in copying his guitar signature.

In many maskanda songs, an unmetred *isihlabo* introduction is generally followed after a few seconds by a metred instrumental introduction, often an ostinato, bringing in the other instruments of the band. These are concertina and/or electric guitar, electric bass guitar, sometimes violin, saxophone or synthesizer and invariably a drum kit or drum computer. Since all vocal and instrumental parts draw on the same tune or riff, and use this material at their own discretion (see dotted lines Figure 1.4), a separation between melody and bass is often misleading. Many maskanda songs are composed around a cyclic riff of cadential progressions (I-IV-V-I / I-VI-IV-I / I-IV-I-V), tonal inflections may be invoked from these heptatonic modes, even without leading tones (Figure 1.3). Many of these features have been retraced to the verse-refrain structures of *boeremusiek*, the periodicity and tonal closure of (Anglican) church hymns (Allingham 1990; Erlmann 1991; Khoza 2009) and the riffs of blues, jazz and vaudeville practices that many South Africans were exposed to in their capacity as migrating farm labourers and urban factory and domestic workers in the late nineteenth and early twentieth centuries (Erlmann 1991; Coplan [1985] 2008b; Ballantine [1993] 2012). However, bi-tonal sensibilities (the D and C fundamentals in Figure 1.4), derived from *umakhweyana* or *ugubhu* gourd bow practices, are just as prominent. They will be discussed in Chapter 6. Clegg's rendering of 'Sab' Inganono' emphatically shies away from the rhythmical fixation of a beat. Jenkins, by contrast, suggests a $\frac{4}{4}$ metre with triplets rather than a rocking $\frac{6}{8}$ metre, through the prominence of the drum with a slow reggae-like skank stroke on the 4th beat of each $\frac{6}{8}$ bar (corresponding with the 2nd and 4th beat of a $\frac{4}{4}$ bar) (Jenkins 2011; Figure 1.3).

When the groove has been established and musical instruments have been introduced, the lead singer (often also the lead guitarist) commences their song, based on the same melodic idea as the instrumental parts. The vocal timbre of the lead singer can be piercing and nasal, or it can be soft and reciting, almost whispering. All these vocal techniques are said to have been derived from *amahubo* choral dance songs and *umakhweyana* gourd bow playing that are considered to be traditional (Zulu) heritage. In both Clegg's and Jenkins's versions, the interaction between lead singer and backing chorus is decidedly antiphonal (Figure 1.4, bars 4 and 8), which is often considered as a hallmark of maskanda's Africanness in its suggestion of communality (Khoza 2009; B. Nkwanyana 2009b). Maskandi, just like gourd bow players, consider their guitar or concertina as a chorus to which they set their vocal creativity as a lead singer (S. Ngcobo 2008f), arriving at the same points in the melody at their own discretion, indicated with the dotted lines in Figure 1.4.

Figure 1.3 'Sab' Inganono', Jenkins and Band (2011: 00'18"–00'25" and 2013 Pt 1: 01'41"–01'49"). Main melody and harmonic progression in g-mixolydian or d-dorian. Transcribed with kind permission from David Jenkins.

Figure 1.4 'Sab' Inganono', Jenkins and Band (2013 Pt 2: 00'03"–00'19"). Heterophonic texture and interaction between lead voice, backing chorus and instruments. Transcribed with kind permission from David Jenkins.

Lyrics of maskanda songs currently cover the whole spectrum of social commentary, stand-up comedianism and love songs. Whereas early street guitar repertory dealt predominantly with issues that the guitarist encountered on their wanderings, maskanda production during apartheid times increasingly shied away from the social engagement (and often criticism) that the wandering guitarists were renowned for. Nkwanyana and Khoza describe how apartheid censors erased tracks on LPs that harboured potential criticism of the establishment, and promoted the songs that addressed abstract or indistinctive themes such as love, happiness or grief (Khoza 2009). Nevertheless, social criticism and the mocking of establishment is still an important aspect of maskanda performance today. The various readings of 'Sab' Inganono''s lyrics, presented earlier, exemplify the importance of the listeners' agency in interpreting the maskandi's igama.

One of the most distinctive aspects of maskanda as opposed to other musical genres that emerged from the experience of forced labour migration is the spoken self-praise *izibongo* passage, after lead singer and backing chorus have presented the main musical and verbal ideas of the song. The tradition of spoken praise and spoken self-praise is long-standing and impressive among many sub-Saharan societies. *Izibongo* – literally the indication of family lineage (or surname) in the Zulu language[8] – is hence one of the most important signifiers of maskanda's traditionality. Whereas the *isihlabo* is the maskandi's signature in instrumental and musical respects, the *izibongo* is the maskandi's signature in vocal and poetic respects.

The prosody (and, by implication, the musicality) of the *izibongo* is another crucial aesthetic criterion by which an audience judges the maskandi's skills and virtuosity. A maskandi is able to phrase elaborate *epitetha ornantia* over quick guitar picking, remaining in the song's groove and melodic ambitus. Just as important, however, are their indications of family lineage and geographical location. The maskandi is thus providing their physical address to the audience, which is functional in the role that maskanda played in courtship. If the girl (or boy, see Chapter 7) likes the maskandi, s/he knows where to find her/him, even if s/he is working elsewhere. Moreover, for wandering migrants in a hostel with many other migrants from a plethora of places, the indication of descent is an important aspect of asserting who they are and where they belong (Ntuli 1990: 302).

Another standard ingredient that emerges in maskanda's form and functions as a powerful sign of tradition is the incorporation of *ingoma* dance routines. Veit Erlmann describes how *ingoma* dance is a 'product of the dramatic socioeconomic changes in Zulu society after the final downfall of the independent kingdom' in 1879 (1991: 98). Like street guitar and concertina practices, *ingoma* dance emerged from colonial encounters, often choreographed by employers as 'spectacular dance competitions from at least 1921' (Erlmann 1991: 101). Erlmann's account was seconded by Sazi Dlamini who explained to me that 'there never was any tradition like large troupes. Of course, there are typical movements associated with *amahubo*, but they are very slow ... by old men, you know. And they don't change' (Dlamini 2011b). Nevertheless, *ingoma* dance is often experienced as precolonial heritage, because of its adoption of *ukugiya* moves in synchronized formats. Jenkins's live performance of 'Sab' Inganono' provides a lucid example of maskanda being linked to traditional *ukugiya* gestures through synchronized *ingoma* routines (Jenkins and Band 2013 Pt 1: 02'05"–02'20").

---

[8] Although *izibongo* (eulogy/eulogies) has often been clarified to me as being derived from *isibongo* (clan name), Rycroft emphasizes the difference between the two: 'the word "izibongo" occurs only with the prefix izi- (class 10) which in Zulu generally indicates plurality. The formal cognate "isibongo" (class 9) does not serve as its singular but has a different meaning .... Dr B.W. Vilakazi claims that the term izibongo is applicable to "any phrase or phrases, sentence or sentences, where the imaginative or emotional language is employed to describe something. Izibongo may be addressed to a person, animal, or any object of emotional excitement" (1938: 106)' (Rycroft 1960: 60). Vilakazi's and Rycroft's interpretation of *izibongo* is broader than some other explanations that reserve the term exclusively for self-praise (Clegg 2009; Dlamini 2011a), tightening the link with *isibongo*.

The developments of *ingoma* dance and maskanda guitar practice as social and political tools to construct difference in colonial and apartheid environments offer many parallels. Erlmann talks about a 'domestication' of *ingoma* dance 'from a militant, oppositional and suppressed form of popular culture to a tourist attraction' (1991: 96) between 1929 and 1939. The word domestication indicates the violent and invasive dimensions of 'homing' (Ahmed et al. 2003: 2). Olsen observes a similar dynamic in the development of maskanda during the height of apartheid cultural policy in the 1960s and 1970s. Interestingly, maskanda's standardization as described above thrived on the incorporation of *ingoma* dance around the same time as it transformed from a solo leisure occupation into a band performance practice. Whereas it was alien to the solo migrant guitarist tradition, *ingoma* dance became a marker of maskanda's Africanness and Zuluness in band format.

Inscriptions of sound

These sonic and visual dimensions of maskanda performance increasingly functioned as markers of a genre because they summoned and suggested a range of earlier musical practices and techniques that will be further outlined in the following chapters. Clegg's and Jenkins's repeated assertion of 'Sab' Inganono''s authority of traditionality concerns precolonial as well as colonial traditionality. The song references colonial wars in South African history, responds to traditional conventions of Nguni poetic expression and musically represents allegedly precolonial musical techniques (a hexatonic/pentatonic tonal sensibility, heterophonic texture) that have been transplanted to guitar and concertina almost unaltered, and allegedly colonially imported musical conventions (heptatonic modality and periodic, motivic form structure). At the same time, the song enables maskandi to find connection with more recent musical idioms considered to come from across the Atlantic, such as reggae, R&B, gospel and jazz. In these respects, the song is emblematic of current maskanda practice in South Africa.

Maskanda's denotation of these practices can be regarded, in Ochoa's words, as inscriptions of sound that occur on the body – human bodies, social bodies, bodies of repertoire – indexing a sound archive (2014: 7). Thus, Jenkins's and Clegg's presence as white Zulus playing, singing and dancing maskanda on the street in a mining suit has several far-reaching epistemological implications that cannot be reduced to a political statement or the problematization of identity articulation. Maskanda's capacity to mimic – in Bhabha's sense of the word – and tweak existing categories of thought and belonging sheds light on these epistemological implications. Maskanda is a realm of signification in which 'semantic snowballing' occurs, a concept central to Thomas Turino's musical application of Peircean semiotics: 'old indexical connotations [between music as sign and the event it signifies] may linger as new ones are added, potentially condensing a variety of meanings and emotions within a highly economical and yet unpredictable sign' (2008: 9). This accumulation and contingency cannot be divorced from what Monson calls the 'aesthetic values of social interaction ... and cultural sensibility' (1996: 8) in musical performance. The concept of sensibility is particularly useful for my understanding of maskanda as a mode of knowing, since it covers the overlap between the capacities of physical senses (sensing how things 'are' or 'work') and cognitive acts of reasoning, inferring and arguing. This unsettles mind–body dichotomies that feature eurogenic conceptions of knowledge so strongly.

Maskanda's mimicking capacity with its indexical immediacy and epistemic contingency not only features maskanda as musical practice (a set of indexical signs), but also the concept 'maskanda'/'umaskandi'/'maskande' (a set of symbolic signs). As Turino observes, symbolic signs, in their capacity to generalize, can create an indexical reality of their own (2008: 16). 'Umaskandi' indicates the actual practice, the abstracted genre and its personified purveyor. Moreover, the coining of the term is situated in a variety of times and places. Zulu jazz guitarist Bheki Khoza situates it in the kind of colonial encounter that is stated in 'Sab' Inganono':

> Immediately after the Bambatha [Rebellion in 1906] … people would find themselves … without the cattle. Then they started to go [to urban areas and mines]. And one of the first persons would bring, after been going to town, the guitar. So, the guitar became very popular in Natal, … and the Boers in Natal, they were playing Afrikaans. You know, they were playing … a version of those Scottish songs. And different things. And the rhythm, of course, that they were hearing. Now … the word *massekande* is actually an Afrikaans word: *musikant*. And the first people who were playing that, they were not playing African music … first, [they] would learn these songs from the Boer people and then [they] go on and say: 'hey, this [is] not fitting my song.'
>
> (Khoza 2009)

Sazi Dlamini situates the emergence of the term 'maskanda' a few decades later, claiming that it 'derived from repressive interactions between Afrikaans policemen and itinerant black musicians. Having fallen foul of apartheid curfew laws, these musicians would be forced to … prove their pass status by singing such Ur-Afrikaans *volksliedjies* as "Sarie Marais"' (Dlamini paraphrased by Davies 2010–11: 194; see also Blignaut *c.* 1931). Even though South Africans from diverse backgrounds experienced these songs as Ur-Afrikaans, Davies remarks that 'the ["Sarie Marais"] tune is actually Scottish, if authenticity remains an issue for you' (2010–2011: 194). Record producer Rob Allingham, by contrast, says he wouldn't be surprised if the term maskanda came to be used only in the late 1980s or early 1990s, when South African music industries – invariably implementing apartheid cultural policy – needed an umbrella term to categorize a range of Zulu street guitar practices that were formerly known as 'Zulu Trad' (2009).

Potentialities of hearing

These various accounts about the emergence of the term agree on two points: maskanda practices are manifold and they preceded the emergence of the name maskanda. Over the years, a diverse range of existing street playing practices on concertina and guitar became categorized as maskanda. Khoza's and Dlamini's account that the first maskandi 'were not playing African music', but rather Boer and Scottish tunes, is seconded by many other oral and written sources (Kirby [1934] 1953: 257ff; Rycroft 1977: 217). Clegg, by contrast, situates the many walking songs that existed in the first half of the twentieth century in the realms of existing African traditions: 'you got all these songs which were learned by every guitarist' (2009). 'The ability [of a maskandi] to … take a traditional song and put in on the guitar was itself acclaimed' (Clegg 1981: 5). Khoza's and Clegg's seemingly opposing claims – 'the first maskandi were (not) playing African music' – unearth the experience of what Dlamini calls the transculturation that emerged from the social and cultural displacement of forced labour migration. Workers knew the musical techniques, songs and forms from their villages, and they also came to know *boereliedjies* and church hymns. Given the situation they found themselves in, it is not surprising that they constructed these repertoires as different, even though these repertoires became increasingly syncretic. Dlamini – like Khoza and Clegg educated with a variety of Nguni musical practices, and eurogenic tonal harmony as well as jazz harmony – described maskanda's syncretism in terms of an 'in-betweenness' with regard to tonality:

> instrumental maskanda is part of that experience of transculturation [and] modernity, which takes all [other] influences: church, school …. But then again, you have this whole spectrum that tends to indigeneity, by way of pentatonic …, or this, what I don't know what to call … : octatonic, if I look at it … There's some[where] in between, you know, between pentatonicism and cyclicity of the diatonic.
>
> (Dlamini 2011b)

The tension between pentatonicism and diatonicism that features in maskanda and many adjoining genres such as isicathamiya and mbaqanga will be further explored in Chapter 6. Dlamini's search for analytical terms to describe what he hears serves here to show that this tension is not a straightforward binary of Nguni pentatonicism versus eurogenic diatonicism, but rather a range of potential ways one could hear maskanda, a potentiality that also features Clegg's account of 'Sab Inganono'.

Clegg noted that 'Sab' Inganono' 'attracted my sense of Celtic resonance', which he specified as the modal key and the $\frac{6}{8}$ metre. Nevertheless, he asserted, '[it] is a very old [Zulu] war song' (Clegg and Band 2007: 02'00"ff; Clegg 2009). His assertion is confirmed by David Jenkins, who after having spoken 'to many Zulu singers and culturalists' concludes that 'Sab' Inganono' is a traditional *ihubo*, an a cappella choral dance song (2016). Yet, by situating 'Sab' Inganono' in Zulu, Afrikaner and Celtic sonic realms, Clegg and Khoza pointed not only to maskanda's syncretic nature but also to the various (and sometimes incompatible) ways in which one can hear a song. Foregroundings of aural experiences are interesting not so much for their indication of musical features, but for the glimpses (or sonic suggestions) they offer of the composite and divergent aural archives that maskanda musickers possess. Such aural archives set the conditions for the ways in which sonic expressions are being continuously (re)inscribed on their bodies, and thus how acoustic assemblages circulate between listening entities.

Assessment of this circulation of acoustic assemblages enables a critical engagement with the agencies of, and exertions of power between, listening entities. 'Sab' Inganono' – to my knowledge – is mainly known through performances and recordings by Clegg and Jenkins. Jenkins stated that his renderings of the song are meant to pay tribute to Clegg and Sipho Mchunu, Clegg's partner in his band Juluka (Jenkins 2016). It is likely that Clegg became familiar with the song through Mchunu, who played the song in Jeremy Marre's 1979 documentary film *Rhythm of Resistance* (Mchunu 1979: 00'27"–01'41"). In this documentary, the song is introduced as a 'new song', suggesting that it is Mchunu's composition, or at least his transplantation of existing musical material to the guitar.[9] Only the start of the song is played serving to introduce the musicianship of Mchunu, and particularly his importance for the emergence of Juluka. As such, Mchunu's rendering of the song is barely available for hermeneutical and critical scrutiny. It cannot become fully part of the feedback loop between listening and speaking, as became clear in my discussion of the song's *isihlabo*, yet it clearly has facilitated this feedback loop to commence and resonate in almost all respects. Mchunu's rendering is present, but only as a 'nearly agential pressure' (Bloechl 2008: 11); as a mere tension against Clegg's and Jenkins's renderings that are available for hermeneutic interpretation through their modes of enunciation (on albums and the internet).

Also, none of the more famous maskandi such as Phuzekhemisi, Mfaz' Omnyama and iHashi Elimhlophe, and none of the local maskandi I worked with, has ever tried their hand on this song. This contrasts sharply with other themes in maskanda practice that are continuously copied, varied and emulated verbally, kinetically and musically by maskandi taking note of each other's work, such as songs about dowry (*lobola*), HIV/AIDS ('Ingculazi Iyabulala'), odes to the Zulu King ('Bayethe') and the calling of ancestors. Although there are many ways of explaining this absence of black agency in the performance of this song (exemplified by the many possible subject positions of the song's protagonist discussed earlier), it poignantly coincides with a similar discursive imbalance in maskanda research that suffers from a similar lack of black agency. This obviously crucially determines who is (re)creating what 'soils of significance' (Hoffman), who is mimicking and menacing which authority (Bhabha) and who participates in the circulation of acoustic assemblages between different listening entities (Ochoa). The unequal power relations between the subject positions of various human musicking bodies, social bodies and bodies of sounding and kinetic repertoire as outlined through my discussion of 'Sab' Inganono' provide some experiential insight into the traumatized societal fabric from which maskanda emerged.

---

[9] Jenkins acknowledges this, but is certain, nevertheless, that it is an *ihubo*.

2

Foregroundings of Maskanda's Styles and Substyles

When maskandi present their igama, they live out a pact of mutual understanding that culminates in a shared set of skills (Monson 1996: 2). This living out takes place not only with the musickers present at the scene, but also with those who came before: the mothers, fathers, aunties, friends and grandparents who have taught the attendants their understandings and skills. In Zulu culture, the role of such ancestors (*amadlozi*) is crucial for the emergence and sustainability of communities and the sharing of experiences. One's *idlozi* or shade is the aspect of being human that 'presents you' (Nzimande 2009), makes you the living person that you are. Rather than a discrete or individual entity, an *idlozi* encompasses all 'the teachings of one's mother and father' (Nzimande 2009). Since death is considered a 'natural continuation of a man's existence' (Berglund [1976] 1989: 80), *amadlozi* are among the living (as respected elderly persons), as well as among the deceased (as ancestors). In all cases, the teachings of the shades 'are there', in Nzimande's words.

Music – be it ritual song (*ihubo*), narration, praise (*izibongo*) or dance (*ukugiya*), as such or in combination – is an immensely important vehicle for communication with ancestors and divinities (Berglund [1976] 1989: 198ff; Olsen 2008a; Nokwe 2009; Nzimande 2009; Dlamini 2011b; B. Nkwanyana 2016b). This communication can take various directions. Musicians can – through their music and musicianship – receive callings from ancestors with tasks and responsibilities. At times, such callings are prompted through the demands of ancestors. At other times, they are prompted through actions by living human beings, notably if they start certain musical practices at certain moments: in the use of specific musical instruments, modes, riffs or specific hymns (*amahubo*). Hence, the use of these musical vehicles can be dangerous, bringing musicians into conditions where they are unable to control themselves (Nokwe 2009). Thus, certain *amahubo* can only be sung by skilled people with a certain degree of knowledge and spiritual power (*amandla*) or seniority (Berglund [1976] 1989: 199; Olsen 2008a). Musicians cannot always rehearse or perform when they might get, or have had, a calling from an ancestor because they are physically affected by it (Nokwe 2009). Here, it is important to recapitulate that a maskanda performance as igama makes the past present and hence proceeds from a diachronous or retroactive as much as from a synchronous or teleological conceptualization of time and tradition. As such, the past is being (re)claimed, enriched with new meaning and reconstituted in the face of the here and now, with unpredictable and contingent outcomes for future and present as much as for past events. The presentation of an igama thus encompasses a condition of *différance*: the attribution of cultural meaning to events is simultaneously deferred and differentiated. Homi Bhabha argues that here, in such a Third Space of enunciation, culture as practice is constructed and located (1994b: 58–9).

As I explained in the Introduction of this book, Bhabha's notion of Third Space as a location of culture serves my aim of making my readers experience the multiplicity of subject positions in maskanda practice that has been (and still is being) shaped by past relationships. Thus, we can sense maskanda knowledge as a temporarily positioned resonance between a self and the world through a sonic and aural (re)organization of space. Foregrounding this multiplicity and its dependence on aural experiences enables me to dig deeper into formations of (musical) knowledge and the power dynamics that constitute it. As much as the presentation of an igama engages with time, in diachronously producing past and present experiences, maskanda performance deals with place (as opposed to space). Places are constructed through various modes of enunciation. They are conceptualized (for instance, as homesteads, rivers to drink from and mountains to see). They are identified through the outlining of musickers' movements and dwellings (from harbours to farms to mines to villages and back). They are also indicated as the specific locations from which musickers were physically expelled, and that remain operative as 'phantom districts' (Clegg 1982: 9; 2009; see also Impey 2018: 94–115) in the articulation of communities, languages, musical styles and cultural customs. Whereas Chapter 1 engaged with articulations of tradition in time-space, Chapter 2 engages with articulations of style in such constructions of place over time.

Locations and movements

Marie Jorritsma observes the continued pertinence of the struggle for land in and for the (cultural) history of South Africa (2011: 3). Angela Impey has provided a painstaking analysis of the continued spatial and environmental rupture through the loss of land and resources that features in the everyday lives of so many South Africans (2018). Geographical locations are loaded with meaning, as is the movement when a struggle over them is lost or won. In maskanda's early years, such attributions of meaning were palpable in the position of many labour migrants as *abaqhafi* or *amagxagxa*, situated in the binary between rural in between urban (*-kholwa*) and rural (*-bhinca*) ways of life (see Introduction). Whereas the *amagxagxa* belonged to neither of these binary poles, due to the uprooting consequences of their migration, many of them were able to combine and reflect on the knowledge and experiences of multiple realities. Continuity and stability lay in what they were able to bring with them: memories, ideas, values, stories, languages, musics, skills. These aspects of self were a stable 'locus', whereas the environment – hostels, villages, contacts, (job) occupations – was unstable and transitory. Many black South Africans still find themselves in this situation. In this respect, maskanda became not only a realm of stability and continuity for many migrants but also 'a mode of passage between locations' (Abels 2012 quoted in Richardson 2016: 123). Impey describes how the pathways (*indlela*), cut out by maskandi as much as mouth harp players, 'were both the physical locus of the walking songs and employed as a metaphor to describe a range of intertwining aesthetic and social configurations' (2018: 64).

In this chapter, I address 'the (re)claiming and (re)processing [through maskanda musicking] of habits, objects, names and histories that have been uprooted' (Ahmed et al. 2003: 9). In order to do so, I explore how maskanda musickers musically and conceptually locate their musicking activities, in regions, communities and eras, but also in stages of their own lives, or in social and political opportunities they have negotiated from communities and relationships. By highlighting the epistemological dimensions of these acts of musicking, I demonstrate that they surpass the need for identity articulation that is often centralized in deconstructivist cultural studies of individual and collective notions of Self and Other.

An important musical means for a maskandi to assert their individuality as a musician, a spokesperson for their community and as empowered citizen is their tune or tuning. Almost all maskandi I talked to asserted that their tune or tuning is unique, on an individual level and on a collective level when tunes are connected to specific regional styles. 'Once I put on a tune, then I am able to play my style', my teacher Shiyani Ngcobo explained (2008f).[1] Via my friend and colleague Kathryn Olsen, I got in touch with Ngcobo (1956–2011) who taught maskanda guitar in the Community Arts Project of the University of KwaZulu-Natal, where I was affiliated as a visiting researcher and lecturer. Like many other maskandi, he seemed to use the noun 'tune' (melody, song) and the verb 'to tune' (to adjust the strings of the guitar) interchangeably. At first, I assumed the difference had been lost in translation (the interview with Ngcobo was carried out with an interlocutor). Only later did I realize that my confusion emerged from my limited aural understanding of maskanda and the guitar. I knew that maskanda guitar tuning deviates from standard guitar tuning (E2,A2,D3,G3,B3,E4): usually, the E4 string is tuned down to D4 (in *isiZulu* style), but many maskandi adopt alternative tunings which they consider to be their own. I also knew that various songs of one maskandi are often based on the same two fundamentals with their harmonic partials, a structure derived from gourd bow practice. What I would call a scale is a maskandi's tuning as well as their tune, because the scale/tune as basic material for a song depends on the tuning of the guitar.

Johnny Clegg explained to me how the pitches to which the guitar strings are tuned affect the opportunities for maskandi to invent tunes around them. Clegg did this by focusing on what Tom Collins calls 'the movement of the guitarist's hands as a guide to [song] construction' (Collins 2006–7: 5). In Clegg's explanation, the structural reliance of Zulu guitar music on gourd bow playing becomes evident in his reference to the two fundamentals on which a tune is based and to which the tuning of the guitar is adapted.

---

[1] Shiyani Ngcobo can be seen playing maskanda guitar on the cover of Charles Keil and Steven Feld's book *Music Grooves* (1994) as a nameless representative of a grooving '[s]treet musician outside a worker hostel near Umlazi Township, Durban, South Africa' (Keil and Feld 1994: iv).

So, when I first heard Zulu street guitar music [in 1967] it was all played in this G-shape. [demonstrates descending: e – d – b – a – g]. This is an A to G shape [referring to the two fundamentals A and G]. [Then] it was a new move to play from the D to the C. [demonstrates: f – e – d – c – a – c] [This] shifted it right out to a different thing [the incorporation of a semitone]. Then, for the ... older styles, they adapted isiCece: wedding songs, and some oooold traditional war songs, into that semitone [plays: d – c – b – g]. Which up here was: [Clegg moves to D-C shape: g – f-sharp – d – c and then completes the pentatonic scale by combining the two: g – f-sharp – d – c – b – g]. And then Sipho [Mchunu], who was quite an experimenter, he took everything down to the bass strings, and he is the only one I ever met who did that ... [plays f – d – c – f – g on the lower strings] So you had different keys and different places which, as the guitar developed, people developed styles around.

(Clegg 2009)

These various 'shapes' or 'domains' on the guitar are connected to styles that indicate a region or occasion. The tunings are preconditions for the realization of styles. They also represent group and individual identities and reveal how individual and group identities intersect in the performance and critique of maskanda. My aim is to provide insight into the operations of the styles' modes of knowledge inscription (i.e. how do style articulations function as epistemology) rather than into the identities they represent.

Style specifications and the situatedness of difference

Maskanda musickers explained and demonstrated various maskanda styles to me; I combine their explanations with the written accounts that exist about these styles. My intention is not to prove these accounts wrong or inconsistent, but rather to provide an insight into the situatedness of difference. By discussing the manifold ways in which maskanda styles are demarcated, and by pointing out the hegemonic position of Clegg's experiences in these demarcation narratives, I intend to reveal, firstly, how musical and extra-musical variables are employed to describe musical style, musical structure and musical change, and, secondly, how these variables mean different things to different people in different circumstances with resulting exertions and negotiations of power. The verbal or musical specification of these variables in the articulation of musical styles is an act of temporary arrest. By distancing oneself from the experience, it is possible to approach an experience again as text on one's own terms and shape it accordingly. Both maskandi and music researchers execute this distancing and subsequent re-approaching in their work.

This process has been extensively theorized in anthropological and ethnomusicological studies (Clifford 1988; Rice 1994). James Clifford observes that 'unruly experience' is transformed into a text, which is a process by which 'unwritten behavior, speech, beliefs, oral tradition, ritual come to be marked as a corpus, a potentially meaningful ensemble, separated out from an immediate discursive or performative situation' (Clifford quoted and paraphrased in Rice 1994: 10). Following Ochoa, I would formulate this as a momentary freezing of the circulation of acoustic assemblages between listening entities. By attributing meaning to an acoustic event or experience, we take a 'snapshot' of something that is inherently transitory, fluid and permeable. Such momentary arrests can acquire extremely violent dimensions, for instance in the imposition of apartheid policies outlined in the Introduction of this book. Nevertheless, the capacity of arresting this circulation belongs to anyone who is able to attribute meaning to an experience: researchers, musicians, listeners, critics, concert and festival organizers, producers and broadcasters. They all take snapshots through multiple and often combined modes of inscription (hearing, singing, speaking, writing, playing, reading) with their own agencies and from a variety of subject positions. These snapshots affect the further (options for) circulation of acoustic assemblages and the participation of various entities. As such, they are powerful exertions and negotiations of power.

It is through the imposing and arresting implications of musickers' inscriptions, that an exchange of, or dialogue about, musical experience and musical epistemology becomes possible, constituting temporary articulated interrelationships between musicking subjects. Through my participant-observation in such exchanges I can shed light on *how* these interrelationships between musicking subjects are constituted and *how* processes of textualization occur. An important aspect of highlighting the multiple ways one can hear maskanda styles concerns experiences of structural and aural undecidability (Scherzinger 2004: 258). These experiences surfaced in the ways Dlamini and Clegg foregrounded their multiple and inconclusive hearings of 'Sab' Inganono' in Chapter 1. Experiences of structural and aural undecidability provide further insight into the malleability of notions of difference beyond a binary frame of correct and incorrect understandings. These experiences enable all musickers to observe the time lag between event and enunciation (Bhabha 1994b: 58-9), because they dwell in the space or moment in which events acquire cultural and epistemological authority. In this process of dwelling, the roles of various modes of inscription (writing, guitar playing, dancing, singing, self-praising) in acts of knowledge formation become perceivable. Thus, a focus on the time lag between event and enunciation enables me to foreground maskanda musicking as a mode of knowing that converses with, and is folded into, modes of knowing that are not maskanda musicking but are featured by a similar time lag, such as academic textualizations.

Musickers associate maskanda styles primarily with peoples and their languages. Almost all styles are described with the Zulu prefix isi-, referring to a language, a tongue, a way of speaking. isiZulu, isiBhaca and isiChunu refer both to languages and to musical styles.[2] 'When you're singing', Khoni Miya explained, 'then your tongue translate[s] the music on its own direction ... translates the music to the maskanda

---

[2] Whereas no systematic research has been carried out in exploring the sounding similarities between, for instance, the language isiZulu and the musical style isiZulu, or isiBhaca, or isiChunu, there are no indications that the musical styles rely on the sounding features of their linguistic equivalents or vice versa.

which is the direction of your tongue' (2009a). Styles depend to a large extent on how the strings of the guitar are tuned, making the guitar 'speak a certain language or dialect' (Khoza 2009). Since the styles are often connected to peoples and the areas in which they live (or used to live), a maskanda style (including its tuning) occupies a similar function as language in being a specific and intrinsic way to express yourself and your community, a way that cannot be easily mastered or even understood by someone outside the community (K. Miya 2009a). Thus, comparisons with language in order to describe maskanda surpass the level of metaphor in many respects. Zulu jazz guitarist Bheki Khoza formulated this as follows:

> I'm not talking Xhosa. I'm not talking Pedi. I'm just talking Zulu – that is the language I speak. You can tune the guitar for different, seven times, still talking Zulu ... as you get into another place there is a different dialect of Zulu. It's a different tuning ... so it's really based on community. And also, remember, there is all kinds of songs, ritual songs, there is also wedding songs, and the harmony – if you have studied harmony – is very easy to identify: 'oh, this is from this chord to this chord, or this from this key to this key.' But then there is different tunings, where ... somebody would tune the dialect and give you the guitar and you won't be able to play. Because [the guitar] is made so it speaks its language. Now they do the same thing with the concertina.[3]
>
> (Khoza 2009)

The intricate connection of maskanda styles with various peoples in South Africa coincides with the ways in which styles are geographically located. Moreover, the use of musical style categories embodies an agency to articulate the regions in which they are said to have emerged and thrived, as well as to map the massive movements of people and communities through and between those regions. Crucial in these mappings, articulations and locations is the natural border of the Tugela River, which also still signifies the cultural difference between the colonial province of Natal (south), including Durban, and the former 'homeland' of KwaZulu (north), symbolizing the core of the Zulu Kingdom as well as colonial farmlands (Figure 2.1). Labour migration forced hundreds of thousands of people from Natal into various parts of KwaZulu and into urban areas, often 'six months a year for agriculture, and for six months to cities to the heavy industries' (Clegg 1982: 9).

The experience of permanent displacement that resulted from this migration enhanced the importance of articulating physical roots, descent and family lineage. Style names such as isiShameni or isiNdwedwe refer to specific geographical locations (Shameni river, Ndwedwe region) where these styles are said to have emerged or

---

[3] Clegg seconds Khoza's account by pointing at the isiNdwedwe style: 'The people from Ndwedwe developed a technique all of their own and introduced the pentatonic scale to the concertinas to the point at which they had to actually undo the concertina, change round the buttons and change around the way the concertina is played. There was a very influential interaction between the guitar and the concertina' (1981: 3).

developed. Like anywhere in the world, the people living in, and originating from, those places are often called by the same name (amaNdwedwe: the people from Ndwedwe). Labour migration also gave rise to a less specific geography often enriched with imaginations of origin and rootedness. Umzansi style, for instance, refers to the diffuse concept of the South Coast to be discussed shortly. Labour migration also caused what Clegg calls 'two cognitive maps' of an area in the minds of people: 'one which I call "phantom districts", the districts which you can't see, which they know through looking at mountains, rivers, etc., … We have some very severe competitions developing between the different phantom districts' (1982: 9). These competitions, as we shall see, were often settled musically.

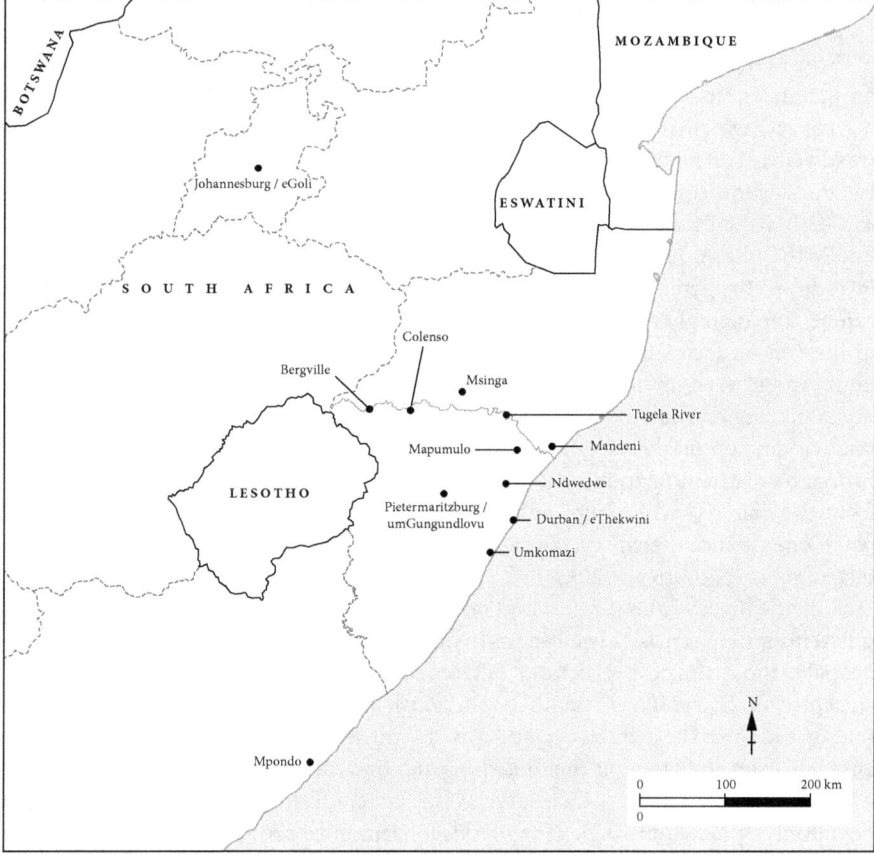

Figure 2.1 Map indicating Tugela River, Mandeni, Msinga, Bergville, Colenso, Mapumulo, Ndwedwe, Durban, Umkomazi, Mpondo, Pietermaritzburg and Johannesburg.

Clegg distinguishes two main styles, isiNdwedwe (south of the Tugela River) and isiChunu from the Msinga area (north of the Tugela River) (2009). In order to show how written accounts of the development and categorization of styles may distort the experience of those who practice and hear these styles, I will compare accounts by Veit Erlmann (1991), Johnny Clegg (1981, 2009) and Bongani Nkwanyana (2013). As mentioned earlier, it is not my intention to prove either one of them right or wrong. Rather, my aim is to reveal how aural experiences of difference are generally less unequivocal than the concepts, categories and comparisons employed to describe such difference, which, in fact, accounts for the accuracy of these experiences of difference as fluid and context-dependent. Once spoken discourse about style categorizations is translated and standardized in order to be written down, the differences become intellectual constructions. Such constructions can provide opportunities for approach and dialogue, but also for imposition and appropriation.

Erlmann gives credit to Clegg in his attempts to distinguish styles (1991:75), referring to Clegg's seminal papers that encompassed a great deal of Clegg's live demonstrations on guitar. These demonstrations have not fully made it into the transcriptions of his papers, which implies a significant loss of information. Erlmann claims that isiNdwedwe is structurally reminiscent of *umakhweyana* gourd bow playing, whereas isiChunu is informed by *imfilitshi* mouth organ practices (1991: 75). Whereas Clegg explicitly seconds the latter part of this claim (Clegg 1981: 7), the former part is only implicitly present in his paper, when he states that '[t]he people from Ndwedwe ... introduced the pentatonic scale to the concertinas' (3). The use of a pentatonic scale can be convincingly explained by *ugubhu* or *umakhweyana* bow playing as a source of inspiration (see Chapter 6 and Titus 2013). The binary that Erlmann sketches, however, between *umakhweyana* bow playing on the one hand, and *imfilitshi* mouth organ playing on the other, is absent in Clegg's paper, nor was it reiterated by any of the maskanda musickers I talked to. Bongani Nkwanyana even emphatically denied Erlmann's distinction, judging it as 'not real', because the differences of style emerge from the dance (and by implication the melodies and rhythms on which one can place one's dance steps), certainly not from the technical affordances of musical instruments (Nkwanyana 2013).

Still, the binary Erlmann employs may be useful to describe structural (sounding) differences between isiNdwedwe and isiChunu styles. Unfortunately, he does not describe those musical structural differences other than referring to the 'chordal structure of ... *imfilitshi* mouth organ music' (1991: 75). To follow his implied line of thought: the pentatonic scale in the more heterophonic isiNdwedwe style emerges from the fact that the *umakhweyana* bow can produce two or three tones, a tone or semitone apart, which serve as fundamentals for overtones that make up a pentatonic or hexatonic scale. The *imfilitshi* harmonica produces tones that respond to the triadic, homophonic sensibilities that isiChunu style became subject to, as I will explain shortly.

Another example of the construction of difference is Erlmann's attempt to connect the major division between isiNdwedwe and isiChunu styles with another crucial style distinction that many maskanda musickers pointed out to me: the difference between isiZulu and isiShameni styles (Khoza 2009; B. Nkwanyana 2009b; Dlamini 2011b). Whereas the difference between isiNdwedwe and isiChunu revolves around geographical location (south and north of the Tugela River) and around musical precursors (*umakhweyana* and *imfilitshi* practices), the difference between isiZulu and isiShameni styles revolves around rural versus urban sensibilities, and around dance routines. In the context of massive forced labour migration, the rural–urban divide became an ever more powerful trope to situate and distinguish musical styles. The interesting and problematic aspect in determining these criteria of distinction is that they overlap to a large extent. It is, hence, not surprising that Erlmann equates isiNdwedwe explicitly with isiZulu style on music structural terms (1991: 101). Many maskanda musickers observe the pentatonic or hexatonic nature of isiZulu style (S. Ngcobo 2009; Dlamini 2011b), highlighting its structural similarities with *umakhweyana* bow playing, and the tuning of the guitar (E2,A2,D3,G3,B3,D4) that enables it to 'speak Zulu' (B. Nkwanyana 2009b).

Qualities of sound

I will address a couple of isiZulu musical features that were pointed out to me in oral and written accounts of this style. At times these features can be explained in terms of tone parameters such as timbre, tonal consciousness/harmony or texture, but for the most part, these features surpass the dimension of a single parameter. In this context it is worthwhile to discuss Tom Collins's method of differentiation between maskanda styles. Collins focuses on 'the movement of the guitarist's hands as a guide to construction' (2006-7: 5). He visualizes the 'choreography' of the maskandi's hands by providing tablatures of his transcriptions. His exploration of this guitar-based composition leads him to the claim that the texture of a maskanda song emerges from the picking style that a maskandi adopts. While pursuing this hypothesis, Collins comes across several 'oriflammes' of isiShameni, isiZulu and isiMandolino styles in the *isihlabo* of Bongani Nkwanyana, whose music he learned to play. In analysing these oriflammes, Collins reveals the many sounding and choreographic aspects involved in determining a style. On the basis of the *isihlabo*, Collins observes that Nkwanyana's isiMandolino style is most emphatically featured by triads, whereas in his isiShameni *isihlabo* they are merely 'implied', because of the 'dyadic content' of the material, and in his isiZulu songs they are rare (2006-7: 12). Moreover, he notes that, even in the most triadic of his styles, isiMandolino, Nkwanyana often employs open fourths in the lower notes of his triads ($\frac{6}{4}$ position in eurogenic analytical jargon), which Collins describes as 'thoroughly Zulu' (13). His observations clarify the difficulty of distinguishing isiMandolino, isiShameni and isiZulu styles on the basis of the use of triads. Thanks to his attention for the choreography of the maskandi's hands, however, Collins is able to diversify harmony and pitch as style-determining musical parameters:

A sound world rich in harmonic overtones is central to the isiZulu style, whose mannerist opening [tablature] coordinate (x,x,x,x,3,0) produces discernible resonance in the upper partials of the underlined strings (x,x,x,x,3,0). The maskanda tuning system (E2,A2,D3,G3,B3,D4) is conspicuously well suited to this idiom, inducing the hypothesis that the desire for resonance between the upper four strings was the main reason why the maskandi deemed the Western tuning system (E2,A2,D3,G3,B3,E4) to be in need of modification. Such extrapolations from the particular to the general are perhaps a little naïve, but the (x,x,x,x,3,0) coordinate is such an oriflamme of isiZulu that one cannot help speculating on its nostalgic symbolism.

(Collins 2006–7: 13–14)

Collins's observation deserves to be quoted at length because it reveals that differences in styles are not always discernible by pitch or harmony, but also by resonance (and by implication: timbre), showing that parameters such as harmony and timbre coalesce. The (x,x,x,x,3,0) coordinate sounds differently according to the use or position of a capo (which is increasingly common in maskanda). In combination with the isiZulu tuning, however, the resonance of the upper four strings will always be a discernible aspect.[4]

Rather than articulating individual sound parameters, most maskandi explained the sonic qualities of maskanda in terms of other musicking practices (playing styles, vocal practices, dance). Musician and university lecturer Sazi Dlamini has superior knowledge of, and skills in, various Nguni musical practices, jazz composition and eurogenic tonal harmony. Yet, he refused to pinpoint the traditional quality of maskanda, and of isiZulu style in particular, in terms of single musical parameters. Confronted with video footage of maskanda dancer Bongekile Ngwabe, who sung backing vocals for maskandi Shiyani Ngcobo during his tour through the Netherlands in 2010 (see Chapter 5), Dlamini asserted that 'her voice is singing old style', which he connected with *ugubhu* and *umakhweyana* gourd bow practices. The sound of the voice, according to Dlamini, needs to fit in with the intricate sound of the *umakhweyana*; they need to be in balance in dynamic, timbral, rhythmical and pitch-related/temperament respects. He emphasized that 'very few people … even within the tradition would recognize this' as old. 'Only the very musical people, like [maskandi] Shiyani [Ngcobo] understand this … connection to tradition' (Dlamini 2011b). To some extent, the sonic intricacies of Dlamini's qualification of 'old style' remained illegible to me due to my limited ability to understand musical sound beyond the sound parameters in which I have been raised.

Maskanda musickers often connect maskanda to tradition by referring to *amahubo*, a cappella choral dance songs. According to Rycroft, Zulu South Africans regard these 'as their highest form of musical activity' (1977: 225). In making this connection,

---

[4] Clegg points out that having two strings at the same pitch also features bluegrass tunings (1981: 8), which clarifies the fact that Northern Hemisphere audiences often associate maskanda with bluegrass.

musickers specify the quality of the sound in a variety of ways. Nkwanyana and Khoza stated that the art of *amahubo* (and hence of maskanda too) revolves around saying a lot with just a few tones. This approximates Dlamini's account of *amahubo* as non-rhythmical, free in time, therefore perceived as slow.[5] I would describe singing in an *ihubo* manner as a continuous attempt to reach a pitch (which is therefore minutely flat for equal-temperament ears). The softness of the falsetto, the abundant voice inflections approaching speech intonation and the density of text provide its quality as a reciting and lamenting cry. Dlamini addressed pentatonic scales, unequal temperament – suggesting that some styles can best be played on instruments with unequal tuning (*ugubhu* gourd bow or *umtsingo* flute) – and timbre as indispensable aspects of 'the old style'. Bongani Nkwanyana, by contrast, does not consider vocal technique to be an issue at all in the distinction between styles. He rather emphasizes metre through the placement of dance steps.

Choreographical geographies

Dance is a musical, social, political and linguistic vehicle for expression in Zulu culture. All the styles that feature maskanda discourse have in some way or another been derived from dance practices. Understanding maskanda's stylistic intricacies is impossible without an understanding of dance, especially *ingoma* dance styles that emerged and developed in the same colonial environment as Zulu street guitar practices. Hence, it is a crucial aspect in the discourse about isiZulu versus isiShameni styles. Many dance events (such as *isicathulo* [gumboot] dance) were accompanied by concertina or guitar, maskanda's most prominent instruments (Clegg 1982: 10; Dlamini 2011b). Despite their colonial history, however, addressed by Erlmann (1991), Clegg (1982) and Meintjes (2003, 2017), both maskanda and *ingoma* signify precolonial heritage for many Zulu South Africans. Again geography – and, by implication, origin and descent – is an important variable in the conceptualization of aural and kinetic experiences.

An important trope in the stylistic situation of both maskanda and *ingoma* is the concept of the 'south coast' (*umzansi*) that, unlike Ndwedwe, Msinga, Colenso and Mapumulo areas, is more difficult to locate geographically (Figure 2.1). Akin to European notions of the 'Orient', potentially ranging from Casablanca to Tokyo, Zulu notions of the 'south coast' indicate an area that roughly contains the villages in Natal and around Durban (including those inland), and this area is expanded or restricted depending on the distinction that needs to be made. In a global context, South Africa itself is sometimes dubbed Mzansi. According to Clegg, seconded by Nkwanyana, the Natal Midlands (roughly between Pietermaritzburg and the Drakensberg mountain range) have always been a point of reference for such geographical indications, since many people were brought there for farm labour:

---

[5] Dlamini also implied that the non-metrical nature of *amahubo* accounts for the fact that strongly rhythmical *ingoma* dance routines in various isiShameni and umzansi styles are colonial constructions rather than precolonial heritage (2011b).

> [t]he word *umzansi* comes from the term *abantu basenzansi*, the people who live below us, and it's a term used by the Zulu living in the Natal Midlands referring to the people who live towards the sea on the coast, and this is also an indication as to where the dance first developed, around Ndwedwe and Mapumulo areas. The people on the coast refer to the dance as *isiZulu*, meaning 'the true Zulu national dance'.
>
> (Clegg 1984: 68)

Clegg's quotation reveals the notions of authenticity that accompany both isiZulu style and umzansi dance, being two sides of the same original coin. The 'south coast' signifies rootedness or home in geographical, historical and cultural respects (with musical and choreographical implications) for those who were forced to work in the Midlands and Durban. Nkwanyana, by contrast, understands umzansi as both original and syncretic. He situates umzansi further inland in the Midlands area including Bergville, rather than in the Ndwedwe and Mapumulo areas, further emphasizing how the idea of umzansi as an imaginary place of rootedness and origin was most powerful in the Midlands (Figure 2.1). According to him, umzansi and isiBegville styles are hence one and the same style:

> The people from the Midland[s], that are called Begville people, they are the one who initiated that umzansi. Because they were able to mix themselves with the people from the south. Even today, this umzansi dance is still residing within the Be[r]gville area. Other people from other areas, it's very difficult for us to copy that pace. I can dance umzansi, but not perfect.
>
> (B. Nkwanyana 2013)

Nkwanyana goes on to say that umzansi was, indeed, initiated by people from the South Coast, indicating how the style, due to the seasonal migration, emerged in more places at once and can be situated and rooted in more places at once. In doing so, he differentiates Clegg's neat classification of styles, even though Clegg admits there are two 'groups of dancers who practice [umzansi] dance, the people of Msinga ... and the people from Bergville' (1984: 64). Nkwanyana's and Clegg's accounts are powerful testimonies of the uprooting of lives that encompassed many decades and a large 'commuting area' in which the indication of descent became ever more important, as a physical as much as an imaginative act being cast in music, dance, and the conceptual articulation of styles.

Zulu countercultures

These articulations of style acquire an additional complexity in the identification of various Zulu communities whom, too often, get reduced to a monolithic Zulu nation. I mention three communities in particular that feature simultaneously as validators of tradition and as countercultures in narratives about maskanda's emergence and development. Their roles are articulated according to a variety of interpretative goals, sometimes in order to stress continuity in a tradition or practice, at other times in order to distinguish between peoples, languages and cultures in South Africa, sometimes in order to illustrate maskanda's emergence as a melting pot of styles and techniques.

The Bhaca people in Mpondo occupy an interesting position in the construction of maskanda as a Zulu performance practice. They fled from King Shaka kaSenzangakhona (c. 1787–1828) (*-bhaca* means to flee in several Nguni languages) and came to embody a specific and 'deep' form of traditionality.[6] Sometimes, their music is opposed to isiZulu style and culture (Khoza 2009). At other times, the Bhaca people, through their eminent vocal tradition, represent the 'south coast' styles as a central inspiration for maskanda performance, close to the village that many maskanda musickers, due to its strong concertina tradition, consider the ultimate cradle of maskanda music: Umkomazi (Hadebe 2008; Clegg 2009; Nzimande 2009). Musickers demarcate isiBhaca style in terms of specific features ('fifth harmonies', 'rhythmical humming' [Khoza 2009; Jenkins 2013a]) that can nevertheless easily feature other styles as well.

Clegg reports that both the Tembu people, who developed isiShameni style in the Colenso, and the Chunu people, who developed isiChunu style in the Msinga, also absconded from the Zulu state in the nineteenth century (Clegg 1981: 3; 1982: 8, see also Impey 2018: 95–9 for the precolonial rivalry between various clans.) Later, isiShameni dance was developed by the Tembu people on the Colenso farmlands to replace inter-district competition in the form of stick fighting matches (*umgangela* in the Zulu language and *uphenge* in the Tembu language) (Clegg 1982: 8). Whereas these competitions were previously prearranged and ritualized, they took on 'a very nasty connotation' (1982: 8) due to the ever-harsher competition over land (and the possibility of being evicted from it). Hence, dance competitions gradually replaced the stick fighting competitions, occupying a similar role with less destructive consequences, which resulted in an 'incredible riot of inter-district dance competitions' (10). Clegg also points out that the social and musical circumstances for the farm labourers who were brought in from Natal to Colenso were very similar to the nearby Msinga (1981: 7), where the Chunu people developed their isiChunu concertina style. Labourers were exposed to Afrikaans homestead life in which the concertina and the *boereorkes* were prominent means of passing the time. The strong concertina tradition of the Chunu people and the emergence of isiShameni dance in the Colenso area can be explained by a combination of these sources of inspiration with existing *imfilitshi* practices (Clegg 1981: 3). It may be for this reason that both isiShameni and isiChunu styles are, each in their own way, but for similar reasons, opposed to isiZulu style. The identification of musical differences between the styles possibly serves the more important goal of emphasizing the political and cultural abscondence of the Chunu and Tembu people.

---

[6] Mxolisi Majozi describes how the Bhaca people hid from Shaka: '-bhaca, in Zulu, means to hide .... They were hiding from Shaka, and if you look at them, they've got marks on their faces. The marks on their faces were created with thorns as a mask to disguise themselves and their leader, so Shaka does not see who is the leader or not when their face is covered in blood. That's where the mark[s] come from' (2011).

However, I have not encountered any maskanda musicker who directly equates isiChunu with isiShameni style, like isiNdwedwe is equated to isiZulu. Clegg, a very competent isiShameni dancer, was not keen to play isiChunu and did not consider himself 'a very good exponent of this particular style' (1981: 7). isiChunu emerged as a concertina practice that could not easily be imitated or copied by those without a concertina, and without the skills to play it. Clegg reports there were hardly 'any exponents of good concertina music' in KwaZulu (3). isiShameni, by contrast, was a dance practice that could more easily spread among farm labour communities. Currently, it seems to stand for a less localized way of playing chord-based rather than heterophonic music. Nkwanyana distinguishes several isiShameni tunings, 'depending on the village you are from' (B. Nkwanyana 2009b), strengthening the umbrella status of the style. isiManjemanje, literally 'now-now', is a hectic dance often in $\frac{8}{8}$ metre (Dlamini 2011b), and isiMandolino is based on the tuning and playing techniques for the mandolin (B. Nkwanyana 2009b). They are often mentioned as isiShameni(-related) styles that prefigured the emergence of mbaqanga.[7] Moreover, Dlamini suggests that isiManjemanje embodies the transition from the characteristic use of I-VI-IV-I ostinati (derived from mission school hymns) to I-IV-V-I ostinati in more recent isiShameni styles. isiKhunzi, Shiyani Ngcobo taught me, is another isiShameni-related style, a fast style, that, as Erlmann testifies, is derived from 'coon' and informed by minstrel and vaudeville practices (1991: 57). Despite the diversity of tunings, Nkwanyana consciously opposes the isiShameni tuning (D2,A2,D3,A3,B3,D4 or equivalents) to the isiZulu tuning of the guitar (E2,A2,D3,G3,B3,D4), by pointing out that in isiShameni many strings are tuned on the same pitch in order to make it easier for maskandi to play triadic chords (B. Nkwanyana 2009b).

The chordal nature of isiShameni styles may have emerged from various colonial encounters. Dlamini explains that the I-VI-IV-I ostinato underlying isiShameni style 'points at a confluence of mission school music and traditional techniques' (2011b). Bongani Nkwanyana and Bheki Khoza claim that the harmonic ostinato, which they describe as a cadential ostinato I-IV-V-I, 'is coming from the Boers' (2009), aligning themselves with Clegg's account of the KwaZulu farmlands. Still, they too emphasize the importance of church hymns in the emergence of isiShameni style as the basis for isicathamiya and mbaqanga genres. 'The more churches we heard, the more we get the amen', Khoza explained, probably hinting at the prominence of the plagal IV-I cadence. Nkwanyana and Khoza also explain in detail how genres like maskanda, isicathamiya and mbaqanga differ from 'a boeresong', describing this difference in terms of timbre and texture rather than harmony or form. 'Rather than playing the root and the fifth [an obvious feature of both church hymns and *boereliedjies*], the bass is always melodic' in isiShameni style, they asserted (Khoza 2009). Despite the relative importance of

---

[7] Mbaqanga, literally 'porridge', signified the 'musical daily bread' for many South African jazz enthusiasts in the 1950s and 1960s. Like maskanda, mbaqanga emerged as a confluence of many existing styles, such as marabi, kwela and traditional dance styles, signifying a black urban lifestyle in the mid-twentieth century. See Meintjes (2003) for a thorough study of this musical genre.

harmony, isiShameni is hence decidedly different from the *boeremusiek*. Moreover, '[the vocal group] Bafana isiColenso', both guitarists explained,

> are singing this Shameni, but in the form of isicathamiya ... [they] put it into Zulu music. That's another thing .... It is not the church .... It is direct from the [Zulu] culture ... adapted from the sounds of *amahubo*. You hear more the counter voices .... When they sing, there is more than one lead ... so it becomes intertwined.
> (Khoza 2009; B. Nkwanyana 2009b)

The quotation cited by Nkwanyana and Khoza serves here to reveal the manifold ways in which difference is constructed. With their explicit reference to the timbre of *amahubo* singing and the heterophonic texture that distinguishes *amahubo* from church hymns, Nkwanyana and Khoza not only describe the 'confluence' of mission school music and traditional techniques (Dlamini 2011b); they also reveal that the distinctions – including musical and structural ones – that are drawn between isiZulu and isiShameni styles (or isiNdwedwe and isiChunu styles, or isiShameni and isiChunu styles) depend on the kind of comparison in which they are used. Since little has been written about the features of these styles, there is little standardization in the description of style features, apart from those provided by Clegg. This absence of standardization might help us rather than hamper us in understanding the use of styles in maskanda practice. It is the focus on structural detail that allows for the description of a relaxed, context-dependent and changeable difference. It is what Martin Scherzinger described as 'the experience of a structural undecidability; one whose irreducible undecidability is less the result of some empirical imperfection (or the "unrecoverable" emic access to the "source of signification" ([Subotnik] 1996: 169)) and more the result of a trace of contingency lodged within the logic of any structure' (Scherzinger 2004: 258). These traces of contingency in maskanda styles shed light on the multiple disruptive and transitory environments that maskanda musickers were exposed to in the period in which maskanda developed in the first half of the twentieth century.

The hegemony of verbal-conceptual snapshots

It is important to reiterate that these undecidabilities are lodged in the concepts rather than in the practices, and only become relevant in verbal discourse. Admittedly, this constitutes the epistemic power of verbal modes of knowledge inscription, since specifications as arrests of inherently fleeting meaning formations facilitate an exchange of, or dialogue about, musical experience, constituting temporarily articulated interrelationships between musicking subjects. Yet, if modes of inscription (hearing, singing, speaking, writing, playing, reading, recording) are not combined in the attribution of meaning to music, these verbal-conceptual snapshots singularly affect the (options for) further circulation of acoustic assemblages and the participation of various listening entities, and become invasive and/or hegemonic.

This became particularly clear to me when I revisited recordings I made of one of the earliest guitar lessons I received from Shiyani Ngcobo who demonstrated on the guitar the particularities of umzansi and esikhulu styles, both of which he categorized as isiZulu styles (S. Ngcobo 2008c). He foregrounded parameters of tradition (when was

Figure 2.2 'Sevelina'. Texture and interaction between lead voice and guitar parts (S. Ngcobo 2008a). Transcribed with kind permission from heir Shiyani Ngcobo.

the style played?), location (where was it played?) and entitlement (who is supposed to play a style?). The interaction of Ngcobo's demonstrations and the necessity for me to make sense of them by conceptualizing them with my own analytical toolkit constituted a temporary acoustic assemblage in which I and Ngcobo participated as listening entities, but indirectly also our musicking forefathers and foremothers, teachers, friends and peers.

As an example of isiZulu umzansi, Ngcobo played the song 'Sevelina' (Figure 2.2; S. Ngcobo 2008a), the very first song he learned as a youngster from his elder brother Bheki Ngcobo a.k.a. Khetuwise on the *igogogo*, a tin can with fishing line as strings (Olsen 2004: 2). I made sense of this song as based on a descending hexachord: e – d – c – b – a – g. Ngcobo demonstrated isiZulu esikhulu style through his song 'Izinyembezi' (The Tears [Figure 2.3; S. Ngcobo 2008b]). This style is considered to be an eminent style (*-khulu* means 'large' or 'grand'). Ngcobo explained that the style has been derived from the concertina being played by senior members of the community: fathers and grandfathers. I distinguished 'Izinyembezi' from 'Sevelina' on the basis of my identification of a hemitonic pentatonic scale with major thirds, a whole tone and two half tones (g – f-sharp – d – c – b). According to Sazi Dlamini, these chromatic sensibilities constitute the traditionality of isiZulu style (Dlamini 2011b).

Figure 2.3 'Izinyembezi'. Voice, lower and upper guitar parts showing the alternation between f-sharp and f, and the insertion of e in the pentatonic scale as well as the presentation of motives A, A', A" and B (S. Ngcobo 2008b). Transcribed with kind permission from heir Shiyani Ngcobo.

Apart from differences in tonal and timbral respect between 'Sevelina' and 'Izinyembezi', I heard differences in rhythm and metre that constitute their form. 'Sevelina' is cast in a closed form. The riff is easily transcribed in a $\frac{12}{8}$ metre. The upper guitar parts and lead voice offer variations to this riff (transcribed in one staff in various grey scales in Figure 2.2). These variations are of equal length, which gives the song a stable and rocking character due to the triplet metre that is applied in many maskanda songs. The fastness of dancing, identified by Bongani Nkwanyana as a feature of umzansi dance, possibly underlies this metrical feel. 'Izinyembezi', by contrast, presents motives that cannot be transcribed in recurring regular bars. It has an unmistakable groove thanks to the ongoing picking in the lower guitar part (transcribed as sixteenth notes in Figure 2.3) that gives the reciting singer his melodic anchor points. In Chapter 6, I will explain such grooves and their chromatic alternations (Figure 2.3) as being inspired by allegedly precolonial gourd bow playing techniques.

Ngcobo's demonstrations do not provide the data to make general claims about differences between umzansi and esikhulu styles, and their similarities as isiZulu styles. As I have explained, I am not particularly interested in these general claims, because they concern the representations rather than the dynamics of knowing, and it is the latter rather than the former that I engage with in this book. The conceptual parameters that I employed to engage with Ngcobo's playing and singing, such as differences in tonality, 'blue notes', vocal timbre, string resonance, texture and groove, as indicated in Figures 2.2 and 2.3, may have been completely irrelevant to Ngcobo, just like I did not consider the intricate connotations of an igama or the dance steps as aural orientation points until I started reading (!) Clegg's and Erlmann's accounts. This demonstrates the contingency of the process of experiencing and interpreting music. It is this contingency and aural potentiality that I want to bring to the fore in this book and celebrate. For it is in this contingency and potentiality that those dynamics of signification, sensation, presentation and meaning formation may be found that may otherwise remain unnoticed, illegible (Bloechl 2008: 20) and/or barred from the realm of 'plausible knowledge' (Bloechl 2008: 6).

Such dynamics also teach us something about global flows and trends of academic knowledge formation, being a predominantly conceptual written mode of knowledge inscription that disavows its contingent dimensions. Post-structuralist critiques have thematized this disavowal for some time now (Derrida [1967] 1997: 85ff), but the implications of this acknowledgement for the role of musicking in the formation of knowledge have only recently started to become theorized comprehensively (Erlmann 2004, 2010; Ochoa 2014; Abels 2016). Epistemic traditions that rely on the written word – which often also rely on a body of written texts that assert a form of monotheism: Judaism, Islam, Christianity – have always valued music ambivalently at best, or outright negatively at worst. In European history, music's non-referential character has been considered problematic throughout. Plato problematized poetry, including music, as potentially anarchic (Plato 2004 [c. 4th BCE]: 65). St Augustine warned that music could be a distraction from God (St Augustine 1992 [397 CE]). Both Catholic and Protestant churches – think of the Council of Trent in the sixteenth century and

Calvin's prohibition of musical instruments in church (Garside 1979) – repeated this warning. Idealist philosophers in nineteenth-century Germany, such as Kant and Hegel, distrusted music for its unspeakable characteristics, openly disqualifying its status as an art (Hegel [1826] 1998; Titus 2016b). Today, parents still warn their children against musics that allegedly trigger sexual, violent or otherwise licentious behaviour (Jackson 1999). Thus, music (and performance at large) is explicitly considered an unsuitable means for the transmission and validation of knowledge and ideas. Rather, as the Colombian philosopher Santiago Castro-Gómez observes (quoted in Ochoa 2014: 13), eurogenic epistemologies proceed from an ocularcentric premise as a safeguard for unequivocality and singularity, and the constitution of unified and controllable selves, aiding the kind of discriminatory knowledge that both Bhabha and Castro-Gómez identify as a foundational aspect of colonialism.

In oral epistemologies, music's status is quite different. Among Zulu South Africans, song, dance and instrumental performance-based practices validate Zulu knowledge and heritage as securely and powerfully as, for instance, a *Sefer Torah* (Torah scroll) validates Jewish knowledge and heritage. This implies that music and dance are considered fully-fledged forms of knowing connoting and denoting specific content, and that they have great epistemic status. It is necessary to state it here in order to decentre the Eurocentric presumptions mentioned above that musical acts of knowing are necessarily less stable, precise or comprehensive than conceptual forms of grasping and differentiation, due to the former's musicality. In this book, I argue the exact opposite: it is the aspiration towards verbal and conceptual unequivocality, stability (fixity) and categorical difference that results in knowledge, ideas and interpretation becoming obscured or even lost. The undecidability of aural experience, by contrast, as well as the equivocality of musical 'explanation' (in its literal form of 'unfolding') account for the multifariousness, richness and potentiality of thought and knowledge formations at large, as Ngcobo's demonstrations of maskanda styles indicate.[8] Such an argument interrogates the almost exclusive reliance of academic discourses (including this book) on writing, and it unearths the process of Eurocentric conceptual appropriations of musical culture that took (and take) place under the guise of 'understanding'.

---

[8] An example of music being an unequivocal and stable form of discriminatory knowledge concerns the realm of identity articulation – through the social and emotional inclusion/exclusion of black or white people, men or women, human or less human people, old or young people, European or non-European people, African or non-African people, etc. This might be the reason why so many music scholars focus on musical identity articulation as an object of research, and why it is difficult to reach beyond it in musicological studies. It is epistemically straightforward and representational compared to other domains of musical epistemology. (See also Abels 2016: 2 for a critique of this scholarly confinement.)

Part II

Maskanda as a Discourse of Power in Post-Apartheid South Africa

3

Ground Level:
The Kushikisha Imbokodo Festival in Durban

In October 2009, I visited maskandi Josefa Nkwanyana a.k.a. Mziwoxolo (1952–2012) in the village of Mandeni, near Tugela River. Joe Nkwanyana had worked in the centre of the national music industry during the apartheid years and in the early transition years during the 1990s. In the early 1980s, he worked with Hamilton Nzimande (1936–2002), who would make a huge name for himself as the producer of Mahlatini and the Mohatella Queens, and who also launched the career (as well as the sound) of legendary maskandi Phuzushukela (see Chapter 1). Nkwanyana released a highly acclaimed album *Ngihamba Nomngani* with Gallo in 1984, of which he never saw a penny, and he toured Norway, Belgium, Mauritius and Mozambique. He worked with singer and actress Tu Nokwe from the late 1980s until 2007. Yet, here he was, in Mandeni, at his parents' home, growing vegetables. 'This one', he said, and pointed at his guitar, 'needs practice but I no longer practice because I am always busy tending the fields. Actually, I should not be playing because it has disappointed me .... It didn't do anything; the knowledge I have did not give me anything' (J. Nkwanyana 2009b).

I spent a whole afternoon with Nkwanyana during which he shared his wide knowledge of maskanda guitar styles, differences between rural and township ways of singing, the permeable line between maskanda and gospel vocal techniques, ways of knowledge transmission through maskanda song and traditional healing and spells. Yet, he was very explicit about the fact that none of this musical and interpretative skill had brought him anything in terms of a sustained career or even a family, as if what he had on offer did not count. Joe Nkwanyana's story is one of the saddest I have encountered during my research into maskanda, even though it is by no means a unique story.

Many Zulu South Africans have some knowledge about how to address ancestors (*amadlozi*). Within such customs and conventions, the ability to administer medicine (*umuthi*) for good or bad causes is considered crucial. There are also experts one can consult for specific problems, illnesses, dangers or challenges in life. Several of them are also musicians. Busi Mhlongo (1947–2010) consciously presented herself as a healer and diviner, an *isangoma*; Nkwanyana's knowledge of *umuthi* plants gave him the status of a herbalist (*izinyanga zemithi*). He provided us with detailed accounts of how plants can be used, to heal or harm people, depending on the intention and the morality of the user.

On more than one occasion, maskandi explained to me how they became affected by various uses of *umuthi*, often in harmful ways. Nkwanyana insisted that he had become ill through the music and that this was the doing of other musicians. S'kho Miya reported similar situations of *umuthi* being planted on stage to jinx and obstruct her performance by making her ill. Berglund observes that sickness and suffering is often explained from friction or tension in social relationships that – in turn – are caused by the breaking of moral standards of living ([1976] 1989: 348). This makes the position of ill people very precarious, because medical intervention will not have any effect if the underlying tensions are not identified and overcome first. Invariably, the ill person has a responsibility in doing this. It may be no coincidence that the maskandi who presented themselves most openly as diviners – Busi Mhlongo and Joe Nkwanyana – were both seriously ill and died from these illnesses.

Epistemic in-betweenness

Engaging with maskanda – whether in performance, in the discursive practices that judge and disseminate it or as an academic object of study – means engaging with its epistemic in-betweenness. On the one hand, maskanda has functioned from its early days as an alternative to written (and often oppressive) epistemologies. Maskanda's purveyors orally transmit, document, negotiate, express and perform events, viewpoints, moral orientations and societal norms that form part of the day-to-day lives of those who were consciously excluded from formal education and knowledge acquisition. On the other hand, maskanda's emergence in the context of forced labour migration enhanced the urgency of adapting this heritage to new, imposed living conditions. Maskanda's musical and verbal dialects, societal values, praises of dignitaries, accounted events (wars, migratory moves), lifestyles and religious beliefs had to be made 'legible' in the framework of apartheid society. The discursive spaces in which maskanda thrives are sites in which this tension can be observed.

In her book about maskanda, Kathryn Olsen describes how maskanda developed from being a private and often acoustic leisure activity to a commercial amplified band enterprise in a studio (2014: 56–70). This development encompassed many decades and was decidedly informed by apartheid cultural policies. Yet, maskanda's manifestations as a solo occupation and a band practice not only constitute a chronological transition. Moreover, the binary between the solo occupation as socially embedded and non-commercial versus the band occupation as socially indifferent and commercial should be approached with care. Clegg emphasizes that records, even in the 1970s, 'were rough and ready' (Clegg 2009). Their commercial appeal was limited to an audience that was in the know about the Zulu guitar on the streets. Currently, maskandi with access to studios, record deals, airtime on radio and TV, and festival stages also play acoustically in private, or at communal events at their (rural) homes. Although maskandi can no longer be seen in the streets of Durban and Johannesburg, maskanda contests in hostels still thrive. Yet, most maskandi in present-day South Africa consciously and explicitly aim to make a living out of maskanda, which they do with various degrees of success.

In Part II of this book, I focus on this aim of professional musicking in South Africa today, because I intend to address how maskanda practice became part of social and commercial institutions and organizational infrastructures of which it never had been part as a leisure guitar practice in the streets and hostels of Durban and Johannesburg. These infrastructures encompass, for instance, music industries, (national) media, concerts, festivals and national and global imaginations of Zulu and South African culture. This implied that maskanda needed to become 'legible' to more people than practising maskandi only, by representing and communicating specific (musical) ideas, heritage, legacies, identities, loyalties and societal behaviour. The fact that maskanda became a powerful and straightforward marker of male Zulu identity, despite its emergence as a hybrid and displaced music practice, can be explained by this requirement of legibility. Moreover, maskanda needed to become legible to an audience that requests music, even though maskanda practice involves much more than musicking. Maskanda musickers also pray, communicate with ancestors, praise or criticize dignitaries, educate the community, narrate histories, soothe tensions, transport people back home and personalize the public space, and more, through maskanda.

Thus, I argue that maskanda's cultural status (including its epistemic and epistemological implications) was increasingly, and still is, being articulated through this requirement of legibility to audiences that are not limited to immediate bystanders and the local community. This resulted in an increasing division of labour in the act of musicking with distinctions between playing, managing, producing, distributing, promoting, and so on, as well as a change in the artistic social status that these jobs represented. The musicker promoting the music gains agency over the creativity of the maskandi, since they can tell the maskandi whether the maskandi's creation is legible to a paying music audience or not. Such divisions of labour provide opportunities as well as restrictions to musicians. These were articulated to me by many maskandi and their managers (Khama 2009; K. Miya 2009a; Nkabinde 2009; B. Nkwanyana 2009) and they have been outlined in detail in the literature about various South African performance practices (Meintjes 2003; Coplan [1985] 2008b; Ballantine [1993] 2012; Olsen 2014). There is a clear intersection of the political representation of maskanda as 'Zulu Traditional' in apartheid times, the stereotypical commercial demands of today's national and international music markets, and the options for self-articulation of creators and listeners of maskanda – an intersection that often sustains existing power relations and discursive regimes. The events I describe in the following three chapters provide some compelling examples of this.

However, my account also shows that maskandi and audiences articulate themselves in a diversity of manners as Zulu people, men, women, musicians, teachers and, indeed, South African citizens through maskanda. Although reified icons of Zulu nationalism, intertwined with stereotypes of African Otherness, are important in maskanda's regional, national and international representation, there is a growing interest among maskanda musickers for those musical expressions that signal Africa's global normativity rather than its Otherness. This translates into an orientation towards global rap, soul, gospel and R&B practices, but also into a conscious 'revamping' of sonic heritage that is experienced as local and traditional. South Africans from all backgrounds and social strata display a keen urge to reconnect with the rest of the world after sustained cultural isolation during the apartheid years. Scholarly attention for the increasing diversity of ways in which maskanda is created and experienced (Nyezwa 2018; De Jong and Madzikane 2020) reveals a socio-cultural horizon in maskanda discourse that surpasses the commodified performance of visuals, sounds and dances that portray Africa as 'a place of savanna and safari' (Meintjes 2003: 225). In the following chapters, I intend to demonstrate the importance of foregrounding the aural experiences of a variety of maskanda musickers.

Hence, this part of the book focuses on the ways in which maskanda musickers with a wide array of agencies shape their professional lives through maskanda, and it addresses in particular the many instances in which musickers work around, tweak, negotiate or even disregard the totalizing implications of imposed imaginations, commodifications and restrictions on their participation. I do this by explaining how auditory engagements with maskanda (as modes of sharing experiences, knowledge and understanding of this music) are located in specific cultural settings of production, distribution, mediation and consumption. In doing so, I identify *the dynamics of circulation* of acoustic assemblages (Ochoa 2014: 22) and I indicate how 'soils of significance' are being (re)created (Eva Hoffman quoted in Ahmed et al. 2003: 9). Ahmed et al. observe that 'affective qualities ... and the work of memory in their making cannot be divorced from the more concrete materialities of rooms, objects, rituals, borders and forms of transport that are bound up in so many processes of uprooting and regrounding' (2003: 9). I employ this observation to substantiate my understanding of maskanda epistemology as multiple, relational and temporarily stable, indicating the inherent 'belatedness' of cultural signification (Bhabha 1994b: 58). In this belated process of signification, assumptions, preconceptions, misconceptions, hunches and experiences interact, and I hope to dissect such interactions in more detail by describing my own belated understanding of this music. This should provide partial insight into the ways we use our voices, bodies and musical instruments to signify, evoke, present, produce, interpret and comment on the world in which we live: how we make sense of our worlds through sound and listening.

Divisions of musicking labour

I structure my description along the lines of Khoni Miya's analysis of the 'levels' of musicking within the music industry – levels that an artist needs to access in order to sustain herself. Miya's account indicates how musickers use stage, production studio and media as spaces in which they shape their careers and their music. Certain skills and forms of knowledge that are central to maskanda practice – such as personal stories or local histories, demonstrations of virtuosity, musical indications of place and descent, messages conveyed by ancestors in dreams or spells for competing musicians – are sometimes barred from these spaces and at other times enter and shape them. By structuring my argument along Miya's observations, I hope to shed some light on the analytical and experiential perspective of those who engage with maskanda as a way of life, since these levels determine the maskandi's ways of life. They point at distributions of power within the various divisions of labour in the South African music industry: who has agency over the musicking process, the artistic result, the economic profits, the cultural capital and hence the production of (epistemic) heritage? My account also indicates the entanglement of my and Miya's thought as well as the representational and agential inequalities in the ways I employ Miya's analysis.

I got in touch with Khoni Miya while I was working with her sister Khombisile 'S'kho' Miya, who leads a maskanda band in Durban. The sisters – Khoni being an afropop singer, S'kho a maskandi – barely survive in the fringes of Durban's urban economy. There is no music industry of note in Durban. For musicians who want to make a living with their skills, Johannesburg is an unquestioned and often unattainable destination. I encountered S'kho Miya coincidentally, attending one of her gigs at the University of KwaZulu-Natal's Centre for Jazz and Popular Music in 2008. She is a woman my age, then in her thirties, with an adult daughter, whom she raised by herself and who recently had to drop out of school because she became a single mother too. S'kho Miya's music, her band and her friendship soon turned out to be my foremost source of conceptual and musical information about maskanda, and, more importantly, they shaped my aural, embodied and emotional attachment to maskanda music and its musickers. Miya encouraged me to join her band Abagqugquzeli (Organizers), later renamed after herself – Khombisile Band – and perform with her. I worked with her from August to October 2008 and from July to October 2009 in the Stable Theatre in Durban, the band's rehearsal venue. I also met her sister there.

Khoni Miya distinguished three levels in the professional career of a South African musician: 'ground level', 'middle level' and 'up level'. On the ground level, one is a more or less independent musician, and in the case of women, like S'kho and Khoni Miya, this implies being a vocalist, since women do not play guitar, concertina or drums. It is obvious to Khoni Miya that a musician has a producer, a choreographer, an arranger and a composer. Often these roles are taken on by one person, and my impression was that S'kho Miya took on all these roles: she composed her own songs, devised her own choreographies and taught these to all (male) musicians and (female) backing singers (including me). Often, there were men present during rehearsals who claimed to be her manager or producer, who helped out with advice concerning dance and rhythm and provided contacts for gigs, but they were clearly not in charge of the artistic process in getting a performance together. S'kho was in charge. Khoni stated that producers never know what a musician needs, only a composer/arranger knows this.

On the middle level, a musician is accessing a music industry through a record company or label. In order to do so, a musician needs a manager who will introduce her to the relevant people in the industry and the wider world. These opportunities for exposure constitute a virtually unattainable step in the career of a South African musician. As I will outline in Chapter 4, the spaces that enable such exposure – (festival) stages, recording studios and media platforms – need to be accessed simultaneously. Without exposure in local, regional and national media it is impossible to secure gigs, and without gigs there are no options to rent an expensive studio for a recording or sign a contract with a record label. And without an album it is virtually impossible to arouse interest from media broadcasters or festival organizers.

The 'up level' is in fact the most problematic level in Khoni Miya's analysis of professional musicianship in South Africa. The music industry has taken over all the roles that producer, manager, choreographer, arranger and composer used to fulfil. The industry can now ditch the producer and 'start squeezing you down' (K. Miya 2009a). The division of labour that follows from the musician's embedding in the industry has made her dependent on this industry. Even though ground, middle and up level do represent a form of artistic and economic advancement for many maskandi, the 'up level' is not necessarily a better position to be in than the 'ground level', as Joe Nkwanyana's case illustrates. Maskandi, producers and media representatives move in and out of these levels. In Chapter 5, I provide a few examples of such 'squeezing', enabled by a commercial demand for cheaply produced black music productions in the post-apartheid era. Many musicians succumb to it through their hopes of eventually climbing onto an overseas stage.

As a female researcher in S'kho Miya's band, I could be part of the musical labour on stage and in rehearsal rooms as well as observe and participate in the (predominantly female) community that stays in the village when (predominantly male) labourers work in town. For Miya and myself, the easiest way to bond was through making music together. On the occasions that I wanted to talk to her about her music, she called her elder sister Khoni, who acted as an interlocutor, since my Zulu was less proficient than S'kho's English. I still regularly visit S'kho and Khoni Miya's village, KwaBhidla, near Highflats, and I remain struck by the similarity between the village's current demography and the one during the apartheid era as documented in the literature. This demography is a direct social consequence of forced labour (Meredith 2007; Coplan [1985] 2008b; Ballantine [1993] 2012): there are no adult men in KwaBhidla, just women, children and elderly people. There is no sewer system, no running water and only occasionally electricity. Those who work in town (nowadays also women like S'kho and Khoni Miya) are supposed to support the village with food and presents when they visit. These visits are rare since transport is expensive. In order to make money they must reside in town in often deplorable temporary lodgings.

Despite their problematic socio-economical position, both Miya sisters have a clear vision of their musical careers, which they pursue with a relentless persistence. In 2008, when I started rehearsing with S'kho Miya in the Stable Theatre, she had the odd gig around Durban. In 2009, when I returned, she possessed a professionally produced demo album recorded in a Johannesburg studio. Next to her plans to release this album (which she did in 2010: *Ungcayi Lweqhikiza*), it enabled her to rehearse the dancers without having to summon (and pay) a band for rehearsal. The drive that S'kho and Khoni Miya displayed to expose themselves and their music, to perform and participate in a network of Durban musicians, despite the very poor material rewards, was decidedly fuelled by their outspoken intention to climb onto an overseas stage.

Khoni and S'kho Miya never made a secret of the fact that they envisaged me – a white woman from Europe with an interest in maskanda – to be their manager who should pave their way to fame and glory on overseas stages. This made my position as a friend highly problematic. From the very start of our collaboration, the sisters were explicit about what they wanted from me, and thanks to their outspokenness I was able to keep reiterating that I had not come to South Africa to become a band manager. They were not the only maskandi who expected this from me (Khama 2009; Ntuli 2009). Why else would I come from Europe to work with a maskanda band? With decades of white colonial guilt complexes on my shoulders, I realized it was problematic, if not impossible, to ignore or neutralize these expectations. S'kho Miya gave me a wealth of data for my research project; what did I give her in return? Fees for my singing and dancing lessons, payment of a hospital bill, occasionally transport or lunch, nothing particularly solid or long-standing. It made me realize how difficult it was to act on Concord Nkabinde's encouragement outlined in the opening sentences of this book: explain – to S'kho Miya and to myself – why and how her music is important to me.

Whereas I could easily empathize with Miya's expectations of me, I was worried by her fixation on this one trajectory towards 'overseas'. I have reiterated time and again what an excellent teacher she is. I could testify of this from my own experience. I suggested that she might be able to earn a better living if we arranged a venue where she could teach many well-to-do Durban kids maskanda dance and song. But she never expressed any interest in this. For her, like for so many South Africans, success could only be achieved at a place other than the one in which she grew up in apartheid times, and in which she eked out her precarious existence.

Female maskanda musicking

Despite all this, S'kho Miya is by no means disempowered. She has agency that impacts greatly on maskanda practice in South Africa and beyond – an impact with musical, social and conceptual dimensions. She is a woman in a musical genre that traditionally thrived in male-dominated spaces such as hostels and mines. Deborah James wrote a detailed study of women's musical agency in migrant conditions, particularly in and from the Northern Province (now Limpopo). She points out how women create and affirm their own senses of home through musical performance that they experience as traditional (James 1999). Yet, Kathryn Olsen observes that this female agency is limited within maskanda practice. Although women maskandi and female maskanda bands are proliferating, most women perform the role of front dancers and singers, with lyrics, sound production, instrumental accompaniment and the release of albums being predominantly in the hands of men. Olsen points out that the lyrics of female bands often take a male perspective and the opportunities for women maskandi to articulate themselves are determined by men (2014: 141–84). This is consistent with the traditional role of women in Zulu society, confined to domestic spaces and caring duties.

S'kho Miya, by contrast, composes her own songs, devises her own choreographies for these songs, puts together her own band, teaches her (male) band members by herself (Figure 3.1), organizes her own festivals and releases her own albums. The band is self-consciously named after her: Khombisile Band. Through the lyrics of her songs (see the Appendix in this book), Miya is outspoken about the position of women in present-day South Africa, taking on issues of polygamy, imposed or forced marriage ('Nith' Angiqome Bani' [S. Miya 2010c]) and problems arising from male dominance in relationships ('Ibhoxongwana' [S. Miya 2010d], 'Wayibulal' Inhliziyo Yami'). Her *izibongo* (to be discussed in Chapter 7) employs decidedly female boasting symbols to draw attention to her musical skill. Her musical and social independence may be the reason why she takes up the traditionally male role of provider in her village. I was unable to establish whether her self-articulation as an independent maskandi would have been possible during apartheid times, when the Zulu community was walled off from societies elsewhere (and successful female artists such as Busi Mhlongo went into exile). However, it was obvious to me that, in 2008, she was respected as a musician and an independent personality by Zulu men and women of all ages.

Khoni Miya's involvement in the friendship between her younger sister and me was in no way limited to being an interlocutor. She regularly expressed to me the importance not only of women shaping their own (musical) careers and lives, but also of women consciously standing up for a collective feminist cause. Her agenda became clear in the way she explained the history of female participation in maskanda (as documented in Chapter 1) and in a range of initiatives she tried, and sometimes managed, to get

Figure 3.1 S'kho Miya instructs the members of her Abagqugquzeli Band during rehearsal at the Stable Theatre, Warwick Triangle, Durban, 3 October 2008.

financial support for, such as the erection of an organization that attends to the needs of female musicians in townships or the organization of an all-female music festival, in order to give exposure to female musicians. It is this latter initiative, the Kushikisha Imbokodo Festival, that I discuss in more detail because it reveals the outreach and impact of 'ground level' musical initiatives on local and wider communities, not only through the performances at the festival itself, but also through it being covered by local media and financially supported by local governments.

David Coplan ([1985] 2008b: 246) and Brett Pyper (2016) have set out to

> show that the mounting of a ... festival [in present-day South Africa] has become a kind of meta-cultural performance in its own right, carrying resonant sedimented historical meanings (whether these are conscious or not) and revealing cultural aspirations that frame the performances of ... musicians themselves (who likewise, like their audiences, can deliberately or unknowingly reinforce or subvert the circumstances of their presentation).
>
> (Pyper 2016: 108)

An important reason for this meta-cultural performativity is the fact that '[f]estivals in various formats, initiated by a range of role players, were a notable feature of public culture within various African communities across the country for much of the twentieth century' (109) reflecting 'attempts to construct a black public sphere in South Africa' (109) despite conscious and often successful efforts by colonial and later apartheid governments to obstruct or destroy such a public sphere.

The importance of the Kushikisha Imbokodo Festival was its conscious attempt to foreground the role of women in the reinforcements and subversions of a public sphere, mentioned by Pyper. During the festival, women not only displayed, but also shaped their Zulu heritage. Thus, they presented themselves as fully fledged maskandi who are supposed to be the guardians of this heritage. It is important to understand such initiatives not as newly developed forms of female emancipation in the post-apartheid years, but as the reclaiming of practices and customs that were very much part of female musicking in earlier times (Gunner 1989; Olsen 2014; B. Nkwanyana 2016c). Thus, I felt I witnessed (and participated in) a (re)creation of 'soils of significance' (Ahmed et al. 2003: 9). At the festival, this recreation occurred through what Ahmed calls 'concrete materialities' in lively conversation with 'the work of memory'. I mention performance practices (the visibility of women as front singers and dancers, independent artists and composers), poetics (the content of the lyrics) and musical sound. In order to further explore this female agency in maskanda performance, I will discuss two performance practices that have increasingly come to signify male agency among Zulu South Africans whereas they used to be prominent female forms of expression too. These encompass the use of *ibhodlo* or 'goat voice' in this chapter and the delivery of *izibongo* (spoken self-praise) in Chapter 7.

On 30 August 2009, a Sunday afternoon, from 12 pm to 5 pm, the Kushikisha Imbokodo Festival took place in the BAT Centre, Durban's community centre for local craft and performing arts. The festival was conceived by Khoni Miya and organized by her and several women and men in her professional network. Organizing a *Kushikisha Imbokodo* (Women's Movement) Festival is not an obvious thing to do in South Africa's Zulu community. Men and women are equal under the progressive post-apartheid South African Constitution, but they have decidedly different roles, and often rights, in many South African communities, such as the Zulu, Indian and Afrikaner ones. In Zulu culture, this is enhanced by the traditional custom of polygamy for men, but not for women. The tradition of *lobola* (dowry) that a man must pay (often in cows or other livestock) to the father of his desired bride furthers the image of women as valuable assets or property rather than as independent human beings. Female musicians told me on several occasions how this image has hampered them in their development as individuals and artists.

Another important determinant of gender relations in Zulu communities is the separation of many Zulu men from their families because of forced labour migration from the late nineteenth century onwards. The displacement and disempowerment of Zulu men that accompanied the forced labour also fostered the antithetical image of the precolonial Zulu man as a strong and fear-inducing warrior, embodied by the nineteenth-century Zulu King Shaka (*c.* 1787–1828). With labour migrancy and Zulu tradition being two formative tropes of maskanda performance, the identificatory categories of 'masculinity' and 'Zuluness' are often conflated in maskanda's performance, and more broadly in South African parlance. Character traits dubbed as 'male', such as strength, discipline, aggression, competitiveness and dexterity, are often also attributed to the Zulu people, and, by implication, to maskandi (see also Meintjes 2017: 5ff discussing the mythologization of the Zulu warrior). The festival showcased ways in which women increasingly appropriate the performance-based and musical signs that previously signified the masculine environment in which maskanda was said to be practised.

Khoni Miya translated 'kushikisha' to me as the movements women make when they dig and plant food for their children. The term can also be used in a figurative sense: women's movement (K. Miya 2009a).[1] 'Imbokodo', the Zulu word for grindstone, also refers to the Zulu saying 'Wathint' abafazi wathint' imbokodo' (Strike the women and you'll strike the rock), that was used on 9 August 1956 when twenty thousand women gathered at the Union Buildings in Pretoria to protest against pass laws for women of colour. With these references to Zulu tradition and anti-apartheid history, Miya effectively put the importance of current female visibility and representation to the fore. She managed to obtain a subsidy from the provincial Department of Arts and Culture (DAC), and media coverage by local media such as the Durban newspaper *Daily News* and the radio station Vibe FM, based in Durban's KwaMashu township. Both sisters also had a decisive role in the artistic set-up of the festival, drawing on their network of musicians and taking a large part of the performance upon themselves in various groups (Figure 3.2).

---

[1] According to Ignatia Madalane, Miya referred to grinding corn with two rocks, traditionally a woman's job (2012).

The Kushikisha Imbokodo Festival

The BAT Centre's main concert hall (seating a few hundred people) was 75 per cent filled. The language of communication was Zulu. The gender balance in the audience was more or less equal, but the performers were entirely made up of women's bands,

Figure 3.2 Khoni Miya performs at the Kushikisha Imbokodo Festival.

with women as front dancers and singers, and men as instrumentalists. Most bands had conventional pop music line-ups of electric guitar(s), bass and drums (with the occasional addition of Latin and/or African percussion). All songs were elaborate, lasting up to ten minutes with extensive *izibongo* spoken praises, and long instrumental interludes that enabled performers and audience members to dance. The audience members were minutely aware of the lyrics, the gestures belonging to specific musical phrases, and they were supposed, and invited, to demonstrate this knowledge with the musicians on stage.

The audience responded very directly to specific dance moves and to *izibongo*, and especially the women in the audience were very vocal in their enthusiasm for local celebrities. These included female maskandi Sgqebhezana, afrojazz singer Melody Ngwane who allegedly receives her songs through dreams and Makhulu Hlope who delivered a wildly received cover of Dorothy Masuka's song 'Into Yam' (Masuka 1959), made famous by Miriam Makeba.[2] Hlope also performed marabi and jive. Khoni Miya participated in several of the backing choruses of these artists and performed a few of her own afrogospel songs that are featured by the voice inflections of gospel, and by a combination of cyclic chord progressions and response choruses in parallel fourths.

Thanks to the translations of Ignatia Madalane, I found out after the event that the agenda of many of the performers had been explicitly feminist. Sgqebhezana addressed her (mixed gender) audience as 'odadewethu' (my sisters) only. Nozuko addressed it as 'zintombi zasemzansi' (girls from South Africa), to which the female part of the audience responded with overwhelming cheers. The repertoire consisted of love songs that spanned a wide range of emotions: the fear of the beloved one's beauty, the hope of never breaking up or the wish of getting married (Makhulu Hlope). Several artists addressed the experience of dating an 'usikhotheni' (a useless person), of being beaten, and being asked for money (Sgqebhezana, S. Miya), of children being left by their father (Hlope) and of the love for one's husband even if he drinks ('Into Yam'). In most of these songs, these troubles were not only identified, but also regretted and sometimes condemned. Since (maskanda) songs often deal with real-life experiences, the lyrics give a compelling insight into the kind of problems women struggle with in present-day South Africa. Khoni Miya always reminded me of these problems when we talked. These explicitly female perspectives on South African daily life were welcomed (or at least accepted and participated in) by all audience members and they were embedded by male MCs who presented their own tongue-in-cheek intermezzos without any gender-specific references. Thus, whereas the title of the festival and the themes addressed by the female artists suggest an outspoken feminist agenda, the event was not a parochial women-only occasion.

---

[2] 'Into Yam is one of the songs that Makeba sings in Lionel Rogosin's clandestine 1959 film *Come Back Africa* about township life in South Africa. The film premiered at the 1959 Venice Film Festival and it was Rogosin who bribed South African officials to let Makeba come to Italy for the presentation. She would not return to South Africa for the next 30 years. Rogosin along with Harry Belafonte financed Makeba's travels to the US and arranged for her to appear on the Steve Allen show in November 1959. The first song she sang on live television in the United States was Into Yam' (Allen 2011).

The non-parochial character of the festival may have been prompted by it being intended to give women maskandi exposure to a broad audience. The enthusiastic reception of the performers by the audience indicated that these women were regarded as artists in their own right. They smoothly moved in and out of various musical and performance genres. In her opening act, Sgqebhezana performed songs that are easily recognizable as maskanda. Prominent features included a melodic bass line, climactic drum rhythms that come to a halt as an indication for the dancers to execute *indlamu* (a stretched-leg kick), drop their feet or jump and long, loud and boasting *izibongo*. By contrast, Nozuko started her slot with a sample of the recently crystalized gospelmaskandi genre. Features include obvious maskanda guitar riffs combined with a laid-back groove and a much less agile bass than a conventional maskanda bass. In her second song, however, her flexible gospel voice instantly switched to the directional and constrained timbre of a maskandi singer. All these styles and techniques seemed to belong to the artists' aural archives. Moreover, all songs were firmly located as South African and Zulu through the language of the lyrics, through call-and-response formulas in parallel fourths and fifths, and through cyclic riffs in I-IV-I$_4^6$-V-I, I-VI-IV-I or similar harmonic progressions. Surely, all music sung and played this afternoon was considered to be indigenous Zulu music: it was shared as insider's knowledge by musicians and audience.

The festival revealed how the female performers appropriated normative performance conventions that are usually, but not always, in the hands of men. These appropriations encompassed the cover of the song made famous by Miriam Makeba as well as a song by Nozuko that sounded strikingly similar in mode and groove to Phuzekhemisi's song 'Bayethe'. Obviously, she drew from a common reservoir of musical material. However, more than drawing on a common repertoire of modes and grooves, it is the appropriation and adoption of vocal timbre that I want to discuss here as an indication of the increasingly empowered female presence on Zulu musical stages.

Ibhodlo

Meintjes has addressed the cultural significance, in national South African and international contexts, of *ibhodlo*, a vocal groan that became commodified and exported in the 1980s and 1990s as a 'lion's roar' through the music of Simon Nkabinde (1937-99), a.k.a. Mahlatini and The Mohatella Queens (hear, e.g., S. Nkabinde 1987: 00'31" and 00'43"). It became a signifier of Zulu cultural heritage and its exoticized equivalent notion of Zuluness (Meintjes 2003: 221-36). I will further unpack this notion of Zuluness in the next chapter. Here it is important to note that the commodified notion of Zuluness as 'strong, proud, aggressive, and posturing' (225) is no longer an exclusively male stage persona. It was self-consciously adopted by several female maskandi at the Kushikisha Imbokodo Festival in front of an audience that clearly did not perceive this as out of the ordinary. The same can be said about the abundance of *izibongo* self-praise. Often experienced as male through its competitive boasting and its alleged central function in courtship, *izibongo* was confidently reappropriated by the artists featuring at the festival, which will be further discussed in Chapter 7.

Meintjes observes that the *ibhodlo* is described as a 'goat voice' in South Africa, with goats being 'commonplace domestic items in rural South African homes' (226).

> The goat voice is a referent that makes less comment than the lion's roar does on the register of the sound, the unpredictability in the moments of utterance, and the range in volume and pitch, while it gives more significance to timbral features – to the gruffness, to its deep-throated vocal production, which produces a feeling of pitch distortion and a constrained resonance, resulting in a pulsating effect. The metaphor also comments on the repetitive presence of the utterance.
>
> (226)

Whether lion's roar or goat's voice, when Mahlatini conquered the world with his *ibhodlo*, the groan was imitated and reproduced by countless South African musicians in order to 'sound Zulu' with all the tribal and warrior-like stereotypes that came with it. It became a musical trope in its own right, also at the Kushikisha Imbokodo Festival. This seconds Meintjes' observation that the *ibhodlo* is currently being 'reclaimed' from 'the sophisticated global arena' (in which Mahlatini's roar became tarnished) for local consumption 'as a local identity marker' (2003: 230ff). Various female artists at the Kushikisha Imbokodo Festival, including S'kho Miya, employed this local identity marker despite the rather uncooperative sound production that affected her intonation (S. Miya 2009c; Figure 3.3). Miya, moreover, uttered a range of grunts and howls that

Figure 3.3 S'kho Miya performs at the Kushikisha Imbokodo Festival and reappropriates the *ibhodlo*. Photograph by Mageshen Naidoo (S. Miya 2009b: 00'20"ff; 2009c).

are often used in maskanda practice and stem from earlier vocal practices such as war cries and *amahubo* singing: 'haibo', 'awu', 'yim lo', 'washa'. Miya scatted these words, rapping them over the instrumental riff of guitar and bass, making musical structures of them on the spot (S. Miya 2009b: 00'20"ff).

Whereas the festival was by no means a women-only festival (men and women were quite equally represented among the audience and on stage with all-male instrumentalists), it did seem to be an exclusively Zulu musical event. I was the only white person in attendance. All bands were dressed in attire that is often associated with precolonial ways of living. Women were wearing long or short colourful skirts with beads on their head, ears and limbs (Figures 3.2 and 3.3), children were wearing Zulu headdresses and men wore distinctive *umbaselwa* dress: bright patched suits traditionally associated with labour migrancy (Figures 3.4 and 1.2).

Only after the festival was I able to reflect on the many sides that my participation in it involved, symbolizing different stances and problems to different people. I had to admit that my presence was significant to the outlook of S'kho Miya's Band and Khoni Miya's festival, and for the audience that watched a white woman enter the stage in Zulu attire singing maskanda in Zulu with a Dutch accent. Although my employment of strategies of Othering was subconscious and unintentional, I did record the alienation I felt when I participated in maskanda. This alienation had a social dimension: I could not understand many of the conversations that were going on about artistic decisions or ideas. It also had a musical dimension: I found it difficult to master choreographies and singing techniques.

Figure 3.4a S'kho Miya's Abagqugquzeli/Khombisile Band at the Kushikisha Imbokodo Festival (S. Miya 2009a). Dancers from left to right: S'kho Miya (lead), Bonisiwe Phungula, Dolly Ndlovu, Nontobeko Mtshare, Pinky Mabaso, Barbara 'Nompilo' Titus.

Figure 3.4b The Abagqugquzeli/Khombisile Band prepares for performance at the Kushikisha Imbokodo Festival (S. Miya 2009a). Photographs by Mageshen Naidoo.

From the start of my engagement with S'kho Miya and her Khombisile Band, she made it clear to me that I was supposed to work towards a performance with them. Whereas the weekly rehearsals in the small rehearsal rooms of the Stable Theatre were a way for me to become musically acquainted with maskanda, for her they served the aim of preparing me for a performance. This could attach me to the band as a potential white manager with international exposure, but also provide the band with a unique and instantly visible (and audible) selling point on stage (Figures 3.4a and 3.4b). I dreaded the moment she considered me ready for it. I noticed that I occupied the role of an unwilling and embarrassed child with a bad rehearsal discipline and a tendency to talk myself out of performance obligations with the argument of incapability and insecurity. In August 2009, Miya decisively put an end to my excuses; she bought me an expensive dance outfit and set a deadline: the Kushikisha Imbokodo Festival.

Maskandi withey

Although the festival was an exclusively Zulu musicking event, it was by no means a culturally exclusivist event. I had expected more surprise at, and less encouragement of, my half-hearted attempt to 'join the club'. Local media picked up on my participation, and a couple of weeks later S'kho Miya and I were invited for an interview at a local radio station, Vibe FM (Vibe FM 2009). The activities of Vibe FM provide another example of musicking at the 'ground level' that exists relatively undisturbed from demands from record companies, government policies or institutionalized and often reified cultural expectations.

Vibe FM continues to broadcast from the Ekhaya Arts Centre in Durban's KwaMashu township and has been set up by local volunteers. Community building is an important impetus behind its establishment. With support from the provincial government, it aims at empowerment of disadvantaged youths through 'various integrated arts and multimedia advancement skills that would increase career opportunities, job creation and practical knowledge'.[3] Radio shows encompass – according to the station's own account – 70 per cent local music, with a lot of maskanda (40 per cent). In 2009, the station featured a daily show completely devoted to maskanda from 7 am to 9 am, with the participation of local maskandi. The atmosphere in the studio was professional and relaxed, all staff were male, and although the audience was addressed in Zulu, the interview with me was conducted in English. The interviewers, DJ Mlungisi and Lungisani, jokingly brought me in as a peculiar specimen of the local maskandi, asking me when my first maskanda album would be released.

DJ Mlu also phrased the question that so many maskanda musickers posed to me, and that Concord Nkabinde identified as a potentially crucial channel of knowledge exchange between me and South African maskanda musickers: 'There are so many forms of music in the world', DJ Mlu stated. 'Why did you choose maskanda to study?' This was one of those instances in which I was able to explain to a larger Zulu audience than just a few bystanders what it is that I was doing and why I was doing it. I explained to DJ Mlu that I am not a performer. Rather than releasing a CD, I intended to write a book about maskanda. I wanted to write this book, because I had never heard music like this until South African friends I met during my college years in Britain exposed me to it. Maskanda's sonic particularity as well as South Africa's notorious loaded history awakened my interest. I implicitly admitted that it was my unfamiliarity with maskanda (maskanda's Otherness) that drew me to it.

The Vibe FM anchor men pointed out that my performance as a white woman from Europe in a Zulu event at Durban's BAT Centre had not gone unnoticed. My Otherness was also a source of fascination for my fellow musickers. They encouraged me to sing with Miya the two-part refrain of her song 'Ngilobole' (S. Miya 2010b), which resulted in idolatrous calls from listeners, thanking me in Zulu. DJ Mlu and I both emphasized Miya's crucial role in my maskanda engagement. Throughout the interview it became increasingly clear to me (although I wasn't able to bring all of it across to the Vibe FM

---

[3] This community building is coordinated by the KCAP (KwaMashu Community Advancement Projects), 'a non-profit organization (012–391 NPO) founded in 1993'. It is 'the only organization that has built its own unique Ekhaya Multi Arts Centre in Kwa Mashu, the oldest township of Durban'. It 'includes facilities such as Ekhaya Computer Lab (with Internet), Music Recording Studio, Theatre Facility, Dance Studio, Workshop Space, and Video Editing multi-media suite and a community radio VIBE FM facilities. The centre involves the community in radio drama and creative script writing, video production, Film Festival, traditional arts and cultural activities and African arts' (KCAP 2015).

listeners) that it is thanks to Miya that I have been able to familiarize myself with the music in many different respects. She has taught me how maskanda is sung, how an *izibongo* is constructed and should be delivered in public, how a song is transmitted to instrumentalists, which dance routines belong to which phrases and how one needs to dress for a performance. Intentionally or unintentionally, she has also provided insight into the daily lives of many maskandi nowadays. But most importantly, she has socially included me, making me part of the band and part of her family, a relationship that lasts up to this day and which does not only concern her, but also her community.[4] As many people pointed out to me, she primarily regards me as an *umuntu* (a human being), and only secondarily as an *umlungu* (a white person), two concepts that often remain mutually exclusive for many black South Africans today. Conversely, I have been able to identify the subconscious reified fixities and fetishes of stereotypical Zuluness in my mind and attitude, thanks to my relationship with Miya and many more maskanda musickers.

Yet, S'kho Miya kept very silent throughout the interview. She seemed subdued and conspicuously on guard. As vocal and present she could be in the delivery of maskandi skills for a large audience, here she was almost vanishing in the corner of that studio (Figure 3.5). Like Sipho Mchunu's seminal role in the foregroundings of the song 'Sab' Inganono', discussed in Chapter 1, Miya's seminal role in presenting maskanda to scholars and audiences from outside South Africa seemed to be swept under the carpet during the radio show, simply by the fact that I was receiving the credits for doing that. I was doing the talking, and I was receiving the idolatrous calls from KwaMashu listeners thanking me for it. I have never been able to discuss this agential inequality with Miya, and ask her whether this was the reason of her silence during our Vibe FM interview, but I am quite certain we both felt it that day, and on many more occasions. As Angela Impey has put it eloquently: 'while I may have learned how to attach meaning to [Miya's] sound, I was ill equipped to interpret [her] silence' (adapted from 2018: 216) for the very reason I was implicated in it. These explicit and, more often, implicit structures of inclusion and exclusion to some extent grow out of the legacy of apartheid's policy of 'separate development'. More importantly, however, they are being sustained through presumptions of Europe's cultural, epistemic and epistemological self-sufficiency and superiority more generally – presumptions that also featured my attitude in the radio studio. This attitude reduced Miya's seminal role to a barely perceivable 'nearly agential pressure' (Bloechl 2008: 11) in the radio broadcast about a maskandi whitey.

Both the Kushikisha Imbokodo Festival and Vibe FM were subsidized by the KwaZulu-Natal provincial Department of Arts and Culture (DAC). The DAC particularly emphasized the community-building aspect of the festival. The DAC's

---

[4] After several visits to KwaBhidla near Highflats, I was given a Zulu name, Nompilo, that, like all Zulu names, indicates the (envisaged) position of the person in the family (in this case, 'mother of health'). The entire Miya family has consistently and exclusively addressed me with this name since 2009.

Figure 3.5 Barbara Titus and S'kho Miya (right front corner) at Vibe FM, 19 September 2009. Photograph by Selby Ngcobo.

Vision and Mission were clearly displayed on posters in the concert venue (Figure 3.6) and in an elaborate address by its deputy manager, Mrs D. N. Ntuli. Both displays emphasized the development of arts and culture as a means for (economic) development and 'to empower citizens through a full an[d] open access to these resources'.[5]

Yet, the fact that I was the only white person present at a KwaZulu-Natal community building event illustrates how separated the lives of Zulu, Indian, Afrikaner, Xhosa and white English-speaking citizens of KwaZulu-Natal still are. Maskandi who perform at events like the Kushikisha Imbokodo Festival or get airtime on a station like Vibe FM are barely able to sustain a living from their musical careers. The cultural implications of their musicking, by contrast, are considerable within their communities. Through the (re)appropriation and (re)grounding of sonic and aural perceptions, maskandi (re)claim authority over cultural heritage in the form of performance practices and ideas. 'Ground level' or community-based musicking provides insight into the complexity and multifariousness of these appropriations and groundings, for instance with regard to the tension between imaginations of overseas (*pesheya*) and home (*ikhaya*), the position of women or the white capitalization on black agency in musical encounter, as demonstrated by musicking acts by Clegg, Jenkins (outlined in Chapter 1) and myself (at Vibe FM).

---

[5] KZN Department of Arts and Culture, Eastern Region, eThekwini North *Mission Statement*, displayed on 30 August 2009 at the BAT Centre, Durban. (Figure 3.6)

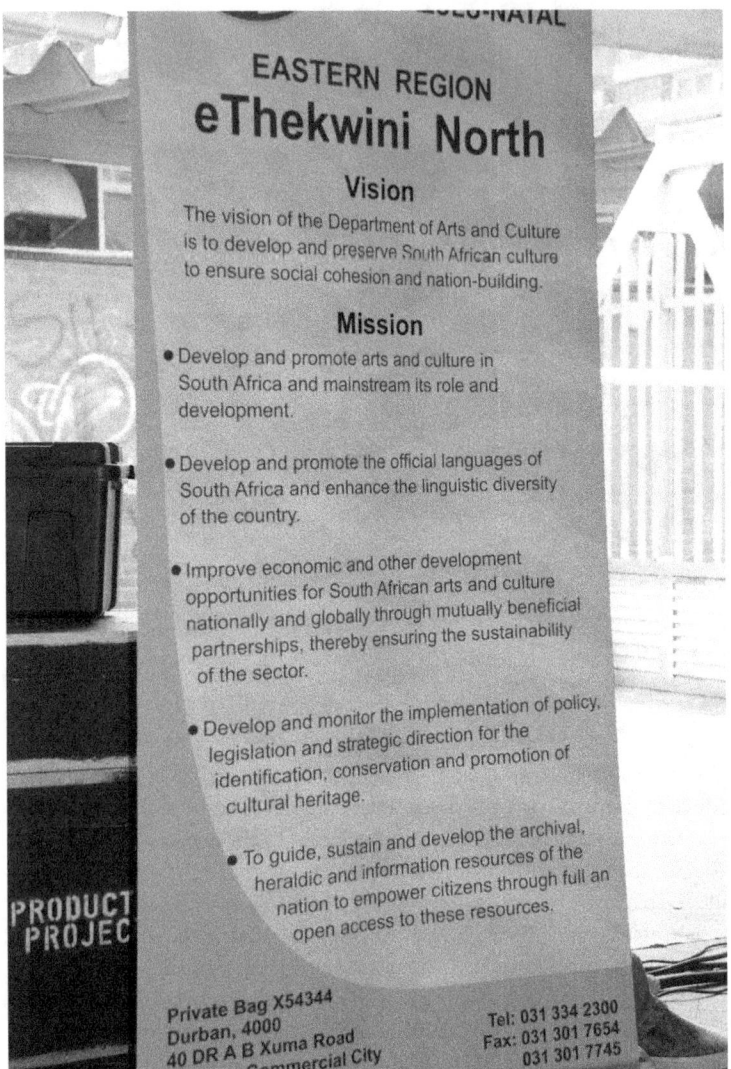

Figure 3.6 DAC Mission Statement at the Kushikisha Imbokodo Festival.

This invites further questions about what this community is and how it is experienced socially and aurally. The rigid categorizations between various groups of people typical of apartheid ideology gave rise to equally rigid distinctions between 'insider' and 'outsider' knowledge. Joe Nkwanyana's biography, outlined at the start of this chapter, illustrates this particularly well. The knowledge that earned him status and respect in his own community did not count outside of it. Then, his illness, allegedly imposed on him 'from outside', forced him back into his community and it was this illness that posed a huge social problem within his community. Thus, what is experienced and articulated as a community provides a form of acknowledgement of skills and ideas that constitutes a body of knowledge. Granting and receiving this acknowledgement is a form of protection from exclusion and isolation and, hence, an exertion of power. Yet, a community itself – not only in apartheid South Africa – is subject to larger dynamics of inclusion and exclusion from which individuals can hardly withdraw. Many of the power struggles that feature in maskanda practices as well as the attempts to make a living out of it are shaped by these dynamics of inclusion and exclusion. They will be subject to further scrutiny in the following chapters.

4

Middle Level:
The MTN Onkweni Royal Cultural Festival in Ulundi

Reified constructions of Zulu identity and 'tradition' is the rhetorical stock-in-trade of prophets and princes, proletarians and politicians because *it is the symbolic embodiment of an internalized, self-defining moral imagination.*
David Coplan, 'A terrible commitment', 1993, emphasis in original

In September 2009, I spent an afternoon at 'J. Mofokeng & Associates (JMA)', an independent theatre, TV and events production company in Johannesburg. I talked to Nomcebo Ngema, Head of Research, and to Nhlanhla Ngwekazi, the anchorman of a then-new TV show about South African traditional music called *Moribo*, produced by Lichaba Nthethe and broadcast every Sunday between 6 pm and 6.30 pm on SABC 1. The South African Broadcasting Corporation (SABC) broadcast one series of twenty-six episodes in 2009 and does not currently broadcast an equivalent or related programme. One of the explicit aims of the TV show was to familiarize a younger generation of South Africans with traditional music, by striking a balance between old and recent repertoire and practices, through dynamic graphics and visuals, and by attracting young presenters. Maskanda – being a signifier of age-old rural techniques clad in current urban musical formats – took a prominent position in the programming of the show.

In my conversations with representatives of media companies, record production companies and musicians, I sensed that musicians have limited opportunities to showcase their skills, especially if they work outside the jazz and pop mainstream. These are musicians in what Khoni Miya would call a 'middle level' stage in their career. Festival and venue stages, production studios, spaces on digital media and airtime on broadcast media are often only accessible in combination. Without being able to access one space, it seems impossible to access another, but once one space has been accessed it remains difficult to stay there and access other performance spaces. S'kho Miya recorded a well-sounding demo album in a privately paid-for Johannesburg studio, with ten songs that showcase a great variety of styles (S. Miya 2009d). She released it independently (S. Miya 2010), but it never achieved what she expected it to do: allow her to acquire airtime on radio and TV or provide her with regular gigs at events and festivals. Shiyani Ngcobo toured internationally and recorded a CD with the London-based World Music Network (S. Ngcobo 2004). Once, I translated a letter from this company for him, which stated that sales lagged seriously behind the money he had received for the CD, and which indicated that the company had not anticipated that his royalties for the CD would not live up to the honorarium he had been paid. Producer Abraham Mija from Gallo indicated that record companies invariably let go of musicians who do not sell.

South Africa has thriving jazz festivals, sometimes with an international outreach,[1] and a range of pop music shows presenting afropop, hip-hop, soul and gospel. Traditional music shows, by contrast, remain sparse. Whenever they get in touch with musicians, Ngema (2009), Ngwekazi (2009) and Nthethe (2011) feel the desperation of their invisibility and inaudibility in mainstream media and music industries. The supply of musicians is much larger than the demand for the music they make, and even seasoned talent scouts and producers admit the business is extremely tough on musicians (Nzimande 2009; Nthethe 2011). Several musicians, including well-educated middle-class ones, reported cases of exploitation by a multitude of concert and festival organizers, and they saw parallels with practices in the South African music industry that prey in particular upon musicians that are ill-informed. These instances of abuse encompass artistic and intellectual robbery (B. Nkwanyana 2009b), the infringement of copyright (B. Ngcobo 2009b), the factual indenture of musicians through killer contracts (Nkabinde 2009; Nthethe 2011) and bribery in the promotion of artists (Nthethe 2011). Cases such as these – both nationally within South Africa and internationally (Salomon Linda's 'Mbube' and Paul Simon's *Graceland* are infamous examples) – have been extensively documented and discussed by a number of musicologists and lawyers (Meintjes 1990; Feld 1996; Meintjes 2003; Wassel 2009; Meintjes 2017: 210–37). South African musicians whom I still communicate with on a regular basis, such as S'kho and Khoni Miya and Bongani Nkwanyana, suggest that the situation has not improved in the decade after I carried out my interviews.

It is impossible to ascertain whether the current lack of regulation of the nation's music industry affects South African musicians more than musicians in (multinational) music industries elsewhere (see Taylor 1997, 2007). Nevertheless, this lack of regulation reminds many South Africans of apartheid machinations of abuse, often with racial and ethnic inequalities of power resonating in the background. Especially after the lifting of the boycott, there was a significant rise in the demand for local 'black' musics, both nationally and internationally. Combined with a large pool of badly educated and economically vulnerable black musicians, this led to a profitable industry that capitalizes on cheap and indentured labour in a similar way as the mining industry did.

Zuz'Muzi producer Tshepo Nzimande and Gallo producer Abraham Mija emphasized the importance of live shows, artist interviews and interested DJs in the process of pushing a track product, whereas many musicians uttered their hope that

---

[1] For an insight into the importance of festival culture in apartheid and post-apartheid South Africa, see Pyper (2016).

they would be scouted for a record deal once they climbed onto the stage of a local, regional or national event or festival (S. Miya 2008a; Khama 2009). The *Moribo* show was conceived with the intention to fill the lacuna of opportunities for exposure on broadcast media. The MTN Onkweni Royal Cultural (MORC) Festival in Ulundi claims to fill a similar void in national exposure for musicians of 'traditional music'. By discussing my presence at the 2009 edition of the festival, I explore the tensions between opportunities and restrictions posed to the participating musicians in artistic, social and political respects. Brett Pyper notes that

> public festivals ... whether at local, provincial or national levels, have tended to become rather ad hoc affairs, sometimes being presided over by cultural brokers who may have learnt to navigate the bureaucratic tender system without having much of a consistent record within the arts and culture sector.
>
> (Pyper 2016: 114)

At the MORC Festival, exposure to (new) audiences and networking opportunities turned out to be difficult to weigh against implicitly and explicitly prescribed modes of expression and a loss of musicians' control over their musical creations and enunciations. Both the lack of industry regulation and the ad hoc character of the festival are cases in point in foregrounding these tensions.

I want to add urgency and poignancy to these tensions by outlining how they tied in with my own engagement with maskanda music and musicians. The artistic and infrastructural opportunities and restrictions posed to the musicians during and after this festival resonated in many respects with ways in which I initially experienced maskanda – aurally, performatively and socially. I foreground this resonance in order to outline how these infrastructural affordances are part of a larger pact of mutual understanding, lived out between maskandi, audiences and their predecessors (Monson 1996: 2), of South African music, of black popular music and of African music that are continuously (re)configured through performance, critique, media distribution and scholarly reflection. They constitute an epistemology: a configuration of knowledge based on a set of assumptions that are so self-evidently associated with maskanda that they are only partly acknowledged by those (including myself) operating within it. By foregrounding aural experiences – through maskanda performance/maskandafication as much as through academic investigation and writing – I aim to shed light on the constitution of such epistemologies.

The MTN Onkweni Royal Cultural (MORC) Festival

The MTN Onkweni Royal Cultural (MORC) Festival was initiated by Senzywsky Musho Shandu, a respected Durban event organizer. Since Shandu had difficulties raising funds for his event, he liaised with one of the members of the Zulu royal house, H.R.H. Prince Africa Zulu (Zulu 2007), who has a strong business network. Over the years, the prince increasingly appropriated the festival (K. Miya 2009b; Nthethe 2011).

This appropriation is obvious in the festival's name, referring to its funders: MTN is one of the larger telecom companies in South Africa, Onkweni is a branch of the Zulu royal house. In my description of the festival, I focus on the close association of 'Royal' and 'Cultural' in the event's name – an association that has always played an important and problematic role in the history of Zulu nationalism (La Hausse 2008: 263ff). The prince conflated these notions to further interests that – as I outline below – had little overlap with the interests of musicians of 'traditional music' as expressed above by Ngema, Ngwekazi and Nthethe.

Musicians from all over KwaZulu-Natal and Gauteng assemble annually in Ulundi, for a Saturday, many of them with national and international exposure and fame. Participants included isicathamiya group Ladysmith Black Mambazo that conquered the world after the release of Paul Simon's album *Graceland* in 1986. Earlier editions of the festival saw Busi Mhlongo (1947–2010) who made a name for herself in exile in Great Britain and the Netherlands before she returned to South Africa after the demise of apartheid. Zibakwakhe Johnston Mnyandu a.k.a. Phuzekhemisi (b. 1962), who performed at the Football World Cup in Japan in 2002, and several national stars, such as Bhekumuzi Luthuli, Thokozani Langa, Bheki Ngcobo (a.k.a. iHashi Elimhlophe) and Madala Kunene, play regularly at the festival. As a meeting place for musicians from all over the country, the MORC Festival enabled musicians such as S'kho and Khoni Miya to liaise with other musicians and become part of their networks. The supra-regional and international outreach of the festival (allegedly with musicians from a variety of African countries), the presence of representatives from (national) media and the involvement of national sponsors made the event a prime example of what Khoni Miya would call a 'middle level' event in a manner that Ngwekazi envisaged it, namely to help musicians from a variety of socio-economic and artistic backgrounds present themselves and be exposed to each other.

Ulundi is a three-hour drive north of Durban. It is a town with a loaded history. Founded by the Zulu King Cetshwayo as the Zulu Kingdom's new capital when he took over power in 1873, it featured in the last battle of the Anglo-Zulu War in 1879. It was captured by the British and the royal kraal was razed to the ground (Knight 2008: 187). From 1981 until its dismantling in 1994, the apartheid government reinstated Ulundi as the capital of the pseudo-independent Zulu homeland KwaZulu, reigned over by Chief Mangosuthu Buthelezi of the Inkatha Freedom Party (IFP). Until 2004, the capital of KwaZulu-Natal province alternated between Pietermaritzburg and Ulundi. Since then, Ulundi has become a sleepy provincial town, and it functions as a base for members of the Zulu royal family.

The status of the Zulu royal house in present-day South Africa is comparable to that of most European royal houses, in having a strong public function, but no official political power. Unofficially, however, royal families in Southern Africa exert considerable power over their fellow citizens, as will become clear throughout this chapter. In the two conversations I had with Prince Africa Zulu after the MORC Festival (Zulu 2009a, 2009b), it appeared that his character was decidedly deformed by royal entitlements and an overabundance of goods and attention. During meals he was indifferent about the choice of food, eventually requesting the flabbergasted waiter to serve him a living mouse. He was unable to concentrate on a subject of conversation, drifting from music event organization to the destination and duration of his months-long holidays in the scope of one sentence. He brazenly admitted that his sole aim of our conversations was to get me in his bed. The royalty of Prince Africa is contested, which he admits himself by boasting that his cousins try to assassinate him when he is on royal grounds (which include Ulundi). He was also exposed as an 'indirect prince' in internet responses to his appearance on the BBC television show *The Undercover Princes* from February to April 2009 (*Undercover Princes* 2009).

It turned out to be impossible to obtain substantive information about the organization, musical orientation and social implications of the MORC Festival from this volatile character. However, my encounters with the prince did reveal how he employed a commodified idea of Zulu culture for furthering his own celebrity status. The opportunities for musicians to acquire national exposure on the festival were determined by this royal interest. In the absence of an artistic vision, the MORC Festival was 'to salute and celebrate the life of the great general, statesman Zulu warrior and a royal prince, His Royal Highness Prince Shingana, son of King Mpande', Prince Africa's great-grandfather.[2] With the slogan '18 hours of heritage' the festival emphasized the inextricability of traditional culture with Zulu royalty.

S'kho Miya and I were both enthusiastic about her being scouted for the festival, since she viewed it as a step forward in her trajectory towards an overseas presence, and I viewed it as a possible alternative to it. Initially, Miya wanted me to perform with her band at the festival, as a continuation of my performance with them at the Kushikisha Imbokodo Festival a couple of weeks earlier. Since I felt insufficiently able to participate fully in a performance, she abandoned the idea. So, rather than travelling with the musicians in a bus on the Friday prior to the event, I hired driver Selby Ngcobo for the Saturday only. I had travelled extensively with Ngcobo (no relation of Shiyani or Bheki Ngcobo) and I often picked his brain since he is a knowledgeable maskanda fan.

Princes and proletarians

The festival was supposed to start at 10 am on 3 October 2009, but on our arrival at the Ulundi Sports Complex at around noon, the sports fields were empty, apart from a large stage with professional light and sound systems and a LED screen. The event was clearly sponsored by MTN and Coca-Cola. In the subsequent hours, tensions were mounting among the musicians and representatives from the press, who were wondering when the event would start. Joseph Shabalala from Ladysmith Black Mambazo told me it was not the first time he was made to wait. 'I'm here out of respect for the young

---

[2] See also the recent update of the festival's aims and vision at the Onkweni Royal Cultural Festival website, http://www.onkweniroyalfestival.com. Note that the Gallery displays pictorial material from 2008 to 2012 in which the 2009 festival is conspicuously absent.

man [Prince Africa Zulu]', he said, 'but this is the second time we meet this situation' (J. Shabalala 2009).

During the hours the maskandi and I waited for the MORC Festival to start, Selby Ngcobo's car gradually transformed into our house, filled with coats, costumes, bags, phones, towels and newspapers (Figure 4.1). Miya and her band members attacked the food I had brought from home: a couple of bananas, cookies, flapjacks. They also started munching on the leftovers of the KFC breakfasts we had had on our way in, tearing the small pieces of chicken from the bones we had left behind. Earlier, Miya had confided to me that she had hardly slept, and she expressed the wish to go back with me to Durban, rather than wait for the musicians' bus to return. Gradually, I managed to assess the situation in which the musicians had to work. A music student from the University of KwaZulu-Natal, where I was teaching as a guest lecturer, was also lined up for performance at the festival, and she told me what was going on.

This student told me that the musicians' bus had taken eight hours to reach Ulundi (normally a three-hour drive). On arrival at 10 pm, the musicians were led to a dancing party in a tent and only around midnight was there food. The musicians could not go to bed before 2.30 am, when they were taken to a school for the night. There were no sheets or blankets and in the morning there was no warm water for showers and no breakfast. She also stated that all musicians were supposed to get ZAR 1,000 per band (consisting of a number of dancers [two to

Figure 4.1 S'kho Miya in performance costume at Selby Ngcobo's car during the MORC Festival.

four], instrumentalists [three to five] and a lead singer), which amounted then to about €10 per person. 'Is this a way for a prince to treat his people?' the student asked rhetorically.

When I checked this story with Miya, she confirmed it. As a provider for her band, she had spent her last money on breakfast for her band members. It struck me that Miya only came forward with her problem after I had expressed my dismay about the musicians being treated like disposable commodities. It had not occurred to me before that Miya was apparently very careful with what she told me. It made me realize how fraught our friendship is with inequalities and implicit expectations. My uneasiness about this grew as the afternoon progressed. Nothing happened in the next few hours, even though all the musicians had long since arrived. At around 2.30 pm I lost patience and I said I would go home if nothing happened within an hour. I immediately saw the panic on Miya's face. If I were to go home before she had performed, she would have to leave the car and change into her costume outside in the field. She would have to wait for the musicians' bus to go back to Durban, which – considering the five-hour delay – meant she would have to spend another night in Ulundi without blankets, warm water or breakfast. I simply could not do that to her. 'I will wait for you', I promised, and I felt trapped, just like the rest of the musicians. I knew that Miya would only be given a chance to enter the stage after all the prominent musicians had done their share and could leave with their own transport. It would be a late night.

By 3 pm things gradually gained momentum. This was partly because members of the royal family had arrived. Lots of Mercedes, BMWs, men in tailored suits, flashy sunglasses and with several wives at their sides approached the stage and entered the VIP tent. The main impetus behind the gradual commencing of the programme – as I found out much later (Nthethe 2011) – was the interference of the sponsor MTN demanding action. At the time, however, I idealistically assumed it was the outright anger of the musicians that made things move ahead. To me, Miya seemed one of their most vocal representatives. She ranted in Zulu at the Master of Ceremonies, roaring with rage and almost in tears. Later she told me that she had said that nobody would enter the stage before they had been able to eat and drink, and before they had seen their money. The message would be delivered to the prince. 'Good for you', I said to Miya. 'And if you don't see your money, you are not going to perform, and you can go back home with me.' 'Exactly', Miya said.

It is tempting to explain her revolt against her situation as an act of empowerment because of my presence (with my own transport) and/or the pressure I had exerted through my impatience. Most other musicians would have to wait for the bus to leave; they were practically being held hostage by the prince. But I haven't found any proof of the fact that my presence had anything to do with her assertiveness in standing up for herself. It was clearly not the first time she and her colleagues had found themselves in this situation, sandwiched and crushed between feudalist and capitalist exploitation. David Coplan notes that, during the apartheid years, policies were aimed at curbing an 'autonomous, self-supporting, culturally relevant

black music world' ([1985] 2008b: 246). The authorities had an interest in festivals being organized poorly and audiences being kept small. '[U]nprofessional, dishonest producers', and 'unreliable participants' left 'players often stranded with no pay' (Coplan [1985] 2008b: 246). In this respect, the MORC Festival was merely the continuation of a standing practice.

Miya's assertiveness and anger, however, did not stick in the weeks that followed. She showed no visible signs of distress or frustration when I told her that the prince intended to commercially exploit the video footage of her performance. She was apologetic about him when I spoke to her several months later. It wasn't his fault that things didn't go smoothly, she said, and if the prince were to ask her again to a gig she would be there (S. Miya 2010e). I realized that, if the eminent Joseph Shabalala was prepared to get hooked for a second time, Miya's response – aimed at getting any gig that could help her survive – would be no different.

Miya was finally able to perform when the sun set, and she almost literally fought her way up onto the stage. She chose to ignore the hastily composed programme with the order of appearance of the various artists and simply demanded her slot, even when the MC was still trying to talk her band members off the stage. With a line-up of two guitars, a bass guitar, synthesizer, drum kit and three dancers she performed two songs, 'Ingculazi Iyabulala' (S. Miya 2009d) and 'Sithi Khuzani' (S. Miya 2010a; Figures 4.2a and 4.2b). Her performance was so powerful and convincing that maskanda fan Selby Ngcobo became a long-term supporter of her band after the festival, attending many of her performances and offering transport for her band with reduced or no costs (Figure 4.3).

Figures 4.2a–b S'kho Miya and her Abagqugquzeli Band on stage at the MORC Festival.

Zulu nation

Much South African research into the country's black popular musics addresses the rising demand for 'local' music in national and international markets after the demise of apartheid in the early 1990s. This demand is satisfied through the employment of cultural symbols (visual, musical, linguistic) that have an apartheid history in being devised to emphasize differences between South Africans. Louise Meintjes, in her book about mbaqanga, reveals how musical instruments, singing timbres and sound production are aimed at constructing a 'Zulu' sound that is not only supposed to represent the largest language group in South Africa, but also helped shape the stereotype of Africanness as 'natural', 'primitive', 'timeless' and 'collective' in an international market. She also outlines how this determines the artistic options for many mbaqanga artists to express themselves (Meintjes 2003: 212, 225–6). Crucial in this construction of Zuluness, according to Meintjes, is the role of sounding and visual media:

> Mediation facilitates the popularization and distribution of Zuluness. Mediation also escalates the flow of Zuluness through technological facility and market-driven principles. It can intensify that feeling of being Zulu by compacting, juxtaposing, and overlaying multiple features into [for instance] a figure like drum sound, which then indexes a world of Zulu-identified worlds and suggests connections to them.
>
> (2003: 211)

Figure 4.3 S'kho Miya and Selby Ngcobo after performance at the MORC Festival.

Meintjes' observation is a powerful example of how indexical signification, mentioned by Turino as a form of meaning formation with 'the greatest emotional potential' (2008: 9), can be used as an instrument of power and suppression. Maskanda performance, too, is a good example of apartheid ideologues' attempts to designate musical practices to certain people and imply they are intrinsic to their 'nature'. At its inception in the early twentieth century, it was impossible to align maskanda to any 'people', 'nation' or language group in southern Africa. During the 1950s, however, state-regulated record companies and media selectively recorded and broadcast predominantly a-political (sometimes censored) maskanda songs in a band setting that highlighted *ingoma* dance and war cries, with maskandi clad in *ubeshu* (animal skin) and/or *umbaselwa* (aestheticized mining suits) dress. These aspects did not necessarily form a part of maskanda's early performance in a solo guitar playing setting. Thus, maskanda increasingly became associated with Zulu culture and identity, an association that lasts up to this day (Figures 4.4a, 4.4b, 4.4c and 4.4d).[3]

Other music practices presented at the MORC Festival, such as isicathamiya, mbaqanga, South African jazz and R&B-oriented afropop genres, have been subject to similar political and commercial dynamics. These can be observed in Prince Africa's appropriation and representation of the MORC Festival's performances. More than about publicizing the event beforehand, the prince had thought about the mediatization and distribution of the festival's performances afterwards by asking *Moribo* producer Lichaba Nthethe, the one talented television producer in South Africa with a heart for traditional music, to shoot footage of the festival.[4] In his conversations with me, the prince openly stated that his priority lay with the opportunity to access various media (national radio, TV and newspapers) in order to increase his celebrity status. The notion of traditional Zulu culture was a means for him to acquire this access. By promoting, mediating and distributing the MORC Festival's performances he was able to bolster his royal image of a chief, benefactor, patron and disseminator of cultural heritage. Research by Fraser McNeill into Venda reggae music (2012) demonstrates that such constellations of power not only revolve around feudal institutions like the royal house per se, but extend into informal spheres in which musicians need to seek out sponsors for the sustenance of their musical careers. The relationship between musicians and their sponsors often develops into a patron–client relationship, leading to fraught structures of dependence and expectations of self-censorship.

---

[3] For an in-depth analysis of this process see Olsen (2014: 56–69). Maskanda producer Tshepo Nzimande emphasized the importance of notions of identity for maskanda sales: 'People, once they get rich, they remember where they come from. [At] corporate events, they want to put in some tradition: "I am a Ndebele, I am a Zulu, I am a Xhosa, I want people to know that I am Xhosa and I am a CEO of Eskom" [a large South African electricity company]' (2009). See De Jong and Madzikane (2020) and Nyezwa (2018) for research into Bhaca maskanda and Xhosa maskanda, respectively.

[4] After finishing his music degrees at the University of the Free State and Northwest University, Nthethe pursued a career as a researcher for current affairs television. He tells hair-raising stories about his interviews with disgruntled citizens and his exposures of corrupt politicians. Obviously, he knew immediately what kind of personality he was dealing with when he met the prince (Nthethe 2011).

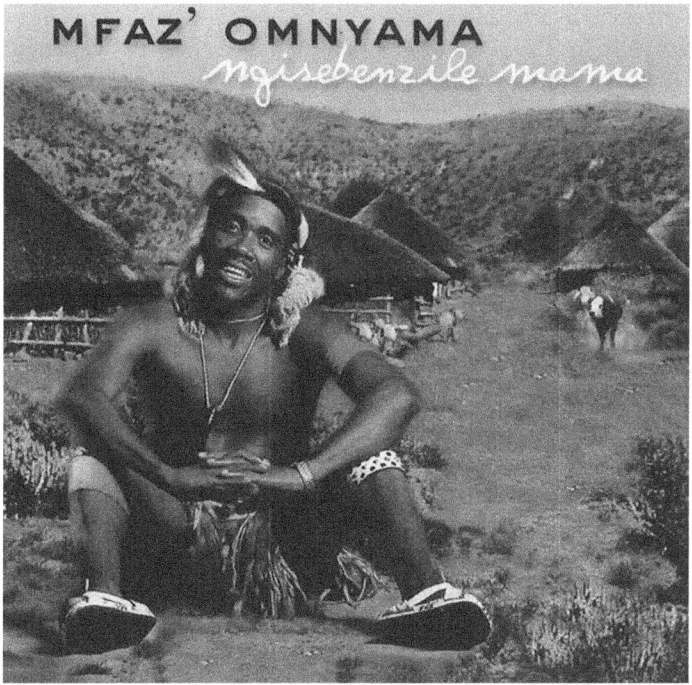

Figures 4.4a–d Album covers of maskanda releases during, and in the early years after, apartheid.

Via online channels (that must have been accessible to sponsors and representatives of the media, but hardly to the musicians he had scouted), the prince promoted the festival in surprisingly universalist and cosmopolitan terms:

> We need to invest in seeing nations coming together, the music is an instrument that one can utilize to bring change in the country and people's lives and [sic] as well as peace in the continent. It is more important than ever before to develop, celebrate and promote African heritage amongst ourselves. This is the opportunity to promote love, peace, the spirit of Ubuntu and prosperity in the continent.
>
> (Zulu 2009c)

There are distinct echoes in this statement of Thabo Mbeki's popularization of the idea of an 'African Renaissance', presented during his deputy presidency under Nelson Mandela in the 1990s. Mbeki argued that collective pride in a (united) African heritage with an emphasis on social cohesion as an essence of African culture would lead to the rise and establishment of Africa as a significant player in global economic and geopolitical affairs (Mbeki 1998a, 1998b). A key concept in this Pan-African ideal, implicit in the deputy president's statement and explicated in the prince's, is 'the spirit of Ubuntu', derived from the Xhosa proverb 'Ubuntu ungamntu ngabanye abantu' (People are people through other people). Cynically enough, ubuntu has become a highly politicized concept in South Africa, which is often used to emphasize difference rather than cohesion, being attributed to black Africans only.

Another aspect that is interesting about the prince's statement is his emphasis on music as an 'instrument' to further the cause of African empowerment. Meintjes (2003) and Gilbert (2007), among others, have addressed the crucial role of (performance) culture in the exertion of political power in South Africa. Meintjes describes how Zuluness was constructed as a 'political position' in the final decades of apartheid rule, particularly through the Inkatha Freedom Party (IFP) that started off as a cultural movement in the 1970s and gradually turned into a violent political body propagating the apartheid state's overall strategy of separate development:

> The process of mobilizing Zulus in support of a political program involved a massive and spectacular utilization of cultural symbols and expressive practices, as well as of 'traditional' sociopolitical structures. IFP political leaders sought to legitimate and increase their own authority by authenticating their links to the leadership of tribal and militaristic distant Zulu past.
>
> (Meintjes 2003: 195)

With the Zulu royal house being prominently represented in the IFP, Prince Africa Zulu's rhetoric and his utilization of cultural heritage seems to be another continuation of standing practices. Praising the quality of Lichaba Nthethe's footage, he addressed the necessity of recognizable visuals (rather than sounds which he did not specify) such as *ubeshu* dress and *ingoma* dance for commercial exploitation. He identified these visuals immediately as essences of Zulu and, by implication, African culture, emphasizing their exotic value for audiences that are unfamiliar with it. Crucial in his intention to promote 'traditional music' was his attempt to describe the Zulu, South African and African culture as synonyms. He subsequently presented this cultural conflation as an appendix to the Zulu royal house (Zulu 2009a).

The prince's exertion of power took place on a startling variety of levels. In a direct way, he was able to determine the movement of musicians (they were unable to return home before they had performed), he determined their financial remuneration (a few euros per person for the entire weekend) and he decided if and when they could sleep, eat or wash. On a more pervasive level, he used his royal status to articulate Zulu culture as an appendix to Zulu royalty by employing his business network to access media that packaged the music performed at the festival into profitable cultural symbols. This strategy seems to be a continuation of the ways in which apartheid recording industries commodified recognizable performance visuals and sounds in previous decades.

Meintjes has convincingly revealed that these visuals and sounds are still recognized worldwide as representations of Zuluness and Africanness that keep them at a safe inferior distance from the 'European Enlightenment': dance as a stylized fight, music as trance, polygamy for men, subservience for women, nepotism among clan members, obedience to the tribal king. The prince's name, Africa Zulu, is an ominous exemplification of such a society that feeds into the fantasy of a culturally, epistemically and epistemologically self-sufficient and superior Europe (Bloechl 2008: 23). In this capacity, such societal visions were used to legitimize the implementation of apartheid ideology. They continue to function in the global presentation of 'Africa' as a 'place of savanna and safari' (Meintjes 2003: 225).

Yet, as Brett Pyper argues, in colonized public spheres music has come to play a particular role in 'mediating the complex and fraught relationships between modernity and tradition, indigeneity and cosmopolitanism, cultural relationships across "racial" lines' (Pyper 2016: 112). Lara Allen and Liz Gunner, moreover, observe that music 'constitutes a large, powerful platform through which public opinion can be influenced', accounting for its function as a 'trenchant political site in Africa' (Allen quoted in Gunner 2009: 29). The prince's appropriation of musical performance for his personal economic and political gain unleashes sentiments and debates in South Africa that provide an insight into the societal cohesion of the Rainbow Nation, and into categorizations of musical and cultural expressions that are present in any multicultural society. Struggling with their apartheid histories, many South Africans are sensitive to, and reflexive about, clashes of belief systems, the curtailing of the freedom of speech, socio-economic inequality and the possible subjugation of cultural symbols to the rhetoric of populists, issues that have become ever more pressing in Europe and North America too. I roughly discerned three responses to the prince's appropriation of musical performance, which illustrate how South Africans comment on the world in which they live through (the experience of) musical performance.

The first response to my account of such exertions of power came from the many South Africans who claim that this packing-and-parcelling has a profound impact on the kind of music maskandi are able to make and how they are able to identify themselves not only as Zulus and musicians, but also as men, women, friends or South African citizens (Nkabinde 2009; Olsen 2009b).[5] Rather than a cultural imperialism, these respondents feel they witness a 'cultural feudalism' with an accompanying disciplinary regime built on a power base of (racialized cultural) capital, media presence and an attitude of superiority (Carton and Draper 2008).

A second response to the prince's appropriation of musical performance is an outcry at the threat it poses to recently gained democratic rights for all South Africans, not only musicians. The members of the Zulu royal family may have no official political power, but they do have solid alternative power structures based on a loyal fan community glued together by a hierarchical attitude and, notably, the commodified idea of Zulu culture and heritage. This fan base can be mobilized at will in a state that has difficulties upholding the law for all its citizens. Hence, several people discouraged me from publishing my observations of, and judgements about, the MORC Festival presented in this chapter.

Those South Africans who are in a process of upward social mobility, in particular, do not take an immediate stance on the prince's abuse of power, but rather view the outcry at his actions as a clash of moral and societal values among people who have lived separate lives for decades. According to them, this clash cannot simply or solely be judged by an outsider from Europe imposing the moral superiority of values of equality and freedom after centuries of European colonial domination and exploitation (Naidoo 2009b; see also Martens 2008).

The sustenance of stereotypes

The validity of all three responses became clear to me once I acknowledged that many of the stereotypes employed by the prince to exert political power also form part of my own experience (including my hearing) of maskanda, which was often belated, and in this belatedness both deferred and diversified (Bhabha 1994b: 58–9). In order to further engage with the belatedness of my understanding I return to Bhabha's notion of stereotypes as fetishes (1994c: 77), addressed in the Introduction of this book.

---

[5] 'People in South Africa do not look beyond their own living environment', Nkabinde claimed, referring to societal confinements in the past. 'They don't dream. They don't envisage. Even if they perform internationally, they do not go outside their hotel room' (2009). I am not sure whether I agree with him completely. S'kho Miya dreams, and she envisages, but those dreams and visions turn out to be very difficult to realize within the confinements of her living conditions.

Stereotypes as fetishes – metaphoric associations with, and metonymic replacements of, culture – keep exerting their influence on human experience. Even when they have been recognised as stereotypes, and we have rhetorically distanced ourselves from them, they keep exerting their influence on human experience.

At the MORC Festival, there was a great variety of musical styles, dress codes, uses of instruments and stagings. Maskanda bands and artists (Imithente, Thokozani Langa, S'kho Miya and her Abagqugquzeli Band) featured next to isicathamiya (Ladysmith Black Mambazo) and mbaqanga groups, gospel singers (Sfiso Ngwane), kwaito artists (L'Vovo Derrango), afropop artists (Khoni Miya) and DJs. The festival organizers claimed there were musicians present from Zambia, Mozambique, one of the Congos, Zimbabwe, Tanzania, Burundi and Malawi, although I have not heard from or contacted these musicians.[6] Like at the Kushikisha Imbokodo Festival, artists would easily switch between, as well as combine, performance conventions of musical genres that I perceive as different from each other. Many musicians bended towards jazz, R&B and gospel idioms through their employment of ninth and eleventh chords in their cyclic harmonic progressions. With regard to vocal technique, artists would switch instantly from florid R&B inflections in one song to a piercing and overtone rich *amahubo* timbre in the next song. Sometimes, R&B harmonies and formats were combined with *amahubo* vocal techniques in one song.

There was also a great diversity in performance formats, ranging from a solo singer with a backing band (Thokozani Langa, Sfiso Ngwane) to extensive dance troupes in which male and female dancers performed a variety of *ingoma* routines and backing choruses (Imithente, Abagqugquzeli). Some groups included elaborate *izibongo* and *ululating* passages. Musicians dressed up in *ubeshu* dress: animal skins with headdresses and beads, with bare feet and exposed abdomens, indicating an (imagined) rural tradition. Others were dressed in *umbaselwa* suits: aestheticized, brightly patched imitations of mining suits that indicate the appropriation of the labour migrant experience (Figure 4.5). A fair number of musicians, however, wore none of these cultural symbols, being dressed in jeans and shirts, which did not distinguish them from any US-based pop artist.

Acknowledging this variety of performance formats, timbral domains and visual clues invalidates the essentialism of stereotypical representations. Stereotypical, binary constructions of difference, such as Zulu tribalism versus European Enlightenment, become untenable in the light of this variety. Conversely, stereotypical representations obstruct the recognition of such (internal) variability. My acknowledgement and understanding of the variety of performance practices at the MORC Festival were belated, maybe for this reason. However, more importantly, even after my

---

[6] Line-up information available at the Onkweni Royal Cultural Festival website, http://onkweniroyalfestival.com/info/history/2009-2/ (Zulu 2009c). I have not been able to verify this information.

Figure 4.5 S'kho Miya and her Abagqugquzeli band in *umbaselwa* dress. From left to right: Mqapheli Hadebe (1st guitar), S'kho Miya (lead vocals), Mtolo (keyboard), Somnyama Ndabandaba (2nd guitar), Wiseman Chiyi (bass). Khayalethu Mkhize (drums) sits in front of the band in the shade.

acknowledgement of this variety, the stereotypical constructions of difference remained operative in my mind and body as Bhabhaesque fetishes. The *continued* epistemic power of these fetishes was far more difficult to acknowledge. Acknowledging their power, after my rhetorical distantiation from them, required the concomitant acknowledgement that I was still assuming an Archimedean point of observation for myself. I still believed – subconsciously – in the objective value of my observations. I still believed I could see without being seen, even if I claimed the opposite. This tension between my unacknowledged position as an observing, categorizing and taxonomizing researcher on the one hand, and my increased feeling of being part of maskanda modes of knowing on the other constitutes the 'doubled origin' (Bloechl 2008: 23) of my knowledge, which is – in essence – a colonial origin. It illustrates the entanglement of scientific and colonial epistemologies.

An example of such a stereotype as fetish was my understanding of male polygamy as an unquestioned part of Zulu custom and tradition, hampering me to recognize the many subject positions in the debate about this practice. Polygamy is secured in the post-apartheid Constitution in accordance with customary law. This implies that polygamy is often exclusively reserved for men. The many ways in which male polygamy is experienced, explained and judged surface in maskanda discourse as a mode of shaping and transmitting knowledge (see the Appendix in this book). In his hit song 'Ngafa' (Xaba and Magubane 2003b), Mandla Xaba (a.k.a. Shwi) takes a subject position that confirmed my reductive understanding of Zulu male polygamy

(Titus 2016a). He emphasizes that men have the right to be in relationships with several women, and he explicitly denies this right to his girlfriends/wives. The rocketing sales of this song indicate that his audience endorses his patriarchal chauvinism, or at least does not object to it. S'kho Miya, in contrast, openly criticizes the custom of talking female family members into polygamous marriages as a second, third or fourth wife in her song 'Nith' Angiqome Bani?' (S. Miya 2010c). Shiyani Ngcobo, too, points out the wrenching consequences of polygamous loyalties to family relations in his song 'Isithembu' (S. Ngcobo 2004), stating that polygamy left him orphaned because his mother could not bear it (see the Appendix). Johnston Mnyandu (a.k.a. Phuzekhemisi), however, pointed out the disruptive consequences of not adhering to such patriarchal lines of family organization for men, women and children (Mnyandu 2009). Whereas Shwi and Phuzekhemisi's propagation of male polygamy enjoys much more public exposure in South Africa than Miya and Ngcobo's criticism of it, the diversity of these viewpoints, rooted in their articulation of specific social and experiential situations, points at the crucial role of maskanda discourse in affecting public debate about societal issues.

I found it difficult to sense and recognize this plurality of thought in the context of deconstructive scholarly explanations of maskanda's role in the articulation of Zulu ethnic nationalism. Coplan describes this articulation as a 'reified', 'embodied' and 'internalized' imagination (1993a: 306). Olsen observes 'a sense of obligation and duty to tradition that was assimilated with the political aspirations and hierarchies of power within the IFP' (2014: 67). Without wanting to invalidate Coplan's and Olsen's analyses, I don't think they tell the whole story about the diversity of articulations of Zulu identity and tradition. When I talked to driver Selby Ngcobo about male polygamy, he told me that in Zulu society there is no divorce. 'So, what do people do if they are unhappy together', I asked. 'The man builds a new house somewhere else', Ngcobo explained, 'and lives there with his new wife. His old wife can also go and live with someone else and if the other man fathers children with her, it is her (estranged) husband's duty to provide for those children and they will carry his name' (Selby Ngcobo 2008b). Ngcobo's explanation prompted me to inform myself about polygynous households and the domains in which women exert power and possess agency (Hammond-Tooke 2008: 63). This diversified my impression of polygamy as the unequivocal suppression of women. I also learned about the ways in which polygynous custom was conveniently Othered as 'barbaric' and 'uncivilized' in colonial discourse in order to rationalize white supremacy, justify invasions and impose colonial infrastructures of oppression (Martens 2008: 126ff).

The persistence of polymetre

A musical equivalent of such belated acknowledgement of persistent stereotypes as fetishes in my thinking was my analytical urge to explain maskanda's rhythmical features in terms of 'polymetre'. This was an experiential as much as a discursive urge. In my attempts to master the dance routines and chorus entries of S'kho Miya's songs, I experienced them as metrically ambiguous (I deliberately use this negative connotation), because I initially struggled to place my dance steps correctly (S. Miya 2008b; Figure 4.6). In order to execute the dance, I had to divide equal units of four beats into equal units of three beats (Figure 4.7). In my close listening of the song in stage, studio and rehearsal environments (see Chapter 8), I sensed that binary and ternary metres were there simultaneously, in the instrumental parts as well as in the dance. Thus, through my notion of 'polymetre', I took my own aural familiarity with an unchanging pattern of downbeats as an unquestioned starting point for aurally as well as conceptually constructing the maskanda Other.

In the wake of music scholars such as Mieczyslaw Kolinski, Simha Arom, Willie Anku and Meki Nzewi, Kofi Agawu has long settled the scores with analytical inventions such as 'polymetre' and 'additive rhythm' that served the systematic aural Othering of musics from the African continent (Agawu 2003: 82–6). Whereas I employed my concept of polymetre (or hemiolas) in order to switch from the one to the other metre when the dance steps required it, for Miya (and other band members) these two metres were both there all the time. She did not need to switch. This underlines Agawu's assertion that there is 'no ethnotheoretical discourse to ground or at least support the notion of polymetre' in African music (2003: 84). Yet, this very notion remained operative in my head as much as in my dancing body – a useful example of how such conceptual inventions reproduce themselves through their impact on aural and bodily experience.

Figure 4.6 S'kho Miya teaching the choreography of the song 'Sithi Khuzani' to Barbara Titus, Stable Theatre rehearsal rooms, Warwick Triangle, Durban. Photograph by Nhlanhla 'Ntshokovane' Shinga (S. Miya 2008b).

Figure 4.7 'Sithi Khuzani'. Placing of the dance steps in relation to bass and guitar parts (S. Miya 2008b). Transcribed with kind permission from S'kho Miya.

When I visited Johnny Clegg at his home in Sandton, I found out it was my culturally situated aural familiarity with an unchanging pattern of downbeats that made me aurally as well as conceptually Other the musical sounds I encountered, a problem that generations of comparative musicologists and ethnomusicologists have foregrounded already. I listened with Clegg and his friend Bafazana Qoma (Buff) to one of the recordings Clegg had made of a dance group from the Umkomazi region (see Figure 2.1) at Jeppe Hostel in Johannesburg (Clegg 2009). We listened to an old *ihubo* called 'Ya Khulum' Ingoma' and we tried to clap along (Umkomazi Dance Group n.d.). Figure 4.8 shows how the notion of polymetre helped me grasp what happened in the chorus, but also hampered me in hearing the tension between a stable rhythmic background and a fluid accentual foreground (Agawu 2003: 84). In accordance with my 'dealing strategy', I have transcribed the *ihubo* in $\frac{3}{4}$ and $\frac{4}{4}$ metre, with the drum covering both possible metres by articulating eighth notes in $\frac{6}{8}$. The metrical ambiguity is created by the fact that the articulation of the words 'Ya Khulum' Ingoma' is timed on different moments in a $\frac{6}{8}$ grid, on the 1st, 3rd, 5th and then on the 1st, 3rd and 6th eighth note of the drum pattern, whereas the drum articulates 1st, 3rd, 4th and 6th notes. The articulation of the syllables determines the emphasis in the bar – an emphasis that keeps changing between 3rd, 5th, and 1st, 3rd and 6th beats of the bar, allowing one to identify equal units of two beats (with three eighth notes [$\frac{6}{8}$ metre]), and three beats (with two eighth notes [$\frac{3}{4}$ metre]). Whereas I needed to switch between these two possibilities of hearing, Buff clapped both rhythms in a regular pattern on 3rd, 5th, 1st, 3rd and 6th eighth notes, where the emphasis on the 1st alternates with the emphasis in the 6th (Figure 4.8, bar 2–3). Through the fixation of distinct metres, I perceive an ambiguity not only between $\frac{6}{8}$ and $\frac{3}{4}$ metres, but also between $\frac{3}{4}$ and $\frac{4}{4}$ metres, because 1st eight note and 3rd eight note in the $\frac{6}{8}$ bar are equally prominent. This creates cognitive dissonance with the classic Eurocentric preoccupation with one downbeat or/as bar line. I am able to *interpret* the ongoing rhythm of the drum as a stable rhythmic background with the text accents constituting a fluid rhythmic foreground. Yet, it remains hard for me to instantly *hear* it as such and reproduce it through clapping or dancing. My Eurocentric preoccupation is the 'embodiment of an internalized, self-defining moral imagination' (Coplan 1993a: 306) as much

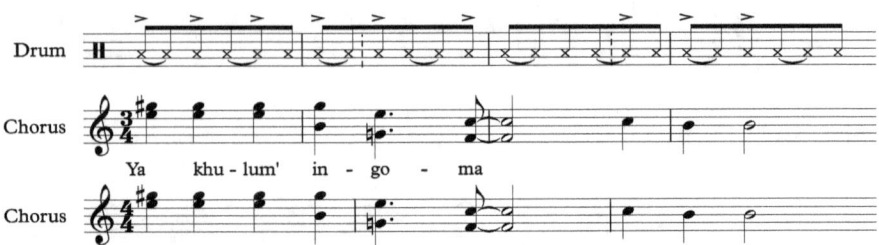

Figure 4.8 'Ya Khulum' Ingoma'. Notation in $\frac{6}{8}$, $\frac{3}{4}$ and $\frac{4}{4}$ metres (Umkomazi Dance Group n.d.).

as 'constructions of Zulu identity and "tradition"' (Coplan 1993a: 306) constitute such an embodiment.

In her song 'Sithi Khuzani', S'kho Miya employs a similar tension between a stable rhythmic background and a fluid accentual foreground (Agawu 2003: 84) that I kept hearing as metrical ambiguity in order to be able to deal with it performatively. She shifts her (and my) dance steps from the 6th to the 5th to the 4th triplet note in what I perceive as a $\frac{6}{8}$ metrical grid (audible in de 2nd guitar), while the drum (on stage) and the programmed percussion (on the album) keep on going in $\frac{4}{4}$ metre (Figure 4.7). The bass, both in rehearsal and on stage, is ambiguous: it can be heard as binary dotted rhythms, but sometimes tends towards a triplet feel. Yet, precisely the fact that it doesn't play triplets causes the various parts to land on their tones on slightly different moments: this makes the song swing. Never did I hear maskanda musickers employ the concept of swing, nor did they associate this musical feature at any time with jazz. Crucial here is that the swing in 'Sithi Khuzani' is visible and kinetically perceivable in the dance rather than audible on hearing only. That makes it so easy to miss out on for those who have been raised with an aesthetic of 'absolute music'. The sacrilege of pure sound implied in this aesthetic was devised for a very specific cultural practice in late-nineteenth-century Central Europe. As the qualification 'absolute' indicates, this aesthetic was devised primarily for the furthering of a 'self-defining moral imagination' (see Titus 2016b).

My analysis also demonstrates that I resort to culturally situated concepts for what I hear ('metrical ambiguity', 'rhythmic swing'). However, I do not have many analytical tools at my disposal for the dance steps I had to place. There is a highly diversified conceptual reservoir in the Zulu language for dance steps, dance genres and dance occasions, because these kinetic dimensions are so much more important for maskanda than for the 'absolute music' from late-nineteenth-century Central Europe. The *ihubo* 'Ya Khulum' Ingoma' illustrates that such metrical and rhythmical gestures as well as the conceptual tools to describe them are part and parcel of *amahubo* practice. Many maskandi know and keep practising these gestures in other formats than *amahubo*. My readers will not learn this conceptual (and hence epistemological) diversity, other than from my interspersed references to *ukugiya, cothoza, indlamu, umqonqo, umgqashiyo, isiShameni, isiZulu, umzansi* and *ingoma* dance routines when they apply to their direct impact on sound or descriptions of sound and/or have sociopolitical implications. This is another representational and epistemological imbalance in my foregrounding of maskandi aural experiences. My foregrounding continues to be shaped by an aesthetic of 'absolute music' in which sound takes precedence over all other musicking parameters. These other/Other musical parameters hence to some extent remained illegible to me. The extent to which they have become legible to my readership is determined by their capacity to serve the explanation of maskanda's sonic aspects.

Despite, or maybe thanks to, their recognized role as colonial cultural fetishes, the concepts of polygamy, polymetre and absolute music enable academics to engage with the dynamics of knowledge formation that surface in various cultural and musicking practices on festival stages, broadcast media and in scholarly arguments. In this chapter the role of these concepts in the sustenance of feudal and colonial exertions of power has been emphasized. They continue to shape the time lag between event and enunciation (Bhabha 1994b: 58–9), even if we distance ourselves from them rhetorically. In the following chapters, more attention will be devoted to the agency of individual musickers to intervene in the liminal space or time lag between event and enunciation. Maskandafication – presenting experiences, encounters and techniques *as* maskanda – is an important dimension of such interventions. Like concepts, individual interventions regulate and disturb the circulation of interrelationships between musicking subjects constituting maskanda's acoustic assemblages (Ochoa 2014: 22). By outlining these interventions, I highlight the ways in which maskanda musickers, consciously and subconsciously, tweak, menace or work around the cultural reductions that often feature acts of musicking worldwide.

5

Up Level:
Shiyani Ngcobo's Tour
through the Netherlands

Being a maskandi is, by default, being political. Maskandi Bongani Nkwanyana (b. 1965) is straightforward about this:

> [T]he SABC ... were puppets of the IFP then [in the early 1990s]. Today they are a puppet of the ANC. And before the IFP they were a puppet of the nationalist [apartheid] government .... I'm no longer receiving any airplay from the SABC, they don't play anything from me! From me they don't. The station that plays my music ... all those are community radio stations, or independent radio stations. But Ukhozi FM, the one that should be playing my music, as a Zulu station – they don't! They don't! ... You know why? I talk too much. I say that I tell the truth whenever the truth is there. I don't care who's doing what. I tell the truth .... They don't like that ... and I don't mind. No one can hamper my career!
>
> (B. Nkwanyana 2013)

Nkwanyana finds himself in a position that enables him to make this statement. He is a successful businessman with his own record label (Kora Records) and he is a chosen representative for the Democratic Alliance (DA) at the City Council of Johannesburg. More than twenty years after the formal dismantling of apartheid, South Africa's many communities often still live in separate worlds in material, cultural and political respects – worlds divided along ethnic lines. Most 'legally black' South Africans will unchangeably vote for the ANC because it is a former liberation movement (with some Zulu nationalists voting for the Inkatha Freedom Party [IFP]), and English- and Afrikaans-speaking white middle classes will generally vote for the Democratic Alliance (DA). Bongani Nkwanyana is a self-declared patriarchal Zulu man who honours his ancestors. He suffered demonstrably under apartheid. His formal education was cut short at the age of sixteen, which forced him to resort to domestic work and work in restaurants. Music, then, was his only way out. His open loyalty to a political party that is often associated with this apartheid legacy, also because it briefly aligned itself to the New National Party, has raised more than one eyebrow among his direct friends and relatives. Yet, Nkwanyana keeps reiterating the necessity for a healthy opposition against the monopoly that the ANC currently holds on political power in so many South African governments.

Social commentary

Nkwanyana's position is also emblematic of the status of a maskandi as a spokesperson for the people. Maskandi take established power bearers to task and give a voice to what would otherwise be left unsaid. Of old, maskanda's status as social commentary (*amaculo akhayo*) is anchored in its capacity to document and historicize the events, experiences and encounters a maskandi was exposed to. The maskandi I worked with always emphasized the 'realness' of their songs. This realness emphatically includes those elements of events and experiences that are generally being epistemically distanced in eurogenic epistemologies as 'supernatural' elements, such as the sensing of ancestors and omens through animals and weather conditions. Yet, these are very much part of 'nature' in Zulu epistemologies (see also Berglund [1976] 1989). Musicking practices facilitate the physical and palpable sounding invocation of these elements through modal, rhythmical, timbral and dynamic musical features. I will further elaborate on this in my analysis of Bongani Nkwanyana's 'Inkunzi Emnyama', in Chapter 6.

During my maskanda guitar lessons, Shiyani Ngcobo instructed me about maskanda composition. These instructions provided ample information about what (his) maskanda transmits, disseminates and negotiates as knowledge. He foregrounded aural and conceptual experiences in close intersection:

> [A] composer makes a song about what he sees in the street. For instance, when a car hits a man and you see the man lying on the street being wounded, you make a song about it and the people will say: 'this man is a good musician, he makes a song about what he sees', and the people will remember what was in the newspaper about this accident. Everywhere you look there is some song. You look at the trees outside and you see the flowers and it can drive you to make a song. Everywhere is a song around you.
>
> (S. Ngcobo 2009, paraphrased by author)

Ngcobo's comparison with a newspaper item is typical of the way in which maskanda still functions as a source of news and interpretation, expressed through lyrics, tunes and dance as an igama. Many maskandi explained to me how seriously they take their task of informing and educating the community they belong to. They conceive of themselves as artists and guardians of their community's heritage:

> When I write songs, I make it a point that there is a message in a song. Some of my songs are telling these stories. And some of them are advising alternatives. And some of them are criticizing.
>
> (B. Nkwanyana 2013)

Clegg asserted that the importance of social commentary in maskanda peaked in the 1940s to 1960s and waned when maskanda became commercially viable in the 1970s (Clegg 2009). Yet, like Bongani Nkwanyana, Shiyani Ngcobo, Joe Nkwanyana and iHashi Elimhlophe, all still address urgent societal problems with their songs, such as the abuse of power by traditional healers (Ngcobo's 'Izangoma' [2004]), the disruptive consequences of polygamy (Ngcobo's 'Isithembu' [2004]), the imposition of the universality of human rights (Joe Nkwanyana's 'Kanti lelungelo libavala') and the dangers of child abuse and the abuse of women. Many songs of the hugely popular maskandi Zibakwakhe Johnston Mnyandu (a.k.a. Phuzekhemisi) are examples of this. Phuzekhemisi, initially together with his brother Kethani, continues to confront Members of Parliament as well as local chiefs with the enduring absence of basic amenities for large numbers of South African citizens ('Imbizo' [1989 - see Figure 4.4b], 'Emapalamende' [1994]). Phuzekhemisi also (literally) played a mediating role in the faction fights between IFP and ANC supporters in the transition years in the early 1990s, which almost cost him his life. Phuzekhemisi's career shows that the commercial viability of maskanda and its social engagement strengthen rather than exclude each other.

Clegg has a point in asserting that maskanda's commercial production submitted it to apartheid cultural policy that censored the songs aimed at social commentary and promoted the songs that limited themselves to general themes. In the words of Bongani Nkwanyana and Bheki Khoza, this policy 'changed maskanda into a very narrow way of talking about women and money and cars' (Khoza 2009; B. Nkwanyana 2009b). These dynamics have been addressed in Chapter 2. Nomcebo Ngema reported that maskanda stopped being exclusively concerned with societal issues much later, with the advance of gospel and R&B influences at the turn of the century: 'I think it is starting to change with the R&B; that's basically about love. Generally, they will be saying: "this girl that I like ... " etc.' (Ngema 2009).

Musickers invariably formulate freedom of expression as an essence of maskanda practice. Maskandi, producers and media representatives all acknowledge that this freedom has always been regulated by the industry and media: sometimes it is fostered, at other times it is curtailed. The close intersection of the performance stage, the recording and production studio and other musicking spaces further tightens the grip of these spaces on the opportunities musickers possess or obtain to express themselves. This tension is most urgent in what Khoni Miya identifies as an 'up level' stage of a musician's professional career. In this chapter, I focus on those maskandi who were able to access those spaces, and I address the ways in which they manage to breathe in the sometimes suffocating embrace of the music industry, the media and political institutions. Whereas musicians working within the industry may earn more money than those working outside of it, like S'kho and Khoni Miya, they hardly enjoy more economic sustainability. Moreover, it is hard to step out of the industry – maybe as hard as it is to get one's foot in it.

Musicking labour migrants

Illustrative in this context is the career of maskandi Nothi Ntuli, whom I encountered in Downtown Studios in Johannesburg in 2009.[1] Ntuli is a highly regarded maskanda

---

[1] Louise Meintjes devotes an insightful paragraph to Ntuli's studio session work. She outlines how his immense experience as a studio musician helps his consociates of the Umzansi Zulu Dancers straddle 'rural, migrant affect' and a 'wider world consisting of the township, the city, and the studio' and 'cultivate' a 'Zulu, contemporary, male, and migrant sociality' (217: 219–20).

guitarist who started his career as a backstage guitarist for the legendary maskandi Mphatheni Khumalo a.k.a. Mfaz' Omnyama (1959–2001). At the MORC Festival in Ulundi, he took on this task for another maskanda celebrity: Thokozani Langa. Often, the biggest maskanda stars do not play live guitar, even if they are live on stage and hold a guitar in their hands. Instead, they focus on the dance (Jenkins 2013b). Skilled but invisible guitarists do the playing for them backstage. Nothi Ntuli is one of the most regularly asked backstage guitarists.

Ntuli described his life to me as that of a labour migrant. The mining or domestic labour that kept people from their homes in the apartheid days now seems to have been replaced by studio work. Ntuli needs all his time to do session work in order to make a living, and the only way to get that work is to be in Johannesburg physically.

> When I am at home there are no people to play with ... And also studios ... it's very hard .... I don't like staying here [in Johannesburg]. It's the whole money situation. Jozi is too difficult .... Every month I have to pay 800 rand for a place to stay. When I am at home, I don't have to pay a cent. [laughs] ... Just to make money and when I have it, I go home and come back.
>
> (Ntuli 2009)

Despite the fact Ntuli is so highly regarded, his solo career never took off. When I talked to him in 2009, he was on the brink of recording and releasing a solo maskanda album, *Sanibonani*, with Zuz'Muzi Records, but this album was only released in 2019. TV presenter Nhlanhla Ngwekazi related how problematic the career of a studio session musician can be:

> You will see them at Downtown Studios as studio musicians, playing bass, playing drums, playing the guitar for somebody, but if you have it in you, you want to show it to the world, you want to perform it. Standing behind the mike in the studio, recording, is not enough.
>
> (Ngwekazi 2009)

Visibility on stage and in TV programmes such as Nthethe's *Moribo* show turns out to be crucial in order to reach beyond the existence of a music labourer with a migratory life. Those who have made a name for themselves and are able to make a comfortable living with their musicianship second this. They explain how much a musician (and manager) need to focus simultaneously on live performance opportunities, record deals and on segments in TV and radio programmes that will reach the required audience (Khama 2009; Mnyandu 2009). Sometimes, record companies are indispensable in offering the logistics to access sufficient sites for the music's promotion. Abraham Mija from Gallo explains:

> What we do, normally ... with the traditional music: if you don't go and perform there, people they won't know. It won't sell .... Okay, you can take it to the paper, but ... people who buy this music, they don't read [the] paper ... [or] the internet

– they don't have internet and all this ... You must go to the ground floor. Where people are. Taxi rank, you go to the bus stops, you go to the railway stations. You know. Like, in Durban station, there you see everybody's always there.

(Mija 2009)

At other times, the musician's manager is taking care of all these duties. Linah Khama (a.k.a. Ebony) is married to one of South Africa's greatest maskanda stars Bheki Ngcobo a.k.a. iHashi Elimhlophe (b. 1959). She set her successful performance career aside in order to manage the successes of her husband. Khama was very open about the necessary requirements if one wants to place a successful artist in the market:

You must be able to know: 'this is what I am worth' ... Because sometimes there are people who come in and they want to cheat you .... If we are going to the stage, we make sure we present [the] name of iHashi like unique.

(Khama 2009)

This also implies that iHashi is taking on musical formats, genres and styles that are either very much at the centre of maskanda discourse or completely outside of it. By rigorously connecting his name to such formats, Linah Khama and Bheki Ngcobo managed to make a 'brand' out of iHashi Elimhlophe. iHashi branded himself through his performance with the two other stars of post-apartheid maskanda – Mfaz' Omnyama and Phuzekhemisi – in the 1997 song 'Sxaxa Mbij", which secured his status among the top three national maskandi artists (B. Ngcobo, Khumalo and Mnyandu 1997). He featured visibly at rallies for the election of Jacob Zuma as president of the ANC in 2009 (B. Ngcobo 2009a), and in between those years he consciously set up crossover projects with artists from other genres and other countries, employing reggae, hip-hop and gospel idioms in his music.

Crossover musicking

These acts of branding have decidedly improved iHashi's visibility as well as his opportunities to record new albums (more than thirty since the mid-1970s) and to win prizes in traditional music segments. Like Bongani Nkwanyana, Linah Khama and Bheki Ngcobo run their own record label (iHashi namamPoni), together with the band in which their children perform. Once they have acquired a certain amount of fame and resources, artists attempt to create their own spaces within the larger industry. Often maskandi help each other by building and sharing their own studios, and by acting as producers for each other's albums. This often leads to interesting artistic exchanges. Mandla Xaba (a.k.a. Shwi from the maskanda duo Shwi noMtekhala) produced the album of the female maskanda duo Izintombi, with his artist name featuring prominently in the album title: *Izintombi zika Shwii* (Ngobese and Ngobese 2009). Jazz guitarist Bheki Khoza was the producer of Bongani Nkwanyana's album *Yash'inkani* (2009a), in which he encouraged Nkwanyana to modulate to different keys and to minor modes, and 'play maskanda inside it .... Find your way in there' (Khoza 2009). Phuzekhemisi produced the 2008 album *Ubuyile Umaqondana Egoli* by the young Bhaca artist Ichwane Lebhaca (Lebhaca 2008). The fact that both Khoza and Phuzekhemisi are established figures in jazz and maskanda realms, respectively, may have enlarged the album's audiences and certainly helped branding Nkwanyana and Lebhaca as artists doing something unique. These examples represent effective strategies of musically and performatively adapting and appropriating sounding and stage material that maskanda musickers encounter in their lives and careers – a foregrounding of one's aural experience in the form of maskandafication.

The necessity felt by musicians to keep expanding their audience, their exposure and their sales is not solely a matter of economic survival or calculating capitalism. Not all of the above-mentioned albums are directly representative of the mass-produced commercial maskanda that is heard and enjoyed in most taxis, supermarkets and other public spaces in KwaZulu-Natal and Gauteng. South African musicians – maskandi and others – also want to get exposed to music from abroad in order to enrich themselves as artists, performers and composers. They intend to expand their artistic idioms and techniques by working with musicians from elsewhere (Kunene 2008; B. Ngcobo 2009b; N. Shabalala 2010). This (re)appropriation of globally current idioms and techniques is another powerful form of maskandafication, after decades of apartheid isolation and an international cultural boycott:

> There is a crossover now, in the international market, in the South African market. Because of the apartheid, most of the things were closed .... I am able now to talk to you, to organize a gig, ... and then we see if it is working. But before we couldn't do it. That's why you see a lot of maskandi going outside.
>
> (Nzimande 2009)

Nzimande notices the current options that musickers possess to exchange ideas, work together and organize and perform crossovers. He instantly translates this into profitable markets. As Louise Meintjes has pointed out in her monograph about mbaqanga (2003), the concept of 'overseas' (as opposed to 'abroad') carries a literal 'other-worldliness'. It is 'over the sea' (*pesheya olwandle*) and stands in stark contrast to 'home' (*ikhaya*), signifying the place where Joe Nkwanyana spent the remainder of his days, and where S'kho and Khoni Miya still live. Crossover musicking is a conscious attempt to narrow the gap between *pesheya olwandle* and *ikhaya*, as we will see in Chapters 7 and 8. Musicians such as Madala Kunene (Kunene and Lässer 1998), Phuzekhemisi (Mnyandu 2007), iHashi Elimhlophe and the late Busi Mhlongo work with musicians from Europe, North America and Latin America. Mhlongo had her 2001 album *Urban Zulu* marketed as 'the maskanda of the new millennium' (Mhlongo 2001) and it received great international acclaim among world music aficionados worldwide. On tour in Canada, Phuzekhemisi chose to work with a Canadian choir that sang in Zulu (Mnyandu 2009). His 2007 album *Sesihlangene* was produced for sports events with an international outreach. It features maskanda songs in English and emerged in collaboration with the Zimbabwean Kennedy Zimba (see also Olsen 2014: 96).

Almost all musicians I talked to mention Mahlatini and the Mohatella Queens and Ladysmith Black Mambazo (LBM) as unquestionable models for the launch of their own international careers, despite the demonstrably unequal options for expression that these collaborations entailed. Yet, for many South African musicians, the displaying of what you have on offer to a foreign audience and the opportunity to be exposed to a new repertoire and hence grow artistically are two sides of the same coin of success, as succinctly phrased by Linah Khama:

> [iHashi] has been abroad several times, he's been to Canada, he's been to India, he's been to China, he's been to Miami, he's been to Hungary, he's been to Russia .... The only thing that hasn't been there is a breakthrough, because nothing has been done, like, big advertisement, big marketing of his music .... Cause most of the time, we got there and represent [our] country. But we want to represent the country and be able to explore ourselves and be able to grow. Like Black Mambazo with Paul Simon .... And it's easy then to sell it to your country, because it's something that they don't have.
>
> (Khama 2009)

In this view, options for expression are enriched through opportunities for the absorption of new styles and techniques, but also for insights into what international audiences value about South African styles and techniques. Meintjes explains how Northern Hemisphere notions of Zuluness and Africanness, as discussed in Chapters 3 and 4, were musically satisfied by Mahlatini and his producers. International musical markers of Zuluness acquired aesthetic status on South African stages, precisely because of their worldwide appeal, a process that Mark Slobin calls 'validation through visibility' (1993: 21). More than thirty-five years after the international successes of Mahlatini and LBM, many of the musical markers that signified their South Africanness – Mahlatini's *ibhodlo*, LBM's mbube-style multipart vocal styles, the inclusion of war cries, florid guitar *isihlabo* and the melodic bass guitar – are abundantly used by South African maskandi to demonstrate both their unique and their mainstream suitability for an international stage.

Shiyani Ngcobo's tour through the Netherlands

The ambiguities of the interaction between maskandi and international audiences, and the implications of these interactions for musicians in South Africa, can be further elucidated by discussing Shiyani Ngcobo's tour through the Netherlands and Belgium in June 2010, the last he undertook before he passed away in February 2011. From 1997 onwards, Ngcobo travelled to France, Norway, Denmark, Germany, Switzerland and Cameroon. In 2000, he played at the Rainforest World Music Festival in Malaysia, where he first caught the ear of the British producer Ben Mandelson. His CD *Introducing Shiyani Ngcobo* (S. Ngcobo 2004) met with great acclaim from music experts worldwide and resulted in an elaborate tour across the

UK with several BBC radio appearances in 2004. In 2007, he performed at Carnegie Hall, New York.

However, unlike iHashi, Ngcobo was hardly known in South Africa; his international success was not reflected in any substantial regional or national exposure. I mentioned his name wherever I could, to maskandi and producers in Johannesburg, to the clearly knowledgeable radio presenters at the KwaMashu township radio station Vibe FM and to festival organizers. None of them showed any visible sign of recognition of this virtuoso maskandi who started his career winning prizes at national maskanda contests in the late 1980s (Olsen 2014: 76). Arguably, Ngcobo's acoustic guitar sound appeals to foreign world music audiences rather than to young urban South Africans. Also, Ngcobo's lack of access to performance venues and local and national airtime in South Africa once again demonstrates the impenetrable entanglement of stage, studio and other spaces to further one's musical career.

Hence, Ngcobo lived (in similar circumstances as S'kho Miya) in the KwaMakhutha township near Durban, surviving on teaching maskanda guitar in the School of Music at the University of KwaZulu-Natal and in an affiliated outreach programme, UKUSA (Olsen 2014: 77). In this capacity, I met Ngcobo when I decided to take maskanda guitar lessons in order to familiarize myself with the sounding and structural aspects of maskanda music. Not surprisingly, Ngcobo did not have any illusions about the promises of the overseas stage, although I have never seen him being bitter or cynical about the discrepancy between his national and international careers. Hence there wasn't so much pressure on our relationship about what he expected from me. He taught me in what developed into a warm and friendly teacher–pupil relationship. This may also have been due to the fact that uBaba uShiyani (as I was supposed to call him) was much older than me.

Ngcobo's tour initially comprised two legs, one in the UK with more than ten shows and one in the Low Countries (Belgium and the Netherlands) with three shows. The British leg was cancelled. The British organizers didn't succeed in raising enough funds. The Dutch world music centre RASA in Utrecht, however, was determined to realize the Dutch leg, so, in collaboration with Kathryn Olsen, who acted as a spokesperson for Ngcobo, they scheduled the tour from 2 to 7 June 2010 with concerts in the Zuiderpershuis in the Belgian town Antwerp, in their own venue RASA in Utrecht, and in the Tropentheater in Amsterdam. My contribution was limited to establishing contact between RASA's artistic director and Olsen. Prior to the tour, Ngcobo produced an album with his band members at the University of KwaZulu-Natal (S. Ngcobo 2010a). I joined the tour as a contact person, local fan and cultural interlocutor, attending all concerts and accompanying the musicians.

The shows in Amsterdam and Utrecht were marketed and presented in the context of a larger 'package deal': a whole evening with live music, a documentary film, interviews with novelists and filmmakers about post-apartheid South Africa, support acts and an afterparty with a DJ. Both evenings were consciously using the fact that the Football World Cup was about to start in several South African cities, with a range of media attention for South Africa on Dutch TV, radio and in cinemas. The RASA show in Utrecht on 4 June was presented as a 'Football Weekend' (Figure 5.1), with video

Shiyani Ngcobo's Tour 123

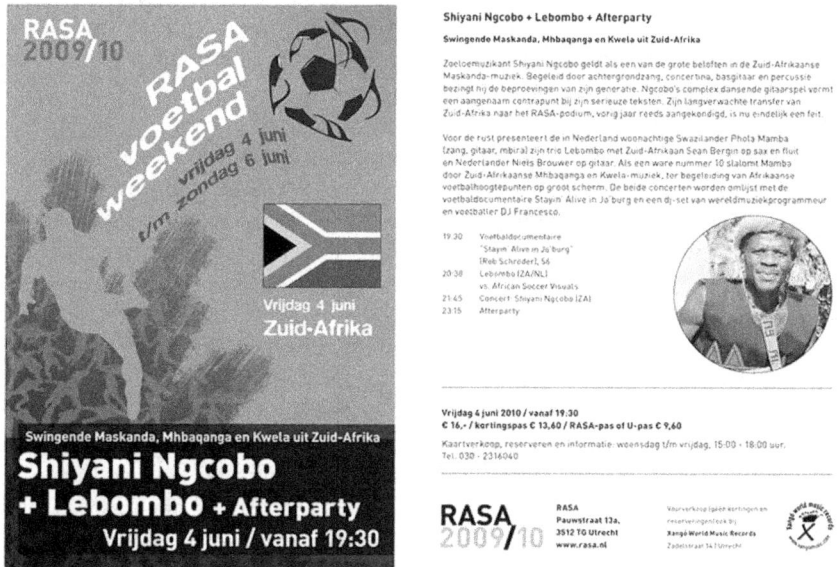

Figure 5.1 Advertising material for Shiyani Ngcobo's performance at RASA, Utrecht, the Netherlands.

footage of football matches being projected as a background to the support act prior to Ngcobo's performance.

The Amsterdam audience on 6 June was invited to 'A Zulu Night'. Despite all these marketing efforts, there were only a few people in the audience: twenty in Antwerp (the only venue that presented Ngcobo's performance without support acts), about thirty-five in Utrecht and about a hundred in Amsterdam. After the show in Antwerp, I talked to Dora Mols, the general artistic manager of the Zuiderpershuis, and we wondered why it is more difficult to get an audience for music from sub-Sahara Africa than it is for West African music. With decades of experience in scouting musicians from Africa, Mols suggested the exposure of francophone Belgium audiences to francophone West Africa might be a clarification. She also asserted that South Africa's cultural isolation from the world during the apartheid years was still not entirely broken by the time we talked. Musicians, except those in exile, hadn't had enough opportunity yet to present themselves to European audiences, which was precisely the problem identified by musicians in South Africa (Mols 2010).

Ngcobo and his band treated the audience to a wide range of songs and styles. The lyrics with their translations had been provided by Olsen, with songs about ancestors ('Thongo lami'), about people who try to steal Ngcobo's musical talents ('Isphiwosami'), about Ngcobo's doubt of God's good intentions because of HIV/AIDS ('Angikholwa') and a praise of King Zwelithini ('Ingonyama'). Ngcobo finished his show in all cases with 'Inhliziyoyami', a song about how he was left by his mother, which he elaborately explained to the audience beforehand. All songs developed into an extensive *izibongo*, and all songs were accompanied by a djembe rather than the drum set that usually features contemporary maskanda. I will elaborate on the presence of this djembe shortly.

A mutual awareness of difference between performers and audience was palpable in all shows. I employ this mutual awareness as a point of focus for my description and analysis of these events, in order to outline discrepancies in understanding maskanda that are epistemic as much as performative. In South Africa, members of the audience jump up, enter the stage and dance on stage *with* the maskandi. In Europe, despite the 'swing set-up' of the concert hall, enabling the audience to dance, performers and audience remained in their fixed positions facing each other. Moreover, the audience, including myself, responded more positively to the songs in pentatonic isiZulu style than the ones in heptatonic isiShameni style, possibly because pentatonic isiZulu style sounds different from the global pop mainstream. My conversations with other musicians and local tour manager Marieke Pieters shed further light on the ways in which such notions of difference were conceptualized. Pieters often escorts bands for RASA, but had never encountered a Zulu band before. We had been travelling with each other for some days in casual jeans and T-shirts. At their first show, when the maskandi were lined up, ready to enter the stage, she was visibly impressed by their *ubeshu* outfits, consisting of leopard skin prints and head gear (Figure 5.2). The maskandi were barefoot with exposed abdomens. I felt equally impressed. I hadn't seen Ngcobo perform very much and never in this outfit.

Figure 5.2 Shiyani Ngcobo and Band in *ubeshu* dress prior to their performance at RASA Utrecht, 4 June 2010. From left to right: Zwelakhe Mnguni a.k.a. Khetelo (concertina), Njabulo Shabalala (djembe), Marieke Pieters (tour manager), Joseph Bhekizizwe Chiliza (bass), Maureen Bongekile Ngwabe (vocals and dance), Shiyani Ngcobo (lead vocals, guitar).

A South African in exile

In Utrecht, Ngcobo's performance was preceded by the group Lebombo as a support act (Figure 5.3) and I got in touch with its South African flautist and saxophonist Sean Bergin (1948–2012), who built quite a reputation for himself in the Netherlands. He left South Africa in 1973, during the height of apartheid. South African music did have a presence in the Netherlands then, but it was very much dependent on images of the Struggle. Making South African music in the Netherlands was by implication taking a political stance against apartheid and Bergin did that both implicitly and explicitly.

After Ngcobo's band had entered RASA's stage in their *ubeshu* dresses, Bergin left after ten minutes into the show. He said goodbye to me and referred to my research: 'Please keep doing this. It is important. But I can't bear this. I need to go now' (Bergin 2010). Marieke Pieters had talked to Bergin more extensively and she told me later what it was he could not bear. 'It's the dress', she said. 'The way they sell themselves by dressing up like savages. Why are they doing that? It hampers them in being appreciated for their musical qualities' (Pieters 2010). Like Bergin, and quite contrary to her awe, prior to the concert (Figure 5.2), Pieters was outraged by it.

I agreed with her to some extent: *ubeshu* can be seen as another stereotype forced upon the maskandi by global imaginations of maskanda's Africanness. Many South African musicians of colour complain about being 'exoticized' when they perform abroad, through requirements of dress, instruments and repertoire (Naidoo 2009a;

Figure 5.3 Lebombo support act consisting of Niels Brouwer (guitar), Phola Mamba (vocals, guitar, mbira) and Sean Bergin (flute, saxophone) at RASA, Utrecht, 4 June 2010.

Nkabinde 2009). For Sean Bergin, this was a clear example of such stereotypification that is forged not only through demands of global capitalism in the music industry, but also through the inheritance of apartheid. In his eyes, the racist stereotypes that featured the society he fled from are now being embraced by musicians as *authentic* means to articulate their identity on an international stage. Yet, his view does not allow for the reality that *ubeshu* dress, for many Zulu South Africans, does indeed belong to the heritage of Zulu culture. Both at the Kushikisha Imbokodo Festival in Durban and at the MORC Festival in Ulundi, I had seen a mindboggling extravagance of *ubeshu* and *umbaselwa* dresses.

So, I played the devil's advocate and I asked Pieters to think about performance conventions of, for instance, classical choirs in Europe. 'My choir dresses up in black gowns, suits and ties when we perform', I reminded her, 'although we never wear that in daily life'. They belong to the *imagined* heritage of middle-class, formerly church-going classical music lovers in Europe, North America and many other parts of the world. Is that a similar commercial demand? Pieters realized that she regarded the articulations of identity that are familiar to her (such as choirs dressed in black) as natural and obvious, whereas she regarded the articulations of identity that are unfamiliar to her (such as Zulu men and women in animal skins) as constructed and contrived.

Pieters' and Bergin's responses to Ngcobo's stage appearance provide valuable information about individual notions of authenticity in European world music discourses. These notions were further complicated by Ngcobo's inclusion of a djembe in his line-up, played by Njabulo Shabalala, replacing the conventional pop music drum set. Whereas percussion often functions as a marker of African music to European audiences, the djembe has only recently emerged on South African stages, possibly through mainstream pop and jazz bands using 'exotic' instruments and through the global appeal of West African musicians such as Youssou N'Dour and Angélique Kidjo. Increasingly, West African percussion is used in South African musics ranging from jazz to afropop, and the young Zulu percussionist Njabulo Shabalala epitomizes this expansion of horizons. When I asked Ngcobo about the djembe, telling him that I had never heard maskanda with a djembe before, he started beaming with pride. 'It is my idea', he said. 'Nobody has ever made maskanda with a djembe before and it works well. It is unique for my music' (S. Ngcobo 2010b).

For Ngcobo, including a djembe signals authenticity in the sense of 'being unique', 'true to himself' and it also signals hybridity by mixing Zulu culture with that of other parts of Africa. For the Dutch audience, however, the djembe signals another kind of authenticity: a welcome confirmation of maskanda's Africanness, since maskanda is played on globally available musical instruments (guitar, bass) that are often framed as Western. An audience poll that I carried out in Antwerp and Utrecht confirmed this need for the confirmation of maskanda's Africanness. From both perspectives, however, the inclusion of the djembe signals difference and is an attempt to articulate oneself in a market that thrives on idealizations of the Other. With all the postcolonial attention for the concept of the Other, the questions 'other for whom?' and 'other than what?' are sometimes lost from sight. Such questions might articulate the epistemic gaps between the various musickers (Ngcobo and his band, Bergin, Pieters, me and other Dutch audience members) participating in maskanda practice. The case study presented here reveals that these questions warrant continued attention. The same Otherness (the djembe) may stand for radically different conceptions of difference (Zulu maskanda, Pan-African maskanda, unique individual maskanda, maskanda of the future, timeless maskanda). These conceptions of difference are cherished by different subjects (audiences, musicians, media representatives and tour operators) with unequal amounts of agency to foreground their conception of difference. All these conceptions are based on (individual archives of) aural experiences and on the various previous foregroundings of aural experiences in musical performance, arrangement, critique and analysis. These inscriptions of sound can tell us something about the circulation of acoustic assemblages between listening subjects, shaping larger (often implicit) theories of sound (Ochoa 2014: 22–3).

Understanding 'Asinankomo'

In order to illustrate how these diverging conceptions of difference are based on a diversity of aural experiences of the same event, I provide a close reading and listening of Ngcobo's performance of his song 'Asinankomo' (We do not have cattle) in the Tropentheater in Amsterdam on 6 June 2010 (S. Ngcobo 2010d). This close reading serves several concerns of this book. Firstly, it pays attention to the disjunctions in the aural experiences of the same event. Such attention helps me acknowledge the agency that maskandi possess in shaping their art according to their own ideas, even if these do not align with the perceptions of the watching and listening audience. There are inevitable epistemic gaps between what maskandi do, say or convey musically and how their utterances are understood. Nevertheless, even in restrictive and disempowering circumstances, maskandi regulate and control the circulation of acoustic assemblages between listening entities (Ochoa 2014: 23), and they assert cultural authority through their intervention in the liminal space between event and enunciation through their musicking (Bhabha 1994b: 58–9). Like my musicking in writing this book, maskandi's musicking hence operates as epistemology, even if we use different modes of knowledge inscription. Secondly, this close reading demonstrates how my belated understanding of 'Asinankomo' exemplifies the formation of colonial knowledge as forged between frontier and metropolis. Thus, my understanding of 'Asinankomo' is double-and-split (Bloechl 2008: 23) with potentially outreaching as well as potentially imperialist implications.

Towards the end of his concert, Ngcobo performed a song with lyrics that were translated in the programme notes as 'We have no cattle, no money, nothing. We are poor' (RASA 2009/10). Only when I showed my video footage of this song to Sazi Dlamini, my colleague at the University of KwaZulu-Natal, more than a year later, did I manage to conceptualize the immense rift in understanding the music that we all heard, a rift between the South African maskandi on stage and the Dutch audience that heard and watched them, including myself. Throughout the tour, I had had the inescapable feeling that South African and Dutch musickers were unable to live out a mutual pact of understanding. Through Dlamini's explanation this feeling now became palpable.

The first indication of this rift was that I, as a semi-skilled maskanda musicker, had not noticed what Ngcobo had been singing about. It is safe to assume that the rest of the Dutch audience must have been as ignorant as I was. Like all maskandi, Ngcobo poses a statement through his song, an igama that cannot be misunderstood if one speaks Zulu and knows how to interpret the dance and dress that Ngcobo employs. Like all igamas, this statement is communicated through a variety of communicative and performance-based modes.

Ngcobo's message is clear: he accuses the *abamhlope* or *abelungu* (whites) of his poverty (Figure 5.4). White people have taken everything away from us (us being non-white people). This accusation is conspicuously absent from the programme notes. The sentence 'Kwashonaphi okwezwe' (Where did the things of the nation go?) refers to what used to belong to the nation or the people of the nation, that is, land, livestock, and so on; but considering the fact that 'you see us with nothing' ('Usibona singena lutho'), it appears that everything has been taken away. Later in the song, Ngcobo refers to water that needs to be bought in shops now, because, like the land and the livestock, it is no longer a natural resource with general access. The same might happen, he suggests, to the air we breathe. In doing so, he connects past, present and future events and attributes historical significance to the acts of bereavement he describes.

Apart from the verbal modes of communication, there are some powerful visual, choreographic and sounding aspects to the posing of this igama that have great persuasive power, and that 'transfer' voices of the past to the present by activating their contained energy and securing an afterlife of events and works, something that is increasingly acknowledged as featuring eurogenic forms of historiography too (Gumbrecht 2004: 21ff; see Titus 2021). Sazi Dlamini observed that Bongekile Ngwabe, the female backing singer and dancer, is dressed as a warrior. She performs male dance routines (S. Ngcobo 2010d: 02'55"–04'20").

> SD: This boy's a hero. He's a warrior. The boy is a warrior! ... dress[es] the woman as a warrior. This is very significant. BT: He's there to ... battle? SD: Yeah ... doing battle ... showing ... respect as well .... [Shiyani] was always original, and very critical with the critics. Everything, from family to the world – this was remarkable. He had a sharp eye. A critical eye for issues, issues around us ... And he sang it.
>
> (Dlamini 2011b)

Many people I showed the video of Ngcobo's performance to wondered why Ngwabe was dressed in the *ubeshu* dress that is usually reserved for men. Her dance routines were also male rather than female. Clegg asserts that 'although young girls are sometimes allowed to dance isishameni, umzansi, umqonqo, only men can represent the district' (Clegg 1982: 13). Here, Shiyani Ngcobo decidedly granted these representational capacities to his female dancer. Having been affected by the critique of Bergin and Pieters, I assumed that Ngcobo had given in to a reductive representation of Zulu culture on an international stage that was disconnected from the day-to-day practice of wearing *ubeshu* dress in Zulu homes and performances. Dlamini's explanation, by contrast, allows for the option that Ngcobo consciously wanted to tell something with

[Verse:]	
Usibona singena lutho	You see us with nothing
Asinankomo	We do not have cattle
Kwashonaphi okwezwe	Where did it/things of the nation, go?
Usibona asinalutho	You see us with nothing
Asinankomo	We do not have cattle
Kwashonaphi okwezwe	Where did it/things of the nation, go?
Ngoba abamhlophe sebaku thathe nkonke	Because the whites have taken everything
Asisenalutho	We do not have anything
Kwashonaphi okwezwe	Where did it/things of the nation, go?
Ngisho abelungu sebaku thathe konke	Whites have taken all/everything
Asisenankomo	We do not have cattle
Kwashonaphi okwezwe lonke	Where did it/things of the nation, go?
Ngoba manje batheng' e supermakete	Because now they buy at supermarkets
Azisekekho iinkomo	There is no more cattle
Akusekho kwezwe mhlabeni	There is nothing left of the nation here on earth
Iimbuzi zithengwa kwabamhlophe	Goats are now bought from whites
Asisenalutho	We do not have anything
Kwashonaphi okwezwe emhlabeni	Where did it/things of the nation, go?
Usibona asinalutho thina	You see us with nothing
Asinankomo	We do not have cattle
Weeee	[Lamentation]
[Chorus:]	
Asinankomo	We do not have cattle
Asinalutho	We do not have anything
Asinamali	We do not have money
Imali yabelungu	Money belongs to the whites
[*Izibongo*:]	
Wadla Nduma Ndumane	Nduma Ndumane ate
Thumbu lenkomo	Cow's intestine
Uyoze ulilahle, sweet mtwana	You will end up giving up, sweet baby
Ntombi yangivimbela	The girl who tried to hinder me
Akwaba nhlungu	It did not hurt
Izayoni ezangivimbela	It is Zion that hindered me.

*** [too rapid to transcribe and translate] ***

Figure 5.4 'Asinankomo'. Lyrics transcribed and translated by Ignatia Madalane and Elias Nxumalo (S. Ngcobo 2010d), with kind permission from heir Shiyani Ngcobo.

Ngwabe's dance and the dress, supporting the lyrics of his song.[2] Moreover, like some of the maskanda songs addressed in previous chapters, 'Asinankomo' directly signifies older Zulu musical practices that represent traditionality for many Zulu South Africans, as well as for those who have not been directly exposed to gourd bow playing and *amahubo* singing. The song is based on an anhemitonic pentatonic scale with a descending motive e-flat – d-flat – b-flat – a-flat – g-flat as overtones of the two fundamentals A-flat and G-flat, a bi-tonal notion that I will explain in Chapter 6 as having been derived from gourd bow practices (Figures 5.5 and 5.6).

There is more to the song's musical features. There are the heterophonic voice entries and embellishments of this motive (S. Ngcobo 2010d: 00'48"–00'56") and the response chorus that moves in the same tonal and motivic realm as the lead singer and bass (02'11"–02'21"). The chorus is harmonized in fourths and fifths, which is often retraced to multipart a cappella choral song (*amahubo*). These sonic markers will be elaborately discussed in Chapter 6. Ngcobo's vocal timbre is sustained and pressured, a bit nasal, but also with a certain lightness in higher registers, mixing it with some falsetto (01'54"). This reciting style is consciously employed for putting a

Figure 5.5 'Asinankomo'. Pentatonic scale derived from two fundamentals. Transcribed with kind permission from heir Shiyani Ngcobo.

Figure 5.6 'Asinankomo'. Main guitar and bass parts (S. Ngcobo 2010d). Transcribed with kind permission from heir Shiyani Ngcobo.

[2] Unfortunately, I was late asking Ngcobo himself what he wanted to convey with this song. By the time I had learned to appreciate the song's many interpretative dimensions, Ngcobo had passed away, less than a year after his Dutch tour, in February 2011.

message across that one cannot miss, but that also suits (colours in with) the timbral aspects of the acoustic guitar and earlier the gourd bow. Thus, mode, texture and vocal timbre of the performance reference and evoke older Zulu practices, constituting the art of telling a history with just a few tones while keeping people engaged.

Dlamini observed that these sounding aspects of the music support the lyrics of the song. They sonically present a Zulu perspective. Dlamini illustrated this by playing and improvising along with the video footage of Ngcobo's performance on a traditional *umtsingo* flute. Thus, he emphasized its isiZulu tuning and pentatonic scale:

> His music is amazing. What connects ... is that they're immensely proud people ... very proud ... It's the kind of song you can play on a bow, you can play it on a traditional flute, you know, it's [like] ... speaking again of that broad sensibility of traditional music.
>
> (Dlamini 2011b)

As I mentioned earlier, for a Dutch audience, these sonic markers may be vague indications of maskanda's Africanness, enhanced by Ngcobo's incorporation of the djembe. For many Zulu South Africans, however, these sonic features signify much more specific epistemologies. It is tempting to interpret Ngcobo's choice for specific musical material as an articulation of *identity*. However, such interpretation obscures Ngcobo's much more important and multifaceted *discursive* validation of specific traditions. His choice represents and constitutes an epistemological position with regard to the problem that the igama thematizes: criticizing the behaviour of white people and outlining the history of this behaviour.

Menacing the Zulu stereotype

Academics do not always sufficiently acknowledge such discursive validations of tradition *as* epistemology.[3] Ngcobo transmitted his ideas on stage with similar critical intentions (not means) as, for instance, an academic historiographer does: to inform and persuade an audience or readership, and to transfer voices from the past to the present by demonstrating how they still work in the present. The experiences Ngcobo describes are still part of the daily lives of many South Africans. Thus, Ngcobo's multi-modal performance of his igama is in many ways a more integral textualization of the complex and multifaceted societal conditions in early-twentieth-century and early-twenty-first-century South Africa than written linear narratives such as those laid down in this book. His performance helps us experience the processes of adaptation, appropriation and domestication that have shaped the lives of those who participate

---

[3] See also Liz Gunner's engagement with 'the place of song *as* debate and as a discursive presence within the public sphere and the body politic'. She also observes that this presence 'has not been fully acknowledged' (2009: 47).

in maskanda, because he immediately produces these processes in the here and now. His maskandafication of these processes is a compelling foregrounding of his (aural) experiences that forms part of circulating acoustic assemblages between listening entities that hear each other hear.

The urgency and topicality of his *igama* were cynically demonstrated by the Dutch audience, including myself, enthusiastically clapping along with the performance, cheering in between lyrics and *izibongo* and happily applauding his complaint. All maskanda performance is directed towards all those present at the scene, but we were completely ignorant of the fact that Ngcobo's complaint may have been directed towards us. This ignorance made us part of the performance of the *igama* in ways we could not imagine. Maskandi and audience inhabited the same soundscape (Smith 1999: 47) in the Amsterdam Tropentheater on that evening in June, yet they knew the world in fundamentally different ways through what they heard. Watching the footage of the show (S. Ngcobo 2010d), Dlamini foregrounded the skill with which Shiyani Ngcobo played with his audience and with their expectations of him as a Zulu musician. Dlamini's analysis through his interview with me as a member of the Dutch audience needs to be quoted in full:

> SD: This is very discursive, what's happening here. It's like … there's a gap, there's disjunction. [The] experience … First of all, no one hears what he's saying – that's number one. They're just looking. And hearing. They don't understand what he says. So even then, that's already like, disjunctive. And Shiyani is trying to communicate something, by both appearance and by the music. Now his appearance … What do you say about this question?
>
> BT: Well, you know, when I, when I look at it from, from a Western perspective, I think it's kind of … for me it's primitive.
>
> SD: Very interesting, it's primitive, very interesting …
>
> BT: Because it's a man …
>
> SD: Skins … Yeah, it's …
>
> BT: … clad in animal skins, and, and you see lots of his body, and …
>
> SD: Yeah, it's, it's prehistoric …
>
> BT: Ja, it's premodern.
>
> SD: Premodern, ja, it's premodern … Which has to do with: identity. Identities and embellishing certain compliments about his identity and how … he is sure it is understood by the world. This [is] what is done …. He knows about the exoticism of his Zulu image. And how it has been presented. By Mahlatini [and the Mohatella Queens]. What I'm saying is that … for him this is not really novice; an embellishing, you know, of expectations, and constructions of identity.
>
> (Dlamini 2011b)

With his analysis, Dlamini elucidated how the exchange of aesthetic expectations between musicians and audiences occurs, with unbridgeable gaps, and with undeniable inequalities of power, but in a far more complex manner than Sean Bergin presented it.

The maskandi are anything but passive victims of commodified cultural stereotypes. Rather, they have active agency in using and embellishing these tropes in ways they see fit. Ngcobo does not primarily intend to please a foreign audience. On the contrary, he teases this audience in a discursive convention common to maskanda performance: as a warning, a sharp joke, an opinionated provocation. Dlamini's comments pinpointed the many roles that the maskandi fulfils: as an observer, messenger, spokesperson for the community, jester, teacher, historiographer and critic. One could interpret Ngcobo's performance of 'Asinankomo' as an act of Bhabhaesque mimicry: he stages his version of the Zulu stereotype as a fetish that resides in the minds of European audiences as a substitute for the Zulu people. He menaces this stereotype by taking command over it and employing it for his aims, enriching its meaning and asserting his own epistemological agency.

All these epistemological implications would have remained illegible to me had I not been able to pick Dlamini's brain and had I bought into Bergin's idea of Ngcobo's performance as a reductive articulation of Zulu identity. Shiyani Ngcobo's agency to tease his audience by making it part of his performance may have remained invisible and inaudible, reduced to nothing more than an unarticulated 'nearly agential pressure' (Bloechl 2008: 11). This near-hidden agency is comparable to Sipho Mchunu's agency in the conception of the song 'Sab' Inganono', discussed in Chapter 1. It is also comparable to S'kho Miya's agency in disseminating maskanda music among larger audiences than her immediate colleagues, discussed in Chapter 3. In all those cases, I, and my readership, have heard and interpreted maskanda once again as 'subaltern' replication rather than subversion of the hegemonies of eurogenic performance practices and eurogenic epistemologies that I think I am able to 'read'.

Beyond the subaltern and hegemony

The problematic aspect of the category of the subaltern being understood in binary opposition to a hegemony was also highlighted by Khoni Miya. My conversation with her strengthened me in my insight that attributing 'subalternity' to a form of expression, in it being 'illegible' or outside hegemonic discourse, robs those who participate in these forms of expression of their expressive agency within the discourse. Many people are able to 'read' Ngcobo's expressions and many of those people can exert cultural authority in decidedly domineering ways. I have demonstrated this in previous chapters with my accounts of the music industry, representatives of the broadcast media and royal festival organizers. What is crucial to take into account is *for whom* Ngcobo's expressions are illegible or subaltern, and *for whom* the various exertions of cultural authority are hegemonic. Miya pointed me towards the existence of such multiple subject positions when she refused to go along with my hypothesis that Dutch audiences don't understand what happens on maskanda stages. She argued that understanding something has multiple (including musical) dimensions that I did not consider in my judgement. Only after my talk with Dlamini did I learn to listen to what she had said:

KM: No, before you are singing you are explaining to them [the international audience]. [S'kho Miya seconds this]. You are explaining to them what you are singing. Somebody like me, I and some of the white people, they learn to come [understand] when they are performing, and some others start dancing but don't understand ... [laughter]. Because now why do they do that ... they just feel the sound ... 'There's a feel that I can dance here, the sound is driving me, but why, why the sounds drive[s] me ... what is this saying?' Because with people's things, with dancing for her [S'kho Miya], ... they are not dancing for enjoying her, what she is singing, they are enjoying the sound. So, it means we have to communicate over there.

BT: Communicate through music?

KM: Ya. It is typical.

(K. Miya 2009a)

Miya emphasizes the possibility of explaining the lyrics to the audience before you start singing, and I have often wondered what would have happened between audience and musicians during the performance of 'Asinankomo' had Ngcobo done that. She argues that there are always people, as well as white people, who know to some degree what's going on, and there are some who don't. But she refuses to assume an *a priori* experiential rift between the participating musickers, since even those who do not understand will enjoy the sound and start moving. This is a crucial mode of understanding: it is hearing rather than reading, and it allows for the option that some people will bring home different aspects from the performance than other people, which is not a vagueness or absence of meaning, but an enrichment of meaning. Her observation was lost on me when I commenced my research, but started to make sense to me when I dug deeper into modes of understanding beyond written and conceptual ones. One of such modes of understanding concerns the expressive prominence and precision of dance in Zulu culture that I touched on in my explanation of the notion of igama in the Introduction, and that has been outlined so richly and viscerally by Louise Meintjes in her book about *ingoma* dance (2017). Another of such modes of understanding concerns the various musically and bodily expressed differences of maskanda styles, outlined in Chapter 2, as well as the female reappropriation of male-dominated sonic practices such as *ibhodlo* and *izibongo*, discussed in Chapter 3.

My belated ability to observe such understandings also made me overlook forms of agency that maskandi possess to shape their musical lives, their artistic ideals and their modes of expression. Musicking shapes social agency – this is what makes music as a mode of knowing such a fascinating topic of research. Obviously, I have learned this from decades of ethnomusicological research, but I was only able to identify these forms of agency practically through my conversations with Dlamini and Miya, including Miya's distinction between ground, middle and up levels of labouring in the South African music industry. The undeniable epistemic gaps and inequalities of power within these acts of *practical identification* (Derrida [1967] 1997: 116 as cited in Scherzinger 2004: 273) reach beyond a simple binary of subaltern and hegemony. I intend to further articulate and substantiate these gaps and power relations in sonic and aural terms in the next three chapters.

Part III

Hearing Maskanda

6

Knowing Zuluness Aurally

In previous chapters (Part II), I outlined *what* maskanda musickers do to make sense of their world through music, sound and listening. In the following chapters (Part III), I focus on *how* they do this. Thus, I intend to provide insight into *how* maskanda musicking 'works' as epistemology. Like in previous chapters, I outline the foregroundings of aural experiences in performance, arrangement, spoken and written feedback and critique, commercial dissemination or academic prose. In Chapters 6 and 7, I describe *what* musickers cast in maskanda idiom or discourse; in Chapter 8, I describe *how* they do this, *how* maskandafication operates. Even more directly than in previous chapters, their foregroundings are complemented, but also distorted, by my own hearings of maskanda. My hearings are presented in several analyses of songs as 'discrete' musical entities, and of the spaces, occasions and instances in which they sound, such as lessons, rehearsal rooms, YouTube channels, (festival) stages, albums and studios. Through these discrete analytical endeavours, I demonstrate the epistemic and epistemological importance of music and performance on the one hand, and I shed light on the performative importance of (music) analysis and scholarship on the other.

Tomie Hahn notes that processes of coming to 'understand' another subculture's sensual orientation can pose 'a sensual dis-orientation' (17) that can redirect associations and undermine stereotypes such as those I outlined in Chapters 4 and 5. Hahn's notion of sensual dis-orientation can be regarded as an implication of what Peter Szendy describes as a 'twofold process of "hearing another person listen"' (Szendy as paraphrased by Erlmann 2004: 18). As Monson (1996: 2) and Scherzinger (2004: 272) suggest, participating in acts of music analysis is a social practice that revolves entirely around hearing another person listen. As such, it can articulate individual and culturally specific sensual dis/orientations. Regarding music analysis as a social practice helps relax the binary of musical versus conceptual modes of knowing. Musical performance and verbal explanation employ different means of inscription but equal degrees of detail and precision in such processes of understanding and are often employed in tandem in both maskanda and musicological practices.

Structural listening and close reading of music help us foreground undecidabilities, and 'traces of contingency' in aural experience (Scherzinger 2004: 258). It might enable us to embrace sensual dis-orientation. Such foregroundings are highly performative endeavours, notably since my analyses initially prompted me to cover up my dis-orientations and undecidabilities. Only when I reflected on this urge did they function as means to identify my analytical insecurities. The exchanges of analytical concepts and ideas between me and my fellow musickers were limited and fraught. I performed much of the analytical work long after I had finished my fieldwork, through reading and rereading (next to hearing) my source material. Thus, my analyses unearth the inequality in the opportunities for all maskanda musickers to foreground our musical experiences and they articulate the belatedness in my understanding of maskanda, identifying my knowledge as double-and-split between epistemological frontier and metropolis (Bloechl 2008: 23–4).

Maskanda indexes a multitude of 'mother cultures' for maskanda musickers, ranging from 'deep Zulu' heritage to globally normative popular musics. Maskanda musickers, including myself, directly experience (through reference and [re]production) these mother cultures while listening to, and participating in, maskanda. By making all these points of reference accessible *as* maskanda, maskanda musicking encompasses a continuous sonic and aural (re)organization of space and (re)assemblage of concepts. This maskandafication reaches beyond the representations of those spaces and concepts, although they are obvious discursive starting points for all maskanda musickers I talked to. Rather, acts of maskandafication constitute interior subjectivities such as experiences of the body, of movement and of consciousness, and they provoke intensities, sensations and affects in their articulation of genres, styles and traditions. Dynamics of maskandafication thus exemplify an aural notion of self, not as a unified and singular 'given' entity, but as a temporary, composite resonance, shifting in a continuous circulation of acoustic assemblages between listening entities (Ochoa 2014: 22–3) and 'anchored in multi-local ties' (Ahmed et al. 2003: 3).

Deep Zulu and urban Zulu knowledge

A prominent discursive trope in the presentation of maskanda as a funnel for ideas, statements and musical practices is its status as Zulu culture. Maskandi derive their cultural authority from a conceptual distinction between 'real' (or deep) and 'less real' (or urban) Zulu music. They clad allegedly rural and traditional sensibilities in musical formats experienced as urban and modern. 'Maskand is not the real Zulu music', Bongani Nkwanyana emphasized. 'Maskand was born of the real music of the Zulus, ... which ... is called *amahubo*' (2009b). In order to authorize the knowledge of what it means to be Zulu, maskanda musickers discriminate between what is supposed to be real (or deep) and what is 'not quite' real (or urban) Zuluness. In doing so, they also interrogate this knowledge. These acts of mimicry (Bhabha 1994d: 86), with authorizing, discriminating and menacing implications, point at the necessity to treat the knowledge about, for instance, what it means to be Zulu not solely as a research subject, but as an epistemology that is in dialogue on equal terms with epistemic and epistemological presumptions of those who do not know what it means to be Zulu (see also Graeber 2015). Sonic details and aural sensibilities that surface in acts of maskandafication harbour the potential for such a dialogue.

What has been packed and parcelled as 'Zulu' during centuries of cultural colonialism and decades of apartheid cultural policy illustrates how modes of knowledge inscription have been made subservient to the colonial aim of articulating controllable cultural identities. In such articulations, musical and epistemic practices that constituted deep Zulu culture – such as *amahubo* choral dance song, *ugubhu* and *umakhweyana* gourd bows, *umtsingo* flute and *isitorotoro* mouth harp practices – became uprooted. Firstly, they were uprooted physically through the massive migration of peoples. Even if they are experienced as precolonial practices, they were profoundly formed by the colonial encounter, in a similar way as *ingoma* dance is a product of the colonial encounter despite its strong precolonial status (Erlmann 1991: 95–111). Secondly, they were uprooted epistemically through the consistent degradation of their musical eloquence. Even though Rycroft reported in the 1970s that *amahubo* a cappella choral dance song is considered to be 'the highest form of musical activity' (1977: 225) in Zulu culture, at present *ugubhu*, *umakhweyana*, *umtsingo* and *isitorotoro* are no longer widely played due to their low social status in being considered culturally and epistemically inferior. Thirdly, they were uprooted culturally by systematic impositions of difference. Zulu *amahubo*, *umakhweyana* and *isitorotoro* practices have Xhosa, Swazi, Sotho and Tsonga equivalents that are currently being regarded as different mainly because of apartheid policy rather than easily perceivable cultural or musical differences (see also Kirby [1934] 1953: 196–7; Impey 2018: 48). This imposition of difference might be on the wane in recent years. Even though maskanda has been purposefully framed as 'Zulu Trad' for decades, many maskandi told me about Xhosa, Venda and Sotho maskanda (Coplan 2008a; Nyezwa 2018; De Jong and Madzikane 2020). At times, musickers used the denomination 'maskandi' in its old-fashioned general sense: a musician's music that could as easily apply to Ghanaian highlife or Brazilian bossa nova as to urban Zulu music.

Nevertheless, the attention for ideas, concepts and musical practices experienced as Zulu is unmistakable (Davies 1992; Titus 2013; Olsen 2014). Maskanda musickers 'strategic[ally] re-appropriat[e]' them and reorganize the space in which they occur (Hahn 2007: 17) by making them perceivable *as* maskanda. Often, globally legible musicking practices, such as jazz, R&B, gospel and hip-hop, are consciously incorporated in such reappropriations. Thus, maskandafication is a reclaiming of 'soils of significance' (Eva Hofmann quoted in Ahmed et al. 2003), validating Zulu culture as both traditional and contemporary, as both unique and open to the world. This points to the multifariousness of epistemologies that can be identified as Zulu.

This active reclaiming is a form of homing and inhabitation that exceeds the involvement of physical movement or dwelling (Ahmed et al. 2003: 3). It is, in Ahmed et al.'s words, a 'regrounding' of what has been uprooted. These acts have not only referential qualities to a place that has been left behind, but also (re)productive qualities that assert a presence (and a future) of new forms of relating and belonging (10). Uprooted practices, objects, names and histories are regrounded as something else (maskanda). This provides insight into how culture is constructed as a contingent and hybrid assemblage of 'not quite' copies of a range of 'mother cultures', that transform, and often distort, normative or established knowledge, practices or skills in unanticipated ways (Bhabha 1994d: 86). Ahmed notes in a similar strain of thought that 'diasporic homes' can 'queer' conventional conceptions of home (Ahmed et al. 2003: 8). Sensual dis-orientations (Hahn 2007: 17) and aural undecidabilities (Scherzinger

2004: 258) are hence significant and under-researched sources of knowledge, whose non-singularity and permeability demonstrate the precision, inclusion and richness (rather than the vagueness or inconclusiveness) of musical modes of knowing as well as non-eurogenic modes of knowing.

Understanding 'Inkunzi Emnyama'

In order to foreground how aural and conceptual modes of knowing are folded into each other, I provide an analysis of Bongani Nkwanyana's song 'Inkunzi Emnyama' (Black Bull). In this song, Nkwanyana self-consciously employs poetic, aesthetic, social and sonic means to articulate uprooted epistemologies; he 'maskandafies' these epistemologies. Both Nkwanyana's song and my analysis of it are an igama, a presentist statement rather than a narratively structured argument. Both igamas are folded into each other. On the one hand, they are difficult to tell apart; on the other hand, they converse with each other on unequal epistemological terms about what it could mean to be Zulu in global orderings of knowledge. They function as lenses (or, rather, hearing aids) through which we can sense the difficulty of sharing skills and understandings of music and through music. However, they also enable us to celebrate the power of the plurality and changeability of knowing emphasized by Monson (1996: 86–8), Hahn (2007: 7) and Ochoa (2014: 22).

Nkwanyana's song has two readily available renderings, a private acoustic version of the song freely available on YouTube (B. Nkwanyana 2014), and an amplified band version on the album *Yash'inkani* (2009a) for sale on the South African music market.[1] By comparing these two versions, I intend to shed light on the ways in which they both serve the articulation of musical and cultural ownership. On the one hand, this ownership is rooted in, and referring to, practices considered to be traditional and even precolonial. On the other hand, this cultural ownership is in continuous dialogue with contemporary musical practices in South Africa and beyond, such as jazz, hip-hop and R&B. My focus on the sonic qualities of these two renderings serves the aim of making my readers 'hear' the sonic and aural ground that maskanda covers in between music practices that are often musically understood as separate genres. A closer hearing of maskanda interrogates such separations. Close listening enables us to approach in both an experiential and a representational manner the time lag that maskanda musicking embodies through its maskandafication: the ways in which it textualizes and 're-spells' (in sound, words, performance gestures, dress, dance routines) existing and new experiences or states of being in the world.

The acoustic version of 'Inkunzi Emnyama' (B. Nkwanyana 2014), available on YouTube, presents an aesthetic of pure sound. The visuals are deliberately kept sober, yet they are extremely effective in foregrounding the sound. We see an empty studio

---

[1] I employ a related analysis of Nkwanyana's song 'Inkunzi Emnyama' in a forthcoming contribution to the volume *Researching Performance, Performing Research*, edited by John Koslovsky and Michiel Schuijer. In this publication, the analysis serves the aim to identify overlaps between academic and performative engagements with music.

with one solitary microphone for the maskandi with his guitar. This image points at the experience of the lone wanderer musician that predates maskanda as a band performance with backing chorus and *ingoma* dancers. The setting centralizes and isolates the performer vis-à-vis a fully attentive, non-participating audience. The experience of oldness is enhanced by the black-and-white visuals. The video clip consciously seems to challenge the current public image of maskanda as an entertainment dance experience, because it foregrounds its igama sonically and verbally as an intellectual exercise. We merely get to see the beat/groove in which the maskandi moves, and a close-up of his face and mouth, making his vowels and consonants.

The layers of meaning the song conveys, like in Ngcobo's equally intricate performance of 'Asinankomo' discussed in Chapter 5, were (and are) not always accessible or legible to me. I am unable to determine how Nkwanyana's lyrics and employment of musical material affirm, question or deviate from existing poetic norms in Zulu and other South African communities. I am unable to gauge the significance of the symbols Nkwanyana uses to strengthen his igama. Interlocutors such as the translators of the song lyrics and Nkwanyana himself explained a variety of issues to me in response to my questions. With these limited means of access at my disposal, I am in a position to convey, firstly, the song's richness and the diversity of options to know the world through maskanda music and, secondly, the process of my familiarization with it.

The poetic aspects of Bongani Nkwanyana's igama contain many references to deep Zulu culture that profoundly impressed the translators Ignatia Madalane and Bongani Mkhonza, but also posed challenges to them. Whereas I felt that a poetic interpretation of the lyrics from my hand would be an impertinent imposition, I was comforted somewhat by Madalane's assertion that 'the born frees who … live in the cities would have no clue what he is talking about' (2016a). Her assertion made me aware of the fact that my unfamiliarity with the music I hear I can compensate for (or, rather, disguise) through the music analytical toolbox I employ to interpret the music. My ignorance concerning Zulu conceptual thought and the experience of 'deepness' as a form of cultural and conceptual eloquence and authority is much more blatant and much more difficult to cover up with academic tools of poetic interpretation. After all, I am not a literary scholar.

The subsequent readings of the lyrics (Figure 6.1) illustrate the diversity of interpretations of the song as well as the process of submission and singularization of the knowledge of Nkwanyana, Madalane and Mkhonza to the aims of my narrative. The story I intend to tell is that of the heritage deemed traditional by maskanda musickers, which has been uprooted during the colonial and apartheid eras and is regrounded by Nkwanyana through maskandafication.[2]

---

[2] Nkwanyana explained that in this song he pays tribute 'to my Grand Father Deliweyo who was known as Nkunzemnyama. He was the well-known and trusted Traditional Healer at KwaZulu, he was trusted by almost all traditional Leadership (*Amakhosi* and *uBukhoso* / Traditional Leaders and Leadership including Isilo [His Majesty] The King). He passed on in 1945' (B. Nkwanyana 2016d). See Chapter 3 for the close intersection of maskandi skills and traditional healing.

[Verse:]
Kukhala insingizi langqunqa lamnyama izulu, laqala layikhipha phezu komsila we gabazane?
Sengithi umam' uyang'phosa.
Isikhwele sendoda siyingozi singambulala umuntu x 3
Umangabe kungowakho ubombelethe 'mhlane ugoduke x 2
Ang' khathali noma ungang' thumela ngezulu.

The southern ground hornbill thunderbird sings, then the clouds turn dark
As if the mother is bewitching me
A man's jealousy is very dangerous, it can kill a person
If [she] is yours put her on your back and go home/fuck off
I don't give a damn even if you can strike me with lightning!

Damn bloody fool[u]
Sishimane ushela kanjani uma ushela ngomuthi x 4
Damn bloody swine
Umangabe kungowakho ubombelethe' mhlana ugoduke x 2
Angikhathali noma ungangithumela ngezulu
Anginandaba noma ungangithumela ngezulu

Damn bloody fool
You coward, how do you pursue/propose to a person/girl using *umuthi*
Damn bloody swine
If [she] is yours put her on your back and go home/fuck off
I don't care even if you can send me a lightning strike
I don't care even if you can send me lightning

[Chorus:]
Yimi inkunzi emnyama
Yimi inkunzi emnyama madoda
Yimi inkunzi emnyama
Nahlaba inkunzi emnyama?

Nahlaba inkunzi emnyama.

I am the black bull / I am the top dog
I am the black bull gentlemen
I am the black bull
Why are you stabbing/sacrificing the black bull?
You stabbed the black bull.

Figure 6.1 'Inkunzi Emnyama'. Lyrics transcribed and translated by Ignatia Madalane and Bongani Mkhonza (B. Nkwanyana 2014), with kind permission from Bongani Nkwanyana.

In my reading of the translation made by Madalane and Mkhonza, 'Inkunzi Emnyama' narrates a protagonist whose wife has been seduced by another man by means of *umuthi* (traditional medicine). This form of seduction is a form of witchcraft, cowardly and deceitful (*isishimane*), which is why the protagonist calls him a 'damn bloody swine/fool' (B. Nkwanyana 2014: 01'26"). More significant than the comparison of the coward with the swine is the protagonist's comparison of himself with a black bull ('Yimi inkunzi emnyama' [02'22–02'42"]). As Johnny Clegg and Louise Meintjes have stated on various occasions (Clegg 1982: 13; Meintjes 2017: 226), the bull is a central symbol of Zulu culture because it represents strength, firmness and endurance, behavioural features that are connected through the concept of *ubukunzi* (bullness). The protagonist boasts that he is the black bull, but also laments that the black bull is being stabbed and sacrificed in the process of deceit. Instantly after his igama that 'you are stabbing the black bull' ('Nahlaba inkunzi emnyama' [02'46"]), Nkwanyana starts humming (ehee-ehee [02'50"–03'25"]) which is a direct indexical sign of the underworld of the ancestors (B. Nkwanyana 2016a) to which the bull now seems to have passed on. There is a subtle poetic build-up to this apotheosis of stabbing the black bull, first in the very first words of the song when the protagonist sees an *insingizi* or southern ground hornbill thunderbird (00'20"), which is a powerful sign of taboo and bad luck among Zulu communities (Madalane 2016a), and subsequently when he claims in general terms that the jealousy of a man is dangerous and can kill people (00'48"–01'09") anticipating, on the one hand, the threat the black bull poses to the coward swine and, on the other hand, the slaughtering of the black bull himself. It seems as if the symbolic death/murder/sacrifice of the black bull embodies the emotional or social death of the protagonist.

When I asked Nkwanyana about the lyrics, he came up with several aspects I had missed. This was partly because maskanda lyrics are never to be grasped fully, unless by those who witnessed the event that it is about, and partly because of my limited knowledge of Zulu epistemologies. Whereas I abstracted the narrator of the event as 'a protagonist', Nkwanyana explicitly stated that the song 'is about me' (B. Nkwanyana 2016d). In the song, Nkwanyana does not have a wife, but is still in the process of courting a girl, and he describes this process as a match in which competitors can disadvantage each other in winning the favours of the girl. Nkwanyana also mentions the concept of a district, in very much the same way as Clegg indicated 'phantom districts', discussed in Chapter 2. They have been geographically dismantled through the erection of Boer farms, but culturally still exist in the competitions between districts and between members of a district. The use of *umuthi* is thus not only the mistreatment of the woman in question, but also an example of cheating in the match, and the potential inducement of a district fight.

Nkwanyana indicates that this fraud is noticed because the thunderbird is heard singing. Like in 'Sab' Inganono', discussed in Chapter 1, the aural symbolism is more prominent than the visual. Also, Nkwanyana makes it clear that he is the winner of the competition, because of his status as a black bull – 'confident, strong and fearless' (B. Nkwanyana 2016d). An *isishimane*, by contrast, is a derogatory term for someone who is afraid of girls – that's why the damn bloody fool needs to use *umuthi* to stand a chance in the match. The black bull politely warns the deceitful competitor of the consequences of his behaviour (00'48"–01'09") and has direct lines of communication with the ancestors about the issue. In the song, this communication is cast in repetitive humming (ehee-ehee [02'50"–03'25"]) in the chorus responses which, as Nkwanyana explained to me, are directly derived from *amahubo*.

I had assumed that the black bull tastes defeat in the song and passes on to the ancestor world. Moreover, I had adopted some kind of Orpheus-derived notion of an underworld as a realm of death after life. However, for Nkwanyana, the ancestor world is part of the here and now, impacting on the fight with the deceitful competitor.

It functions as a realm of power rather than of defeat. In Nkwanyana's own reading, the stabbing of the black bull is a dangerous irritation and provocation for the feud to commence, not a defeat or slaughtering, as I had read it, let alone a symbolic or sacrificial death.

It is safe to assume that the epistemic discrepancies between my reading of the lyrics in translation and Bongani Nkwanyana's poetic intentions have their musical equivalents in the many ways we can hear his music. Yet, in making sense of what I hear I can employ an elaborate collection of analytical tools that I have practised during years of music lessons and academic training. They enable me to cover up my ignorance of Zulu musicking practices by framing them with my own set of tools. As has been outlined in countless earlier ethnomusicological publications, this cover-up potential constitutes the hegemony of institutionalized academic modes of knowing. In order to acknowledge and curtail this power, I emphasize three epistemic procedures. I highlight instances of my own aural undecidedness about what it was that I heard. I focus on sound parameters such as timbre, voice b(l)ending techniques and resonance as structural compositional devices that cannot readily be represented in eurogenic modes of transcription and representation. I explain forms of equivocality as inclusive, rich and precise aural constituents of maskanda's cultural, epistemic and epistemological authority rather than as inconsistencies or unclarities. All these forms of curtailing academic epistemic power exertions point to the performativity of the analytical practices I have been raised in. Thus, I hope to do justice to the many ways in which relationships between listening entities are continuously 're-assembled' in maskanda practice (Ochoa 2014: 23), and to take less of a 'snapshot' of the circulation of acoustic assemblages between listening entities.

Multivocality

In an earlier publication, I reported that I only properly started to grasp maskanda's close connection to *umakhweyana* and *isitorotoro* idioms when I visited Bongani's distant cousin Joe Nkwanyana in Mandeni, Tugela in October 2009 (Titus 2013). He explicitly stated as well as demonstrated how his maskanda skills were indebted to the *umakhweyana* and *isitorotoro* playing of his mother. The aspects that I centralized in this analysis were those aspects that I could easily describe in prose and transcribe in staff notation: tonality, rhythm, metre and texture. With regard to these sound parameters, I could draw on a considerable body of research, pointing out the tonal, temporal and textural similarities between maskanda guitar and song on the one hand, and *umakhweyana*, *isitorotoro* and *amahubo* practices on the other. Timbre, resonance and voice b(l)ending, however, remained practically unaddressed in my publication, simply because I had not developed an ear for them as potentially structural compositional devices.

Many maskanda songs, especially those in isiZulu style, thrive on the alternation of two fundamentals. This alternation is said to have been derived from the sounds that emerge from beating the string of the *ugubhu* or *umakhweyana* gourd bow (Rycroft

1977: 221; Clegg 1981: 2; Erlmann 1991: 75; Collins 2006–7: 2). Beating the undivided string of the *ugubhu* produces two tones (either stopped or un-stopped) that are a semitone apart. The divided string of the *umakhweyana* produces three or sometimes four tones that are a whole tone or a semitone apart. The two unstopped ones are the most audible ones with the richest overtone spectrum, so *umakhweyana* practices often also rest on a bi-tonal notion. The intricacies of gourd bow playing do not primarily lie in the production of these tones, but in the barely audible overtones that emerge from the instrument's resonator, usually a calabash, that is muffled or amplified by holding it further or closer to one's body (Impey 1983: 10–12). Joe Nkwanyana's mother played the song 'Molomolo Mama' on the *umakhweyana* (Figure 6.2), a cradle song asking whose child this is (see the Appendix in this book). The song develops from the fundamentals B, A and G-sharp. By playing along some overtones of the *umakhweyana* fundamentals (A and G-sharp) in a higher register on his guitar, Joe Nkwanyana 'filtered out' a descending pentatonic scale: e – d-sharp – b – a – g-sharp that articulated maskanda's distinctive tonal orientation (pentatonic or hexatonic scales based on the overtones of two adjacent fundamentals of the bow) as well as its heterophonic texture (Titus 2013: 296–7).

This play with string resonance and resonator filtering is clearly audible in Bongani Nkwanyana's 'Inkunzi Emnyama', a song that he instantly confirmed to me as a song in isiZulu style (B. Nkwanyana 2016b). 'Each and every string [of the guitar] must *speak* like I do', Nkwanyana asserted, in order to 'represent the voices' (2009b). Nkwanyana plays the two fundamentals (F and E-flat) that are central to the song in regular ongoing alternating motion, and fills in the overtones in broken chords on his guitar (Figure 6.3) resulting in an anhemitonic minor pentatonic scale of d-flat – b-flat – a-flat – f – e-flat. As explained in Chapter 2, not only this pentatonic scale, but also the play with resonance can be regarded as an 'oriflamme' (Collins 2006–7: 14) of isiZulu style that is conceptualized as traditional. In 'Inkunzi Emnyama', Nkwanyana plays the upper tones (f' and e-flat') on more than one string in order to amplify them through resonance, which is enhanced by the octaves (f – f'; e-flat – e-flat') fifths and fourths (B-flat – e-flat – b-flat – e-flat') sounding on the lower strings. Yet, triadic sensibilities are not absent in

Figure 6.2 'Molomolo Mama'. Voice, bow and guitar in the first verse (Mrs Nkwanyana 2009a: 02'00"). Transcribed with kind permission from heir Mrs Nkwanyana.

Figure 6.3 'Inkunzi Emnyama'. Motive A and B (B. Nkwanyana 2014: 00'20"–00'33"). Transcribed with kind permission from Bongani Nkwanyana.

what could be heard as an orientation towards d-flat, when Nkwanyana commences his motive C on that tone, supported by the f that sounds along (Figure 6.4).

It is tempting to construct a linear historical narrative from *amahubo* as a precolonial heritage to the *umakhweyana* bow as an instrument that the Zulu took over from the Tsonga people in the early nineteenth century (Princess Magogo kaDinuzulu quoted in Rycroft 1977: 256) to musics that emerged in labour migrant environments in the

Figure 6.4 'Inkunzi Emnyama'. Motive C (B. Nkwanyana 2014: 01'25"–01'30"). Transcribed with kind permission from Bongani Nkwanyana.

early twentieth century. Yet, all these practices existed side by side for a considerable amount of time and influences must hence have been reciprocal. Songs that emerged from the overtone series of bows and mouth harps could get later vocal renderings in *amahubo* as much as vice versa. Still, the way in which *amahubo* texture underlies *umakhweyana* bow practice and the ways in which *umakhweyana* players reference this *amahubo* heritage have found their way into the scholarly literature (Rycroft 1977; Impey 1983; Davies 1992). Impey observes that the structural similarities between *umakhweyana* practice and *amahubo* encompass: (1) the bow providing an ostinato phrase comparable to the constant (although not always continuous) chorus voice-part; (2) one or more 'singers'/parts joining in at a later point (staggered entries); and (3) an overlapping relationship between solo and chorus phrases (1983: 13) in motivic and tonal respects. An *amahubo* chorus presents contrasting material to the lead singer in a lower and narrower ambitus, but within the same tonal framework (Titus 2013: 296–7).

In all maskanda songs – 'Sab' Inganono' and 'Inkunzi Emnyama' are clear examples – questions can be asked about who is speaking, with which voice or part and whether these voices can be heard simultaneously or subsequently. Sometimes these voices depart from each other, at other times they fuse. As I will outline below, this multivocality of subject positions and the multimodality of expression in sonic, conceptual and performative respects ties maskanda directly to earlier practices and validates these earlier practices as culture, heritage, eloquence and knowledge. The multifariousness of maskanda musicking thus underlies the genre's epistemic and epistemological authority. Many maskanda musickers told me that the traditionality and skill of a maskandi can be judged from the way a maskandi is able to adopt the vocal techniques and timbres of an *amahubo* or bow singer (Dlamini 2011b), how a maskandi is able to blend with their instrument as a simulated chorus. Gourd bow players as well as maskanda guitarists (S. Ngcobo 2008f) regard their instrument not as extensions of their own musicking body, but rather as a simulation of an *amahubo* chorus (Rycroft 1977: 225). The roles of lead singer, chorus and bow player are redistributed in the practice of solo maskanda guitar practice, a capacity of multitasking that labour migrants were forced to develop on their long walks from home to work and back. Thus, often a maskandi responds in antiphonal manner to their own *igama*.

The multivocality of maskanda texture is further complicated by the ways in which a maskandi is able to suit their voice not only to the various roles a maskandi occupies (a lead singer setting their vocal creativity against a chorus), but also to the instrument they play. Blending or contrasting one's voice with a specific musical instrument implies the ability to hold a middle ground between singing and playing. This ability has important precedents in gourd bow, and notably *isitorotoro* mouth harp playing that many maskandi identified as seminal to their maskandi skills. Angela Impey has elaborately discussed the history, use and status of the mouth harp for her research into the Swazi equivalent of the *isitorotoro*, the *isitweletwele* (2018: 45–70). She also explores the middle ground between singing and playing the instrument.

Whereas the different roles a maskandi assumes seem to articulate the differences between possible voices and perspectives, the voice blending capacities facilitate the concordance of voices, parts and articulations. It interrogates an unequivocal distinction between voices, or between instrumental and vocal parts. Gradually, I developed an ear for the possibility that this blending did not primarily concern pitch or rhythm, but rather timbre and resonance, aspects I had disregarded in my published analysis of Mrs Nkwanyana's song 'Molomolo Mama' on *umakhweyana* and Shiyani Ngcobo's song 'Siyafunda' (Titus 2013: 300ff). In my engagement with this lacuna here I demonstrate once more the performative and culturally situated dimension of (music) analysis. An analysis is work in progress. It is an accumulation and continuous adaptation of enunciated experiences and observations. In combining these experiences and observations, an analysis constitutes in itself a circulation of acoustic assemblages between listening entities in space-time. This circulation accounts for the inherent belatedness of knowing.

Nkwanyana assumes his position of lead singer in relation to his guitar as chorus by means of the igama he poses: in a descending vocal line in speech rhythm that spans almost two octaves (a-flat' – B-flat) (B. Nkwanyana 2014: 00'20"–00'29"; Figure 6.3: Motives A and B). Here, Nkwanyana really speaks, even if he is singing, adapting to the rhythm of Zulu speech with vowels, consonants and inflections of words and sentences as leading elements in his performance (00'20"–02'22"). The large ambitus of his melodies seems to be consciously tailored towards emphasizing the tonal variation in Zulu speech. He always starts in a high register above c', without using any falsetto, emphatically pressing out the sound in order to reach the high note. Like those of many maskandi, his voice hence sounds slightly constrained, but also clear, almost piercing. This gives his performance an urgency that suits his igama – a message that one should not take lightly or try to ignore. The contrast between the instrumental groove (as chorus) and the lead vocals is enhanced by the fast $\frac{6}{8}$ metre of the broken chords in the guitar and the $\frac{4}{4}$ metre in the speech rhythm of the voice. The layers of three-against-two metre (Figure 6.3: bars 2, 5, 6 and 8 among others) emphasize the independence of the parts, and hence the song's heterophony, in which each voice is audibly represented, because they reach the respective fundamentals (F and E-flat) and reciting tones (b-flat and a-flat) just after each other through their staggered entries.

In the chorus parts (B. Nkwanyana 2014: 02'20–03'25" and 04'24"–05'07"), however, the timbre of Bongani Nkwanyana's voice is much rounder and smoother than in his lead-singer passages. Occasionally, he does use falsetto to reach the notes above c'. Since the chorus parts are meant to facilitate the lead voice, laying a tapestry of rhythm and mode that can be used as a starting point for the vocal creativity of the lead singer (see Figure 6.3 for such tapestry in the guitar), the timbral spectrum of Nkwanyana's 'chorus voice' (see Figure 6.9) is adapted to providing such a tapestry. However, it is important to note that the distinction between the various sound parameters in this analysis is artificial to a large extent, since as much as the timbre, it is the register, the rhythm, the ambitus and the tonal material of the imagined chorus that constitutes its tapestry function. Thus, the solo singer takes on the role of chorus due to his 'tapestry vocal capacities'. Maskanda musickers often directly linked these vocal capacities to *amahubo* which are 'the most important songs in a person's life' (J. Nkwanyana 2009b), and which are purely vocal (B. Nkwanyana 2009b). The instruments (gourd bow, guitar, concertina) merely function as a substitute for the chorus, facilitating the wish to -*hubo* on one's own.

Bongani Nkwanyana's manner of interacting with his instrument 'as chorus' is reminiscent of that of Mrs Nkwanyana on *umakhweyana*. In 'Molomolo Mama', the only directly audible tones of the song are the three fundamentals of the bow in a descending motive B (open upper portion of the string), A (stopped lower portion of the string) and G-sharp (open lower portion of the string), as well as the vocal reciting tone e'. The bow functions as a chorus playing a continuous riff in a variety of grooves that can be transcribed as quasi-dotted sixteenth notes (Figure 6.2).³ Impey observes that in both *amahubo* song and *umakhweyana* bow playing, the lead singer will add variations to the call phrase of the song, whereas the chorus (either physical or imagined through the instrument or through the lead singer's response to their own lead) remains constant throughout (1983: 13). In many maskanda songs this lead-chorus contrast is obvious through the wider voice range that the lead singer employs as opposed to a narrower ambitus they cover in the chorus parts. In 'Molomolo Mama', this contrast between the motivic material of the gourd bow and that of the lead singer (diversified in pitch, rhythm, timbral and dynamic respects) is instantly audible on first hearing (Mrs Nkwanyana 2009a: 00'10"–00'13"; Figure 6.2).

The above analysis demonstrates that, as much as in motivic structure or ambitus, the contrast between imagined lead singer and chorus is audible in the differences between vocal timbres that Bongani Nkwanyana adopts in his performance of these roles. The manners in which lead voice and chorus are distributed among what I would identify as musical parts is a structural compositional device in Nkwanyana's song 'Inkunzi Emnyama'. It determines the development of the song in time. The lead singer seems more important at the start of the song, with his wide ambitus and his

---

[3] As Impey states, it is unlikely that such riffs have been derived directly from vocal practices, since they are too rapid and continuous (1983: 14). The rhythm transcribed as dotted sixteenth notes (see Figure 6.2) is not as straightly dotted as the notation suggests. The rhythmical articulation is precise and consistent, just not easily representable in staff notation durations.

elaborately recited igama (B. Nkwanyana 2014: 00'20"–02'20"). The imagined chorus becomes increasingly dominant towards the end of the song with more repetitive groovy material in a narrower ambitus, suggesting a circular motion around reciting tones a-flat and b-flat (B. Nkwanyana 2014: 02'20–03'25" and 04'24"–05'07"; Figures 6.8 and 6.9). The imagined chorus communicates just the one central message: 'you stabbed the black bull'.

Voice blending and resonance as a structural compositional device

The play with multivocality involves not only the articulation of differences between possible voices and perspectives, but also the acoustic blending of them. These voice-blending capacities interrogate an unequivocal distinction between voices and complicate the notion of musical 'parts' that can be transcribed in a 'score'. To my ears, this blending did not primarily concern pitch or rhythm, but rather timbre and resonance. Groove and motivic development seemed subservient to a distinct intensification and increased density of resonance. This increased density of resonance as a structural compositional device (indicating the structural implications of playing with various degrees of multivocality) was audible in 'Inkunzi Emnyama' and in 'Molomolo Mama' on *umakhweyana*. It can best be illustrated, however, through Mrs Nkwanyana's song 'Mthembu kaMthele' on *isitorotoro*.

Mrs Nkwanyana played the *isitorotoro* with a fundamental E-flat forming harmonics on 3rd (b-flat), 4th (e-flat), 7th (c+) and 9th (f) partials of E-flat. The scale that emerged from this material encompassed three expanded major second intervals ([f — e-flat] [e-flat — d-flat-/c+] [d-flat-/c+ — b-flat]) in between f' and b-flat (Figure 6.5).

The pitches of the overtones in this natural harmonic row were not fixed, but bended through the resonances of mouth, throat and chest cavities. These bends could take up a major second, going from one pitch to a lower pitch or moving up and back again to the same pitch. The shape, size and direction of the bend in combination with the articulation of the mouth harp's tongue constituted the groove of the song, and its

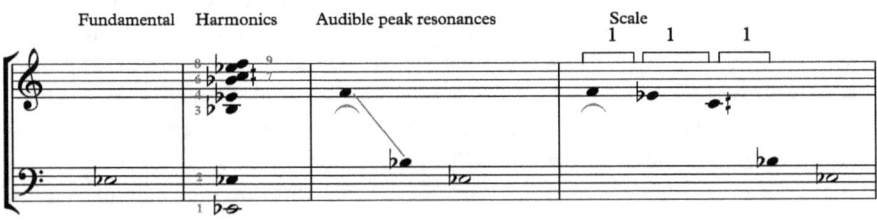

⌢ = bending ± quarter tone – whole tone

1, 2, 3 = harmonic partials

Figure 6.5 'Mthembu kaMthele'. Fundamental E-flat, audible harmonic partials, peak resonances and resulting scale. Transcribed with kind permission from heir Mrs Nkwanyana.

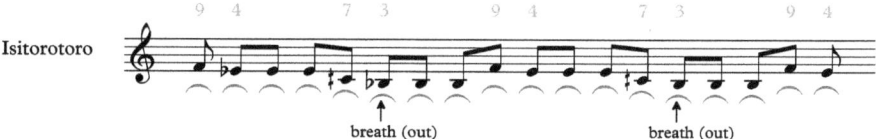

Figure 6.6 'Mthembu kaMthele'. Starting motive sounding through harmonic partials (Mrs Nkwanyana 2009b). Transcribed with kind permission from heir Mrs Nkwanyana.

quasi-linguistic articulation in formants. The sensation of pitch as movement rather than position in Mrs Nkwanyana's *isitorotoro* playing helped me acquire an aural sensitivity for the aesthetic importance of pitch inflections and formant spectrums in the constitutions of maskanda vocal techniques, tunes and styles.

The groove of the riff is realized not only through articulation of the mouth harp's tongue and formants, but also through breathing in and out in a rhythmical manner (Figure 6.6). All these modes of articulation are meant to make the more or less distinct overtones resonate with each other. The development of the song is realized through the art of making this resonance richer, denser and more intense. Mrs Nkwanyana does this by letting the overtones follow in quicker succession (the articulated rhythm is intensified) and bringing the motive displayed in Figure 6.6 back to a core of fundamental/4th harmonic partial (unison/octave e-flat) and 3rd harmonic partial (fifth b-flat) (Figure 6.7). This apparent reduction of 'pitches' is in fact an intensification, not only because the rhythm accelerates, but also because the overtone spectrum expands in register on top of 3rd and 1st/4th harmonic partials only (Figure 6.7). As explained in Chapter 2, this enhancement of resonance is actively sought by maskanda guitarists in their tunings of the guitar and the doubling of pitches on various strings simultaneously. These tunings and doublings enable the structural development of resonance within the course of a tone, pitch or note (which unveils the limitations of such concepts for what one hears) as well as within the course of a song.

Bongani Nkwanyana, too, increasingly shortens and compresses his motivic material that is eventually brought back to his insistent chorus humming (Figure 6.8). Like in Mrs Nkwanyana's song 'Mthembu kaMthele', the intensification of the overtone spectrum is a crucial parameter in the aural experience of this compression. The most compelling example of this is the development of Motive A, when all motives have been presented and elaborated already. The start of this motive (A") is compressed in merely four tones of the scale (a-flat – e-flat – d-flat – b-flat), transcribed in hardly more than one bar ranging over almost one octave (Figure 6.9: bar 2). The dense and quick progression through the tonal material contrasts with the moments when the voice is silent, opening up the texture (bars 1 and 3). However, these moments of thinner texture are immediately filled up again by an extension of the motive diving further down to E-flat and restating a shortened 'chorus' rendering of this extension immediately afterwards (bar 5). The movement of the voice that was interrupted through the thickening and thinning of texture (when he reached the end of his statement) is now becoming a continuous movement, in line with

Figure 6.7 'Mthembu kaMthele'. Starting motive being brought back to a core of 1st/4th (e-flat) and 3rd (b-flat) harmonic partials (with bends to adjacent tones) (Mrs Nkwanyana 2009b). Transcribed with kind permission from heir Mrs Nkwanyana.

the continuous groove of the guitar. This musical development occurs during the plot of the narrative: 'I am the black bull, you are stabbing the black bull, why are you stabbing the black bull?' This textural fusion of singing and playing gives the song its sense of direction and is even slightly climactic. The pronunciation of the words 'inkunzi emnyama' is not only the semantic verbal core of the song, but also the musical motivic core of the song, being submitted to constant repetition culminating in the *amahubo* humming invocation of the ancestor world (Figure 6.8).

The structural employment of the enhancement of the overtone spectrum is also demonstrated in Motive A'' (Figure 6.9: bars 3–5): a quasi-choral response to Nkwanyana's own igama uttered in bar 2. Despite the thickening of the texture, the motivic material that Nkwanyana sings as response chorus becomes increasingly more economical (bar 5). One of the two tonal centres in the song, the f, becomes less important, being increasingly absent from the song's vocal part. It is through this reduction of tonal material and of the ambitus of the voice that the contrast between lead vocals and response chorus is audible, also in a solo performance. The ambitus of the lead singer is one and a half octave [a-flat' – E-flat], whereas the ambitus of the imagined 'chorus' is a fifth [e-flat' – A-flat] circling predominantly around one reciting tone B-flat. This reduction of tonal material and ambitus links the song directly to similar practices in *amahubo* choral dance song.

This structural enhancement of the overtone spectrum supports the musical and poetic intensification of the song and provides a groove to which the lead singer can develop their vocal creativity. In 'Inkunzi Emnyama', this capacity of the chorus is audible in Nkwanyana's 'Ehee-ehee' chorus parts as communications with the ancestor world (Figure 6.8). The transition to the humming turns the song into an integral invocation and even exorcization that will directly affect the possibilities of the evil competitor to act, as an antidote to the *umuthi* that he has used. Thus, Nkwanyana not only narrates a story with this song; he also impacts on the story *with* his song that poses an igama in sounding and verbal respects shaping a communicative realm where past and present, and the natural and the supernatural cannot be readily separated.

Many maskanda songs can be said to develop in terms of an elaborate motive (B. Nkwanyana 2014: 00'20"–00'25"; Figure 6.3) being increasingly reduced to a motivic

Figure 6.8 'Inkunzi Emnyama'. 'Chorus' communications with the ancestor world as an exorcization of the evil competitor (B. Nkwanyana 2014: 02'51"–03'25"). Transcribed with kind permission from Bongani Nkwanyana.

Figure 6.9 'Inkunzi Emnyama'. Motive A" with extension and 'chorus' response (B. Nkwanyana 2014: 02'22"–02'50"), preceding the 'chorus' communication with the ancestor world represented in Figure 6.8. Transcribed with kind permission from Bongani Nkwanyana.

core (02'50"–02'51"; Figure 6.8) as a basis for composition. Timbral (denser overtone spectrum), melodic (narrower ambitus) and formal (climactic) interaction between voice and instrument can be articulated as driving this development. Yet, considering the repeated hearings and rereadings of primary and secondary sources I had to carry out in order to perform these observations, it is no exaggeration to state that these are my creative as much as scientific acts resembling the manners in which the sounding performance of this music transmits knowledge. Performance and analysis are folded into each other as of modes of knowing. They may be using different modes of knowledge inscription, but they operate as knowledge in a similar way in being a succession of observation, identification, selection, extraction and reconceptualization of features. The only difference is that maskandi do this sonically rather than merely conceptually. The foldedness of African maskandi and metropolitan academic epistemic procedures enables me to reiterate the fallacy of Europe's alleged cultural and epistemological self-sufficiency.

Beyond the paradigm of music-and/as-identity

Maskanda's epistemic implications surface on various levels. It has a signifying power, being in active (and sometimes provocative) dialogue with the musical practices mentioned above (Monson 1996: 86–7). It functions as an index; musickers experience maskanda (as sign) together with allegedly precolonial ideas, (hi)stories, names and customs (as signified objects) (Turino 2008: 8). Maskanda musickers provide a 'double vision' to the heritage maskanda presents: maskanda mimics those ideas, techniques, sensibilities and capacities that have been disavowed in decades of apartheid segregation, oppression and cultural isolation and repeats them 'as something *different* – a mutation, a hybrid' (Bhabha 1994e: 111). In them being repeated, these ideas and capacities become reinstalled (authoritative mimicry) as well as interrogated (menacing mimicry). As such maskanda is also a conscious act of what Sara Ahmed calls 'homing' (Ahmed et al. 2003: 9): encompassing acts of (re)creating 'soils of significance', reclaiming and reprocessing habits (singing techniques, tonal material), objects (riffs, songs), names (*ihubo, igama*) and histories (about the black bull or the thunder bird) that have been uprooted. All these acts of signifying, mimicking and homing carry 'sensual dis-orientations' (Hahn 2007: 17) and 'traces of contingency' (Scherzinger 2004: 258) with them that demonstrate the epistemic strength rather than weakness of conceptual inconclusiveness.

Rather than once again attributing a guarding-identity-and-tradition role to maskanda musicking, it is important to keep an eye out for these epistemological dimensions. Bongani Nkwanyana, like most maskandi, is not merely respelling deep Zulu heritage; he is in active dialogue with global sounds and practices, such as jazz, soul, funk, gospel and R&B. Jazz in particular has always occupied a culturally authoritative position in South Africa. It has always been experienced as an aural space where black aesthetic and epistemic agency could thrive, even during the apartheid years (Ballantine 1999, [1993] 2012; Muller and Benjamin 2011; Ramanna 2016). Moreover, South Africa's segregated communities found opportunities to meet each other and music together on jazz stages and events. They felt equally entitled to re-appropriate this US and globally appealing heritage with consistently reiterated roots in Africa (Gilroy 1993). Hence, tapping into jazz does not make Nkwanyana's music in any way less Zulu, and it harbours as much material for the observation of how musical modes of knowing work. This is another indication that reaching beyond the paradigm of music-as-identity is urgently needed.

When I first heard the studio-produced version of Bongani Nkwanyana's 'Inkunzi Emnyama' on his album *Yash'inkani* (2009a), I did not instantly recognize it as the same song. The album was recorded in the studio of Nkwanyana's own recording company, Kora Records. It was produced by jazz guitarist Bheki Khoza. Trumpet player Hugh Masekela and vocalist Noxolo Radebe make guest appearances on the album (although not in this song). The orientation towards (South African) jazz, notably in Khoza's sound production, is clearly audible on the entire album. Although the sound of acoustic (2014) and studio-produced (2009a) renderings of the song are wildly different, the aim of comparing them is to reveal that they are very much part of the same practice. For most maskandi, playing acoustically on one's own and playing electrically with a band are two sides of the same coin, which both form part of contemporary maskanda musicking.

The album arguably illustrates how maskandi seek artistic and aesthetic connections with contemporary music practices that are not (yet) associated with maskanda and that usually have a more globalized or cosmopolitan status than maskanda: jazz, R&B, hip-hop, gospel and soul. At the same time, the album is a powerful example of the maskandafication of these idioms, in an artistically self-conscious manner appealing to both jazz and maskanda audiences and hence manoeuvring within the demands of market profitability. I highlight a couple of examples to provide insights into how Nkwanyana (the composer and lead performer) and Khoza (the producer) do this.

One of the sound markers of their orientation towards jazz is the inclusion of a horn section and an acoustic piano, which is unusual for maskanda. The acoustic piano replaces the common synthesizer, and the horn section competes with the lead guitarist/singer in taking on 'chorus tapestry' roles: providing a smooth timbral, rhythmic and harmonic foundation against which the lead singer can set their vocal creativity. Thus, on the album *Yash'inkani* the horn section has a central position. The song 'Ishumi Lompondo' starts with a typical pentatonic *isihlabo* that explores the mode, the ambitus and the general atmosphere of a maskanda song, but this *isihlabo* is not executed through guitar or concertina but by the horn section. The song is audibly heterophonic in a classic *amahubo* sense with transparent staggered entries that feature almost all acoustic maskanda guitar texture. In this song, however, the staggered entries are distributed over the whole band, including the horn section and drums. The horn section is also prominent in the song 'Iiyabhubha' in which it improvises on the dense descending guitar fingering in hexatonic mode presented earlier by Nkwanyana on the guitar. The song 'Intambo' features a recognizable maskandi melodic bass, but the bass also has a harmonic jazz function in adding chromatics that appeal to jazz as much as gourd bow sensibilities. In the song 'Umona', typical sustained maskanda vocal timbres and equally typical parallel fourths and fifths in the backing chorus are accompanied by funk beats. In 'Umahangula'/'Home sweet home', characteristically South African harmonic ostinatos (I-VI-IV-I or I-IV-V-I) that evoke marabi and mbaqanga sensibilities end up in jazzy II-V-I cadences with added 9ths to them. A closer analysis of the song 'Inkunzi Emnyama' demonstrates that all these sonic markers do not hamper one from hearing it as maskanda.

Although the horns only play in the intro and outro of 'Inkunzi Emnyama', they decisively set the terms for the jazzy and triadic feel of the song. In maskandi terms, they constitute the *isihlabo*, the signature of the maskandi and the exploration of the song's rhythmical and tonal material. As shown in Figure 6.10, the horn section (consisting of two trumpets or fluegelhorns) moves in dotted swing rhythms, and in parallel thirds, within a heptatonic d-flat major mode (g-flat and c have been added to the anhemitonic pentatonic mode of the acoustic version discussed earlier). D-flat is the unequivocal tonal centre of the song, and the alternation of two fundamentals F and E-flat, which determined the acoustic version, is not absent, but, in my ears, it becomes subservient to this tonal centre.

Figure 6.10 'Inkunzi Emnyama'. Intro with horn section and bass (B. Nkwanyana 2009a: 00'00"–00'14"). Transcribed with kind permission from Bongani Nkwanyana.

One of the ways in which the swing of the song is realized is through the tension between binary and ternary metres that also features in the acoustic version of the song. The guitar moves in $\frac{6}{8}$ metre; bass, lead voice and backing chorus move in $\frac{4}{4}$ (Figure 6.11). It seems as if composer (Nkwanyana) and producer (Khoza) have aimed to emphasize those musical aspects that appeal to both maskanda and jazz audiences. This is also suggested by the use of the piano that melodically echoes the statements of the lead voice, in high octaves, adding 7th and 9th chords to it. This harmonizes the maskanda melodies, but also cleverly emphasizes the typical maskanda texture of staggered entries, derived from *amahubo* dance song. The jazz harmonization is thus happily married to the heterophonic texture of the maskanda idiom. The bass – like in all maskanda, clearly audible in the sound production, and taking on a quasi-melodic role in the heterophonic texture – balances elegantly between jazz and maskanda idioms. It functions (literally) in the context of D-flat major in dominant-subdominant-tonic progression, but also represents the alternation of two fundamentals (E-flat and D-flat) that (harmonically) support the alternation of fundamentals in the guitar (F and E-flat). Still, the c and g-flat are pretty much absent in the core of the song, when there are no horns, so the pentatonic feel of the song remains intact (B. Nkwanyana 2009a: 00'14"–00'37").

The studio rendition of 'Inkunzi Emnyama' is shorter than the acoustic one, made for a market that expects three-minute formats, but the structure of the song is comparable, with Motives A, B and C being individually elaborated and compressed in similar ways as in the acoustic version. These motives carry the same textual ingredients: the narration of the bad omens (A [2009a: 00'14"–00'19"]), of clouds turning dark (B [00'19"–00'24"]), variations of these motives warning the evil competitor that the jealousy of a man can kill (00'39"–00'53") and the cursing of the competitor as an

Figure 6.11 'Inkunzi Emnyama'. Lead voice, guitar and bass in $\frac{6}{8}$ and $\frac{4}{4}$ metre (B. Nkwanyana 2009a: 00'14"–00'37"). Transcribed with kind permission from Bongani Nkwanyana.

isishimane and bloody swine/fool (C [01'09"–01'21"]). Like in the acoustic rendering, the chorus (this time summoned rather than imagined) adopts a prominent role when all main motives have been presented and the *igama* has been stated by the lead singer several times (01'38"–02'06"). This happens in the same adaptation of Motive A as in

Figure 6.12 'Inkunzi Emnyama'. Transition from Motive C to Motive A" in bass, with involvement of backing chorus and lead voice (B. Nkwanyana 2009a: 01'30"–01'40"). Transcribed with kind permission from Bongani Nkwanyana.

the acoustic version, when Nkwanyana boastfully states he is the black bull, through an intensification of texture and ambitus, but in this version, the transition is being jazzed up.

The transition is directly audible and hence more delineated than in the acoustic version through a seeming acceleration and reduction of harmonic rhythm in the bass. From a movement in dotted rhythms, the bass suddenly changes into a movement of quarter notes with a lot of swing (Figure 6.12: bar 5). It seems as if the bass is only being kept in its groove by the backing chorus, singing the same pitches in steady $\frac{4}{4}$ metre. This gives a sensation of faster rotation of harmonic material, although this is all a matter of effect, supporting the suggestion of a boast: the metre remains unchanged, and the cycle of moving from one fundamental to another remains four beats. Yet, the rhythmic swing enhances the directional speed of the song, in combination with the thickening texture/resonance of the backing chorus in parallel fourths and fifths, and the shortening of motives in all parts, that are repeated in quicker succession (Figure 6.12: bars 5–8).

Township style and rural style

It is tempting to associate the prominence of rhythmic swing in the development of the song unequivocally with jazz practices. As has become clear, however, *amahubo*, *isitorotoro* and *umakhweyana* practices also rely on rhythmic flexibility in combination with voice bending. Bongani's distant cousin Joe Nkwanyana demonstrated differences in vocal renderings of the song 'Wentandane Zobaba', which he distinguished as 'township style' and 'rural style' (J. Nkwanyana 2009a). Responding to, and building on, the singing of the young singer and actress Nandi Khumalo (J. Nkwanyana 2009a: 00'03"–00'06"), who was at the scene as an interlocutor, Nkwanyana demonstrated township style singing with voice inflections up to a third and very flexible metre (00'29"–00'33").[4] For his rural style rendering, by contrast, he indicated a steady metre with metric grid. The timbre of his voice was more focused, his falsetto less floating, and hence his pitch was more fixed. Through his emphatic demonstration of this directional rural style sound in pitch and duration, those who were present at the scene instantly felt compelled to join in for a multipart vocal rendering. The rhythmical and metrical elements seemed to determine the way in which singers used their voice (J. Nkwanyana 2009a: 00'44"–01'03"; Figure 6.13). The sensation of the groove being 'locked' in Joe Nkwanyana's demonstration of rural style was aroused by the regularity in (clapped) metre as much as by the timbre of the fifth and fourth harmonies that realized a solid and steady timbral spectrum. This same steadiness and solidity in timbral and metric respects feature Bongani Nkwanyana's backing chorus in the album version of 'Inkunzi Emnyama' (B. Nkwanyana 2009a: 01'38"–02'06"; Figure 6.12: bars 5–8). Hence, I perceived this chorus as keeping the swinging bass on track.

Like in so many maskanda songs, the various parts lay a tapestry of groovy, timbral harmonic sound that facilitates the lead singer to cry out, in this case up to a b-flat', and to start scatting motives. In the studio rendering of the song, Bongani Nkwanyana has more opportunity to do so than in the acoustic version, since he doesn't need to fill in the chorus parts by himself. He takes this opportunity that is not often allowed in maskanda, but often enough in jazz. In contrast with the acoustic version of the song, where he was shortening motives and filling up textures, Nkwanyana is here primarily trying to reach higher in his voice in longer sustained tones before the horn

---

[4] Louise Meintjes accounts the testimony of maskandi Nothi Ntuli (see Chapter 5) who also distinguishes between township and rural styles. In Ntuli's and Meintjes' accounts, the generational differences are important, compelling Meintjes to describe the 'fashionable township sound' as 'a sound that forgets the rural homestead' (2017: 219). Yet, Meintjes also indicates that 'criticism of a township-sounding vocal becomes an assertion of a self that incorporates rural, migrant affect along with the urban and wider world consisting of the township, the city, the studio' (219). It is exactly this criticism that Joe Nkwanyana levelled at the younger Nandi Khumalo's singing. In such criticism I see the time lag between event (the singing) and enunciation (its denomination as a style with concomitant aesthetic judgement) as a location of culture. Meintjes, too, observes that 'two kinds of work [are] being done [in the studio]: the work of recording a song and the work of cultivating sociality' (219). This time lag also points at the circulation of acoustic assemblages between listening entities (the Umzansi Zulu Dancers, Ntuli, Meintjes; Joe Nkwanyana, Khumalo, me) that hear each other hear while maskandafying ideas, sounds, techniques, postures and articulations of self.

Figure 6.13 'Wentandane Zobaba'. Multipart rendering in 'rural style' (J. Nkwanyana 2009a: 00'40"). Transcribed with kind permission from heir Josefa Nkwanyana.

section (in synthesized sound this time) start their outro. Nkwanyana sings his long tones in a maskandi way: sustained, with pressure, without falsetto and with rich overtone spectrums (2009a: 03'18"–03'34"). 'We *hubo* that song' (Nkwanyana 2013), he told me repeatedly, indicating that the timbre and technique of *amahubo* song as an outcry to the community is employed in contemporary musical practices as a form of appropriation.

The incorporation of horns in both intro and outro also seems to add a theatrical dimension to the song in suggesting a procession that passes by and vanishes out of earshot. This is enhanced by the fact the intro (00'00"–00'14"), played on acoustic instruments, is more foregrounded and prominent than the outro played on synthesized trumpets/fluegelhorns, suggesting that the sounds come from a distance (04'20"–04'45").[5] It is tempting to associate this with globally appealing jazz funeral traditions of First and Second Lining as well as with Capetonian *ghoema* parades, suggesting a shared experience of indenture between black musicians from the Southern United States and South African labour migrants as wanderer musicians.

With this album, Nkwanyana and Khoza have created their own space of musical and aesthetic operation, because they are financially more or less independent (see Chapter 5). They forge opportunities for artistic collaboration and musical exchange by drawing on a range of music practices that are experienced and heard as locally and globally normative and culturally authoritative. As indicated in Part II, there are not many maskandi who can afford themselves such artistic experiments. Nkwanyana's album maskandafies jazz and funk idioms, self-consciously exposing these idioms to his audience *as* maskanda in similar ways as he presents *amahubo*, *umakhweyana* and *isitorotoro* idioms to his audience *as* maskanda. His studio version of 'Inkunzi Emnyama' indexically signifies all these idioms: maskanda musickers directly experience them

---

[5] I am grateful to Nishlyn Ramanna for pointing this out to me.

through this song *as* maskanda. Such experiences harbour 'sensual dis-orientations' (Hahn 2007: 17) and 'traces of contingency' (Scherzinger 2004: 258) that account for the epistemic strength of this song. Through its provocation of sensations and affects through the temporary articulation of genres, styles, and traditions, maskanda practice constitutes a continuous sonic and aural (re)organization of time and space. These (re)organizations indicate the agency of maskanda musickers to maintain the circulation of acoustic assemblages between listening entities as a mobile, fluid, and inclusive process, even after decades of apartheid attempts to arrest such circulations.

7

At Home in the World

A comparison of the acoustic and studio-produced renderings of Bongani Nkwanyana's 'Inkunzi Emnyama' demonstrates the unsustainability of an *a priori* binary opposition between old, local or timeless musical and epistemic sensibilities on the one hand, and modern or global ones on the other. South African maskanda musickers do not necessarily consider the amplified album version of 'Inkunzi Emnyama' any less traditional or less indigenous than the acoustic rendering. Moreover, the acoustic rendering possesses as much global credibility as the album one. Yet, *Moribo* anchor man Nhlanhla Ngwekazi admits that musical practices vanish from a collective cultural memory: 'There are many genres of which I hear back at home when, you know, old men get drunk and they call you and say: "back in the day, we used to sing this kind of music, this way," and you say: "wow I have never heard this"' (Ngwekazi 2009). Record producer Tshepo Nzimande, however, commenting on the wildly popular song 'Ngafa' (2003) by the maskandi duo Shwi noMtekhala, describes how existing musical styles as well as aural sensibilities are sustained and re-spelled thanks to the compatibility of Zulu and African American ways of musicking:

> if you know Soul Brothers, it will be more slowish, slow jam type of ballad, but in a Zulu way. That's why it's easy for [Shwi and Mtekhala] to adapt to an R&B song .... They brought that R&B feel. And the way the guy [Shwi] was singing: he has got soul. Because that is another thing: maskandi – there is that cry sometimes, when it is a revelational song or there is a cry for my family or there is that joy getting a fresh love .... They will dress in a modern way, but when they get on stage you see they are Zulus .... They don't lose that taste, no no no no.
>
> (Nzimande 2009)

'Ngafa', based on the riff of Marvin Gaye's 1982 R&B song 'Sexual Healing' (Figure 7.1), secured the rise of an entirely new, and hugely popular genre: maskandiR&B (Titus 2016a). As the name suggests, it appeals to maskanda and R&B audiences in equal degree through the employment of sonic markers and production practices that can be heard as maskanda as well as R&B. These sonic markers encompass a melodic bass with an (isiShameni) I-V-VI-III/V-IV-I harmonic progression, tensions between multiple metres, vocalities that were described by Nzimande as 'slow in a Zulu way'[1] and having 'soul' (Nzimande 2009), and techniques of tone bending or producing a 'cry'. These techniques feature both the *ihubo* sound on which maskanda thrives and the gospel sound on which R&B thrives, albeit in different ways.

This sonic material is regrounded in a kind of – what I would call – contemporary South African 'hyper-gospel': triadic harmonies and homophonic church-like reciting styles with motives that are cut up into smaller parts circling around motivic main tones (Xaba and Magubane 2003b: 00'33"–00'37"; see Titus 2016a for an in-depth analysis of this song). Thanks to the abundance of Pentecostal churches (Anderson 2001; Pew Research Center 2006), this sound currently has an immense appeal to many South Africans. Although 'Ngafa' was released almost twenty years ago, it remains emblematic for genres such as maskandiR&B and gospelmaskandi. They continue to constitute much of the mass-produced and mass-distributed commercial maskanda that is heard and enjoyed in most public spaces in South Africa, such as taxis, supermarkets and at festivals. Bands and artists such as Shwi noMtekhala, Izintombi, Imithente as well as maskanda stars iHashi Elimhlophe, Phuzekhemisi, Thokozani Langa and Bhekumuzi Luthuli (1961–2010) work with and within these highly popular musical formats.

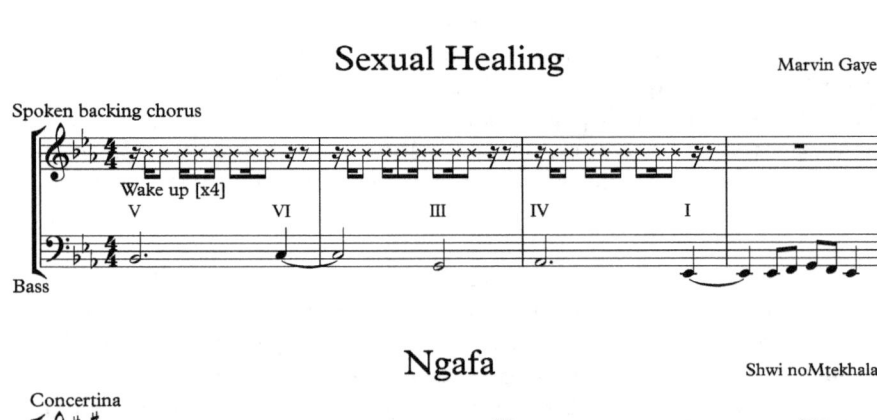

Figure 7.1 Marvin Gaye's riff for 'Sexual Healing' (1982) and Shwi noMtekhala's riff for 'Ngafa' (2003). Reproduced with kind permission from Titus 2016a.

---

[1] In traditional Zulu *amahubo* choral dance song, the more divine and elevated subjects are sung and danced more slowly. Doing this requires authority and initiation and is hence done by more senior members of the community (Olsen 2008a).

Thus, for Ngwekazi and Nzimande, maskanda's alleged specificity as Zulu music and its potential to converse with musics from elsewhere are two sides of the same coin. Many other maskanda musickers seconded this (K. Miya 2009a; Ndladla 2009; Ntuli 2009). They convey the Black Atlantic message (foregrounded in their aural experiences of maskanda) that African music is African music, regardless on which side of the Atlantic Ocean it has been conceived (see Gilroy 1993: 81). It is this cosmopolitan predisposition that I want to bring to the fore as musical, cultural and epistemic agency that shapes the current creation and appreciation of maskanda in South Africa. Even if the overseas stage remains unattainable for many maskandi, they consciously bring the world into their homes in asserting African cultural and epistemic agency as globally normative instead of illegibly subaltern or Other.

Izibongo

The role of spoken praise poetry in maskanda, and in Zulu culture in general, exemplifies this agency. US-American rap and hip-hop lifestyles increasingly become reference points for young black South Africans, and these are often appropriated by the explicit mentioning of the cultural and structural similarities with the eminent artistic traditions of spoken praise, including self-praise (*izibongo*) in southern Africa. I provide insight into these appropriations by providing a close analysis of two exceptional and emblematic instances of spoken praise related directly to maskanda performance. Firstly, I address S'kho Miya's *izibongo*, through which she reclaims this tradition as a female as much as a male practice. Secondly, I address Mxolisi Majozi's rap song 'DJ Gogo' in which he praises his grandmother and employs maskanda sonic idiom to negotiate his position in a national and global hip-hop scene.

Literature on *izibongo* acknowledges the many stances and perspectives that an *imbongi* (praise poet) or a maskandi presents, not only in the renderings of their *izibongo*, but also in their song lyrics. Thomas Pooley, following Gunner and Gwala (1991: 1), emphasizes how closely *izibongo* has always been related to song (especially song inciting to war dance: *izigiyo*) and dance (*ukugiya*), and hence, how praises became 'iconic to the minstrel art of umaskandi' (Pooley 2016: 11). Each in their own ways, literary scholars Ashlee Lenta (2004) and Judith Coullie (1999) describe praise poetry as a kind of (auto)biography. It is 'simultaneously past and present-directed in that [it] represent[s] the individual as a result of his past, while propelling him into the present/future as a figure remade by his autobiographical telling' (Lenta 2004: 60). Coullie explains that

> [t]he subject of the poem is defined, identified, recognised, named adjectivally for living auditors and for the ancestors. The subject is situated in an almost unpunctuated stream of time, from the past of the ancestors to the future generations who may invoke the subject through the performance of the praises.
> (1999: 75)

Clegg implies that the interactive dimension of such a production of presence revolves around a tension being built up between semantic and prosodic meaning:

> These two are, in fact, juxtaposed in a jarring way but in a way that is very pleasant and you have to open your ears, again, and listen to the words, what he's saying, appreciate the cadence, the fall, the way he structured the words as he's saying them and at the same time, listen to the way he's controlling the melody line. He hasn't lost one beat as he's doing it.
>
> (1981: 4)

Pooley gives further detail of this tension building as a form of what Leroy Vail and Landeg White call 'public poetry'. Praise poets, including maskandi, offer a 'stream of comment' speaking directly to the people and their lived experiences and thus offer 'a map of experience' to those people. Pooley provides this detail by focusing on the 'supra-textual elements specific to the mode of delivery' such as speed, control, percussive articulation and carefully weighted phrasing (Pooley 2016: 19ff). This mode of delivery implies a manipulation of spoken Zulu that encompasses the assimilation and concatenation of syllables as well as an impact of depressor consonants (fricatives, clicks and plosives). This impact lowers the pitch and lengthens the vowels of the following syllable, resulting in a generally down-drift intonation that compromises on the semantic meaning of words in the tone language that Zulu is. These actions, Pooley argues, may lead to ambiguities in the interpretation of the lyrics which are appreciated and applauded by an understanding audience. A maskandi

> relies on patterns of alliteration, assonance, repetition, and concatenation of words and vocables to achieve a convincing performance. These articulatory features are their own music. They simultaneously conceal the meaning of the lyrics, which employ imagery that is aphoristic, obscure, or even deliberate gobbledygook. In these ways, *izibongo* place considerable cognitive demands not only on the performer but on listeners too.
>
> (19)

Pooley's account of this 'aesthetic of concealment and ambiguity' (19) is reminiscent of Ingrid Monson's musical application of Henry Louis Gates's concept of 'signifying' as a speaking style (1996: 86–8). Signifying is a provocative, interactional, participatory and hence multiply authored activity of word play and individual statements that constitute notions of internal dialogism (Bakhtin as paraphrased in Monson 1996: 87). Such internal dialogism involves

> (1) Multiple semantic meanings that vary according to and are defined in relation to one another and the socio-cultural context in the present and (2) the temporal context in which ideas are expressed and defined in relation to a history of competing social or cultural discourses.
>
> (Monson 1996: 87)

These fields of tension – concerning the perception of the past in the present, multiple indications of place and descent, individual and collective agency, and the living out of a pact of mutual understanding between musicians, audiences and their predecessors (Monson 1996: 2) – can tell us something about ways in which knowledge is relational and interactive, and how it comes about sonically and aurally.

Like maskanda itself, *izibongo* has always also been done by women, but came to be placed increasingly in the hands, ears and minds of men.[2] At the Kushikisha Imbokodo Festival, discussed in Chapter 3, female maskandi Sgqebhezana and S'kho Miya unleashed enthusiastic responses from the audience with their *izibongo*. Sgqebhezana took time to develop and repeat her *izibongo*, as a conscious signifying practice: for the audience participation to build up. Miya interacted with the audience through boasting and scatting. The importance of *izibongo* at this festival illustrates Bongani Nkwanyana's explanation and diversification of *izibongo*'s functionality in courtship:

> traditionally women also self-praise. Most of the time, women used to be the best traditional dancers and/or *amahubo* lead singers, and they were praised when singing or dancing. What recently disturbed women from self-praising is the fact that most instruments they play involve [the] mouth a lot, i.e. mouth organ (*imfiliji*), *umakhweyana*, *isitorotoro/isitolotolo*, flute (*umtshingo*), etc. In that way, they found it inappropriate to let the instrument go quiet whilst self-praising and continue [with the] instrument [after] finish[ing]. That sounds disruptive. Now that nowadays we are backed by a band, that give[s] them advantage to praise themselves.
>
> (B. Nkwanyana 2016c)

Moreover, Nkwanyana continued, it was not only the men who 'gave their address' to girls via *izibongo*, as outlined in Chapter 1. Young women also attracted young men through the same praising practice 'to follow them for courtship' and it was 'very fashionable to have plenty of young men following. It was sort of a competition as to who is followed by many men' (B. Nkwanyana 2016c). In this respect, Nkwanyana concluded, there is not much difference between traditional courtship rituals and current ones: 'Nowadays it is still happening in a form of Twitter, Facebook, WhatsApp, WeChat, Instagram, etc.' (B. Nkwanyana 2016c).

Nkwanyana's explanation of women's agency in *izibongo* and courtship was seconded on many instances by research into female *izibongo*, such as by Liz Gunner (1989). It points at a growing awareness among musickers (including researchers) that maskanda was by no means an exclusively male practice, certainly not in the early days, as I demonstrated in Chapter 1 with citations from Khoni Miya and Tshepo

---

[2] An example of early female spoken praise is provided by Princess Constance Magogo (1900–1984) in her rendering of the song 'Kwabase sabulawa nguDingane' (Each day we are killed by Dingane). She accompanies herself on the *ugubhu* gourd bow while lamenting the notorious daily slaughter of subjects by King Dingane in the 1830s (Magogo KaDinuzulu [n.d.] 1972: 02'30"–02'55"). Although the song was recorded by Hugh Tracey in 1972, the princess's practice reaches back decades earlier.

Nzimande. Thus, the *izibongo* performed by women at the Kushikisha Imbokodo Festival are as emblematic for the practice of Zulu spoken self-praise as the abundant examples of male *izibongo* available on recordings and in academic literature (Vilakazi 1938; Rycroft 1960; Ntuli 1990; Gunner and Gwala 1991; Olsen 2014; Pooley 2016). However, in being delivered by women they also acquire specific meaning for those attending the *izibongo* performance.

In her thesis about maskanda, Nollene Davies distinguishes between two 'portions' in a typical *izibongo*. The praise passage starts with the identification of the *imbongi/maskandi* encompassing personal information, descent and family lineage. This passage of the *izibongo* is consistent for each song of an individual maskandi and is rich with idiomatic language. This self-identification is followed by a social critique or narrative that ties in with specific themes of the song. The igama of the song is foregrounded here through direct criticism, satire, advice, praise or humour (Davies 1992: 31 quoted in Pooley 2016: 15). D. B. Ntuli further diversifies the two portions identified by Davies, observing that a maskandi typically starts with a preamble directed at a second person urging them to listen (Awuzwe-ke …), to talk back (Khuluma nazo …) or to take hold or grab what the maskandi is bringing to the floor (Zibambe …) (1990: 304). Clegg emphasizes that this must be done 'in a certain acceptable way' (1981: 4) in order to have impact. After this preamble, it is good form to start praising someone else (Ntuli 1990: 304). From my own experience, I have seen that this person can either be present at the scene or be someone important to the maskandi. Only after this praising of others, Ntuli argues, does the maskandi subtly start focusing on themself, locating themself ('the father who begets me', 'the river from which I drink', 'the mountain I can see from my home'), presenting their name, surname, praise name, paternal lineage and remarkabilities of their own appearance (304).

The virtuoso rubs the breasts

I carry out a close reading of S'kho Miya's *izibongo* on her album *Ungcayi Lweqhikiza* (2010) in order to delve deeper into the intricacies of this idiom. In more than one respect, her *izibongo* can be placed in *izibongo* conventions as described above. The *izibongo* is similar for each song on her album, in text and delivery, even if the grooves and tonalities of the songs differ. This points at the role of *izibongo* in a song as the maskandi's signature (see Chapter 1), delivering a continuity in the presentation of the artist, independent from the content of the song lyrics. Miya's *izibongo* is spoken as fast as possible, complying to the conventional *izibongo* practice of privileging the fastness of the delivery over the rhythm of speech (Ntuli 1990: 305; Pooley 2016: 26). She keeps the number of breath pauses to a minimum and they always coincide with the beginnings and endings of verbal phrases. If the verbal phrases are short, she recites them without pause.

Miya's *izibongo* could not be transcribed and translated in full (Figure 7.2), for reasons mentioned by Clegg and Pooley. It harbours instances of doubt, the need for additional clarifications, explanations and reservations. These reservations demonstrate the epistemic and epistemological richness of the *izibongo* in its play with

Awu! Wayenza indaba ufune ivhaka elizoza emva kwako kanti kuziqhauka igagu uqobo lwalo	Awu! You made the news [you created a situation], you wanted to be followed by an 'ivhaka' [someone who doesn't know how to sing], but there came an 'igagu' [someone who is extremely talented, like a virtuoso]
Lalela ngempelake wethu ngoba mina uMaqomboza amajongosi … ngizohlikahlikiza wonke amabele a gqwele isifuba la kubede uhlelo.	Listen very carefully because I, Maqomboza amajongosi … I will rub all these breasts that are covering the entire chest areas and the programme will be messed up.
Ngasho mina ntokazi kaMiya hayi madoda phansi lapho eXXX langiqamuka khona Kanti umfula engiphuzawo ngiphuza uMhlabatshana Kusho mina uMaqomboza amajombosi ehlabathini. Intsizwa engizalayo Umhlakaza Nhlansi Ngubaba wami ongizalayo lowo.	I, daughter of Miya… no men [exclamation], there at XXX where I come from But the river where I drink, I drink at Mhlabatshane It is I, Maqomboza amajombosi ehlabathini. The man who gave birth to me is Mhlakaza Nhlansi That is my father who gave birth to me.
Uthini wena? Deda endleleni awuboni ngiyadlula	What did you say? Get out of the way, can't you see I'm passing by?
Siphelile isikhathi sokushishiliza manje. Ivume wethu.	The time to play [fool around] is over. Agree to it.
Ngisayo kujikijela ngayo induku engayilanda phansi kaNduku esigodi Hee, ziyahlafunya iintambo lapho izigiqi XXX	I am still going to throw a staff [stick] which I fetched down there by XXX Hee, threads [cables] are being eaten there with guitars [cables to amplify instruments, thus meaning busy being 'chewed', i.e. by the sounds of the music?])
Kanti zihlafunya osix mabone umfo owakhalele XXX	But they chew six mabone [common saying unknown to translators]
Ehamba naye osomnyama umfo kandabandaba bayamazi eMandeni	[She] is going/accompanied by the black one, the man from Mandeni.
Injani makunje. Akuyona? Akuyona? Hiyo! Helele!	How it is when it is like this. Isn't it, isn't it? It is! Helele!

Figure 7.2 S'kho Miya's *izibongo* from her album *Ungcayi Lweqhikiza* (S. Miya 2010a: 02'20"), transcribed and translated by Elias Nxumalo and Ignatia Madalane, with kind permission from S'kho Miya.

tension between semantic meaning and prosodic dramatic presence, its intimacy of sharing this mystery with those present at the scene, and its direct, often provocative address of this audience, demanding something in return.

Miya starts off by addressing a second person ('You made the news') moving on gradually to praising herself, and at the end of her praise she also praises others. She urges the audience to listen up (*lalela*) (S. Miya 2010a: 02'20") before she tells us that she is the one who rubs the breasts in circular motion (02'27"), that she is from the *isibongo* (family line) of Miya (02'32"), which river she drinks from (02'37") and which father gave birth to her (02'43"). After having introduced herself she moves on to the actual events that we are attending by addressing all those 'present' in and outside the studio ('get out of the way' 'no more fooling around' [02'47"]). She describes what she is doing and will be doing ('mess up the programme because everyone goes wild', 'cables are being chewed/eaten by guitars' [02'57"]) and acknowledging those who perform with her (03'02"). Miya situates herself as a subject in a classic *izibongo* manner. The stream of time presenting her as a subject is connected with the stream of time of the performance, by addressing the audience directly and demanding a response, either verbally ('Ivume wethu' [agree to it] [02'50"]) or physically ('Deda endleleni awuboni ngiyadlula' [Get out of the way, can you not see that I am passing by?] [02'46"]) In this way, she is also demanding physical space in the here and now. Thus, the flow and presence of the performance becomes part of the autobiographical flow and presence of the subject.

This autobiographical presentation has decidedly female, if not feminist, pretensions. Miya uses explicit female imagery to present a boasting self-praise that sounds aggressive, rough and defiant – features that are generally associated with masculinity. Crucial is her reference to herself as an *igagu* (virtuoso) that does *ukuhlikahlikiza*: 'rubbing in circular motion' all these breasts that are covering the chest area. This will mess up the programme and make things fall apart, because everyone will go wild by it. This seems to be the primary way in which she casts her self-proclaimed status as an *igagu*, and she demands the audience to listen (*lalela*) to it, rather than to watch it, making the metaphorical bridge between the imagery of her breast metaphor and the sound of her music. She also explicitly calls herself an *intokazi* (girl/daughter) of her father, rather than a child – the artist on stage and the persona of the self-praise is a woman, asserting this in an affirmative manner, groaning, howling, shouting and demanding responses.

Crucial in this respect is the fact that the verb *ngizohlikahlikiza* (I rub in circular motion) is not only a conceptual but also a sonic marker of her *izibongo* with the alliterating doubling of syllables hli-ka quickly after each other and the aspirated h just in front of the l (S. Miya 2010a: 02'27"). In *izibongo* generally, there is no particular attention to rhyme, but much attention to alliteration and the use of lowering consonants (d, z, mb, ng, y) and heightening consonants (n, k,) in order to bring melody to the self-praise (Rycroft 1960: 72; Pooley 2016: 23). Generally Miya's *izibongo* has an uplifting character due to the abundant use of heightening consonants such as k and click sound q. Miya is not reciting at the top of her voice though (which Rycroft identified as a feature of *izibongo* [1960: 61]), she uses chest voice with ample low-register sounds (2010a: 3'30"–03'33"), possibly to sound more aggressive and more male. The lengthening of penultimate syllables that Rycroft described as one of the most characteristic features of spoken praise is obvious in Miya's praise (02'51": '-weeeth[u]').

My analysis of Miya's *izibongo* frames it as a female implementation of emblematic *izibongo* conventions reiterating the continuity of *izibongo* tradition as a manner for both women and men to articulate themselves and present their lives, lineages, wishes, concerns and qualities. Yet, positioning her performance practice in this way is an example of epistemological invasion, since I am in the position to establish this largely from what I know about *izibongo* from other researchers (Rycroft 1960; Clegg 1981; Ntuli 1990; Davies 1992; Pooley 2016) and on the basis of a textual transcription and translation carried out by interlocutors of a sounding event that is reproducible and consistent on an album. My knowledge is multiply authored, and my hearing of Miya's *izibongo* is forged into the thrust of the theoretical frame that I have acquired from academics rather than maskandi. My aural engagement shaped itself gradually, on repeated listening to the recordings of Miya's released album, in interaction with my growing insight into the lyrics, and with my support for Khoni and S'kho Miya's emancipatory agenda outlined in Chapter 3. My interpretation of Miya's *izibongo* is based on reading a text rather than on hearing an event or a voice, freezing them in printed prose. It is a compelling example of how written knowledge becomes hegemonic in a global society that prefers written contracts over oral agreements and which has been foundational to centuries of colonial expansion and exploitation.

Yet, I argue that maskanda musickers – and notably maskandi – can be said to 'read' their experiences as 'texts' too, by extracting these experiences from their environment and reapproaching them on a maskandi's own terms through a variety of expressive modes: speech, sounding structures, dress, performance – as a maskanda song. Acts of maskandafying existing practices and idioms are clear examples of such textualizations. S'kho Miya consciously reflects on her position as a female maskandi in a stable recorded 'text'. Bongani Nkwanyana consciously regrounds and rereads *amahubo*, *umakhweyana*, *isitorotoro* and jazz techniques and sounds; Shwi noMtekhala consciously interpret Marvin Gaye's song 'Sexual Healing' as well as *ingoma* and isiShameni dance, by making them accessible *as* maskanda. Although these enunciations may have fewer hegemonic implications than my readings and textualization, they are certainly not devoid of exerting cultural authority and even repression, exemplified, for instance, in the male chauvinist cultural normativity that 'Ngafa' celebrates: Shwi blames his many girlfriends for his infection with HIV/AIDS, demanding monogamy from them to facilitate his polygamous lifestyle. Thus, maskandafication is a mode of interpretation and negotiation of cultural, artistic and epistemic norms in local, national and global realms.

Hip-hop

South African hip-hop artist Mxolisi Majozi a.k.a. Zuluboy (b. 1976) is similarly enmeshed in artistic and cultural conversations between South African and global musicking trends, but from a different perspective: he uses global forms of musical expression as a funnel to present maskanda to a larger audience as traditional heritage. Closer investigation of his music and his explanation of it shows an alternative way of engaging with musical heritage that South African musicians consider theirs (be it globally available or locally marked music), and how they position themselves as post-apartheid South African citizens and world citizens. Nhlanhla Ngwekazi emphasized that Zuluboy raps, but

> I don't call his rap, because he does it the praise singing way, which has been there, I believe ... even hip-hop came from that, you know, it has been there for ... centuries. Ja, he does that style, so I call him maskandihop. It's the first time I hear something like that, but he's Zuluboy, he fits that.
>
> (2009)

Much of this qualification of oldness is informed by the language in which Zuluboy raps: mainly Zulu with the odd English phrase or Afrikaans word. Typicalities of Zulu speech, such as the frequent occurrence of consonant combinations mb, ng, nz, nt, and hl that do not often occur in English, the click sounds x, q, and c, and interpolations such as 'Eish', 'Awu' and 'Haibo' enable listeners to situate Majozi's recitation in southern Africa.

Majozi presents himself consciously as a hip-hop artist and says he keeps his distance from the traditional music scene. Nevertheless, he actively thematizes Zulu culture and tradition in many of his songs, with regard to lyrics, musical idiom, performance style and dress, which he elaborately contextualized during my interview with him as an attempt to 'represent where we're from as Africans, using our resources'. 'We have so many instruments we can explore', he continued. 'If hip-hop in the States made it through Motown, why can't we sample our indigenous stuff?' (Majozi 2011).

Indeed, *amahubo*, spoken praise, self-praise and (war) chanting feature in Majozi's rap songs prominently and are consciously situated in traditional scenery comprising village homesteads and *ubeshu* dress. More recent musical markers of Zulu cultural identity, isicathamiya and maskanda, emerge in his songs too, often presented in an urban street culture that South Africans to date associate with the experience of hostel life. Majozi intensively collaborated with maskandi such as Bhekumuzi Luthuli, iHashi Elimhlophe, Nothi Ntuli and Busi Mhlongo. 'We started working with samples we cut from the hostels, we started putting it into hip-hop time .... I use maskandi as a communication tool, trying to preserve the existence of my identity through the music. Maskandi is what I grew up listening to' (2011). Still, Majozi claims to reinscribe this heritage in his own way. Rather than merely reproducing and sampling it, he consciously retakes command of his own heritage after its exposure to apartheid representations: 'I call my albums' names after books I've read, like, *Inqolobane* [*Yesizwe*] was the first book I read in the Bantu education system in our schools ... I am trying to revamp it and respell it in my own view of society today' (2011).

Majozi's ambitions are not limited to a regeneration and reclaiming of identity among the Zulu. He also repeatedly referred to the idea of Africa and, by implication, 'African culture' as the cradle of mankind. 'Poetry is just an English form of praise', he argued, implying that not only the globalized, and primarily North American, recitation practices that he participates in are indebted to the long-standing tradition of African recitation, but the (colonial) British poetic traditions too (2011). His claim (which is contested) to have coined the name of the genre skandihop relies on this idea: 'I started a genre called skandi-hop, where I mix maskandi and hip-hop .... Skandi is a metaphor: if you're fixing something, you say "kanda, skanda." Skandi-hop: we are fixing hip-hop' (2011). Arguing that '[US-]Americans are very, very limited with their hip-hop' (2011), Majozi sees the conscious employment of African musical resources as a double-edged sword: fixing US-American culture by reinvigorating Zulu culture. The idea of bringing hip-hop, and African American culture in general, back to its roots (which are often described as 'African') has been widespread among many South African and indeed African American musicians for a long time (see, for instance, James Brown, Bill Withers, Stix Hooper in Levy-Hinte 2008). It has historical, geographical, ideological and structural dimensions, which all surface in the South African appreciation of skandihop.

Majozi's conscious branding of himself in South African national media as a global urban streetwise hip-hopper with a Zulu heart accounts for his success. His music complies to a diversity of audience expectations simultaneously, in a similar way as Shiyani Ngcobo's inclusion of a djembe in his band satisfied multiple audience expectations at once (see Chapter 5). Moreover, the possibility to explain songs in both localized Zulu South African and globalized North American terms bolsters South Africa's participation in a global exchange of cultural expression after years of cultural boycott during the apartheid era. It is in this context that Zulu heritage and tradition are constructed.

Granny rocked the parties

Majozi explicitly distances himself from kwaito, which – as Gavin Steingo has convincingly demonstrated (2016: viii) – is often erroneously dubbed 'South African hip-hop'. Rather, Majozi's songs are deliberate musical attempts to forge cultural connections between traditions worldwide, in particular to show the Africanness of global musical idioms such as rap, hip-hop, blues and jazz. To illustrate this, I will discuss Majozi's nostalgic song 'DJ Gogo' from his 2008 album *Inqolobane* (Grain Hut) in more detail, in which he uses the sound and image of the maskanda guitar as a marker of Zulu heritage (Majozi 2008). I see his forging of cultural connections between South Africa and North America as occurring along two 'axes': the axis connecting Zulu spoken praise with global rap idioms, and the axis connecting maskanda guitar tradition with global imaginations of the blues. These connections have musical, discursive and visual components that I will discuss in further detail.

The song is a panegyric to *ugogo* (grandmother), who represents the protagonist's childhood in many respects (Figure 7.3). By presenting her as a DJ rocking the parties ('rocka amaparty'), Majozi is able to refer verbally to a range of musical influences that shaped his youth, notably soul (James Brown), R&B (The O'Jay's) and funk (The Commodores). His historical situation of this music as old music is enhanced by the references, pointed out to me by Ignatia Madalane, to olden-day television shows

Taking you back one two

[Chorus:]
Gogo wam' waw' DJ
Dlala uJohn Patton nama Commodores

Turn and slide nje ngama O'Jays
Ek se ugogo wam' waw' DJ
Sivuswa iphunga le Mr. Min ecleana amavinyl every Sunday

My grandmother was a DJ
She played John Patton and the Commodores

She turned and slided like the O'Jays
I say my grandmother was a DJ
We were awakened by the scent of Mr Min [cleaning product], cleaning vinyls every Sunday

I'm taking you back to the day when the elders used to play
Ama-afro nama perm asading' igel ne spray

When afros and perms still needed gel and spray

Good or bad I'm telling you things were okay
Se ugogo waw' DJ every Sunday
Nangama stay-away agqcok' ubell bottom ogrey
Shay' ithombe zeblack and white
Kwehlisa uk'woma ngePine-nut

Grandmother DJ-ed every Sunday
Even of stay-away [days], wearing grey bell bottoms
Taking black and white photos
Quenching thirst with Pine-nut [cool drink that used to be famous]

Kusuka amaphepha kusala amakhatebokisi

Ngoba ugogo waye rocka amaparty

Papers flew, boxes remained [Zulu saying: 'things were hot, hectic, happening, etc.']
Because grandmother was rocking the parties

uGogo wey' DJ
S'khule sinukelwa isinkwa, si-iron-a amashirt nama tripling
Ngilungisela ukuya emsembenzini
uMalume aboyin' icathulo
noGogo way' busy naboni adlala ingoma zasemandulo
Mzubana sikhula nomculo, shaw' mzimba nomphefumulo
Chess ngizole ray niyi chairs ne-itulo
Okukhand' le khulu, umalume a change iRayban ibhuko
Kwelika Bra Daki no Zuko
uGundi no FK imbungulo usaw' Sdumo

Ngisa gqcokhel' ama-easter ngiphet' ispade

Grandmother was a DJ
We grew up smelling bread, ironing shirts with triplings
Preparing to go to work
While uncle was shining his shoes
Grandmother was busy playing songs from the olden days
When we grew up with music, it hit the body and soul
[XXX chess XXX chairs]
The one with a big head, uncle changing Rayban [sun] glasses
At [or with] Bro Daki and Zuko
Gundi and FK, and the bedbug S'dumo [from sitcom S'gud Is Nice]
While I was still used to dress up for Easter while holding a spade

Bafethu ngikhule ngishay' ibow tie ngikhiphe ugogo on a date	Brothers I grew up wearing a bow tie, taking out my grandmother on a date
Ukhala ngok'gula ugogo ushesha aw'shaye ngespuit	When you cried sick, grandmother would hit you with a *spuit* [rubber syringe]

[Interlude:]

[Chorus:]

Sas'sabhukeli uHe-man noShera	We used to watch He-man and Shera
Ungamazi uCaiphus noMalindi kaNtuli sithi washiwa	If you didn't know Caiphus and Malindi Ntuli, you were left behind
Siya emarket siyobamb'e iLexiton 'iyonake leyo'	We went to the market to smoke Lexiton, 'that is the one' [advertisement slogan]
Ifa lakaMthethwa ne *Hlala Kwabafileyo*	The inheritance of the Mthethwas and *Staying amongst the Dead* [TV drama series]
uLulu Ubuyile, egqoke uwanika ebobokileyo	*Lulu Has Returned*, wearing torn clothes/shoes [Zulu drama series]
Ngikate iMellow Yellow Floshem, Dum-shaya	waiting for Mellow Yellow Floshem, Dum-shaya
Crokett & Jones, Champion Jack, James Brown no Clarence Carter	Crokett & Jones, Champion Jack, James Brown and Clarence Carter
Sweet Job noMkatakata, iverse sengithengile iBhatata	Sweet Job and Mkatakata, the verse I have now bought the sweet potato
Na mapantsula alahlela amaparty	Pantsulas throwing parties
Solala siphuph' inyobisi ne-inyoka zika Magamba	We are going to sleep dreaming about [inyobisi] and Magamba's snakes
Sibona ngowethu uOstrich uKhananda	Seeing Ostrich, Khananda ourselves
Ushaya amakispane ngebrand new leathers uvhez' umkhaba	Dressed or wearing [amakispane] and brand-new leather, showing his big stomach
Sweet Job noMkatakata	Sweet Job and Mkatakata
Hai lezi baf'wethu ezabadala badala bomzubana	Yeah (eish) brothers these are/belong to the elders, elders of long ago
Ngingazinge manje ngoba yazi k'thini	I now don't know what to say
Sesibona s'phusha amatransi itwana	We are now pushing transports [cars], and girls
Kodwa manje yaziyini baf'wethu	But now, you know what, my brothers
Ak'safana nak'dala baf'wethu asikhumbuleni abantu bak'dala	Things are not the same as the olden days, brothers let us remember the elders
Sihloniphe abantu abadala	Let us respect the elders

Hola

Figure 7.3 'DJ Gogo'. Lyrics, transcribed and translated by Ignatia Madalane (Majozi 2008).

(*Sgudi's Nice*: 'uGundi no FK imbungulo usaw' S'dumo' [Gundi and FK, and the Bedbug S'dumo], *Hlala kwabafileyo* [Staying Amongst the Dead] and *uLulu ubuyile* [Lulu Has Returned]), advertisement slogans (Lexiton cigarettes: 'iLexiton iyonake leyo' [Lexiton, that is the one]) and celebrities. These direct references are embedded in more pervasive and less explicit ways of showing that 'things are not the same as in the olden days' ('ak'safana nak'dala'). Granny not only rocked the parties, but also used the *spuit* (rubber syringe) when kids cried sick and their digestion systems needed to be cleansed. In the meantime, 'uncle was polishing his shoes' ('umalume aboyin' icathulo'). These more opaque impressions of past times are supported by the visuals in the video clip, which shift between present-day South African urban images (taxi buses, blocks of flats and trendy shops) and images that fit the music he describes (1960s microphones, old-fashioned suits and vinyl record shops). As the song progresses, the old-fashioned (segregated) township setting becomes more prominent, showing families participating in *ingoma* dance routines and maskanda guitarists playing their riffs. The song ends with a call for respect for the elders ('Sihloniphe abantu abadala'). This call acquires an extra layer of meaning when the white neighbours enter the scene. Initially they complain about the noise, being confronted with a soundscape that they have never formed part of for obvious reasons, but eventually they join the party.

With regard to the development of the narrative, Majozi's rap refers to maskanda performance in several respects. Firstly, the call for respect for the elders is regarded as an inalienable aspect of Zulu tradition that features in many maskanda songs and praises. Like a maskandi, Majozi passes on a message (an igama) with a lesson in it.[3] The nature of the lesson (respect for elders, reconciliation with white people, good citizenship), too, makes him more of a South African maskandi than a US hip-hop artist who occupies the role of a societal outcast. Secondly, Majozi gives an autobiographical account while praising grandmother rather than himself. Like in many *izibongo*, past and present intersect in his narrative. Moreover, narrative and epistemological workings of *izibongo*, observed by Judith Coullie ('[t]he subject [being] situated in an almost unpunctuated stream of time, from the past of the ancestors to the future generations'; 1999: 75), apply to Majozi's rap song too.

The first axis of comparison between South African *izibongo* and North American rap serves to demonstrate how Majozi plays with conventions of both traditions, and hence, aurally shows how they overlap. Views about potential historical, stylistic, societal and structural similarities between (sub-Saharan) African spoken praise practices on the one hand, and globalized urban rap practices on the other differ greatly. Superficial similarities are relatively easy to observe and substantiate. Both encompass improvised or precomposed poetry recited to an implicit or explicit beat. (Hi)story-telling and the formation of individual and group identities are obvious functions for all these

---

[3] Majozi explains that the traditional preeminent position of elders has become problematic in post-apartheid South Africa: '[H]ow it used to operate before: the guy with the highest position in the job in the neighbourhood would get respect. Even when you're chilling together, he would be the one that's talking all the time, and the others would listen. So now it's different, cause the kids are making more money than their elders have ever seen' (2011).

practices. Giving praise to oneself or an elder, courting girls and (not) acquiring or possessing material goods are recurring tropes in these practices, which often emerge in environments with a high incidence of (urban) deprivation, group hierarchy negotiation and (street) competition. It is very hard to interpret these similarities as exclusive features that indicate a historical continuity between the musical practices. Nevertheless, notions of a Black Atlantic culture thrive on the historization of US-American hip-hop culture as inspired by West African and Jamaican spoken praise traditions, serving a range of ideological and political purposes (Gilroy 1993: 34).

As explained earlier, South African musickers increasingly engage with such notions in order to further South Africa's cultural participation in the world. Majozi's rap subtly negotiates a middle ground between these *izibongo* features and global rap conventions. This is audible not only in 'DJ Gogo', but also in songs which lean more emphatically on a US-American hip-hop idiom such as 'Bayethe'/'Hail to the King' [Majozi 2006]. 'Hail to the King' or 'Bayethe' in Zulu language is a song ridden with references to deep Zulu culture in language, visuals and music. Its title comprises an age-old practice of giving praise to the king that is also adopted by many maskandi. Almost all maskandi I know have a song in their repertoire called 'Bayede' or 'Bayethe'. In Majozi's 'Bayethe', the idea of *izibongo* as a praise is consciously thematized, with samples of elder praise poets (*izimbongi*) and an *amahubo* call-and-response structure that is cast in hip-hop idiom. Majozi said about this: 'we started chopping samples we cut from the hostels, putting it into hip-hop time'. It is quite a literal musical expression of Majozi's intention to 'sample and work and compose identity and put it into hip-hop' (Majozi 2011).

Generally, Majozi's recitation is slower than the *izibongo* recitation of many maskandi, because its function is different. He wraps his particular main story and message into the rap, material that in maskanda is reserved for the song lyrics. Hence, the requirement of semantic understanding is much more leading in his rap than it is for maskandi or Zulu praise poets (*izimbongi*). Majozi's flow of the poetry clearly leans towards globalized rap conventions with a steady $\frac{4}{4}$ metre that excludes the metrically ambivalent aspects of *izibongo*. Majozi's recitation tends towards what Adam Krims calls a percussion-effusive rap: 'not necessarily quick', with 'fairly regular and predictable rhythmic patterns' and 'focused points of staccato and pointed articulation, often followed by brief caesuras that punctuate the musical texture' (Krims 2000: 51). As a consequence, the 'downdrift intonation' characteristic of (maskanda) *izibongo* (Davies 1992: 78; Pooley 2016: 23) is absent in many (but not all) of Majozi's rapped sentences; he even slightly ascends in pitch at the end of sentences in order to sustain his listeners' attention to the next sentence.

While Majozi's delivery is clearly percussion-effusive, he plays with the tension between the manipulated speech-effusive rhythms in Zulu spoken praise and the percussion-effusive regular metre of global rap by integrating the lengthening of penultimate syllables, and the shortening or omission of ultimate ones (Majozi 2008: 02'52"–02'54"), which is characteristic of Zulu speech and is sublimated in *izibongo* (see Rycroft 1960: 73). Majozi devotes much attention to alliteration (which is also important in *izibongo* [00'38"–00'43"]) and combines this with attention to rhyme (which is unimportant in *izibongo*, but important in rap [00'13"–00'35"]). This is another way for him to embellish his globalized rap practice with an aura of Zulu traditionality, which enables his audience, such as the earlier quoted Ngwekazi, to hear it as both global rap and local praise poetry.

Blues

The second axis of comparison concerns the sonic markers of maskanda and blues. It serves to demonstrate how Majozi employs maskanda idiom in order to appeal to both globalized North American and domestic South African audiences, bolstering his explicit aim to 'fix hip-hop' by reinvigorating 'limited' North American practices with 'our indigenous stuff' (Majozi 2011). The maskanda sound is a structural element in the texture of 'DJ Gogo' that both sets maskanda apart from and integrates it with the other musical references that make up the song. The way in which Majozi positions the maskanda sound is emblematic for his treatment of tradition as a meaningful aspect of the day-to-day lives of young South Africans.

A solo bass guitar opens the song with a distinctive old-fashioned blues-rock sound that explores a minor pentatonic scale circling around a. The sound of the bass guitar, the regularity of the pitches (a fourth above and a fourth below the final a) and the swing in the three-against-two metre makes it an iconic specimen of blues sound (Majozi 2008: 00'01"–00'08"; Figure 7.4). The alleged antiquity of the presented musical heritage is supported through the visuals, showing the artist's name (Zuluboy) and the title of the song ('DJ Gogo') in gothic script, in sober white on black.

In maskandi terms, the introduction functions as an *isihlabo*, even if it does not sound like an *isihlabo*. It is a solo guitar exploring the range of a scale and the rhythmic and melodic opportunities of a theme. Whereas such a function features many introductory passages in musics worldwide (think of a *prelude* in European traditions or an *alap* in South Asian traditions), the *isihlabo* comes most readily to mind for an audience that knows maskanda and hears maskanda's later role in this song. The exploratory function of this musical introduction, however, is just a suggestion. From the archaic minor pentatonic scale, the scruffy blues-rock sound and the loose ambivalent swing of the triplets, the song abruptly shifts towards a relentless, thin, 80-bpm beat with a chord on f that works as a shock in two ways, relying on both pentatonic blues sensibilities and heptatonic pop sensibilities (00'08"). The f-chord is alien in the pentatonic scale a – c – d – e – g, but also functions as an emblematic

minor pentatonic on a

Figure 7.4 'DJ Gogo'. Bass guitar introduction (Majozi 2008: 00'01"–00'08").

deceptive cadence (VI) in a-minor. From a rough intruder, this chord soon develops into the new tonal centre in a nine-note blues scale, as a chromatic variation of F-major. Tonally, rhythmically and timbrally, the discrepancy between 'then' and 'now' could not have been harsher, but the reliance on blues idiom remains intact. The nine-note blues scale on F (f – g – a-flat – a – b-flat – c – d – e-flat – e – f) adopts the typical use

Figure 7.5 'DJ Gogo'. Twelve-bar blues scheme with changes and *isihlabo* motive (Majozi 2008: 00'13"–00'40").

of blue notes on the 3rd (a-flat) and 7th (e-flat) degrees that alternate with naturalized 3rd (a) and 7th (e) degrees. Moreover, the song is cast in a standard twelve-bar blues scheme, and it does not deviate from this standard in any way throughout, as if blues theory has been the starting point for its conception. Each change is carefully prepared in the bass's key signatures and in the addition of a seventh to the triad before each change (2008: 00'13"–00'40"; Figure 7.5).

Hence, harmonically, 'DJ Gogo' can easily be explained as a mainstream rap song thriving on blues conventions. With regard to melody and texture, however, there are references to maskanda for those who recognize them, and these references are used musically and visually to conjure up the atmosphere of grandmother's time in the township. The most direct borrowing of maskanda idiom is a short descending guitar motive that signifies the start of an *isihlabo* through its quick repetition of tones on one pitch before it cascades towards a lower pitch as rest point (00'09"–00'10").

The *ukupika* character of the descending steps and the resonance of the strings situate the motive as a Zulu street guitar sound. Meintjes describes how, already in the early 1990s, the maskanda guitar style 'distinctly flags the sound as South African in the World Music market and as a local production in the domestic market' (2003: 157). Being sampled, the rhythmically free cascading character of the *isihlabo* motive is cast in the regular electronic beat of the song, acquiring a decidedly metric function in the second half of each bar in the blues scheme, which – in the bass too – speeds up towards the next bar (Figure 7.5). In this way, the motive sounds like an *isihlabo* motive, but clearly has no *isihlabo* function; rather, it is a marker of the Zulu street guitar sound and street musicianship which also appears in the visuals of the video clip.

This *ukupika* sonic marker of maskanda sound is both integrated and set apart in the song. It is set apart in timbre and tonality. The motive contains an e-natural as opposed to an e-flat in the melody of the synthesizer and the harmonizations of the chords, emphasizing the accidental 'blue' nature of the flats in the chords. The guitar part is, moreover, more acoustically produced than the other parts of the song, sounding 'in the front' of the sound production, close by and immediate. Its *ukupika* sound contrasts with the smooth homophonic harmonizations of the bass, drum, synthesizer and saxophone parts.[4] In other respects, the *isihlabo* motive is a crucial structural element of the texture of the song that displays a combination of heterophony and structural polyphony that features both blues (Kubik 1999: 108) and maskanda in very different ways. Apart from the changes in the blues scheme there are no suggestions towards modulation in the song and the instrumental material is quite sober and steady in order to open up space for the rap content, flow and delivery (Krims 2000: 48–9). The melodic material in synthesizer/violin, saxophone and maskanda guitar is presented in heterophonic texture with all instruments 'reciting' on f and landing on c

---

[4] This might illustrate Majozi's statement that US-American hip-hop is so limited because 'they digital[ize] analogue [stuff] and we have so much instruments that we can explore!' (Majozi 2011).

as a rest point, each in their own pace, rhythm diminution and melodic variation. In this respect, too, the song refers to both maskanda and blues idioms.

The combination of heterophony and structural polyphony emerges in maskanda in a rather different context than it emerges here. Much maskanda is featured by cadential ostinatos (I-IV-V-I or equivalents) that are circular rather than functional in harmonic respect. These ostinatos are employed as a motivic riff cast in a heterophony of staggered entries. In Majozi's song, however, the staggered entries have fixed positions in the development of the blues progression. This progression can be heard as an extended cadential ostinato (I-IV-I-V-IV-I), but the duration of twelve bars ensures that the perception of a harmonic progression on the one hand, and the perception of a motive on the other take place on different perceptual levels. This is an often-experienced outcome of sampling. In maskanda, isicathamiya or marabi, by contrast, motive and progression become more or less fused. Still, the employment of the maskanda guitar *isihlabo* motive in each bar, as a repeated diminution of the melody in the synthesizer (Majozi 2008: 00'44"–00'48"; Figure 7.5), arouses the suggestion of staggered entries that features so many local South African popular musics.

Heterophony and pentatonicism signify blues as much as maskanda in the ears of Zulu South Africans. Majozi cleverly uses this double reference to position himself in current national and international music industries, and to create a new and individual sound by aurally foregrounding and appropriating the overlaps between local and global musical conventions. As cited earlier, Majozi regards these acts as a conscious 'revamping' and 'respelling' of the cultural heritage he grew up with 'in my own view of society today' (2011). Often this cultural heritage was constricted, fraught and made reductive through apartheid exertions of power and Majozi uses the agency he has now to revamp and respell it.

Beyond narratives of gain and loss

It is tempting to interpret Majozi's attempt to incorporate maskanda into hip-hop as an opposite action to Nkwanyana's incorporation of jazz idiom into maskanda and Shwi noMtekhala's appropriation of R&B as maskanda. Yet, it is my aim to demonstrate that all these appropriations are part of a larger aural space in which maskandi are now able to move around. I will further explore this space in Chapter 8. It is important to note here that the initiatives by Nkwanyana, Shwi noMtekhala and Majozi stand in a long and powerful maskanda tradition of aural and sonic appropriation and cultural articulation. Bongani Nkwanyana and Bheki Khoza mentioned in particular the early maskandi Sipho Khoza (a.k.a. Thwalofu), Moses Mchunu and Mphatheni Khumalo (a.k.a. Mfaz' Omnyama) as champions of 'playing their maskanda' into other musics, with conscious appropriative agency:

> [Thwalofu] did chorales. Some maskandas are very good with that. They get a church song and actually *colonize* .... There is a lot of guitar playing ... One person who was very good with that was Moses Mchunu. He started to play songs for the

church. Moses Mchunu is after Phuzushukela. He was an early maskande .... And also, when I heard the recording of Mfaz' Omnyama, you know, he did songs from the Zion church, and I thought it was great, not realizing that somebody had done that twenty years ago: Moses Mchunu.

(Khoza 2009, emphasis added)[5]

The musical, social and aesthetic references to globally available musics addressed in Chapters 6 and 7 give rise to two mutually exclusive narratives about maskanda's future. One of these narratives proceeds from the idea that maskanda is dying (Clegg 2009; Khoza 2009; B. Nkwanyana 2009b; Olsen 2009a); the other claims that maskanda's future is a bright one (Ngwekazi 2009; Ntuli 2009; Nzimande 2009). The pessimism of the former narrative often concerns musical features (lack of skill, sound production drowning the heterophony), content of the song texts (love songs rather than social commentary, swearing) and performance practice (moved from the street to an often exploitative music industry). Clegg asserts that '[t]he musical street repertoire is gone. It is finished. Basically because it is perceived to be backward .... I am just amazed at how quickly it has gone' (2009). Many of these maskanda musickers clarify their sense of loss with a paradoxical set of arguments. On the one hand, they lament maskanda's orientation to other musical genres, both nationally and internationally. 'Nowadays there is this kind of Shameni that is being played which sounds more like mbaqanga', Nkwanyana stated (2009b), whereas Clegg pointed out the stylistic orientation towards hip-hop: 'In order for it to survive it has to look at hip-hop rhythms, ... to market itself as being not a relic' (2009). On the other hand, they observe reductive tendencies in which the 'war chanting, dancing, stick fighting, *giya*, maskanda: that's all kind of relegated to a kind of recycling into a new version which is more tame' (Clegg 2009), and that Louise Meintjes explains through Steven Feld's notion of schizophonic mimesis (Feld 1996):

As the sound is separated from its source by means of electronic technology and as reproductions are further reproduced in the image of versions of itself already in circulation, the referent becomes increasingly diffuse .... What carries farthest about the referent is its sensuality and feeling. Though diffuse, difference is made resonant.

(Meintjes 2003: 185)

The *isihlabo* motive in Majozi's 'DJ Gogo' is a textbook example of such a procedure: the sound is being disconnected from the source that produced it and starts functioning as an autonomous referent, representing a generalized or diffused genre, practice or (group) identity. Yet, Majozi's incorporation of such a maskanda referent is a continuation of

---

[5] Nkwanyana and Khoza suggest that this was how mbaqanga emerged. Khoza: '[Mbaqanga]'s a whole different thing. It's a new sort gospel .... It's one string .... It's like [church] hymns [as opposed to *amahubo* hymns] played by a person ... with a maskandi background' (Khoza 2009; B. Nkwanyana 2009b).

a long-standing maskanda practice. It is a form of maskandafication being directly comparable to the incorporation of the *ihubo* sound and the *umakhweyana* texture in much (early) maskanda, discussed in Chapter 6: sounds and textures that emerged from specific affordances of these practices and instruments acquired their own function as maskanda sound in maskanda guitar playing, and became recognizable as traditional maskanda sound even to those who are unfamiliar with amahubo or umakhweyana sound. All these examples provide insight into how dynamics of musical change rely on such disconnections. These disconnections encompass the danger of reification and reduction (as demonstrated by Feld and Meintjes), but also enable musical sounds to acquire renewed referential capacities in a form of 'semantic snowballing' (as demonstrated by Turino 2008: 9). These disconnections also allow for the articulation of an aural notion of self, not as a unified and singular 'given' entity, but as a continuously shifting assemblage 'anchored in multi-local ties' (Ahmed et al. 2003: 3).

The escalating reproduction of sonic elements that were part of the earliest maskanda music took place through etic technological instruments (the concertina and guitar) that dominated musical practices worldwide and have pushed a good deal of indigenous musical instruments into oblivion. The only difference between maskanda's emergence and more recent forms of schizophonic mimesis – and this may be a crucial difference – is the speed and density of the circulation in musical skills being subjected to industrial and computational techniques and global flows of capital. That being said, the guitar and concertina, too, have been industrially produced and globally distributed for many centuries now. The prominence of the guitar pushing out bow and mouth harp was lamented by scholars in the past (Mayr 1908: 257; Hornbostel 1928: 42; Kirby [1934] 1953: 257–8 quoted in Rycroft 1977: 216ff) in similar terms as electronic means of reproduction are interrogated now for the production of African music. This indicates that the process of schizophonic mimesis – contrary to what the noun 'mimesis' suggests – is as much perceptive/a esthesic as it is productive/poietic. It encompasses the twofold process of 'hearing another person listen' (Szendy 2001) and begs deeper engagement with its subject-dependent aural dimension rather than with its status as an objectified inscription of a specific sound.

Many maskanda musickers do not think in terms of musical gain and loss. They adopt a more fluid or gradual interpretation of cultural change. This interpretation pertains to a more optimistic narrative about maskanda's prospects: maskanda bridges gaps between generations, encouraging the youth to take an interest in their tradition; it interacts with musical developments elsewhere in the world, enabling South Africa to culturally participate on an international stage; and maskanda performance professionalizes rapidly, offering maskandi an opportunity to move up the social ladder through their musicianship. These opportunities demonstrate maskanda's continued capacity to sonically and aurally (re)organize time and space in its provocation of sensations and affects through the articulation of genres, styles, traditions and new forms of cultural and epistemic eloquence.

Skandihop, maskandiR&B and gospelmaskande, as well as the interpretation of them as genres that negotiate the features of hip-hop, R&B, gospel and maskanda, can be easily theorized as hybrids in the Bhabhaesque sense of the word: what is disavowed in the presentation and establishment of a stylistic stereotype 'is not repressed but repeated as something *different* – a mutation, a hybrid' (Bhabha 1994e: 111). However, experiences of hybridity are necessarily always ephemeral: as soon as the term maskandiR&B has taken root in popular parlance, a new genre has emerged with criteria based on implicit knowledge and aural experience with accompanying requirements of authenticity. This constitutes the perceptive/a esthesic agency of schizophonic mimesis. Borrowed sounds and adopted techniques are no longer perceived and experienced as borrowings and adoptions (or reproductions and circulations), but as intrinsic features that demarcate a new genre. It is this process that Ana María Ochoa Gautier theorizes as an acoustic assemblage constantly circulating between listening entities (2014: 23) and that Homi Bhabha describes as a Third Space of enunciation: the time lag between an event and the moment when this event has acquired a cultural authority through an enunciation. The genre maskanda itself epitomizes this space of agency and intervention. Chapter 8 will provide further insight into *how* musickers shape this intervention through maskanda practice as a mode of knowing.

8

Sharing Aural Space

All maskandi I talked to were emphatic about the fact that their maskandi skill cannot be copied or mimicked by any other maskandi, and that those other maskandi are just as unique. Yet, as we have seen, they claim command of musical idioms that range from *amahubo* to hip-hop. The tension between maskanda's universalism (intrinsic to the name 'umaskandi') on the one hand, and its uniqueness on the other surfaces in maskandi's exclusivist rhetoric combined with an inclusivist and eclectic use of styles and idioms. This tension enables me to address in this chapter not only *what* is being cast in maskanda idiom (outlined in Chapters 6 and 7), but also *how* this is done. In rehearsal rooms, on stages and in studios, maskanda crystalizes from a range of styles and techniques that are not maskanda, but with which it shares an aural space. In this space, where musickers hear each other hear and engage in a feedback loop between listening and speaking, I participated in the dynamics of maskandafication: foregrounding aural experiences through maskanda performance.

Shiyani Ngcobo told me that 'maskanda is all about creating your own thing, not copying from other people' (S. Ngcobo 2008f). Johnny Clegg identified this capacity as one of the main aesthetic criteria to judge a good Zulu guitar song: *ubugaku* (composition) (Clegg 2009). Madala Kunene emphasized that he had long stopped playing maskanda, and was now doing his own thing, based on musical material that he calls the Madala-line and which he keeps carefully secret: 'My tunings are very secret …. I am not imitating anyone …. No one is telling me what I must do.' When I asked him to relate his skills to those of Shiyani Ngcobo or Phuzekhemisi, he confided to me that he cannot play what Phuzekhemisi plays ('I can just play me') and Phuzekhemisi cannot play what he plays (Kunene 2008). Yet, this capacity of a maskandi's unique *ubugaku* is always embedded in a larger aural and cultural space. Being a prolific backing guitarist for R&B, mbaqanga, gospel, maskanda and soul artists, Nothi Ntuli emphasized that he can play any of these styles, and can play 'to that music [my] maskanda' (Ntuli 2009).

Kathryn Olsen explained that playing your own maskanda is not just a matter of adopting a specific style or technique; it concerns the music that makes you the person that you are. Skills are intrinsic to the maskandi from a specific background, or family or region (2008b). Hence, they are not readily exchangeable or commodifiable. Thus, maskanda is not merely a performance or musicking practice but a way of life. 'Maskande is something like: you don't learn it from somebody else. You are born like it. It is something from yourself', Khoni Miya explained to me (2009a). Ntuli specified this singularity as knowing what it means to be Zulu: 'Maskanda comes from being Zulu. It can't be done by somebody who grew up in another location, because [maskandi] do something that you grew up with from home' (Ntuli 2009).

Your road of growing

Maskanda producer Tshepo Nzimande contextualizes Ntuli's remark, reiterating Bongani Nkwanyana's distinction between deep and urban Zulu knowledge – a distinction that indicates who is and who is not able to understand what it means to be Zulu:

> [Maskanda]'s not exactly about being a Zulu, but ... there is somewhere where it reminds them, where they reflect to, so if you are not a Zulu it's not gonna be easy for you to understand: when we were young as Zulus, how does our father speak to us? And when we have some functions, which songs do we sing? Or ... when there's a new-born baby in the family, how do we welcome that baby? So that's why they are saying: [maskanda] is traditional, because it is something that you *grow with*. It's your road of growing.
>
> (Nzimande 2009, his emphasis)

This sense of belonging also features Bheki Khoza's account of Bongani Nkwanyana's musical skill:

> Why I suggested that you should speak to Bongani [Nkwanyana], is because he breathes [maskanda]. He breaths it .... Because for me, I am half/half. The fact [is] that I grew up in the township, he grew up in the farms.
>
> (Khoza 2009)

These farms were not the traditional villages supposedly harbouring deep Zulu custom (as discussed in Chapter 6). They were the Boer farms where many South Africans carried out seasonal labour. Maskanda's dispersed places of emergence – among farm labourers, an urban workforce and rural villagers – all feature Khoza's statement to frame the hierarchy he poses between, on the one hand, the farmland experiences described by Clegg in Chapter 1, and, on the other hand, the township and hostel environments that suggest a less organic 'road of growing'.[1] Thus, Ntuli's statement

---

[1] Angela Impey observes the tight intersection of a metaphorical and a physical 'road of growing'. In metaphorical sense the pathway (*indlela ezikhula*) is a 'patterned social practice' as well as 'the meanings people bring to their experiences' (2018: 64). This is what Nzimande points at: 'the way we do things here.' It carries the notions of 'a physical pathway used by humans but created either by oxen dragging a plow from homesteads to fields, or by the habitual routes of wild animals' (64). The physical and metaphorical dimensions of these pathways are crucial in the attribution of meaning to maskanda as an itinerant musicking practice, as Nzimande's choice of words ('it is your "road of growing"') testifies.

that '[maskandi] do something that you grew up with from home' can be interpreted in many different ways that all need cultural validation and ownership. Thanks to this multiplicity of individual and collective authentications, maskanda absorbs many musical idioms that are subsequently conceptualized as traditional or 'belonging to us'.

Maskanda musickers asserted that maskanda is recognizable as maskanda through the maskandi's vocal skills. Khoni Miya explained this as follows:

> It's the voice to sing. When you're singing then your tongue translate[s] the music on its own direction. Translates the music to the maskanda which is the direction of your tongue. I mean: your tongue or your sound, your song from your inside. Say somebody is listening to you, he is hearing that you: 'He sounds like maskanda'. You just hear the sound of the person when it sings …. I am not singing you, but I can hear what sound of music you are singing …. Because if you are singing maskanda, they hear the sound of maskanda.
>
> (K. Miya 2009a)

Miya's emphasis on the 'tongue' as the ultimate determinant of the maskanda sound is important. She seems to regard the tongue both as a physiological organ (producing the sound 'from your inside') and as a linguistic concept ('your tongue translates the music [in] its own direction'). This embodied production and translation of maskanda is individually determined and makes you the maskandi that you are. It also indicates where you come from and to what community you belong. Hence, one can only master these 'tongue skills' if one 'breathes it' (Khoza 2009), if one has 'grown with it' (Ntuli 2009; Nzimande 2009), if one has been 'breastfed' with it (J. Nkwanyana 2009b), or if one is 'born like it' (Mija 2009; K. Miya 2009a). By emphasizing this vocal capacity as inherent, although also variable according to musicians or occasions, these musickers imply that one's maskandi vocal skills reflect one's 'road of growing' (*indlela ezikhula*).

Jenkins articulated a variety of ways in which 'the voice to sing' makes a song a maskanda song (Jenkins 2013a). He identified a narrating falsetto voice that presents quick descending motives informing the audience about the story or scene that is being told. Often, this technique is described as a soft, lamenting, reciting style. It is a traditional *amahubo* convention of narrating 'the history with just a few tones' (Khoza 2009), which Mxolisi Majozi described as unmetred: 'there is no real time' (Majozi 2011). Nevertheless, such manners of reciting are often presented in a repetitive loop that suggests rhythm in the regularity of motivic arrangement rather than in the articulation of tones.

A more forceful 'voice to sing' than the narrating falsetto is employed by Bongani Nkwanyana in the acoustic version of 'Inkunzi Emnyama', discussed in Chapter 6. This call is high in pitch with a deliberately constrained use of a forceful chest voice. At times, like in S'kho Miya's music, it can be minutely flat for equal-temperament ears. The lead vocal entry of almost all maskanda songs starts in this way, either with a powerful entry on the high reciting tone ('Inkunzi Emnyama' [B. Nkwanyana 2014: 00'20"], 'Asinankomo' [S. Ngcobo 2010d: 00'47"], 'Ngilobole' [S. Miya 2010b: 00'40"]) or with rhythmic activity in lower registers in order to launch the voice into its cry (such as in Ngcobo's 'Siyafunda' [see Titus 2013: 300] or S'kho Miya's 'Sithi Khuzani' [S. Miya 2010a: 00'29"]). The peculiarity of this sustained vocal timbre distinguishes maskanda from the elaborate voice inflections of US-American 'black' musics, such as gospel and R&B.

Maskandi often employ *amahubo* and isiBhaca 'voices to sing' to assert their traditionality (see Chapter 2). Bongani Nkwanyana explained the spiritual importance of such vocal techniques. He was able to connect directly with the ancestor world through his ehee-responses in the chorus parts of both solo acoustic and album versions of his 'Inkunzi Emnyama' (B. Nkwanyana 2014: 02'50"–03'25"). He explained that this practice was directly derived from the *amahubo* convention to start singing and end up humming in order to come closer to the *amadlozi* (ancestors) (B. Nkwanyana 2016a). Jenkins also demonstrated the deep resonating humming voice which occurs in solo and chorus settings. The timbre is in many ways comparable to the sustained cry of the solo maskandi, but through the multipart singing, the parallel fourth and fifth harmonies further expand the overtone spectrum of the timbre, locking the sound into its pitch and rhythm as one sonic event (Jenkins 2013a). Louise Meintjes describes this vocal technique with great precision and comprehension as 'the unwavering voice' in her book about *ingoma* dance (Meintjes 2017: 62–91).

Grammaticalizations of the voice

Such vocal techniques function as test cases for one's understanding of a range of traditions that are experienced through sound. I realized this when I attempted to approach the timbral spectrum of S'kho Miya's voice, who taught me the backing choruses of some of her songs. During one of the rehearsals in Durban's Stable Theatre, I managed to produce a sustained cry by putting more pressure and volume on my vocal cords, and by searching for the 'pulsating resonance' in the fourths I sang in harmony with Miya in the backing chorus of her song 'Sithi Khuzani' (S. Miya 2009a: 00'21"–00'33"). Miya was so delighted that she went to fetch people from the street to show them I could do it. Having read the academic retracings of maskanda's musical features to Zulu musical heritage (discussed in Chapter 6 and Titus 2013), I assumed that I was finally able to produce a marker of Zulu heritage. Zuluness, however, was not an issue for the hastily fetched audience. Thabani Mahlobo, a man I came to know as Albert, testified to that: 'There is no difference in culture. You listen and then you sing. Good. Good. Your skin is white, and my skin is dark, but still another colour than S'kho's skin, but if we cut ourselves it's all the same blood' (Mahlobo 2009; see also Titus 2019).[2]

Rather than reducing this vocal skill to a marker of Zuluness, whatever that may be, I theorize it in more general terms as a marker of eloquence. In her book about listening and knowledge in nineteenth-century Colombia, Ochoa addresses the

---

[2] I have employed Mahlobo's comments in an earlier publication (Titus 2019: 10ff) with the specific aim to outline modes of musical dwelling and sonic territorialization.

requirement of eloquence among the Colombian upper classes, and notably its vocal dimensions as a training of the voice to 'guarantee a proper relation between voicing [and] pronunciation ... in order to produce a desired political idea of the person' (2014: 18). She specifies this 'grammaticalization of the voice' as an aspect of a culture focused on literacy and on eurogenic philosophical demands of distinguishing man from animals and spirits. I think, however, that there are more forms of vocal eloquence that have an equally important function in producing 'a desired political idea of the person' without any concern of (eurogenic) ideas of anthropocentrism and literacy. My vocal eloquence of singing the backing chorus of 'Sithi Khuzani' with a sustained cry and a pulsating resonance indicated that I could '*hubo* the song' (B. Nkwanyana 2013) – I shared a cultural understanding of what was being stated through the igama of the song in word, sound and gesture (see also Coplan 1993b: 42 for the demonstration of eloquence through its embodiment in song). It is this sharing of understanding that I want to address in greater detail.

The rehearsal room, the stage and the studio are spaces that can easily be considered as cultural impositions of global capital. They can be explained as what Ochoa calls 'technologies of the legible [that] made and still make sound circulation possible' (2014: 7). They can be opposed to the spaces in which maskanda is said to have sounded when it emerged: en route from village to town, in hostels, on Boer farms, in village kraals, at banks of rivers. Many studio and stage performances of maskanda consciously (re)produce those 'original' spaces, through the scenic constructions in videos,[3] the *ubeshu* or *umbaselwa* dress on stage, and also through sonic markers identified in Chapter 6. Grammaticalizations of the voice and the development of specific forms of sonic eloquence are central to such (re)productions. Rehearsal room, stage and studio facilitate and affect the affordances of maskanda musickers to hear each other hear, to participate in a feedback loop between listening and speaking/singing/playing and to shape forms of sonic eloquence as (re)groundings of what has been uprooted. In Part II, I have indicated that access to, and employment of, one of these spaces depends on access to the other(s). In this chapter, I address the sonic and aural implications of the mutual co-dependency of rehearsal room, stage and studio. The outlining of these implications demonstrates the importance of combined scholarly attention for 'interdisciplinary studies of music and identity' and 'close readings of music works and performances' (Monson 1996: 3).

Beyond binaries of inclusion and exclusion

I address these sonic and aural implications by discussing my participation in S'kho Miya's song 'Sithi Khuzani', on stage and in rehearsals. I relate these observations to a

---

[3] See, among many other examples, the songs 'Imbizo' (Z. and K. Mnyandu 1989), 'Lolo sizi olungaka' (Khumalo 1995), 'Imali' (Xaba and Magubane 2003a), 'Ngafa' (Xaba and Magubane 2003b) and 'Hail to the King' (Majozi 2006).

close listening of the studio-produced and recorded rendering of 'Sithi Khuzani' that Miya intends to sell as a commercial product and as a showpiece for the launch of a sustainable national and international musical career. There are several sonic features in rehearsal, stage and album situations that provide information about the various ways in which maskanda is in constant dialogue with musical achievements and ideas elsewhere (both geographically and historically). This accounts for the exclusivist rhetoric that maskandi adopt in their inclusive and eclectic music practices. Maskanda shares an aural space with numerous kinds of musics, and it articulates its own forms of eloquence, its own voice grammar, its own sound production and its own engagement with riffs and grooves through this sharing. Such articulations result in many forms of maskanda practice that are not always directly comparable and could not all be covered in this book.

I draw on rehearsals I participated in of S'kho Miya and her Abagqugquzeli Band (later renamed Khombisile Band) in September and October 2008, and in July and August 2009 in the Stable Theatre in Durban (S. Miya 2008b). I also draw on the performance of 'Sithi Khuzani' I participated in at the Kushikisha Imbokodo Festival on 30 August 2009 at the BAT Centre in Durban (S. Miya 2009a) (see Chapter 3). Finally, I draw on the studio production of this song, which I neither participated in nor attended, for the album *Ungcayi Lweqhikiza*, released in 2010 by Sagiya Productions in Johannesburg (S. Miya 2010a).

I choose 'Sithi Khuzani' for analysis because its 'maskanda status' is contested. Khoni Miya asserted that the song is 'not maskande', and S'kho Miya seconded this, yet I analyse it as a maskanda song, since I heard it as such. This serves my aim of demonstrating how maskanda's status as a genre depends on the sharing of an aural space with what is not maskanda. I also aim to highlight the role of foregrounding aural experiences, in spoken discourses, musical performances and academic writings, in the articulation of maskanda as a genre. Musicians adopt techniques and styles that they classify today as maskande, but in the past as afro-maskande or gospelmaskande, or as afropop, afrojazz or mbaqanga. The analytical observations of the versions of the song, by me and my fellow musickers, are temporarily valid enunciations of social and sonic events. They are performative acts as much as the sounding renderings of the song, and in no way final dissections of autonomous 'works'. Yet, they have the capacity of taking a 'snapshot', presenting their temporary validity as ultimate (academic) knowledge.[4]

'Sithi Khuzani' is cast in a hexatonic mode with a melodic bass and intricate descending motives in picking style (*ukupika*) on two guitars. On her album, S'kho Miya includes an elaborate *izibongo*. Her vocal techniques in particular pay tribute to traditional forms of eloquence, audible in register, melodic shape and notably timbre. Miya 'guarantee[s] a proper relation between voicing [and] pronunciation ... in order to produce a desired political idea of the person' (Ochoa 2014: 18): her igama

---

[4] In this context it is important to note that Miya is presently not involved in maskanda performance. The live performances and the album she is working on she categorized as afropop, 'not maskande' (S. Miya 2018).

is a classic maskanda outcry, being arch-formed, with rhythmical movement in the lower start and ending passages, being sustained at the top note (S. Miya 2010a: 00'28"–00'36"; Figure 8.1) and being directional and pressured in timbral respect. At the end of each longer tone, Miya inflects her voice, sliding from her reciting tone f', to her starting tone c' with small melodic embellishments that are reminiscent of Mrs Nkwanyana singing accompanied by the *umakhweyana* gourd bow (Mrs Nkwanyana 2009a: 00'10"–00'58"; see Figure 6.2).

Miya's sustained cry is musically and dramatically relevant in the outcry of '-ma-a-ma' denoting a lady that is being excluded from the community, because of her gossip (see the lyrics in the Appendix). Like all maskandi songs, the statement is a message with a lesson: remember that all people are like other people ('Umuntu uya fana nabanye 'bantu'), a Zulu rendering of the Xhosa proverb 'Ubuntu ungamntu ngabanye abantu'. The backing chorus has a similar sustained timbral spectrum as the lead voice, that is enhanced by the parallel fourth harmonies on the longer tones (S. Miya 2010a: 01'12") on 'khuza-a-ni'. The harmonies boost the timbral spectre of the tones, expanding the sound in range and dynamics. Moreover, due to the constrained vocal technique, the harmonies sound in pulsations that are reminiscent of Mahlatini's *ibhodlo* technique (Meintjes 2003: 226), discussed in Chapter 3.

However, apparently, there are ways in which 'Sithi Khuzani' does not appeal to the traditions that maskanda is supposed to recreate and reproduce. The song is obviously not cast in isiZulu style. It is hard, if not contrived, to hear the melodic prominence of two fundamentals that may be said to underlay the hexatonic mode: A-flat and B-flat (during the rehearsals) or F and G (on the album, being performed a minor third lower). Since these fundamentals do not alternate, they suggest a unitary tonal centre on A-flat (in rehearsal) or F (on the album), rather than a bi-tonal one. The bass riff

Figure 8.1 'Sithi Khuzani'. Melodic shape of the lead voice (S. Miya 2010a: 00'28"–00'36"). Transcribed with kind permission from S'kho Miya.

Figure 8.2 'Sithi Khuzani'. Bass riff (S. Miya 2008b). Transcribed with kind permission from S'kho Miya.

moves conveniently between an a-flat (or f) as tonic and an e-flat (or c) as dominant (Figure 8.2; see also Figure 4.7).

Yet, there are many songs with one tonal centre that are unequivocally experienced as maskanda, such as Phuzekhemisi's song 'Imbizo' (in B-major) or Shwi noMtekhala's 'Ngafa' (in A-major; see Figure 7.1). Moreover, there is a suggestion of (or sonic reference to) the alternation between fundamentals in the guitar parts in rehearsal, stage and studio versions of 'Sithi Khuzani' (Figure 8.3). In all renderings, the guitarist 'plays with' these motives by chromatizing them. Chromatic sensibilities are not exceptional in isiZulu styles if the mode is based on fundamentals that are a semitone rather than a whole tone apart (see Chapter 6). Again, chromaticism can be heard as a sonic reference to traditional soundscapes. However, the chromatic excursions that the guitarist displays in 'Sithi Khuzani' do not belong to an imagined overtone series of the bow that fit the mode, and the motives are not limited to the alternation of two fundamentals, but occur on various pitches (see also Figure 8.5). Hence, the guitarist is using bow-derived idiom in his own maskandi way, which implies that the alternation of tones has become an independent feature of maskanda idiom itself. It can be viewed as another example of schizophonic mimesis (Feld 1996), and as a process in which a musical event acquires an added enunciated cultural function in becoming self-referential on top of its referencing potential to gourd bow traditionality. This is an example of what Turino describes as 'semantic snowballing' (2008: 9).

I do not know whether the doubtful maskanda status of 'Sithi Khuzani' in the eyes of some maskanda musickers is due to these modal and motivic aspects of the music.

Figure 8.3 'Sithi Khuzani'. Guitar motives suggesting an alternation between two adjacent tones with chromatic additions (S. Miya 2008b). Transcribed with kind permission from S'kho Miya.

My inclination to regard this doubtful status as a problem is illustrative of the binary thought patterns in which I have been raised. This inclination points, once again, at the performative character of my analyses.

Another example of problems that arose from my binary frames of reference was my strict aural separation between programmed and live rhythm sections. I was inclined to describe the programmed rhythm sections as mechanistic, constraining maskanda's metrically ambiguous sensibilities. I appreciated the live rhythm sections, by contrast, as being capable of accounting for those sensibilities (see also Olsen 2014: 58ff). Some aspects of the percussion on the album version of 'Sithi Khuzani' have been programmed. These include the hi-hat in sixteenth notes, a snare drum with eighth notes on the second half of every other quarter note, and a synthesizer motive that presses the song in a firm rhythmical and modal grid (Figure 8.5). Nevertheless, the rhythmical and metrical ambiguities are not drowned by the programming. On the contrary, they enable the musicians to work around the beat on their own terms. As becomes clear in Figure 4.7, the placement of the dance steps, the dotted rhythm in the bass and the variation in the use of syncopated and triplet rhythms by the guitar demonstrate how the musicians are comfortably locked together in the same groove, while they take rhythmical liberties that make the song swing. The chromatic sliding of the guitars (Figures 8.3 and 8.4) enhances the feeling of being free and directed simultaneously (S. Miya 2010a: 01'26"–01'46").

In staff notation this swing becomes manifest in an unclassifiability with regard to dotted and triplet rhythms. This representational binary, too, is deceptive. All these binaries (*either* dotted *or* triplet rhythms, *either* double *or* triple metre, *either* programmed *or* live percussion, *either* tonal *or* bi-tonal) shaped my aural predisposition to use potentially derogatory qualifications such as 'undecided' or 'ambiguous' to describe 'Sithi Khuzani'. In the past, these qualifications facilitated the strict separation between colonizers and the colonized, and currently they reproduce this separation in the rifts between my aural predispositions and foregroundings, and those of my fellow musickers.

In rehearsal rooms, studios and on stages as global 'technologies of the legible' (Ochoa 2014), maskanda musickers bend along with, as well as interrogate, those rifts. One particularly domineering globally legible technology is the electric amplification that became an inalienable aspect of maskanda when Phuzushukela first accessed South African industries and media in the mid-twentieth century. Sazi Dlamini values this development as a 'rockification of maskanda':

> [T]his is basically acoustic music. But once it gets tampered on, even on stage, maskanda never ever sounds nice …. It drowns out the soloistic anchoring of the craft … [the] mastery of instruments …. Maskandi is a solo person – an instrumentalist … One person. [And their] story. Which may be echoed in a vocal chorus – not with any other instruments – a vocal chorus, and quietly without

amplification. That's why Shiyani [Ngcobo] goes down well when he's playing alone …. Then you can hear the finger work, and hear how intricate the voice, and the slidings, you know: all that! So, this [amplified staging] is like alienating the music. And that's [why] in this setting, it's only … it's echoing all the abominations that have happened to the craft, because of the studio production … it's just echoing that. [Long silence] Rockification of maskanda.

(2011b)

Dlamini is not alone in observing that maskandi's attempts to mimic an amplified studio sound on stage undermine the craftsmanship of the genre. Bongani Nkwanyana complains that, through these attempts, contemporary maskanda sounds more like (homophonic) mbaqanga: 'Their guitar is clumsy. The skill of the instrument has deteriorated beyond recognition' (2009b). Phuzekhemisi warns that 'instruments can kill one another' in the sound production (Mnyandu 2009). Joe Nkwanyana notes that 'a band is like a hiding bush for lots of people' (2009b). Producer Lichaba Nthethe indicates how the sound ideal from the studio is rooted in artistic indifference: 'I went to a couple of recording sessions where a guy would record a fourteen-track album in a day! And that for me was, like, shocking … and the engineer would be sitting on the other side, and he doesn't care about the quality' (Nthethe 2011).

Many musickers observe that this lack of artistic commitment is often compensated for by an aesthetic ideal of loudness that, moreover, suits the occasion of dancing that became part and parcel of maskanda when it turned from a solo

Figure 8.4a 'Sithi Khuzani'. Reservoir of motives employed by Guitar 2 in texturing the song (S. Miya 2008b, 2010a). Transcribed with kind permission from S'kho Miya.

practice into a band practice. Since artistic access to the stage depends so much on access to the studio, the social status of having recorded an album makes aesthetic ideals from the studios normative on stages. During his tour in the Netherlands, even Shiyani Ngcobo himself, the master of intricate guitar picking, demanded the sound producers at Utrecht's world music stage RASA boost the volume of bass and drums, against their advice and approaching an aural pain barrier for the audience (S. Ngcobo 2010c).

'Sithi Khuzani''s instrumentation on the Kushikisha Imbokodo Festival stage largely overlapped with the song's rendering on the album *Ungcayi Lweqhikiza*: lead vocals, backing chorus, two guitars, bass, drums and (on the album) a synthesizer. The sound production on the festival stage, however, was dramatically different from the album, and in an outright paradoxical way: the (formerly studio-enabled) amplification was implemented on stage, but not in the studio recording of the song. This indicates that the amplified sound ideal has acquired its own dimension of schizophonic mimesis (Feld 1996). The sound production on stage suffered demonstrably from the amplified sound ideal resulting in a complete drowning of the guitar picking (S. Miya 2009a). The production on the album, however, is transparent and multilayered, giving room to guitar picking, to vocal intricacies in lead voice and backing chorus, and to the interaction of various instrumentalists (S. Miya 2010a).

The bass on the album rendering of 'Sithi Khuzani' is barely audible. Instead, the second guitar (being more strongly amplified than the first guitar) takes on the role of a melodic bass. It plays the characteristic motives that alternate pairs of tones (Figure 8.3). It sets the groove by hovering in between duplet syncopated and triplet rhythms. It also harmonizes the melodies through its chromatic sliding. The guitarists draw from a reservoir of motives (Figures 8.4a and 8.4b) that are to some extent similar to each other. The variation in the employment of these motives lies in what they are contrasted with: the verse and chorus parts of the singers. In an ever-changing constellation of parts, this enables a heterophonic texture with each part reaching the same note at their own discretion (see square brackets in Figure 8.5).

Figure 8.4b 'Sithi Khuzani'. Reservoir of motives employed by Guitar 1 in texturing the song (S. Miya 2008b, 2010a). Transcribed with kind permission from S'kho Miya.

Figure 8.5 'Sithi Khuzani'. Ways in which guitarists set their material against lead singer's verse, enabling a heterophonic texture. Transcribed with kind permission from S'kho Miya.

The rehearsal room as a space of intervention

These descriptions and notations of stage and studio performance provide some insight into the processual aspects of maskandafication, but they are better suited to visually represent results than operations. Such operations of maskandafication (*how* are experiences maskandafied?) can be better observed in the rehearsal room. In the rehearsal room, musickers continuously heard each other hear. It was a space of continuous intervention. I recorded the 'emergence' of Miya's song 'Ngilobole' (see the Appendix for lyrics) in September 2008. The song crystalizes in mutual collaboration between S'hko Miya and the musicians from the melodic material that Miya offers. She instructs a bass player, whom she told me was skilled in gospel but not yet in maskanda (S. Miya 2008d). The transmission of skills is never a one-way process. She sings a refrain to the guitarist and bass player, and the bass player is obviously unfamiliar with the tune (S. Miya 2008a: 00'37"–00'54"). As soon as the instrumentalists take over the tune (00'54"), they start fiddling around with it and make it their own. After a few minutes, an ostinato crystalizes in the bass guitar (02'00"), with the guitar elaborating on it and Miya singing her verse lines to it (04'00"). Since she instructed the bass player like she instructed me – demonstrating an individual motive or a dance routine, and expanding it once she thought I had got it – I gradually became aware of my own creative agency in maskanda performance, even if I faithfully tried to mimic what she was doing.

Genres and styles that I perceived as different became permeable during the rehearsals with Abagqugquzeli, in a similar way that they were permeable at the Kushikisha Imbokodo Festival (Chapter 3) and the MORC Festival (Chapter 4). During the rehearsals' breaks, much needed by the dancers (including me), the instrumentalists continued playing and shifted their attention, without one beat of rest, to different songs and styles, often in the same mode or scale.

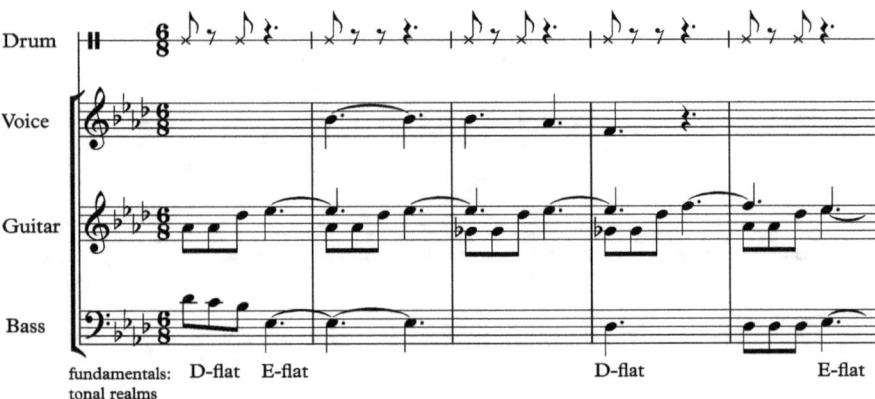

Figure 8.6 Jamming in isiZulu style during the break of the Abagqugquzeli rehearsal, Stable Theatre, Durban, 16 September 2008. Guitar picking in $\frac{6}{8}$ metre with alternating E-flat and D-flat tonal orientations, with drumbeats and bass line (Abagqugquzeli 2008: 00'00"–05'20"). Transcribed with kind permission from S'kho Miya.

I recorded a sample of such a gradual shift in style (Abagqugquzeli 2008). The lead guitarist moves from playing the Guitar 2 riffs of 'Sithi Khuzani' (Figure 8.4a) to one of his own songs. The bass player and drummer don't know the song, but jam along in isiZulu style with $\frac{6}{8}$ metre, a musical world similar to Bongani Nkwanyana's song 'Inkunzi Emnyama': the guitarist picks the same tone on different strings, alternating between e-flat and f, evoking the fundamentals E-flat and D-flat of an imaginary gourd bow, and playing a melodic line in a higher register on top of it (Figure 8.6). The tonal material is hexatonic (f – e-flat – d-flat – b-flat – a-flat – g-flat). His igama is cast in a typical arch form, with a long sustained cry prepared by a quick ascending line in a lower register and concluded with a quick descending line. The bass player highlights the fundamentals. The drummer adds beats on 1st and 3rd eighth notes in the bar, creating an ambiguity between $\frac{6}{8}$ and $\frac{3}{4}$ metres that also features 'Inkunzi Emnyama' (see Figure 6.3).

The bass player and drummer compliment the guitarist with his song (in English, probably because of my presence) and keep jamming in the same mode, but turn towards playing a root progression (Abagqugquzeli 2008: 05'20"–06'20") emblematic for Salomon Linda's famous song 'Mbube' (Linda and The Evening Birds 1939) that furthered the establishment of an entire genre: isicathamiya (Figure 8.7). The b-flat becomes more prominent as a structural base note, further emphasizing a hexatonic rather than pentatonic sound world (06'20"). The mbube riff at the Stable Theatre, however, is cast in a much slower pace than the *wimoweh* groove that acquired international fame. Rather, this riff moves in a very slow ballad-like motion, something that was identified by Tshepo Nzimande as a feature of maskandiR&B: 'That's why all the maskanda artists change to slow jams, to ballads' (Nzimande 2009). Again, contrary to the homophonic structure of the mbube genre, the guitarist starts to 'fill in' the slow riff with dense guitar picking, taking the middle ground between broken chords, poppy licks, and staggered entries texture, this time in duple rather than triple metre. With the maskanda 'being played into' the mbube riff, it occurred to me that maskanda, mbube, R&B, gospel, mbaqanga and marabi (that was next on the menu of the musicians [09'38"]) form part of an aural space that many musicians in South Africa feel 'at home in'.

In South Africa, vocal timbres and the choice of scales/tunings are important parameters for observing the permeability of genre boundaries. From the ballad-style-with-maskanda-guitar rendering of a mbube-like song, the musicians in the Stable Theatre started jamming on a riff with the same tonal material, this time with

Figure 8.7 Mbube riff for a jam during the break of the Abagqugquzeli rehearsal, 16 September 2008 (Abagqugquzeli 2008: 06'20"–09'19"). Transcribed with kind permission from S'kho Miya.

Figure 8.8 Marabi riff for a jam during the break of the Abagqugquzeli rehearsal, 16 September 2008 (Abagqugquzeli 2008: 09'34"–11'30"). Transcribed with kind permission from S'kho Miya.

a c added to it (09'19"–09'34"). This evoked a heptatonic chord-driven soundscape emblematic for a swinging and circling marabi harmonic and melodic ostinato. The bass moved up and down from I to IV to I with a part in contrary motion (moving down and up) on top of this (Figure 8.8). When Miya and I had finished our break, she commenced the first line of her song 'Ngilobole' (11'30"), and the musicians knew instantly where to go. From the very start of the rehearsal onwards, more than an hour earlier, they had not been silent for one second. Like Monson, I intend to stress the interactive, participatory and dialogical character of such discourse that is 'multiply authored' (Monson 1996: 87) and intended 'to keep interaction at the highest possible pitch of creative intensity' (88). This discourse not only takes place between musicians in the rehearsal room, but also on stage between musicians and audiences, and in mediatized form when people enjoy maskanda on record or radio in a taxi bus or in another public space.

Maskandafying the unhomely

In his themed issue about South African jazz, Nishlyn Ramanna succinctly summarizes existing scholarly insights into this sharing of sonic and aural space that certainly does not only apply to maskanda practice:

> In popular and scholarly discourse in South Africa, the term 'jazz' may reference a broad range of local urban black popular musics, from marabi to African jazz to kwela to jive, as well as international and U.S.-American styles such as swing, bebop, hard bop, Latin jazz, fusion, smooth jazz and even (albeit to a lesser extent) jazzy popular musics like R&B, soul, and funk. Common to the musical materiality of all these styles are (many if not all of) the following musical elements and approaches that Olly Wilson (1996) and others (Shepherd 1991; Berliner 1994; Kernfeld 1995; Ramanna 2005) have described as emblematic of African-American musical culture: heterogeneous and pliable timbral conceptions; stratified percussive

musical textures; cyclical structures; dual accentuation schemes; inflected rhythms and pitches; improvisation; signifying gestures, and participatory and communal musical conceptions. These musicking practices voice the double consciousness (Du Bois 2003 [1903]) of Black Atlantic culture (Gilroy 1993).

(2016: 7–8)

Ingrid Monson describes similarly fluid boundaries between African American music genres in the United States that can be observed through shared rhythmic feels, bass lines and numbers of repetition (1996: 195). Ramanna's understanding of Black Atlantic culture points at the intersection of Ahmed's concepts of homing as a 'gathering of "intimations" of home' (2003: 9) and Bhabha's notion of the unhomely as a displacement in which 'the borders between home and world become confused' (1994a: 9). Establishing a temporarily positioned resonance between a self and the world depends on this necessity to always look at, or hear 'one's self through the eyes [and ears] of others' (Du Bois [1903] 2010: 9). The Bhabhaesque unhomely points at two experiences simultaneously. Primarily, it points at the diversity of penetrating gazes and aural predispositions one must expect and adapt to. Secondarily, it points at the monolithic potential of these gazes confirming and reifying one another in one public gaze or aural disposition that imposes on the private. I argue that maskandafications, such as those in Miya's rehearsal room at the Stable Theatre in 2008, constitute a way of dealing with this condition. Illustrative for this kind of musicking is the use of the synthesizer by one and the same musician: as a drum computer, as a concertina for maskanda, as a Hammond organ for soul or gospel and as a marimba for jazz. This use is comparable to the use of the guitar in early maskanda practice: employed as an *amahubo* chorus, an *umakhweyana* gourd bow, an *isitorotoro* mouth harp and an *imfilitshi* mouth organ. This mimicking capacity of a musical instrument is a powerful sonic indicator for Nothi Ntuli's remark that he can play 'any style', and 'play his maskande into it' (Ntuli 2009). Whereas the genres are being distinguished conceptually and experientially, their idioms and gestures are easily combined in such a way that one genre functions as a funnel for, or a denominator to foreground, another.

I just described maskandafication as a reactive response towards an imposed condition of unhomeliness. However, it may be more appropriate to frame it as an active assertion of a cosmopolitan predisposition that emphasizes African cultural and epistemic agency as globally normative instead of illegibly subaltern or Other. Cosmopolitanism – as a set of predispositions that include both the comprehension of local specificity and an openness to the wider world – depends on opportunities to be mobile in corporeal, imaginative and virtual respects (Ahmed et al. 2003: 4). These opportunities can be, and are, realized in music and performance. Rather than becoming confused (Bhabha 1994a: 9), *pesheya olwandle* (overseas) and *ikhaya* (home) become combined. The musical connections maskandi make between global and local, individual and communal experience, and the debates about the value of these connections they engage in, are self-conscious acts of decolonization with an autonomous artistic agency. These acts of decolonization take place in a combination of globally 'legible' spaces of music making: the rehearsal room, the studio and the stage. Musickers are in a position to (re)produce these spaces according to the (re)organization of their remembered, contained, adapted and renewed senses of belonging, at home as much as in the wider world.

This maskandafication has epistemological implications that display overlaps with operations of scholarly knowledge both within and beyond music research. Before I touch on this in the Conclusion of this book, I return to Khoni Miya, who assured me that 'Sithi Khuzani' 'is not maskande'. Yet, I have come to hear the song as such, and to such an extent that I am able to analytically substantiate my hearing. This unmasks the practice of music analysis as a creative rather than as a formalist manner of understanding, and also raises further questions about what understanding maskanda implies. There are feedback loops between individual and communal forms of musical agency in the articulation of styles, between vocal and instrumental techniques and between opinions about good musicianship. There are sonic resonances between studio, stage and rehearsal rooms in the aural and aesthetic norms those spaces and their audiences impose. The most important and least acknowledged feedback loop, however, concerns the one between various 'literacies' or forms of 'inscription' (note my deliberate reliance on metaphors of writing) that engender the aural predispositions that musickers adopt in hearing and interpreting maskanda. These literacies encompass academic musicological interpretation, music analysis and music notation, but just as much the symbolism of deep Zulu custom, the command of a variety of African American musical 'languages', the semantic power of dance or forms of vocal eloquence as well as eloquent silence (Impey 2018: 215–17). The epistemological implications of these feedback loops have not been addressed exhaustively in this book and offer a range of starting points for further research.

Conclusion: Maskanda Epistemology

In this book, I have directed my fascination for musical epistemology – how people know music and how we make 'sense of the world with our ears' (Abels 2016: 11) – towards an engagement with the ways maskanda musickers foreground their aural experiences. They do this through various modes of expression and inscription in various spaces and places, such as rehearsal rooms, stages and studios. Maskandi maskandafy ideas, experiences and encounters by making these accessible and enjoyable *as* maskanda. Acts of maskandafication take shape in riffs, tunes and cries (the *hubo*-ing of igamas) as well as in dance, dress and spoken (self-)praise. All maskanda musickers – listeners, producers, critics and researchers as much as musicians – participate in this maskandafication. They (re)ground uprooted cultural heritage and musical techniques through new and familiar musical formats, through aesthetic and critical judgement of songs, and through academic prose and analysis.

In order to provide insight into acts of maskandafication, I have employed various modes of argumentation. Sequential narratives of how I came to know maskanda have accompanied more diachronous presentist accounts (igamas) of events and experiences in my encounters with other maskanda musickers. These accounts have been flanked as well as contrasted with eurogenic close readings and transcriptions of maskanda songs as 'works'. With this diversity of narratives, accounts, close readings and transcriptions I hope to have demonstrated the multimodality of knowing, pertaining to various forms of conceptual, embodied and aural thought. This multimodality accounts for the performative character of academic research. I also hope to have emphasized the plurality of maskanda performance and tradition, to the extent that there is no one way of practising maskanda, and no one way of hearing maskanda. There are many maskandas in this world, within South Africa and beyond. Many South African maskandi identified musicians from other parts of the world as fellow maskandi (Mnyandu 2009; Nkwanyana/Khoza 2009). This suggests that maskanda musicking is a way of being in the world, possibly, although not necessarily, as outlined in previous chapters rather than as an articulate set of styles. It also indicates that the modes and conventions of practising, hearing and knowing maskanda covered in this book are necessarily partial.

I have outlined my personal road towards understanding maskanda in embodied, emotional, sensual and intellectual respects. I have aimed to take my readership along this road, both experientially and intellectually, through written prose (see also Hahn 2007: 20). Those instances in which I experienced disjunctions between my understanding and those of my fellow musickers are particularly important for the intersection of experiential and intellectual dimensions of my argument. These disjunctions often surfaced in the absence of certain maskanda musickers in existing maskanda discourse, or in my belated or missed acknowledgement of their presence. For example, I was only able to coherently reproduce my understanding of Shiyani Ngcobo's song 'Asinankomo' (Chapter 5) and Bongani Nkwanyana's song 'Inkunzi Emnyama' (Chapter 6) thanks to the intervention of interlocutors such as Sazi Dlamini, Ignatia Madalane, Bongani Nkwanyana himself, Elias Nxumalo, Concord Nkabinde, Nandi Khumalo and Bongani Mkhonza.

In many cases, the epistemic gaps between my understanding of what my fellow musickers told me or taught me on the one hand, and their understanding of it on the other were not bridged. It may have been this confrontation (the not-understanding or multiple disconnected understandings) that was most insightful for all those involved. These gaps indicate the distance between my academic and aural tools, and those of my fellow musickers, but they also show the entanglement of these tools. By means of a conclusion, I'd like to substantiate this entanglement in the following paragraphs.

Analytical shortfalls

There were numerous instances in which my academic tools – postcolonial theory, staff notation, the privileging of certain sound parameters such as tonality, form, texture and metre – fell short of reproducing and accounting for maskanda's sonic events and aural experiences. I have not been able to outline in scholarly prose the differences between *umzansi* and *esikhulu* isiZulu styles, demonstrated by Shiyani Ngcobo (Chapter 2), Dlamini's identification of 'singing old style' (Chapter 2) or Joe Nkwanyana's distinction between rural and township styles (Chapter 6). The richness, malleability and concomitant precision of these distinctions and identifications have been put across in musical sound, but not in singular concepts. This insight compelled me to start raising questions about the epistemic norms and premises in which I have been raised.

Martin Scherzinger identifies such instances of analytical shortfall as 'the experience of a structural undecidability; one whose irreducible undecidability is less the result of some empirical imperfection … and more the result of a trace of contingency lodged within the logic of any structure' (2004: 258). Scherzinger seems to suggest that close listening and close reading as culturally located social acts can identify those undecidabilities, which makes them, to some extent, shareable as epistemic potential. As I hope to have substantiated in this book, I situate this undecidability less in musical structure than in aural predisposition and perception. The traces of contingency tell us something not only about the sounds we hear, but also about our abilities and limitations to hear. These abilities and limitations, in turn, are often determined by the modes of knowledge inscription we use.

These instances of shortfall have proved particularly useful for pointing out the importance of music as a mode of knowing as well as the importance of scholarly analysis as a creative, performative act. Through these instances, I could observe pertinent similarities in the modes of operation between maskanda and academic epistemologies. Maskanda shares an aural space with musicking practices that are not considered to be maskanda, but without which it cannot exist as maskanda (Chapter 8). Musicology shares an epistemic space with modes of knowing (music, sound, expression, performance) that it does not fully acknowledge as epistemologies, yet it exists in a constant feedback loop with these other/Other modes of knowing in order to assert its status as epistemology. The parallel between these modes of operation substantiates Steven Feld's coining of the notion of acoustemology that accounts for the epistemic workings of sound and music as much as for the performative workings of academic research. As I outlined in the Introduction and demonstrated throughout this book, both maskandafication and academic research exert power in their similar modes of operation. Both encompass an encounter, an observation of the features of what is encountered, a distantiation in the extraction of these features from their environment, and a renewed approach of those features on one's own terms.

At other times, disjunctions between my hearings and those of my fellow musickers were softened, when our understandings of what we were doing came to be synchronized for the occasion or when they became permanently transformed. This required a great deal of adaptation from all sides. Insight into the problematic epistemic status of music in global orderings of knowledge (Chapter 2), the endurance of cultural stereotypes as fetishes in my own mind and body (Chapter 4) and the acknowledgement that S'kho Miya's song 'Sithi Khuzani' can be both maskanda and not-maskanda at the same time (Chapter 8) were the main permanent transformations in my understanding of maskanda. Yet, it is far more difficult to provide an answer to Nkabinde's crucial question posed in the Introduction of this book: 'what [will] the impact of your work ... be on how maskanda musicians think about themselves and about their music?' (Nkabinde 2009).

Silences

My relative silence in response to Nkabinde's urgent question is best 'presented' through those instances in which I sensed 'a nearly agential pressure' (Bloechl 2008: 10) from maskanda musickers. These pressures encompass figures, gestures and styles that have remained indiscrete in hermeneutic respect (11): Sipho Mchunu's compositional creativity in the conception of 'Sab' Inganono' (Chapter 1), S'kho Miya's agency in presenting her music to an audience overseas (Chapter 3) and Shiyani Ngcobo's deep Zulu knowledge in the Amsterdam Tropentheater (Chapter 5). Often these near-absences were caused by equally unarticulated expectations in the nooks and crannies of all our minds and bodies. I increasingly learned how these expectations relied on colonial and apartheid pasts and on current political and economic restrictions in access to global 'technologies of the legible' (Ochoa 2014: 7), such as stages, studios and rehearsal venues. Sometimes these expectations were raised simply by me being there, unwittingly exerting my white privilege.

These conditions have immediate and far-reaching consequences for many maskanda musickers. Up to now, the overseas stage has remained an unattainable destination for S'kho Miya (Chapter 3). Nothi Ntuli needed ten more years to make a name for himself as an independent maskandi (Chapter 5). Joe Nkwanyana passed away without having a penny left from his national and international careers (Chapter 6). I am aware that on many more occasions in my account such absences, near-absences and nearly agential pressures have remained entirely unaccounted for, unavailable to hermeneutic interpretation and critical assessment, simply because I, as 'despatialized' omniscient author (Santiago Castro-Gómez quoted in Ochoa 2014: 13), do not have the means to explicate or even experience/sense them. Hence, many ways in which maskandi themselves understand their aural experiences – through maskanda performance, through aesthetic and critical judgement, or through their everyday maskandi routines (as a way of being in the world) – remain unarticulated in this book.

Although I have attempted to 'spatialize' my authorial knowledge, by culturally situating my intellectual premises and analytical tools, I have not yet found a way to work around the centralization and privileging of it. This has compelled me to use this privilege for the demonstration of the dynamics of knowledge formation. The knowledge presented in this book is multiply authored, indebted to maskandi epistemologies and academic epistemologies without being unequivocally situated in either of them. Its modes of operation are performative as much as scientific. In these respects, it is double-and-split, making the maskandi knowledge accessible only in as far as it is 'legible' within the requirements of academic premises. While this does not distinguish this book from any recent ethnography, it acquires an additional urgency in the book's focus on knowledge formation per se. Taking to heart Kofi Agawu's plea to devote more attention to sameness rather than difference (2003: 169), I have focused on maskanda's epistemic and performative overlaps with the scholarly practices I feel at home in.

Appropriations and transubstantiations

This focus is an act of severe cultural appropriation. It forces maskanda practices and enunciations in an epistemological framework that I feel confident in. This epistemological framework presupposes a 'general, relatively context-free' connection between the sign and the object it signifies, that depends entirely on negotiated agreement and definition (Turino 2008: 13). Being the single author of this book, I have a disproportionate agency to determine the terms of negotiation. An important distortive outcome of such negotiation concerns the very concept of maskandafication as one way to foreground one's aural experiences. In employing this concept, I present maskanda performances as musical textualizations of what maskandi encounter. This textual interpretation is a reductive account of sense making engaged with the re/presentation of 'something else'. Maskanda practice entails much more than musically textualizing events and experiences. It also operates in ways that are very different from ethnography. There is much to say for the observation that maskanda practice is incomparable to what I am doing in my academic universe. This is another account of the partiality of this book about maskanda and about processes of sense making and knowledge formation.

The book's focus on maskanda as a musicking act with representationalist hermeneutic potential has been thoroughly formed by eurogenic epistemological preoccupations, such as objectification, dissection and interpretation (Viveiros de Castro 2013; Mamdani et al. 2016: 8 as cited in Buthelezi 2017: 18; Mundy 2018). Admittedly, many maskanda musickers (Mija, Nzimande, Ngwekazi, Majozi) highlight and laud the maskandi's ability to cast issues and ideas of a specific community into performance-based musical styles, poetic idioms and choreographies. This ability substantiates the maskandi's role as a validator of (Zulu) tradition. However, maskanda is more than music and more than hermeneutics. Pleas for the decolonization of thoughts and minds in recent years (Brown 2020) are just starting points for reaching beyond such concepts and perspectives. They suggest that research projects such as the one I carried out between 2008 and 2018 need to take shape on completely different terms, and perhaps no longer by me.

Thus, presenting maskanda as epistemology also comes down to what Hans Ulrich Gumbrecht describes as a magical act of 'transubstantiation': one substance distant in time and space is made present in another substance that occupies space in the here and now (2004: 29). Ethnography generally thrives on this form of transubstantiation: 'unruly experience' is transformed into a text, and in this process 'unwritten behavior, speech, beliefs, oral tradition, ritual come to be marked as a corpus, a potentially meaningful ensemble, separated out from an immediate discursive or performative situation' (Clifford quoted and paraphrased in Rice 1994: 10). Many scholars recognize this as an attempt at performing magic (Stocking 1992: 53; Tomlinson 1993; Gouk 2004: 90; Maskens and Blanes 2013: 268; Graeber 2015). My attempt at presenting maskanda as epistemology thrives on a similar procedure but in a more totalizing form. It is in many ways comparable to the attempts of early ethnomusicologists, such as Jaap Kunst and Arnold Bake, to describe non-European musics as fully-fledged 'art' (Kunst 1931). Such compliance to eurogenic notions of *art, knowledge, music* and *culture* is a politically sensitive epistemic problem in itself that I have only been able to address by emphasizing the cultural situatedness of these terms. Their hegemony remains more or less intact, especially since they are so inextricably intertwined with the mode of knowledge inscription that I employ to reach my academic peers: writing.

At the same time, this appropriative act of magic has enabled me to foreground the appropriative and transubstantiative agency of my fellow maskanda musickers; after all, their epistemic practices can operate in similar ways as my scholarship does. In the academic realm, the substances that occupy space in the here and now may encompass written prose or tenured academic affiliations. In the realm of musical practice, these substances also encompass gestures, sounds, touches and other experiences of bodies as well as inscriptions on (organic and non-organic) bodies (Gumbrecht 2004: 29). I have described these experiences and inscriptions as textualizations and maskandafications in this book: making ideas, statements and musical practices accessible *as* maskanda.

Double-and-split

I have adopted Homi Bhabha's notion of mimicry, with authorizing, discriminating and menacing implications, for my elucidation of how such maskandafying acts of transubstantiation work not only in maskanda performance, but also in this book. Firstly, in processes of maskandafication, cultural authority is asserted and established. The songs 'Sab' Inganono' (Chapter 1) and 'Inkunzi Emnyama' (Chapter 6), Shiyani Ngcobo's demonstration of isiZulu styles, Sazi Dlamini's demonstration of 'old style' (Chapter 2), S'kho Miya's *ibhodlo* and *izibongo* performances (Chapters 3 and 7) and the establishment of new maskandi genres such as skandihop and maskandiR&B (Chapter 7) assert and confirm cultural authority. They do this through the articulation of Zulu tradition and Zulu modernity, of Africa's normativity in the world, and of male and female cultural agency. Maskanda is authoritative knowledge, confirming existing categories of difference.

Secondly, through these categories of difference, musickers distinguish between those who can understand these cultural intricacies and those who cannot. They also articulate their command over these categories of difference as fluid and permeable experiences and assertions. Distinctions between maskanda's substyles and their geographical locations (Chapter 2), Khoni Miya's identification of 'Sithi Kuzani' as a song that is 'not maskande' (Chapter 8) and Thabani Mahlobo's acknowledgement that I could now use my voice in such a way as to *hubo* a song (Chapter 8) account for maskanda's capacity as discriminatory knowledge. In this capacity maskanda asks questions about what it means to understand these cultural intricacies, often leading to deferred, diversified or contingent answers.

Thus, thirdly, as much as cultural authorities are confirmed and distinguished, they are being undermined through maskanda. What is the authority of deep Zulu culture if it is clad in urban musical and poetic formats? What happens to patriarchal societal norms if women compose and perform explicitly feminist songs and *izibongo* self-praise on festival stages, through broadcast media and in recording studios? What are the implications for notions of eloquence and aesthetics if maskanda modes of sonic, poetic and moral articulation become more widely accepted as epistemic and artistic expressions? Such questions point at maskanda's capacity of being menacing knowledge, interrogating subject positions, relationships between listening entities and cultural identities. The processes of maskandafication constitute a liminal space of intervention (and, I would add, of magic). In this space, the conditions of expression as well as the performative, institutional and subconscious implications of a musical or cultural event are not yet determined or fully comprehensive and hence not completely enunciated. This is what Bhabha identifies as a time lag between event and enunciation, a Third Space. Maskanda, I have argued, like many musicking practices worldwide, embodies this Third Space. The potential for contingency as well as intervention in this time lag is realized in acts of maskandafication, offering insights not only into how culture as practice is constructed and located (Bhabha 1994b: 58–9), but also into how knowledge is shaped and transmitted.

Dwelling in this time lag provides some opportunity to observe the disjunctions outlined at the start of this Conclusion from a less centralized perspective, in a somewhat more diversified and diffused and less totalizing gaze or hearing. Processes of maskandafication foreground how musickers reclaim command over the cultural stereotypes as fetishes that have been imposed on them for centuries of colonial imaginations and decades of apartheid policy. During his tour through the Netherlands in 2010, Shiyani Ngcobo menaced the stereotype of the Zulu clad in animal skins, exported by Mahlatini in the 1980s to global stages as a marker of (South) African cultural presence (Chapter 5). Through his skandihop, Mxolisi Majozi actively revamps and respells the books he had to read in the apartheid Bantu education system 'in my own view of society today' (Chapter 7). Through blatantly feminist musicianship, S'kho and Khoni Miya (re) appropriate musical practices, such as *ibhodlo* and *izibongo*, that disproportionally came to be placed in the hands, ears and minds of men during the apartheid years (Chapters 3 and 7). Thus, all these musickers reground practices, experiences and events that have been uprooted. They (re)create 'soils of significance' (Hoffman in Ahmed et al. 2003: 9), and develop notions of home that have not only referential qualities to a place left behind, but also (re)productive qualities that assert a presence (and a future) of new forms of relating and belonging in the world (Ahmed et al. 2003: 9).

The parallel between my description of how my body (including my brain) came to know maskanda on the one hand, and my in/ability to observe the absences and presences of my fellow maskanda musickers in such acts of knowledge formation on the other is situated in the etymological relation of the words 'to acknowledge' and 'knowledge'. Bhabha demonstrates that even acts of disavowal and denial constitute a powerful form of acknowledgement (1994c: 66). Hence, knowing is not primarily a capacity to read (immaterial) 'meaning' into a material form, but to acknowledge the presence and substance of this material – which can be done in innumerable different ways that are necessarily culturally situated and that determine dynamics of inclusion and exclusion as outlined in Chapter 3.

I have provided numerous examples of such acknowledgement in maskanda practices. Maskandi acknowledge presences through the *hubo*-ing of R&B riffs and jazz cadences (Chapters 6 and 7) and in their search for gourd bow resonances on the maskanda guitar's strings (Chapters 2 and 6). Listeners acknowledge presences in observing multiple subject positions in an old Zulu war song (Chapter 1). Maskandi also acknowledge the presence of others (including ancestors/shades) in the spiritual trumping of a competitor in courtship through the vocal and sonic qualities of a song (Chapter 6), or in the provocation of an audience through the performance of an igama (Chapter 5). I have acknowledged maskanda's presence as epistemology. This enabled me to develop an ear and an eye for the presence of those who acknowledge presences like I acknowledge presences. This 'knowing' is simultaneously self-centred and relational. In hearing another person hear (Szendy in Erlmann 2004), we participate in a feedback loop between listening and speaking (Carter 2004: 55). We search and acquire a temporarily positioned resonance between a self and the world through sound, gestures, performances, prose and many other modes of expression and inscription.

Outlining how maskanda epistemologies and scholarly epistemologies are folded into each other also enables me to decentralize eurogenic modes of knowing as self-sufficient. Setting these terms of comparison, too, is an ambivalent endeavour, in Bhabha's sense of the word. Rather than submitting maskanda to a role of scholarly research object only, it is an attempt at making scholarly modes of knowing converse with maskanda epistemologies. At the same time, it employs maskanda instrumentally, mining Southern Hemisphere riches for the refinement of Northern Hemisphere theory (Buthelezi 2017: 17). My ambivalent knowledge and understanding of maskanda wants to be in two places at once, simultaneously fearing and desiring to engage in acts of Othering maskanda. It is double-and-split (Bhabha 1994b: 52), like most knowledge conceived in colonial circumstances (Bloechl 2008: 23).

The demonstration of this ambivalence of my knowledge throughout this book is my way of trying to undermine the fantasy of Europe's cultural and epistemic self-sufficiency (Bloechl 2008: 23) and of accounting for the colonial conditions in which I worked. Sonic and aural experience is a particularly useful realm to do this. Ochoa references Patrice Maniglier in observing how the sonic in eurogenic (colonially distributed) history 'was simultaneously constituted as a dimension of knowledge, that is, as something that needs to be judged as representations ... and as a dimension of sentience, that is, as a phenomenon that involves "an internal variability"' (Maniglier paraphrased in Ochoa 2014: 21). In my account of maskanda practice as epistemology, I hope to have been able to relax the binary tension between knowledge as representative, singular, coherent and unified versus sentience as plural, variable and inconsistent. Musicking practices as much as scholarly practices contain all these features if one develops an eye and an ear for them. This should compel (music) scholars to 'acknowledge' and reconsider the doubtful epistemic status that music, sonic expressions and aural experiences enjoy in many written (including European) intellectual histories (see Chapter 2).

Beyond the harnessing of vulnerabilities

More than twenty years ago, Ingrid Monson demonstrated that knowledge can be conceptualized as the living out of a pact of mutual understanding between musicians, audiences and their predecessors that culminates in a shared set of skills (1996: 2). This book is meant as a corroboration of that insight, and I have intended to bring across how difficult it is to *acknowledge* the implications of this insight. Processes of sharing contain instances of intimacy, togetherness and satisfaction, but also of alienation, embarrassment, reluctance, oppression and submission for all those involved. Providing insight into knowing as a relational (Born 2010; Cook 2012; Feld 2015), dialogical (Monson 1996) or (atmo)spherical (Abels 2013) capacity requires engagement with all these vulnerabilities.

Such engagement warrants questions about my use of theory in this book. I have employed theoretical frameworks of Sara Ahmed, Homi Bhabha, Olivia Bloechl, Jacques Derrida, Ana María Ochoa Gautier, Christopher Small and Peter Szendy as tools of translation. These frameworks enable comparison of maskanda musicking with (sonic) cultural practices in various times and places. However, I also instrumentally employed my insights into maskanda practice as means to further bolster and elucidate their theoretical concepts and perspectives. Many of these theorists advance explicitly inclusivist and decolonial agendas, also with regard to epistemology. Nevertheless, my attempt to theorize maskanda modes of sense making within these frames has both inclusive and imperialist potential.

The inclusive potential can be said to encompass the strains of thinking beyond existing modes of representation, performance and relation that I was able to touch on in the wake of the theoretical premises that I summarized in this conclusion. In Chapters 1, 3 and 5, I was able to point at nearly agential pressures that I might have failed to notice without Bloechl's conceptualization of such pressures (2008: 10) and without Ochoa's attempt to 'read the archive against the grain' (2014: 4). In Chapter 4, I could outline – thanks to Bhabha's application of these Freudian and Lacanian concepts – how cultural stereotypes remained active as fetishes in my body, my senses and my mind, even after I had acknowledged them and rhetorically distanced myself from them. In Chapters 2 and 4, I demonstrated the need to reach beyond the deconstructivist study of cultural identity. This helps us address less palpable and less representational epistemic agencies in musical practice and performance. In Chapters 5 and 6, I demonstrated the need to reach beyond the binary of subaltern and hegemonic subject positions. This might enable us to observe more diversified, temporary, context-dependent and fluid opportunities for maskandi to exert power and relate to other listening entities. In Chapter 7, I demonstrated the need to reach beyond the equally binary narrative of cultural loss and gain. This might enable us to adopt a more rhizomatic account of cultural development, interaction and appropriation. I could not have articulated these 'beyonds' without the help of above-mentioned scholars and theorists.

However, throughout this book, I have not been able to say much yet about these 'beyonds'. These 'beyonds' encompass the aural experiences of those who consider maskanda a way of life. They encompass the semantics of dance steps, styles and gestures. They encompass the phantom districts, the structural compositional devices, the musical techniques, the poetic intricacies and eloquent silences that I have not seen or heard or sensed. They remain 'beyond' in relation to established modes of knowledge inscription and literacies. My articulation of maskanda as a Third Space of enunciation (Bhabha), as a musicking practice that enables the circulation of acoustic assemblages between listening entities (Ochoa), as a recreation of soils of significance (Hofmann in Ahmed) in which people hear each other hear (Szendy) leading to a perennial deferral as well as diversification of meaning formation (Derrida) have also been ways to harness the insecurities and vulnerabilities that were part of my participation in maskanda practice. This harnessing constitutes the imperialist potential of theory and analysis, even if it is aimed at a decolonization of thoughts and minds.

This brings me back to Concord Nkabinde's question posed in the first sentences of this book: why I had come to South Africa to study maskanda. I was unable to phrase a coherent answer to that question because I would have to explicate all those vulnerabilities that I sensed so powerfully (I knew them) without having the words (or theories) to express them conceptually. Much of this precariousness of knowing became painfully palpable when S'kho Miya and I were interviewed for the Vibe FM radio show in KwaMashu township (Chapter 3). I was asked the very same question there, and I brushed over my own vulnerabilities: S'kho Miya had shared something with me for which I received and took the credit. Reflecting on this appropriation, in hindsight, I wondered how to remove its epistemological underpinnings that inevitably sustain the premises of (European) colonization at large (Agnew 2008; Bloechl 2008; Ochoa 2014; Radano and Olaniyan 2016; Mundy 2018; Brown 2020). I gradually realized that such removal starts with the persistent acknowledgement of the vulnerability and precariousness of the temporarily positioned resonance between a self and the world – a resonance that is a precondition for knowledge and understanding to materialize. For it is such resonance that enables listening entities to circulate in fluid, though not necessarily unified, (acoustic) assemblages. This implies that the continuous effort to find resonance and to establish a community, tradition or identity can only succeed with the acknowledgement of the possibility of losing it again in living, flexible and multifarious social and acoustic constellations.

Appendix: Song Lyrics and Translations

'Sab' Inganono'

Transcription and translation by Ignatia Madalane and Elias Nxumalo, with kind permission from David Jenkins (Clegg and Band 2007, 2011; Jenkins and Band 2011, 2013).

[Verse:]
We sab' inganono
[Lead:] Ubalekelani?

Is he / [Hey] are you afraid of the cannon?
[Why] is he / are you running away? / Don't run from the gun

We sab' ukuduma kwayo
[Lead:] Lashona

He is / You are afraid of its sound
The sun has set / He is dead [terrified]

[Chorus:]
Wathukuthela,
We sab' ukuduma kwayo
Wathukuthela,
We sab' inganono

He / You got angry,
He / You got afraid of its sound
He / You got angry,
He / You got afraid of the cannon

[Lead:] Ubalekelani?

[Why] is he / are you running away? / Don't run from the gun

[*Izibongo* Clegg 2011:]
Thatha Mfezi
Zibambe Skegi
Vikela Eshobeni
Bayamzonda abantu
bamzondela ngoba uthanda umculo waba ntwana

Take Mfezi
Hold Skegi
Protect Eshobeni
They hate him
because he likes music of children

*** [too rapid to transcribe and translate] ***

[Verse:]
Zafik' ezakithi ukushona kwelanga

We (warriors) are coming in thousands when the sun sets

Zafik' ezakithi nodumo lwazo

We (warriors) are coming in thousands with thunderous sound

[Lead:] Lashona

The sun has set / He is dead [terrified]

[Chorus Clegg 2011:]
We nsizwa ubalekelani? [Hey] why are you running away?

[Chorus Jenkins 2013:]
Shi hom, hom – Shi hom [War song incantations]

'DJ Gogo'

Transcription and translation by Ignatia Madalane (Majozi 2008).

Taking you back one two

[Chorus:]
Gogo wam' waw' DJ — My grandmother was a DJ
Dlala uJohn Patton nama Commodores — She played John Patton and the Commodores

Turn and slide nje ngama O'Jays — She turned and slided like the O'Jays
Ek se ugogo wam' waw' DJ — I say my grandmother was a DJ
Sivuswa iphunga le Mr. Min ecleana amavinyl every Sunday — We were awakened by the scent of Mr Min [cleaning product], cleaning vinyls every Sunday

I'm taking you back to the day when the elders used to play
Ama-afro nama perm asading' igel ne spray — When afros and perms still needed gel and spray
Good or bad I'm telling you things were okay
Se ugogo waw' DJ every Sunday — Grandmother was a DJ every Sunday

Nangama stay-away agqcok' ubell bottom ogrey — Even of stay-away [days], wearing grey bell bottoms
Shay' ithombe zeblack and white — Taking black and white photos
Kwehlisa uk'woma ngePine-nut — Quenching thirst with Pine-nut [cool drink that used to be famous]

Kusuka amaphepha kusala amakhatebokisi — Papers flew, boxes remained [Zulu saying: 'things were hot, hectic, happening, etc.']
Ngoba ugogo waye rocka amaparty — Because grandmother was rocking the parties

uGogo wey' DJ — Grandmother was a DJ

S'khule sinukelwa isinkwa, si-iron-a amashirt nama tripling — We grew up smelling bread, ironing shirts with triplings

Ngilungisela ukuya emsembenzini	Preparing to go to work
uMalume aboyin' icathulo	While uncle was shining his shoes
noGogo way' busy naboni adlala ingoma zasemandulo	Grandmother was busy playing songs from the olden days
Mzubana sikhula nomculo, shaw' mzimba nomphefumulo	When we grew up with music, it hit the body and soul
Chess ngizole ray niyi chairs ne-itulo	[XXX chess XXX chairs]
Okukhand' le khulu, umalume a change iRayban ibhuko	The one with a big head, uncle changing Rayban [sun] glasses
Kwelika Bra Daki no Zuko	At [or with] Bro Daki and Zuko
uGundi no FK imbungulo usaw' Sdumo	Gundi and FK, and the bedbug S'dumo [from sitcom *S'gud Is Nice*]
Ngisagqcokhel' ama-easter ngiphet' ispade	While I was still used to dress up for Easter while holding a spade
Bafethu ngikhule ngishay' ibow tie ngikhiphe ugogo on a date	Brothers I grew up wearing a bow tie, taking out my grandmother on a date
Ukhala ngok'gula ugogo ushesha aw'shaye ngespuit	When you cried sick, grandmother would hit you with a *spuit* [rubber syringe]

[Interlude:]

[Chorus:]

Sas'sabhukeli uHe-man noShera	We used to watch He-man and Shera
Ungamazi uCaiphus noMalindi kaNtuli sithi washiwa	If you didn't know Caiphus and Malindi Ntuli, you were left behind
Siya emarket siyobamb' iLexiton 'iyonake leyo'	We went to the market to smoke Lexiton, 'that is the one' [advertisement slogan]
Ifa lakaMthethwa ne *Hlala Kwabafileyo*	The inheritance of the Mthethwas and *Staying amongst the Dead* [TV drama series]
uLulu Ubuyile, egqoke uwanika ebobokileyo	*Lulu Has Returned*, wearing torn clothes/ shoes [Zulu drama series]
Ngikate iMellow Yellow Floshem, Dum-shaya	[waiting for Mellow Yellow Floshem, Dum-shaya]
Crokett & Jones, Champion Jack, James Brown no Clarence Carter	Crokett & Jones, Champion Jack, James Brown and Clarence Carter
Sweet Job noMkatakata, iverse sengithengile iBhatata	Sweet Job and Mkatakata, the verse I have now bought the sweet potato
Na mapantsula alahlela amaparty	Pantsulas throwing parties
Solala siphuph' inyobisi ne-inyoka zika Magamba	We are going to sleep dreaming about [inyobisi] and Magamba's snakes
Sibona ngowethu uOstrich uKhananda	Seeing Ostrich, Khananda ourselves

Ushaya amakispane ngebrand new leathers uvhez' umkhaba	Dressed or wearing [amakispane] and brand-new leather, showing his big stomach
Sweet Job noMkatakata	Sweet Job and Mkatakata
Hai lezi baf'wethu ezabadala badala bomzubana	Yeah (eish) brothers these are/belong to the elders, elders of long ago
Ngingazinge manje ngoba yazi k'thini	I now don't know what to say
Sesibona s'phusha amatransi itwana	We are now pushing transports [cars], and girls
Kodwa manje yaziyini baf'wethu	But now, you know what, my brothers
Ak'safana nak'dala baf'wethu	Things are not the same as the olden days, brothers let us remember the elders
asikhumbuleni abantu bak'dala	
Sihloniphe abantu abadala	Let us respect the elders
Hola	

'Sithi Khuzani'

Transcription and translation by Ignatia Madalane and Elias Nxumalo with kind permission from S'kho Miya (S. Miya 2010a).

[Verse:]	
Niyambona lomama	Do you see this mother/woman?
Niyambona lomama	Do you see this mother/woman?
Bayamkhipa inyumbazane	They are isolating her [remove her from the group].
Sebemkhipa inyumbazane	They are isolating her.
Bathi uthanda izindaba	They say she likes to gossip
Uqabanisa omakhelwane	She makes neighbours quarrel
Bayamkhipha inyumbazane	They are isolating her from their group
Niyambona lomama ongaphesheya.	Can you see this mother/woman who is on that other side?
[Chorus:]	
Sithi khuzani webakhiti	We request that you reprimand
Sithi khuzani webakhiti	We request that you reprimand
Isono esingaka emhlabeni.	Such a sin in this world.
Senzenjani?	What should we do?
Sithi kahleni webakhithi	We say it is enough, our people
Awu kahleni webakhithi	Awu, we say it is enough, our people
Umuntu uya fana nabanye 'bantu	A person is the same as other people
Umuntu uya fana nabanye 'bantu.	A person is the same as other people.

'Ngilobole'

Transcription and translation by Ignatia Madalane and Elias Nxumalo, with kind permission from S'kho Miya (S. Miya 2010b).

Kikikikikikiki, lelele	[Ululating]
Uyokikiz' umame	Mother will ululate
Lelelele, kikiki	[Ululating]
Uyokikiz' umama	Mother will ululate
[Verse:]	
Ngiyolotsholw 'ekhaya awubheke	I am going to be lobola-ed at home, look
Awubheke	Look
Ngiyolotsholw 'ekhaya awubheke	I am going to be lobola-ed at home, look
Awubheke	Look
Isoka lam' selithumela abakhongi	My boyfriend is sending negotiators/representatives
Ukuthi bayo ng'lobola	That they can lobola me
Isoka lami selithumela 'bakhongi	My boyfriend is sending negotiators/representatives
Bayo phemba ubuhlobo	To [come and] build [family] relations
Kubazali bam'	From my parents
Ujabula umama	Mother is happy
Elilizela umama	Mother will ululate
Ethathe isikhwili ubaba,	Father will take isikhwili [spear or knobkerrie],
liyothokoza idlozi	the ancestors will be happy,
agiyele abakhongi	he will dance for the negotiators/representatives
[Chorus:]	
Seliyongilobola isoka lami liyongobol' ekhaya	My boyfriend is going to pay lobola at my home
Seliyongilobola isoka lami liyongobol' ekhaya	My boyfriend is going to pay lobola at my home
Ngiyakwa mama ongemama	I am going to a mother who is not a mother [mother-in-law]
Sengiyo kwaba ngigcagce	I am going to bring gifts and get married
Ngihlanganise ithongo lasemzini nelakithi	Connecting my ancestors together with that of the other family
We mnghanami wenzani?	My friend, what are you doing?
We mnghanami kawubheke	My friend, take a look
Ukuziphatha kahle kuleth'i mpumelalo kimina	Being well behaved has brought me success

'Nith' Angiqome Bani?'

Transcription and translation by Ignatia Madalane and Elias Nxumalo with kind permission from S'kho Miya (S. Miya 2010c).

[Verse:]
Lomuntu uyangithanda; angazi nifunani	This person loves me; I don't know what you want
Nithi ngimale ngiqome bani?	You say I must refuse him / break up with him and be with whom?
Lomuntu uyangithanda, uyangondla, uyangiphilisa	This person loves me, he looks after me, he makes me well
Nithi angimale ngiqome bani?	You say I must refuse him and date whom?
Nithi angimale ngiqome yiphi?	You say I must refuse him and be with whom exactly?

[Chorus:]
Hayi, angeke ngivume	No, I won't agree [to this]
Ngeke kulunge ukucitha umuzi wedoda	It won't be acceptable to break a man's home
Hayi, angeke ngivume	No, I won't agree [to this]
Ngeke kulunge ukucitha umuzi wedoda	It won't be acceptable to break a man's home
Akekho umuntu onelungelo lokuhlukanisa nima nomyeni wami	No one has a right to separate me from my man
Akekho umuntu onelungelo lokuhlukanisa mina nomyeni wami	No one has a right to separate me from my man
Lomuntu othandwa yini	The person that you like
Ufuna ukungiganisa esithenjini	Wants me to be in a polygamous [marriage]
Lomuntu othandwa yini	The person that you like
Mina angithandi ukushadela esithenjini	I don't like getting into a polygamous marriage
Mina angifuni ukushadela esithenjini	I don't want to be married in polygamy
Hayi, ngeke ngivume, ngeke kulunge ngicithe umuzi wendoda	No, I won't agree, I won't agree to break a man's home

[Verse:]
Lomuntu uyangithanda; angazi nifunani	This person loves me; I don't know what you want
Nithi angimale ngiqome bani?	You say I must refuse him / break up with him and be with whom?
Lomuntu uyangithanda, uyangiwondla, uyangiphilisa	This person loves me, he looks after me, he makes me well

Nithi angimale ngiqome bani?	You say I must refuse him and date whom?
Kodwa nithi angimale ngiqome bani?	You say I must refuse him and date whom?

[*Izibongo*:]

Awu! Wayenza indaba ufune ivhaka elizoza emva kwako kanti kuziqhauka igagu uqobo lwalo	Awu! You made the news [you created a situation], you wanted to be followed by an 'ivhaka' [someone who doesn't know how to sing], but there came an 'igagu' [someone who is extremely talented, like a virtuoso]
Lalela ngempelake wethu ngoba mina uMaqomboza amajongosi … ngizohlikahlikiza wonke amabele a gqwele isifuba la kubede uhlelo.	Listen very carefully because I, Maqomboza amajongosi … I will rub all these breasts that are covering the entire chest areas and the programme will be messed up.
Ngasho mina ntokazi kaMiya hayi madoda phansi lapho eXXX langiqamuka khona	I, daughter of Miya … no men [exclamation], there at XXX where I come from
Kanti umfula engiphuzawo ngiphuza uMhlabatshana	But the river where I drink, I drink at Mhlabatshane
Kusho mina uMaqomboza amajombosi ehlabathini.	It is I, Maqomboza amajombosi ehlabathini.
Intsizwa engizalayo Umhlakaza Nhlansi	The man who gave birth to me is Mhlakaza Nhlansi
Ngubaba wami ongizalayp lowo.	That is my father who gave birth to me.
Uthini wena?	What did you say?
Deda endleleni awuboni ngiyadlula	Get out of the way, can't you see I am passing by?
Siphelile isikhathi sokushishiliza manje. Ivume wethu.	The time to play [fool around] is over. Agree to it.
Ngisayo kujikijela ngayo induku engayilanda phansi kaNduku esigodi	I am still going to throw a staff [stick] which I fetched down there by XXX
Hee, ziyahlafunya iintambo lapho izigiqi XXX	Hee, threads [cables] are being eaten there with guitars [cables to amplify instruments, thus meaning busy being 'chewed', i.e. by the sounds of the music?])
Kanti zihlafunya osix mabone umfo owakhalele XXX	But they chew six mabone [common saying unknown to translators]
Ehamba naye osomnyama umfo kandabandaba bayamazi eMandeni	[She] is going/accompanied by the black one, the man from Mandeni.
Injani makunje.	How it is when it is like this.
Akuyona? Akuyona?	Isn't it, isn't it?
Hiyo! Helele!	It is! Helele!

'Ibhoxongwana'

Transcription and translation by Ignatia Madalane and Elias Nxumalo with kind permission from S'kho Miya (S. Miya 2010d).

[Verse:]

Kodwa yini?	But what is this?
Kodwa yini le engiyibona ngamehlo ami?	But what is this that I am seeing with my eyes?
Yini le engibamba ngesandla?	What is this that I am holding in my hands?
Ngabe yinsizwa noma yibhoxongwane?	Is this a man or a useless person?
Ngabe yinsizwa noma yibhoxongwane?	Is this a man or a useless person?
Yini le engiyibona ngamehlo ami?	What is this that I am seeing with my eyes?
Ma uyinsizwa ngiyekele, ngiyahamba, liyosha ibodo ekhaya, awekho amanzi	If you are a gentleman let me go home, pots will get burnt at home, there is no water
Ma uyinsizwa ngiyekele ngiyahamba, liyosha ibodo ekhaya, awekho amanzi	If you are a gentleman let me go home, pots will get burnt at home, there is no water
Kodwa yini, yini le engiyibona ngamehlo ami?	But what is this, what is this that I am seeing with my eyes?

[Chorus:]

Mus' ukungibambezela, unjalonje awazi nokweshela	Do not delay me, as you can't even propose to a lady properly
Buyela kwelakini bakutshele ukuthi inthombi ishelwa kanjani	Go back home so that your people can tell you how to propose to a woman
Mus' ukungibambezela, unjalonje awazi nokweshela	Don't delay me, as you are you can't even propose to a lady properly

'Isithembu'

Transcription and translation unknown (S. Ngcobo 2004).

[Verse:]

Min' isithembu ngiyasizonda.	I hate polygamy.
Nalasihambe khona.	I want nothing to do with it.
Ngoba sangixoshel' umama.	Polygamy chased my mother away.
Ningibona nje ngiyintandane,	Today I am an orphan,
Ngoba sangixoshel' umama.	Polygamy chased my mother away.
Ningibona nje ngiyintandane,	Today I am an orphan,
Min' isithembu ngiyasizonda.	I hate polygamy.
Nalasihambe khona.	I want nothing to do with it.

[Chorus:]

Min' isithembu ngiyasizonda.	I hate polygamy.

Nalasihambe khona.	I want nothing to do with it.
Ngoba sangixoshel' umama.	Polygamy chased my mother away.
Ningibona nje ngiyintandane,	Polygamy made me an orphan,
Mina' isithembu ngiyasizonda.	I hate polygamy.

'Sevelina'

Transcription and translation by Ignatia Madalane with kind permission from heir Shiyani Ngcobo (S. Ngcobo 2008a).

WeSevelina, WeSevelina	Sevelina, Sevelina
WeSevelin' uyabaleka.	Sevelina you're running away.
WeSevelin' uyangishiya.	Sevelina you're abandoning me.
Awu! Nokungentombi kuzenz' intombi.	Every girl thinks she is beautiful.
Siyakubona nokungensizwa kuzenz' insizwa.	Now every boy thinks he is a man.

'Izinyembezi'

Transcription and translation by Ignatia Madalane with kind permission from heir Shiyani Ngcobo (S. Ngcobo 2008b).

[Verse:]

Umuntu obulala abantu	[you are] A person who kills people
Umuntu obulala abantu	[you are] A person who kills people
Unamalini ebenke?	How much money do you have in your bank [account]?
Umuntu obulala abantu	[you are] A person who kills people
Umuntu obulala abantu wee	[you are] A person who kills people
Unamalini ebenke?	How much money do you have in your bank [account]?
Kodwa benzeni abantu?	What did people do [to deserve to be killed]?
Kodwa benzeni abantu?	What did people do?
Wena uhamba ubulala abantu	You go around killing people.
Kodwa benzeni abantu be nkosi?	What did God's people do [to deserve to be killed]?
Kodwa benzeni abantu?	What did people do?
Wena uhamba ubulala abantu	You go around killing people
Igazi lomuntu liya khuluma	A person's [your victim's] blood speaks
Igazi lomuntu liya khuluma, ndoda	A person's [your victim's] blood speaks, man
Mus'u kubulala abantu	Stop killing people

[Chorus:]
Izinyembezi	Tears
Izinyembezi	Tears
Ngiyakucela ngemali yezinyembezi	I am pleading with you, my friend, with tears' money
Izinyembezi	Tears
Izinyembezi	Tears
Ngiyakucela ngemali yezinyembezi	I am pleading with you, my friend, with tears' money

'Asinankomo'

Transcription and translation by Ignatia Madalane and Elias Nxumalo, with kind permission from heir Shiyani Ngcobo (S. Ngcobo 2010d).

[Verse:]
Usibona singena lutho	You see us with nothing
Asinankomo	We don't have cattle
Kwashonaphi okwezwe	Where did it/things of the nation, go?
Usibona asinalutho	You see us with nothing
Asinankomo	We don't have cattle
Kwashonaphi okwezwe	Where did it/things of the nation, go?
Ngoba abamhlophe sebaku thathe nkonke	Because the whites have taken everything
Asisenalutho	We don't have anything
Kwashonaphi okwezwe	Where did it/things of the nation, go?
Ngisho abelungu sebaku thathe konke	Whites have taken all/everything
Asisenankomo	We don't have cattle
Kwashonaphi okwezwe lonke	Where did it/things of the nation, go?
Ngoba manje batheng' e supermakete	Because now they buy at supermarkets
Azisekekho iinkomo	There is no more cattle
Akusekho kwezwe mhlabeni	There is nothing left of the nation here on earth
Iimbuzi zithengwa kwabamhlophe	Goats are now bought from whites
Asisenalutho	We do not have anything
Kwashonaphi okwezwe emhlabeni	Where did it/things of the nation, go?
Usibona asinalutho thina	You see us with nothing
Asinankomo	We do not have cattle
Weeee	[Lamentation]

[Chorus:]
Asinankomo	We do not have cattle
Asinalutho	We do not have anything
Asinamali	We do not have money
Imali yabelungu	Money belongs to the whites

[*Izibongo:*]

Wadla Nduma Ndumane	Nduma Ndumane ate
Thumbu lenkomo	Cow's intestine
Uyoze ulilahle, sweet mtwana	You will end up giving up, sweet baby
Ntombi yangivimbela	The girl who tried to hinder me
Akwaba nhlungu	It did not hurt
Izayoni ezangivimbela	It is Zion that hindered me.

*** [too rapid to transcribe and translate] ***

[Verse:]

Usibona singena lutho	You see us with nothing
Asinankomo	We do not have cattle
Kwashonaphi okwezwe	Where did it/things of the nation go?
Amanzi athengwa ezitolo	Water I bought at the shops
Kwashonaphi 'kwezwe	Where did it/things of the nation go?
Imbuzi zithengwa kwabamhlophe	Goats are bought from the whites
Asisenalutho	We do not have anything anymore
Kwashonaphi okwezwe emhlabeni	Where did it/things of the nation go?
Usibona nje asinankomo	You see us like this we do not have cattle
Awa asinalutho	We do not have anything
Kwashonaphi 'kwezwe	Where did it/things of the nation go?

'Inkunzi Emnyama'

Transcription and translation by Ignatia Madalane and Bongani Mkhonza, with kind permission from Bongani Nkwanyana (B. Nkwanyana 2009a, 2014).

[Verse:]

Kukhala insingizi langqunqa lamnyama izulu, laqala layikhipha phezu komsila we gabazane?	The southern ground hornbill thunderbird sings, then the clouds turn dark
Sengithi umam' uyang'phosa.	As if the mother is bewitching me
Isikhwele sendoda siyingozi singambulala umuntu x 3	A man's jealousy is very dangerous, it can kill a person
Umangabe kungowakho ubombelethe 'mhlane ugoduke x 2	If [she] is yours put her on your back and go home/fuck off
Ang' khathali noma ungang' thumela ngezulu.	I don't give a damn even if you can strike me with lightning!
Damn bloody fool[u]	Damn bloody fool
Sishimane ushela kanjani uma ushela ngomuthi x 4	You coward, how do you pursue/propose to a person/girl using *umuthi*'

Damn bloody swine	Damn bloody swine
Umangabe kungowakho ubombelethe' mhlana ugoduke x 2	If [she] is yours put her on your back and go home/fuck off
Angikhathali noma ungangithumela ngezulu	I don't care even if you can send me a lightning strike
Anginandaba noma ungangithumela ngezulu	I don't care even if you can send me lightning
[Chorus:]	
Yimi inkunzi emnyama	I am the black bull / I am the top dog
Yimi inkunzi emnyama madoda	I am the black bull gentlemen
Yimi inkunzi emnyama	I am the black bull
Nahlaba inkunzi emnyama?	Why are you stabbing/sacrificing the black bull?
Nahlaba inkunzi emnyama.	You stabbed the black bull.

'Molomolo Mame'

Transcription and translation by Ignatia Madalane and Elias Nxumalo, with kind permission from heir Mrs Nkwanyana (Mrs Nkwanyana 2009a).

Molomolo mame, molomolo baba	Oh dear mother, oh dear father
Molomolo baba, molomolo mame, molomolo baba	Oh dear father, oh dear mother, oh dear father
Uyosala egad'wathina	The child is left to be looked after by us
Ingane kabani, ingane kamama, ingane kababa	Whose child is this, it is mother's child, it is father's child.
Ushiyingane, ushingile	They left their child, they [the parents presumably] have gone crazy
Ingane kabani, ingane kamama, ingane kababa	Whose child is this, it is mother's child, it is father's child.
Uyosala egad'wathina	The child is left to be looked after by us
Ushiyingane, ushingile	They left their child, they've gone crazy

'Ngafa'

Transcription and translation by Ignatia Madalane (Xaba and Magubane 2003b).

Ngafa, ngafa, ngafela ubala	I am dying, I am dying, dying for nothing
Wooo, ingabe yini?	Ooooww, what is this?

Bayangitshela lapha ngihamba khona	They tell me everywhere I go
Bathi kimi hi zintombi zami.	That it is my girlfriends.
Umanginghena esibedhlela	When I enter a hospital
Ngiyo funa usizo lwempilo yami	Looking for help relating to my health
Bafike bathi, hamba baba a wuna lutho	They tell me to go, saying there is nothing wrong [with me]
Uma nginghena emtholampilo	When I go to hospital
Ngiyo funa usizo lwempilo yami	Looking for help relating to my health
Bafike bathi, hamba baba awuna lutho	They tell me to go away saying there is nothing wrong
Aaaaaa ngo moya wami	[There is nothing wrong] with my spirit
Aaaaaa nge mpilo yami	[There is nothing wrong] with my health
Awungitshele we Nobuhle wami	Tell me, my Nobuhle
Wena ngangi thandana nawe, wangi baqa nabangaki?	Since I've been involved with you, how many people did you combine/cheat me with?
Kawungitshele	Tell me
[Response:] Babebabili	There were two of them
Awungitshele we Nomusa wami	Tell me, my Nomusa
Wena ngangi thandana nawe, wangi baqa nabangaki?	Since I've been involved with you, how many people did you combine/cheat me with?
Ngithi awungitshele	Tell me
[Response:] Babebathathu	There were three of them
Kwakungamele ukuthi ningi baqe nabantu aba ningi	You [plural] were not supposed to combine me with many people
Ngoba nani niyazi ukuthi kulomhlaba kunezifo	Because you [plural] know that in this world there are diseases
Kwakumele nithande mina ngedwa	You [plural] were supposed to love me alone
Awungitshele Sindisiwe wami	Tell me, my Sindisiwe
Wena ngoba ngihlala nawe endlini, bangaki na, ongi baqe nabo?	Since I stay with her at home, how many people did you cheat on me with?
Dali wami	My darling
Ngicela ukukhuluma iciniso kuwe	May I please be honest with you
Baningi.	There is too many of them.
Ngeke ngi ba cede.	I won't finish them [counting]
Ah himihlola, himihloya yani?	Ah strange absurdity What strange absurdity/nonsense is this?
Wangi bulala Nobuhle wami	You killed me, my Nobuhle
Kanti unjani	What kind of a person are you?
Ngikuthembe kangaka	I trusted you

Wangi bulala sthandwa	You killed me my love
Hawu kanti unesandla ekufeni kwami	Ow, so you have a hand in my death/dying
Wangi bulala Nomusa wami	You killed me, my Nomusa
Wangi bulala sthandwa.	You killed me my love.

References

Abagqugquzeli (Organizers)/Khombisile Band (2008), Sharing Aural Space, 16 September, Stable Theatre Rehearsal Room, Warwick Triangle, Durban.

Abels, Birgit (2012), 'For the Love of Soundscapes: Sama Dilaut Cultural Identity, the Sensory Experience of Travelling at Sea, and the Acoustic Claiming of Space', in Birgit Abels, Hanafi Hussin and Matthew Santamaria (eds), *Oceans of Sound: Sama Dilaut Performing Arts*, 97–108, Hildesheim: Olms (Göttinger Studien zur Musikwissenschaft; 3).

Abels, Birgit (2013), 'Hörgemeinschaften: Eine musikwissenschaftliche Annäherung an die Atmosphärenforschung', *Die Musikforschung*, 3: 220–31.

Abels, Birgit (2016), 'Restless, Risky, Dirty (An Introduction)', in Birgit Abels (ed.), *Embracing Restlessness: Cultural Musicology*, 1–16, Hildesheim: Olms (Göttinger Studien zur Musikwissenschaft; 6).

Agawu, V. Kofi (2003), *Representing African Music: Postcolonial Notes, Queries, Positions*, London: Routledge.

Agnew, Vanessa (2008), *Enlightenment Orpheus: The Power of Music in Other Worlds*, New York, NY: Oxford University Press.

Ahmed, Sara, Claudia Castañeda, Anne-Marie Fortier and Mimi Shellery, eds (2003), *Uprootings/Regroundings: Questions of Home and Migration*, Oxford: Berg.

Allen, Siemon (2011), 'Miriam Makeba – Tracks Less Travelled (1958–98)', in Chris Albertyn, Matt Temple, Nick Lotay and Siemon Allen (eds), *Electric Jive Blog*, 9 October. Available online: http://electricjive.blogspot.nl/2011/10/miriam-makeba-tracks-less-travelled.html (accessed 27 March 2021).

Allingham, Rob, prod. (1990), *Singing in an Open Space: Zulu Rhythm and Harmony, 1962–1982*, Cambridge, MA: Rounder Records CD 5207.

Allingham, Rob (2009), Personal communication (together with Kathryn Olsen), 29 June, Hemingway Café, Glenwood, Durban.

Anderson, Allan (2001), *African Reformation: African Initiated Christianity in the 20th Century*, Trenton, NJ: Africa World Press.

Augustine, Saint ([397 CE] 1992), *Confessions*, transl. and ed. James J. O'Donnell, Oxford: Oxford University Press.

Ballantine, Christopher (1999), 'Looking to the USA: The Politics of Male Close-Harmony Song Style in South Africa during the 1940s and 1950s', *Popular Music*, 18 (1): 1–17.

Ballantine, Christopher (2000), 'Gender, Migrancy, and South African Popular Music in the Late 1940s and the 1950s', *Ethnomusicology*, 44 (3): 376–407.

Ballantine, Christopher ([1993] 2012), *Marabi Nights: Jazz, 'Race' and Society in Early Apartheid South Africa*, Scotsville: University of KwaZulu-Natal Press.

Barz, Gregory F. ([1997] 2008), 'Confronting the Field(Note) in and out of the Field: Music, Voices, Texts, Experiences in Dialogue', in Gregory F. Barz and Timothy J. Cooley (eds), *Shadows in the Field: New Perspectives for Fieldwork in Ethnomusicology*, 2nd edn., 206–23, New York, NY: Oxford University Press.

Bergin, Sean (2010), Personal communication, 4 June, World Music Centre RASA, Utrecht, the Netherlands.
Berglund, Axel-Ivar ([1976] 1989), *Zulu Thought-Patterns and Symbolism*, London: Hurst.
Bhabha, Homi K. (1994a), 'Introduction: Locations of Culture', in *The Location of Culture*, 1–18, London: Routledge.
Bhabha, Homi K. (1994b), 'Interrogating Identity', in *The Location of Culture*, 40–65, London: Routledge.
Bhabha, Homi K. (1994c), 'The Other Question: Stereotype, Discrimination and the Discourse of Colonialism', in *The Location of Culture*, 66–84, London: Routledge.
Bhabha, Homi K. (1994d), 'Of Mimicry and Man: The Ambivalence of Colonial Discourse', in *The Location of Culture*, 85–92, London: Routledge.
Bhabha, Homi K. (1994e), 'Signs Taken for Wonders: Questions of Ambivalence and Authority under a Tree outside Delhi, May 1817', in *The Location of Culture*, 102–22, London: Routledge.
Blignaut, Chris A., and The Melodians (*c.* 1931), 'Sarie Marais'. Available online: https://www.youtube.com/watch?v=AYe2lqQcues (accessed 27 March 2021).
Bloechl, Olivia A. (2008), 'On Colonial Difference and Musical Frontiers: Directions for a Postcolonial Musicology', in *Native American Song at the Frontiers of Early Modern Music*, 1–32, Cambridge: Cambridge University Press.
Born, Georgina (2010), 'For a Relational Musicology: Music and Interdisciplinarity, Beyond the Practice Turn', *Journal of the Royal Musical Association*, 135 (2): 205–43.
Brown, Danielle (2020), 'An Open Letter on Racism in Music Studies Especially Ethnomusicology and Music Education' (12 June). Available online: https://www.mypeopletellstories.com/blog/open-letter (accessed 27 March 2021).
Buthelezi, Mbongiseni (2017), 'Why Are You Learning Zulu Again?', *Safundi: The Journal of South African and American Studies*, 18 (1): 16–19.
Butler, Judith (1988), 'Performative Acts and Gender Constitution: An Essay in Phenomenology and Feminist Theory', *Theatre Journal*, 40 (4): 519–31.
Byl, Julia (2014), *Antiphonal Histories: Resonant Pasts in the Toba Batak Musical Present*, Middletown, IN: Wesleyan University Press.
Carter, Paul (2004), 'Ambiguous Traces, Mishearing, and Auditory Space', in Veit Erlmann (ed.), *Hearing Cultures: Essays on Sound, Listening and Modernity*, 43–63, Oxford: Berg.
Carton, Benedict, and Malcolm Draper (2008), 'Bulls in the Boardroom: The Zulu Warrior Ethic and the Spirit of South African Capitalism', in Benedict Carton, John Laband and Jabulani Sithole (eds), *Zulu Identities: Being Zulu, Past and Present*, 591–605, Scotsville: University of KwaZulu-Natal Press.
Chakrabarty, Dipesh ([2000] 2007), *Provincializing Europe: Postcolonial Thought and Historical Difference*, Princeton, NJ: Princeton University Press.
Chikowero, Mhoze (2015), *African Music, Power, and Being in Colonial Zimbabwe*, Bloomington, IN: Indiana University Press.
Childs, Peter, and Patrick Williams (1997), 'Bhabha's Hybridity', in Peter Childs and Patrick Williams (eds), *An Introduction to Post-Colonial Theory*, 122–47, London: Prentice Hall.
Clarke, Eric (2005), *Ways of Listening: An Ecological Approach to the Perception of Musical Meaning*, Oxford: Oxford University Press.
Clayton, Martin (2001), 'Towards a Theory of Musical Meaning (in India and Elsewhere)', *British Journal of Ethnomusicology*, 10 (1): 1–17.

Clegg, Jonathan (Johnny) (1981), 'The Music of Zulu Immigrant Workers in Johannesburg: A Focus on Concertina and Guitar', in Andrew Tracey (ed.), *Papers Presented at the Symposium on Ethnomusicology*, 2–9, Grahamstown: International Library of African Music.

Clegg, Jonathan (Johnny) (1982), 'Towards an Understanding of African Dance: The Zulu isiShameni Style', in Andrew Tracey (ed.), *Papers Presented at the [2nd] Symposium on Ethnomusicology*, 8–14, Grahamstown: International Library of African Music.

Clegg, Jonathan (Johnny) (1984), 'An Examination of the Umzansi Dance Style', in Andrew Tracey (ed.), *Papers Presented at the 3rd Symposium on Ethnomusicology*, 64–70, Grahamstown: International Library of African Music.

Clegg, Jonathan (Johnny) (2009), Personal communication, 1 October, Sandton, Johannesburg.

Clegg, Jonathan (Johnny) (2011), 'Sab' Inganono'. Available online: https://www.youtube.com/watch?v=dEjdf4_TZrs (accessed 27 March 2021).

Clegg, Jonathan (Johnny) and Band (2007), 'Sab' Inganono', in Johnny Clegg (prod.), *My Favourite Zulu Street Guitar Songs*, Johannesburg: Scatterlings Club DVD.

Clifford, James (1988), *The Predicament of Culture: Twentieth-Century Ethnography, Literature and Art*, Cambridge, MA: Harvard University Press.

Clifford, James, and George E. Marcus (1986), *Writing Culture: The Poetics and Politics of Ethnography*, Berkeley, CA: University of California Press.

Collins, Tom (2006–7), 'Constructing Maskanda', *SAMUS: South African Music Studies*, 26 & 27: 1–26.

Cook, Nicholas (2012), 'Anatomy of the Encounter: Intercultural Analysis as Relational Musicology', in Stan Hawkins (ed.), *Critical Musicological Reflections: Essays in Honour of Derek B. Scott*, 193–208, Aldershot: Ashgate.

Coplan, David B. (1993a), 'A Terrible Commitment: Balancing the Tribes in South African National Culture', in George E. Marcus (ed.), *Perilous States: Conversations on Culture, Politics, and Nation*, 305–58, Chicago, IL: The University of Chicago Press.

Coplan, David B. (1993b), 'Ethnomusicology and the Meaning of Tradition', in Stephen Blum, Philip Bohlman and Daniel Neuman (eds), *Ethnomusicology and Modern Music History*, 35–48, Urbana, IL: University of Illinois Press.

Coplan, David B. (1994), *In the Time of Cannibals: The Word Music of South Africa's Basotho Migrants*, Chicago, IL: The University of Chicago Press (Chicago Studies in Ethnomusicology).

Coplan, David B. (2002), 'Sounds of the "Third Way": Zulu Maskanda South African Popular Traditional Music', in Mai Palmberg and Annemette Kirkegaard (eds), *Playing with Identities in Contemporary Music in Africa*, 104–16, Uppsala: Nordiska Afrikainstitutet.

Coplan, David B. (2008a), Personal communication, 24 September, Melville, Johannesburg.

Coplan, David B. ([1985] 2008b), *In Township Tonight! Three Centuries of South African Black City Music and Theatre*, Chicago, IL: The University of Chicago Press (Chicago Studies in Ethnomusicology).

Coullie, Judith (1999), '(Dis)Locating Selves: Izibongo and Narrative Autobiography in South Africa', in Duncan Brown (ed.), *Oral Literature and Performance in Southern Africa*, 61–89, Oxford: Currey.

Curtis, Meagan E., and Jamshed J. Bharucha (2009), 'Memory and Musical Expectation for Tones in Cultural Context', *Music Perception: An Interdisciplinary Journal*, 26 (4): 365–75.

Davies, James (2010–11), 'Report: The Fifth Congress of the South African Society for Research in Music. Rhodes University, 23rd–25th June 2011', *SAMUS: South African Music Studies*, 30 & 31: 191–4.

Davies, Nollene (1992), 'A Study of Guitar Styles in Zulu Maskanda Music', M.Mus. Thesis, University of Natal, Durban.

De Jong, Nanette, and King Madzikane II Thandiszwe Diko (2020), 'Maskanda, Umkhosi wokukhahlela and the Articulation of Identity in South Africa', *Journal of the Royal Musical Association*, 145 (1): 167–90.

Derrida, Jacques ([1967] 1997), *Of Grammatology*, transl. Gayatri C. Spivak, Baltimore, MD: Johns Hopkins University Press.

Dlamini, Sazi (2011a), Personal communication, 3 July, en route Grahamstown–Port Elizabeth.

Dlamini, Sazi (2011b), Personal communication, 7 July, University of KwaZulu-Natal, Durban.

Douglas, Mary ([1970] 1996), *Natural Symbols: Explorations in Cosmology*, London: Routledge.

Du Bois, W.E.B. ([1903] 2010), *The Souls of Black Folk: Essays and Sketches*, Auckland: The Floating Press.

Erlmann, Veit (1991), *African Stars: Studies in Black South African Performance*, Chicago, IL: The University of Chicago Press (Chicago Studies in Ethnomusicology).

Erlmann, Veit (1996), *Nightsong: Performance, Power, and Practice in South Africa*, Chicago, IL: The University of Chicago Press (Chicago Studies in Ethnomusicology).

Erlmann, Veit (1999), *Music, Modernity and the Global Imagination: South Africa and the West*, Oxford: Oxford University Press.

Erlmann, Veit, ed. (2004), *Hearing Cultures: Essays on Sound, Listening, and Modernity*, Oxford: Berg (Wenner-Gren International Symposium Series).

Erlmann, Veit (2010), *Reason and Resonance: A History of Modern Aurality*, New York, NY: Zone Books.

eThekwini Online (2005), 'Maskanda'. Available online: https://web.archive.org/web/20050308095019/http://www.durban.gov.za:80/eThekwini/Tourism_and_Leisure/the_arts/music/zulucontemporary/ (accessed 28 March 2021).

Fabian, Johannes (1990), *Power and Performance: Ethnographic Explorations through Proverbial Wisdom and Theater in Shaba, Zaire*, Madison, WI: University of Wisconsin Press.

Faure, William C., dir. (1986), *Shaka Zulu*. Los Angeles: Harmony Gold USA. Available online: https://www.youtube.com/watch?v=77IzOo4JVaY (accessed 27 March 2021).

Feld, Steven (1981), '"Flow like a Waterfall": The Metaphors of Kaluli Music Theory', *Yearbook for Traditional Music*, 13: 22–47.

Feld, Steven (1982), *Sound and Sentiment: Birds, Weeping, Poetics, and Song in Kaluli Expression*, Philadelphia, PA: University of Pennsylvania Press.

Feld, Steven (1996), 'Pygmy Pop: A Genealogy of Schizophonic Mimesis', *Yearbook for Traditional Music*, 28: 1–35.

Feld, Steven (2015), 'Acoustemology', in David Novak and Matt Sakakeeny (eds), *Keywords in Sound*, 12–21, Durham, NC: Duke University Press.

Garside, Charles Jr. (1979), *The Origin of Calvin's Theology of Music, 1536–1543*, Philadelphia, PA: American Philosophical Society.

Gaye, Marvin (1982), 'Sexual Healing', from *Midnight Love*, New York, NY: Columbia LP PC 38197. Available online: https://www.youtube.com/watch?v=auw56ai2z-M (accessed 27 March 2021).

Gilbert, Shirli (2007), 'Singing against Apartheid: ANC Cultural Groups and the International Anti-Apartheid Struggle', *Journal of Southern African Studies*, 33 (2): 421–41.

Gilroy, Paul (1993), *The Black Atlantic: Modernity and Double Consciousness*, London: Verso.

Gonsalves, Neil (2009), Personal communication, 4 October, The Rainbow Restaurant, Pinetown, Durban.

Gouk, Penelope (2004), 'Raising Spirits and Restoring Souls: Early Modern Medical Explanations for Music's Effects', in Veit Erlmann (ed.), *Hearing Cultures: Essays on Sound, Listening and Modernity*, 87–105, Oxford: Berg.

Graeber, David (2015), 'Radical Alterity is just another Way of Saying "Reality": A Reply to Eduardo Viveiros de Castro', *Hau: Journal of Ethnographic Theory*, 5 (2): 1–41.

Gumbrecht, Hans Ulrich (2004), *Production of Presence: What Meaning Cannot Convey*, Stanford, CA: Stanford University Press.

Gunner, Liz (1989), 'Songs of Innocence and Experience: Women as Composers and Performers of Izibongo, Zulu Praise Poetry', in Cherry Clayton (ed.), *Women and Writing in South Africa: A Critical Anthology*, 12–39, Marshalltown: Heinemann Southern Africa.

Gunner, Liz (2009), 'Jacob Zuma, the Social Body and the Unruly Power of Song', *African Affairs*, 108 (430): 27–48

Gunner, Liz, and Mafika Gwala, eds (1991), *Musho: Zulu Popular Praises*, East Lansing, MI: Michigan State University Press.

Hadebe, Josiah Sillo (2000), 'Izwe Alithuthuki by Phuzekhemisi as Sung in KwaZulu-Natal: Maskandi Song as Social Protest Analysed as an Oral-Style Text', MA Thesis, University of Natal, Durban.

Hadebe, Thembinkosi Dennis (2008), Personal communication, 20 August, 137 Penzance Road, Glenwood, Durban.

Hahn, Tomie (2007), 'Introduction – Sensual Orientations', in *Sensational Knowledge: Embodying Culture through Japanese Dance*, 1–21, Middletown, IN: Wesleyan University Press.

Hammond-Tooke, W. D. (2008), 'Cattle Symbolism in Zulu Culture', in Benedict Carton, John Laband and Jabulani Sithole (eds), *Zulu Identities: Being Zulu, Past and Present*, 62–8. Scotsville: University of KwaZulu-Natal Press.

Hegel, Georg W. F. ([1826] 1998), 'Die Musik', ed. Alain Olivier, in Friedhelm Nicolin and Otto Pöggeler (eds), *Hegel-Studien* 33, 26–52, Hamburg: Felix Meiner Verlag.

Hickox, Douglas, dir. (1979), *Zulu Dawn*. Movie drama, Samarkand/Zulu Dawn NV. Available online: https://www.youtube.com/watch?v=r1tMgptVe7I (accessed 27 March 2021).

Hoffmann, Anette (2020), *Kolonialgeschichte hören: Das Echo gewaltsamer Wissensproduktion in historischen Tondokumenten aus dem südlichen Afrika*, Wien: Mandelbaum.

Hornbostel, Erich M. (1928), 'African Negro Music', *Africa: Journal of the International African Institute*, 1 (1): 30–62.

Hughey, Matthew W. (2009), 'Cinethetic Racism: White Redemption and Black Stereotypes in "Magical Negro" Films', *Social Problems*, 56 (3): 543–77.

iHashi Elimhlophe (White Horse) [*see* Ngcobo, Bheki].

Impey, Angela (1983), 'The Zulu Umakhweyana Bow: Ndabisehlele Myeza and Her Songs', BA (Hons) Thesis, University of Natal, Durban.

Impey, Angela (2018), *Song Walking: Women, Music, and Environmental Justice in an African Borderland*, Chicago, IL: The University of Chicago Press (Chicago Studies in Ethnomusicology).

Izintombi (Young Ladies) [*see* Ngobese, Bongekile and Tholakele Ngobese].
Jackson, T. (1999), 'Music: A Venture with a Note of Caution', *The Financial Times*, 27 July.
James, Deborah (1999), *Songs of the Women Migrants: Performance and Identity in South Africa*, Edinburgh: Edinburgh University Press.
Jenkins, David (a.k.a. Qadasi) (2013a), Personal communication, 27 March, Skype.
Jenkins, David (2013b), Personal communication, 15 July, 137 Penzance Road, Glenwood, Durban.
Jenkins, David (2016), Personal communication, 12 September, Email.
Jenkins, David and Band (2011), 'Sab' Inganono', from *Child of Africa/Ingane yase Afrika*, Johannesburg: Gallo CD XRW-R60-VEH-1. Available online: https://qadasi.bandcamp.com/track/sab-inganono (accessed 27 March 2021).
Jenkins, David and Band (2013), 'Sab' Inganono', live at The Village, Dublin, Ireland, 27 April. Available online: https://www.youtube.com/watch?v=3zAivKhIzTo (Part 1) and https://www.youtube.com/watch?v=FgaYu_t8Pdc (Part 2) (accessed 27 March 2021).
Jorritsma, Marie (2011), *Sonic Spaces of the Karoo: The Sacred Music of a South African Coloured Community*, Johannesburg: University of the Witwatersrand Press.
KCAP (KwaMashu Community Advancement Projects) (2015), 'Ekhaya Multi Arts Centre (EMAC)'. Available online: http://kcap.co.za/about-us (accessed 27 March 2021).
Keil, Charles, and Steven Feld (1994), *Music Grooves: Essays and Dialogues*, Chicago, IL: The University of Chicago Press.
Khama, Linah (a.k.a. Ebony) (2009), Personal communication (together with Bheki Ngcobo), 23 September, Downtown Studios, Johannesburg.
Khoza, Bheki (2009), Personal communication (together with Bongani Nkwanyana), 23 September, Restaurant Mimmos, Eastgate Shopping Centre, Johannesburg.
Khumalo, Mphatheni (a.k.a. Mfaz' Omnyama) (1995), 'Lolo Sizi Olungaka', from *Emazweni Baba*, Johannesburg: Gallo. Available online: https://www.youtube.com/watch?v=NH-LJDnPdW0 (accessed 27 March 2021).
Kirby, Percival R. ([1934] 1953), *The Musical Instruments of the Native Races of South Africa*, Johannesburg: Witwatersrand University Press.
Kisliuk, Michelle ([1997] 2008), '(Un)Doing Fieldwork: Sharing Songs, Sharing Lives', in Gregory F. Barz and Timothy J. Cooley (eds), *Shadows in the Field: New Perspectives for Fieldwork in Ethnomusicology*, 2nd edn., 183–205, New York, NY: Oxford University Press.
Knight, Ian (2008), '"What Do You Red-Jackets Want in Our Country?" The Zulu Response to the British Invasion of 1879', in Benedict Carton, John Laband and Jabulani Sithole (eds), *Zulu Identities: Being Zulu, Past and Present*, 177–89, Scotsville: University of KwaZulu-Natal Press.
Koenis, Stef (2018), 'Jaap Kunst: Early Ethnomusicological Research and the Voice of Indonesia', MA Thesis, University of Amsterdam.
Krims, Adam (2000), *Rap Music and the Poetics of Identity*, Cambridge: Cambridge University Press.
Kubik, Gerhard (1999), *Africa and the Blues*, Jackson, MS: University Press of Mississippi.
Kunene, Madala (2008), Personal communication, 29 August, Playhouse, Durban.
Kunene, Madala, and Max Lässer (1998), *Madamax*, prod. Robert Trunz. Zurich: Impact Music CD 898-51.
Kunst, Jaap (1931), 'Et tu, Matthee', *De Gids* 95 (4): 268.

Kursell, Julia (2017), 'Experimental Cylinders – Experiments in Music Psychology Around 1900', *Journal of Sonic Studies*, 13 (28 May). Available online: https://www.researchcatalogue.net/view/324247/324248 (accessed 27 March 2021).

La Hausse de Lalouvière, Paul (2008), '"Death is not the End": Zulu Cosmopolitanism and the Politics of the Zulu Cultural Revival', in Benedict Carton, John Laband and Jabulani Sithole (eds), *Zulu Identities: Being Zulu, Past and Present*, 256–72, Scotsville: University of KwaZulu-Natal Press.

Lebhaca, Ichwane (2008), *Ubuyile Umaqondana Egoli*, prod. Zibakwakhe Johnston Mnyandu, Johannesburg: Gallo CD 41009.

Lenta, Ashlee (2004), 'Reading the Individual in Community: Personal Izibongo as Autobiographical Performance', *English in Africa*, 3 (1): 59–75.

Levy-Hinte, Jeffrey, prod. (2008), *Soul Power: The Legendary Concert during Muhammad Ali's Rumble in the Jungle*, Sony Classics Documentary Movie 6115.

Linda, Solomon, and Solomon Linda's Original Evening Birds (1939), 'Mbube', Johannesburg: Gallo GE829. Available online: https://www.youtube.com/watch?v=mrrQT4WkbNE (accessed 27 March 2021).

Lucia, Christine, ed. (2005), *The World of South African Music: A Reader*, Newcastle-upon-Tyne: Cambridge Scholars Press.

Madalane, Ignatia (2012), Personal communication, 5 April, Facebook Chat.

Madalane, Ignatia (2016a), Personal communication, 7 July, Email.

Madalane, Ignatia (2016b), Personal communication, 5 September, Email.

Madalane, Ignatia (2016c), Personal communication, 15 September, Email.

Madalane, Ignatia (2021a), Personal communication, 26 March, Email.

Madalane, Ignatia (2021b), Personal communication, 6 May, WhatsApp

Magogo KaDinuzulu, H.R.H. Princess Constance ([n.d.] 1972), 'Kwabase sabulawa nguDingane', from *The Zulu Songs of Princess Constance Magogo KaDinuzulu*, prod. Hugh Tracey, Grahamstown: International Library of African Music (Music of Africa Series; 37).

Mahlatini and The Mohatella Queens [*see* Nkabinde, Simon 'Mahlatini'].

Mahlobo, Thabani Albert (2009), Personal communication, 31 July, Stable Theatre, Warwick Triangle, Durban.

Majozi, Mxolisi (a.k.a. Zuluboy) (2006), 'Hail to the King', from *Masihambisane*, Johannesburg: Native Rhythms CDNATIVE (WCP) 001. Available online: https://www.youtube.com/watch?v=WLlsXyljVcM (accessed 27 March 2021).

Majozi, Mxolisi (2008), 'DJ Gogo', from *Inqolobane*, Johannesburg: Native Rhythms CDNATIVE (WCP) 007. Available online: https://www.youtube.com/watch?v=3DXt3AiKXPs (accessed 27 March 2021).

Majozi, Mxolisi (2011), Personal communication, 7 July, Bambanani Restaurant, Melville, Johannesburg.

Mamdani, Mahmood, Lyn Ossome and Suren Pillay (2016), 'Our Mission' *The MISR Review* 1, 6–8.

Manana, Pinky et al. (2021), '"Maskandi Experience": Exploring the Use of a Cultural Song for Community Engagement in Preparation for a Pilot Sterile Insect Technique Release Programme for Malaria Vector Control in KwaZulu-Natal Province, South Africa 2019', *Malaria Journal* 204. Available online: https://doi.org/10.1186/s12936-021-03736-9 (accessed 28 July 2021).

Martens, Jeremy (2008), 'Enlightenment Theories of Civilisation and Savagery in British Natal: The Colonial Origins of the (Zulu) African Barbarism Myth', in Benedict Carton, John Laband and Jabulani Sithole (eds), *Zulu Identities: Being Zulu, Past and Present*, 122–32, Scotsville: University of KwaZulu-Natal Press.

Maskens, Maïté, and Ruy Blanes (2013), 'Don Quixote's Choice: A Manifesto for a Romanticist Anthropology', *HAU: Journal of Ethnographic Theory*, 3 (3): 245–81.

Masuka, Dorothy (1959), 'Into Yam', performed by Miriam Makeba in the film *Come back Africa*, prod. Lionel Rogosin. Available online: https://www.youtube.com/watch?v=Buod66bq0cg (accessed 27 March 2021).

Mayr, Franz (1908), 'A Short Study on Zulu Music', *Annals of the Natal Government Museum*, 1 (2): 257–68.

Mbeki, Thabo (1998a), 'The African Renaissance, South Africa and the World', Speech delivered at the United Nations University on 9 April. Available online: http://archive.unu.edu/unupress/mbeki.html (accessed 27 March 2021).

Mbeki, Thabo (1998b), 'The African Renaissance Statement of Deputy President, Thabo Mbeki', presented via the SABC, Gallagher Estate on 13 August. Available online: http://www.dirco.gov.za/docs/speeches/1998/mbek0813.htm (accessed 27 March 2021).

McClary, Susan ([1991] 2002), *Feminine Endings: Music, Gender, and Sexuality*, Minneapolis, MN: University of Minnesota Press.

Mchunu, Sipho (1979), 'Sab' Inganono', in Chris Austin and Jeremy Marre (dirs), *Rhythm of Resistance*, London: Harcourt/Virgin.

McNeill, Fraser (2012), 'Making Music, Making Money: Informal Musical Production and Performance in Venda, South Africa', *Africa*, 82 (1): 93–110.

Meintjes, Louise (1990), 'Paul Simon's *Graceland*, South Africa, and the Mediation of Musical Meaning', *Ethnomusicology*, 34 (1): 37–73.

Meintjes, Louise (2003), *Sound of Africa!: Making Music Zulu in a South African Studio*, Durham, NC: Duke University Press.

Meintjes, Louise (2017), *Dust of the Zulu: Ngoma Aesthetics after Apartheid*, Durham, NC: Duke University Press.

Meredith, Martin (2007), *Diamonds, Gold and War: The Making of South Africa*, London: Simon & Schuster.

Mfaz' Omnyama (Black Woman) [*see* Khumalo, Mphatheni].

Mhlongo, Victoria Busisiwe (2001), *Urban Zulu*, prod. Will Mowat, London: EMI Records: CD Melt2000.

Mija, Abraham (2009), Personal communication, 23 September, Gallo Offices, Johannesburg.

Miya, Khoni (2009a), Personal communication, 20 August, Circus Circus Restaurant, Musgrave Shopping Centre, Durban.

Miya, Khoni (2009b), Personal communication (together with S'kho Miya), 29 October, Musgrave Shopping Centre, Durban.

Miya, Khoni (2010), Personal communication (together with S'kho Miya), 20 July, BAT Centre, Durban.

Miya, 'S'kho' [Khombisile] (2008a), Transmission of 'Ngilobole' riffs by S'kho Miya to guitarist and bass player, 16 September, Stable Theatre Rehearsal Room, Warwick Triangle, Durban.

Miya, 'S'kho' [Khombisile] (2008b), Transmission of 'Sithi Khuzani' dance steps by S'kho Miya to Barbara Titus, 16 September, Stable Theatre Rehearsal Room, Warwick Triangle, Durban.

Miya, 'S'kho' [Khombisile] (2008c), Personal communication, 9 August, Circus Circus Restaurant, Musgrave Shopping Centre, Durban.
Miya, 'S'kho' [Khombisile] (2008d), Personal communication, 9 October, Circus Circus Restaurant, Musgrave Shopping Centre, Durban.
Miya, 'S'kho' [Khombisile] (2009a), 'Sithi Khuzani', live at the Kushikisha Imbokodo Festival, 30 August, BAT Centre, Durban.
Miya, 'S'kho' [Khombisile] (2009b), Live interaction with the audience at the Kushikisha Imbokodo Festival, 30 August, BAT Centre Durban.
Miya, 'S'kho' [Khombisile] (2009c), 'Ingculazi Iyabulala', from unreleased demo album for *Ungcayi Lweqhikiza*.
Miya, 'S'kho' [Khombisile] (2009d), Personal communication (together with Khoni Miya), 29 October, Musgrave Shopping Centre, Durban
Miya, 'S'kho' [Khombisile] (2010a), 'Sithi Khuzani', from *Ungcayi Lweqhikiza*, prod. Atlas Philani Duma, Johannesburg: CDSagiya 002.
Miya, 'S'kho' [Khombisile] (2010b), 'Ngilobole', from *Ungcayi Lweqhikiza*, prod. Atlas Philani Duma, Johannesburg: CDSagiya 002.
Miya, 'S'kho' [Khombisile] (2010c), 'Nith' Angiqome Bani?', from *Ungcayi Lweqhikiza*, prod. Atlas Philani Duma, Johannesburg: CDSagiya 002.
Miya, 'S'kho' [Khombisile] (2010d), 'Ibhoxongwana', from *Ungcayi Lweqhikiza*, prod. Atlas Philani Duma, Johannesburg: CDSagiya 002.
Miya, 'S'kho' [Khombisile] (2010e), Personal communication (together with Khoni Miya), 20 July, BAT Centre, Durban.
Miya, 'S'kho' [Khombisile] (2018), Personal communication, 30 December, KwaBhidla, Highflats, KwaZulu-Natal.
Mnyandu, Zibakwakhe Johnston (a.k.a. Phuzekhemisi) (2007), *Sesihlangene*, featuring Kennedy Zimba. Johannesburg: Gallo.
Mnyandu, Zibakwakhe Johnston (2009), Personal communication (together with Kathryn Olsen), 4 September, BAT Centre, Durban.
Mnyandu, Zibakwakhe, and Kethani Mnyandu (a.k.a. Phuzekhemisi noKethani) (1989), 'Imbizo', from *Imbizo*, Johannesburg: Gallo. Available online: https://www.youtube.com/watch?v=HvSVtUEaXOc (accessed 27 March 2021).
Mnyandu, Zibakwakhe, and Kethani Mnyandu (1994), 'Emapalamende', from *Emapalamende*, Johannesburg: Gallo. Available online: https://www.youtube.com/watch?v=0vjgOJhNP-w (accessed 27 March 2021).
Mols, Dora (2010), Personal communication, 3 June, Zuiderpershuis, Antwerp, Belgium.
Monson, Ingrid T. (1996), *Saying Something: Jazz Improvisation and Interaction*, Chicago, IL: The University of Chicago Press (Chicago Studies in Ethnomusicology).
Muller, Carol Ann (1999), 'Chakide – the Teller of Secrets: Space, Song and Story in Zulu Maskanda Performance', in Duncan Brown (ed.), *Oral Literature and Performance in Southern Africa*, 220–34, Oxford: Currey.
Muller, Carol Ann (2004), *South African Music: A Century of Traditions in Transformation*, Oxford: ABC-Clio.
Muller, Carol Ann, and Sathima B. Benjamin (2011), *Musical Echoes: South African Women Thinking in Jazz*, Durham, NC: Duke University Press.
Mundy, Rachel (2018), *Animal Musicalities: Birds, Beasts, and Evolutionary Listening*, Middletown, IN: Wesleyan University Press.
Mziwoxolo (House of Peace) [*see* Nkwanyana, Josefa].

Naidoo, Mageshen (2009a), Personal communication (together with Concord Nkabinde), 28 July, Bangkok Wok Restaurant, Wilson's Wharf, Durban.
Naidoo, Mageshen (2009b), Personal communication, 14 October, Glenwood, Durban.
Ndladla, Zweli (2009), Personal communication, 23 September, en route Melville–Downtown Studios, Johannesburg.
Ngcobo, Bheki (a.k.a. Hashi Elimhlophe) (2009a), Live with 'Zulu Dance Group Performing at ANC Final Rally for Zuma's Presidency', Ellis Park Stadium, Johannesburg, April. Available online: https://www.youtube.com/watch?v=9NydxjMFmWU (accessed 27 March 2021).
Ngcobo, Bheki (2009b), Personal communication, through interlocutor Linah Khama, 23 September, Downtown Studios, Johannesburg.
Ngcobo, Bheki, Mphatheni Khumalo and Johnston Mnyandu (1997), 'Sxaxa Mbij", from *Izingqungqulu Zomhlaba/Pulling Together*, Johannesburg: Gallo B00005YAZH. Available online: https://www.youtube.com/watch?v=qhuR1LTGf-0 (accessed 27 March 2021).
Ngcobo, Selby (2008a), Personal communication, 15 August, en route Glenwood–Wilson's Wharf, Durban.
Ngcobo, Selby (2008b), Personal communication, 4 October, en route Glenwood–PheZulu.
Ngcobo, Selby (2009), Personal communication, 3 October, en route Ulundi–Durban.
Ngcobo, Shiyani [S.] (2004), *Introducing Shiyani Ngcobo. Zulu Guitars Dance: Maskanda from South Africa*, prod. Ben Mandelson, London: World Music Network INTRO 101CD. Available online: https://www.youtube.com/watch?v=Z2y8txs8ZcA&list=OLAK5uy_lGG_jl1h62ZyUwtAYjTEajGXbKjuYjrKQ (accessed 28 March 2021).
Ngcobo, Shiyani [S.] (2008a), 'Sevelina', 30 August, University of KwaZulu-Natal, Durban.
Ngcobo, Shiyani [S.] (2008b), 'Izinyembezi', 30 August, University of KwaZulu-Natal, Durban.
Ngcobo, Shiyani [S.] (2008c), Personal communication, 30 August, University of KwaZulu-Natal, Durban.
Ngcobo, Shiyani [S.] (2008d), Personal communication, 6 September, University of KwaZulu-Natal, Durban.
Ngcobo, Shiyani [S.] (2008e), Personal communication (together with Kathryn Olsen), 20 September, en route Umlazi–Glenwood.
Ngcobo, Shiyani [S.] (2008f), Personal communication, through interlocutor Thokozani Khuzwayo, 21 October, University of KwaZulu-Natal, Durban.
Ngcobo, Shiyani [S.] (2009), Personal communication, 7 October, University of KwaZulu-Natal, Durban.
Ngcobo, Shiyani [S.] (2010a), *Shiyani Ngcobo Featuring Njabulo Shabalala*, prod. Jürgen Bräuninger and Kathryn Olsen, Durban: UKZN School of Music Studio.
Ngcobo, Shiyani [S.] (2010b), Personal communication, 3 June, Zuiderpershuis, Antwerp, Belgium.
Ngcobo, Shiyani [S.] (2010c), Performance of various songs, 4 June, World Music Centre RASA, Utrecht, the Netherlands.
Ngcobo, Shiyani [S.] (2010d), 'Asinankomo', live at the Tropentheater, Amsterdam, the Netherlands, 6 June. Available online: https://www.youtube.com/watch?v=aSS3M2LLHpg (uploaded with kind permission of Shiyani Ngcobo and accessed 27 March 2021).

Ngema, Nomcebo (2009), Personal communication (together with Nhlanhla Ngwekazi), 22 September, J. Mofokeng & Associates (JMA) Offices, Melville, Johannesburg.
Ngobese, Bongekile, and Tholakele Ngobese (a.k.a. Izintombi) (2009), *Izintombi zika Shwii. Usizi*, prod. Khethonjani Dludla and Mandla Xaba (a.k.a. Shwi), Johannesburg: Zuz'muzi Music.
Ngwekazi, Nhlanhla (2009), Personal communication (together with Nomcebo Ngema), 22 September, J. Mofokeng & Associates (JMA) Offices, Melville, Johannesburg.
Ngwekazi, Nhlanhla (2013), Personal communication, 29 May, Facebook Chat.
Nhlapo, Phindile (1998), 'Maskanda: The Zulu Strolling Musicians', MA Thesis, University of the Witwatersrand, Johannesburg.
Nkabinde, Concord (2009), Personal communication (together with Mageshen Naidoo), 28 July, Bangkok Wok Restaurant, Wilson's Wharf, Durban.
Nkabinde, Simon 'Mahlatini' and The Mohatella Queens (1987), 'Thokozile', from *Thokozile*, prod. West Nkosi. Johannesburg: Gallo. Available online: https://www.youtube.com/watch?v=YcH4cPqykF0 (accessed 28 March 2021).
Nkwanyana, Bongani (2009a), 'Inku[n]z'emnyama', from *Yash'inkani*, featuring Noxolo Radebe and Hugh Masekela, prod. Bheki Khoza, Johannesburg: Kora Records CD KORA 003.
Nkwanyana, Bongani (2009b), Personal communication (together with Bheki Khoza), 23 September, Restaurant Mimmos, Eastgate Shopping Centre, Johannesburg.
Nkwanyana, Bongani (2013), Personal communication, 23 July, Park Station, Johannesburg.
Nkwanyana, Bongani (2014), 'Inkunzi Em[n]yama'. Available online: https://www.youtube.com/watch?v=jUZyNzwye-Q (accessed 28 March 2021).
Nkwanyana, Bongani (2016a), Personal communication, 8 May, Email.
Nkwanyana, Bongani (2016b), Personal communication, 9 May, Email.
Nkwanyana, Bongani (2016c), Personal communication, 11 May, Email.
Nkwanyana, Bongani (2016d), Personal communication, 6 August, Email.
Nkwanyana, Josefa (a.k.a. Mziwoxolo) (1984), *Ngihamba Nomngani*, prod. Hamilton Nzimande.
Nkwanyana, Josefa (2009a), 'Wentandane Zobaba', 20 October, Tugela, Mandeni, KwaZulu-Natal.
Nkwanyana, Josefa (2009b), Personal communication, through interlocutor Nandi Khumalo, 20 October, Tugela, Mandeni, KwaZulu-Natal.
Nkwanyana, Mrs (2009a), 'Molomolo Mama', filmed by Vumelani Mchunu, 20 October, Tugela, Mandeni, KwaZulu-Natal.
Nkwanyana, Mrs (2009b), 'Mthembu kaMthele', filmed by Vumelani Mchunu, 20 October, Tugela, Mandeni, KwaZulu-Natal.
Nokwe, Tu (2009), Personal communication, 18 August, KwaMashu Arts Centre, KwaMashu.
Nthethe, Lichaba (2011), Personal communication, 12 July, Bambanani Restaurant, Melville, Johannesburg.
Ntombela, Sipho Albert (2016), 'Maskandi: A Critical Discourse Analysis of Indigenous isiZulu Songs', *Southern African Linguistics and Applied Language Studies*, 34, 109–20.
Ntuli, D. B. (1990), 'Remarks on Maskandi Poetry', *South African Journal of African Languages*, 10 (4): 302–6.

Ntuli, Nothi (2009), Personal communication, through interlocutor Ignatia Madalane, 22 September, Downtown Studios, Johannesburg.
Ntuli, Nothi (2019), *Sanibonani*, Johannesburg: Content Connect Africa (CCA).
Nyezwa, Mxolisi (2018), 'Listening with One Ear – Maskandi Lyrics and their Potential to Revitalise isiXhosa Poetry', *New Coin Poetry*, 54 (2): 118–23.
Nzimande, Tshepo (2009), Personal communication, 23 September, Zuz'muzi Music Offices, 83 Von Brandisstreet, Johannesburg.
Ochoa Gautier, Ana María (2014), 'The Ear and the Voice in the Lettered City's Geophysical History', in *Aurality: Listening and Knowledge in Nineteenth-Century Colombia*, 1–29, Durham, NC: Duke University Press.
Ochoa Gautier, Ana María (2016), 'Acoustic Multinaturalism, the Value of Nature, and the Nature of Music in Ecomusicology', *boundary 2*, 43(1): 107–41.
Olsen, Kathryn (2000), 'Politics, Production and Process: Discourses on Tradition in Contemporary Maskanda', M.Mus Thesis, University of Natal, Durban.
Olsen, Kathryn (2004), 'Shiyani Ngcobo and Maskanda', in *Introducing Shiyani Ngcobo: Zulu Guitars Dance. Maskanda from South Africa*, sleeve notes, London: World Music Network and Riverboat Records, INTRO101CD.
Olsen, Kathryn (2008a), Personal communication, 11 September, University of KwaZulu-Natal, Durban.
Olsen, Kathryn (2008b), Personal communication (together with Shiyani Ngcobo), 20 September, en route Umlazi–Glenwood.
Olsen, Kathryn (2009a), Personal communication, 9 September, University of KwaZulu-Natal, Durban.
Olsen, Kathryn (2009b), Personal communication, 15 October, University of KwaZulu-Natal, Durban.
Olsen, Kathryn (2014), *Music and Social Change in South Africa: Maskanda Past and Present*, Philadelphia, PA: Temple University Press.
Pew Research Center (2006), 'Historical Overview of Pentecostalism in South Africa'. Available online: http://www.pewforum.org/2006/10/05/historical-overview-of-pentecostalism-in-south-africa/ (accessed 28 March 2021).
Pewa, Elliot Sagila (2005), 'The Philosophical, Behavioural and Academic Merit of uMaskandi Music', PhD Thesis, University of Zululand, Richards Bay.
Phuzekhemisi (Drinker at the Chemist's) [*see* Mnyandu, Zibakwakhe Johnston].
Pieters, Marieke (2010), Personal communication, 4 June, World Music Centre RASA, Utrecht, the Netherlands.
Plato ([4th century BCE] 2004), *Republic* Book II, transl. Benjamin Jowett, New York, NY: Barnes and Noble Classics.
Pooley, Thomas M. (2016), 'Umaskandi Izibongo: Semantic, Prosodic and Musical Dimensions of Voice in Zulu Popular Praises', *African Music*, 10 (2): 7–34.
Pyper, Brett (2016), 'Jazz Festivals and the Post-Apartheid Public Sphere: Historical Precedents and the Contemporary Limits of Freedom', in Nishlyn Ramanna (ed.), *South African Jazz Culture: Texts, Contexts, and Subtexts*, 107–22, Berlin: Verlag für Wissenschaft und Bildung (world of music new series; 5 [2]).
Qadasi (White Person) [*see* Jenkins, David].
Radano, Ronald, and Tejumola Olaniyan, eds (2016), *Audible Empire: Music, Global Politics, Critique*, Durham, NC: Duke University Press.
Ramanna, Nishlyn (2005), 'Jazz as Discourse: A Contextualised Account of Contemporary Jazz in Post-Apartheid Durban and Johannesburg', PhD Thesis, University of KwaZulu-Natal, Durban.

Ramanna, Nishlyn (2009), Personal communication, 9 October, Gmail chat.
Ramanna, Nishlyn (2016), 'Introduction: Discursive Flows in South African Jazz Studies—Texts, Contexts, and Subtexts', in Nishlyn Ramanna (ed.), *South African Jazz Culture: Texts, Contexts, and Subtexts*, 7–29, Berlin: Verlag für Wissenschaft und Bildung (world of music new series; 5 [2]).
RASA (2009/10), 'Shiyani Ngcobo', Programme notes for the performance on Friday 4 June, Utrecht: RASA.
Rice, Timothy (1994), 'Dancing in the Scholar's World', in *May It Fill Your Soul: Experiencing Bulgarian Music*, 3–15, Chicago, IL: The University of Chicago Press (Chicago Studies in Ethnomusicology).
Richardson, John (2016), 'Ecological Close Reading of Music in Digital Culture', in Birgit Abels (ed.), *Embracing Restlessness: Cultural Musicology*, 1–16, Hildesheim: Olms (Göttinger Studien zur Musikwissenschaft; 6).
Rycroft, David K. (1960), 'Melodic Features in Zulu Eulogistic Reciation', *African Language Studies*, 1: 60–78.
Rycroft, David K. (1977), 'Evidence of Stylistic Continuity in Zulu "Town" Music', in *Essays for a Humanist: An Offering to Klaus Wachsmann*, 216–60, New York, NY: The Town House Press.
Scherzinger, Martin (2004), 'The Return of the Aesthetic: Musical Formalism and Its Place in Political Critique', in Andrew Dell'Antonio (ed.), *Beyond Structural Listening? Postmodern Modes of Hearing*, 251–77, Berkeley, CA: University of California Press.
Seeger, Anthony ([1987] 2004), *Why Suyá Sing: A Musical Anthropology of an Amazonian People*, Urbana, IL: University of Illinois Press.
Shabalala, Bhekizizwe Joseph (2009), Personal communication, 3 October, MORC Festival, Ulundi.
Shabalala, Njabulo (2010), Personal communication 5 July, en route Utrecht–Antwerp, the Netherlands.
Shabalala, Njabulo (2013), Personal communication, 11 July, BAT Centre, Durban.
Shandu, Thulile Pearl (2007), 'Pitch Black Language: The Quest for Language Purity in isiZulu popular music', *Muziki: Journal of Music Research in Africa*, 7 (4): 263–77.
Shumba, Kemist and Anna Meyer-Weitz (2019), 'Addressing the Socio-Cultural Drivers of HIV/AIDS through Indigenous Music: A Critical Discourse Analysis of Selected Songs by Maskandi Group, Izingane Zoma', *African Renaissance*, 16 (4). Available online: https://journals.co.za/doi/10.31920/2516-5305/2019/16n1a7 (accessed 21 July 2021).
Shwi noMtekhala [*see* Xaba, Mandla and Rodgers Magubane].
Simon, Paul (1986), *Graceland*, prod. Paul Simon. Burbank, CA: Warner Brothers, WPCR-12417. Available online: https://www.youtube.com/watch?v=ToKsXHRh7Yo&list=PLf MjFFywDtbTGW1fdXnUpTZMTMbSv2yKJ (accessed 28 March 2021).
Slobin, Mark (1993), *Subcultural Sounds: Micromusics of the West*, Hanover, NH: Wesleyan University Press.
Sloboda, John A. (1985), *The Musical Mind: The Cognitive Psychology of Music*, Oxford: Oxford University Press.
Small, Christopher (1998), *Musicking: The Meanings of Performing and Listening*, Middletown, IN: Wesleyan University Press.
Smith, Bruce R. (1999), *The Acoustic World of Early Modern England: Attending to the O-Factor*, Chicago, IL: The University of Chicago Press.
Solis, Gabriel (2012), 'Thoughts on an Interdiscipline: Music Theory, Analysis, and Social Theory in Ethnomusicology', *Ethnomusicology*, 56 (3): 530–54.

Steingo, Gavin (2016), *Kwaito's Promise: Music and the Aesthetics of Freedom in South Africa*, Chicago, IL: The University of Chicago Press.

Sterne, Jonathan (2003), *The Audible Past: Cultural Origins of Sound Reproduction*, Durham, NC: Duke University Press.

Stocking, George W., ed. (1992), *The Ethnographer's Magic and Other Essays in the History of Anthropology*, Madison, WI: University of Wisconsin Press.

Subotnik, Rose R. (1996), *Deconstructive Variations: Music and Reason in Western Society*, Minneapolis, MN: University of Minnesota Press.

Sykes, Jim, and Gavin Steingo, eds (2019), *Remapping Sound Studies*, Durham, NC: Duke University Press.

Szendy, Peter ([2001] 2008), *Listen: A History of Our Ears*, transl. Charlotte Mandell, New York, NY: Fordham University Press.

Taylor, Timothy D. (1997), *Global Pop: World Music, World Markets*, London: Routledge.

Taylor, Timothy D. (2007), *Beyond Exoticism: Western Music and the World*, Durham, NC: Duke University Press.

Tenzer, Michael, ed. (2006), *Analytical Studies in World Music*, Oxford: Oxford University Press.

Titus, Barbara (2008), 'Global Maskanda, Global Historiography? Some Preliminary Enquiries', *SAMUS: South African Music Studies*, 28: 43–54.

Titus, Barbara (2010), 'Maskandi Whitey: An Outsider's View', *South African Labour Bulletin*, 34 (1): 63–5.

Titus, Barbara (2013), '"Walking like a Crab": Analyzing Maskanda Music in Post-Apartheid South Africa', *Ethnomusicology*, 57 (2): 286–310.

Titus, Barbara (2014–15), 'Some Implications of Being Undone by Music: A Response to Christopher Ballantine', *SAMUS: South African Music Studies*, 34 & 35: 521–8.

Titus, Barbara (2016a), '"There Is that Cry Sometimes": Negotiations and Exertions of Power in South African Maskanda Music', in Charissa Granger et al. (eds), *Music Moves: Musical Dynamics of Relation, Knowledge and Transformation*, 107–33, Hildesheim: Olms (Göttinger Studien zur Musikwissenschaft; 7).

Titus, Barbara (2016b), *Recognizing Music as an Art Form: Friedrich Theodor Vischer and German Music Criticism, 1848–1887*, Leuven: Leuven University Press.

Titus, Barbara (2016c), 'Review of "Music and Social Change in South Africa: Maskanda Past and Present" by Kathryn Olsen', *world of music (new series)*, 5 (1): 209–12.

Titus, Barbara (2019), 'Introduction: Dwelling in Musical Movement' in Barbara Titus (ed.), *Dwelling in Musical Movement: Making Home in and through Music*, 7–22, Berlin: Verlag für Wissenschaft und Bildung (world of music new series; 8 [1]).

Titus, Barbara (2020), 'Review of "Dust of the Zulu: Ngoma Aesthetics after Apartheid" by Louise Meintjes', *Ethnomusicology*, 64 (1): 174–8.

Titus, Barbara (2021), 'The West in Musical Retrospect: The Historiographical Implications of South African Maskanda Music', in Reinhard Strohm (ed.), *Transcultural Music History: Global Participation and Regional Diversity in the Modern Age*, 99–122, Berlin: Verlag für Wissenschaft und Bildung (Intercultural Music Studies; 24).

Tomlinson, Gary (1991), 'Cultural Dialogics and Jazz: A White Historian Signifies', *Black Music Research Journal* 11 (2): 229–64.

Tomlinson, Gary (1993), 'Approaching Others (Thoughts before Writing)', in *Music in Renaissance Magic: Toward a Historiography of Others*, 1–43, Chicago, IL: The University of Chicago Press.

Turino, Thomas (2008), *Music as Social Life: The Politics of Participation*, Chicago, IL: The University of Chicago Press (Chicago Studies in Ethnomusicology).

Umkomazi Dance Group (n.d.), 'Ya Khulum' Ingoma', recorded by Johnny Clegg at the Jeppe Hostel in Johannesburg.

Undercover Princes, The (2009), Four-part documentary series, aired from 12 February to 12 April on BBC Three Television. Available online: https://www.bbc.co.uk/programmes/b00gtkyq/episodes/guide (accessed 28 March 2021).

Vibe FM (2009), Interview with Barbara Titus and S'kho Miya on 19 September, Ekhaya Arts Centre, KwaMashu, Durban.

Vilakazi, B. W. (1938), 'The Conception and Development of Poetry in Zulu', *Bantu Studies* 12: 203–44.

Viveiros de Castro, Eduardo (2013), 'Cannibal Metaphysics: Amerindian Perspectivism', *Radical Philosophy* 132: 17–28.

Wassel, Deborah (2009), 'From Mbube to Wimoweh: African Folk Music in Dual Systems of Law', *Fordham Intellectual Property, Media & Entertainment Law Journal*, 20 (1): 290–326.

Wikipedia (2021), 'Maskandi'. Available online: https://en.wikipedia.org/wiki/Maskandi (accessed 28 March 2021).

Xaba, Mandla, and Rodgers Magubane (a.k.a. Shwi noMtekhala) (2003a), 'Imali', from *Wangisiza Baba*, Johannesburg: Bula Music 153. Available online: https://www.youtube.com/watch?v=XykwJQFKQYA (accessed 28 March 2021).

Xaba, Mandla, and Rodgers Magubane (2003b), 'Ngafa', from *Wangisiza Baba*, Johannesburg: Bula Music 153. Available online: https://www.youtube.com/watch?v=5PAbByejoTY (accessed 28 March 2021).

Zemp, Hugo (1978), 'Aspects of "Are" Are Musical Theory', *Ethnomusicology*, 23 (1): 37–67.

Zulu, Africa (2007), 'The Personal Website of His Royal Highness, Prince Africa Zulu'. Available online: http://www.princeafricazulu.org/ (accessed 28 March 2021).

Zulu, Africa (2009a), Personal communication, 5 October, Beverley Hills Hotel Umhlanga, Durban.

Zulu, Africa (2009b), Personal communication, 8 October, Gateway Shopping Centre and Palm Hotel, Durban.

Zulu, Africa (2009c), MTN Press release; accessed on 21 July 2011, now removed. Comparable information available online: http://onkweniroyalfestival.com/ (accessed 28 March 2021).

Zuluboy [*see* Majozi, Mxolisi].

Index

fn indicates a footnote that contains new material.
ill indicates an illustration

A
Abagqugquzeli (Organizers)/Khombisile
    Band 76*ill*, 96, 98–9*ill*, 107, 108*ill*,
    190, 198–9
  author joins 73, 74, 83 + *ill*, 84 + *ill*
  jamming session 198*ill*, 199–200 + *ill*
Abels, Birgit 1, 2, 64, 65*fn*, 210
  quoted 48, 203
acoustemology (Feld) 7, 205
acoustic assemblage 18–20, 63, 113, 132
  circulation of 44–5, 61, 148, 159*fn*, 161,
    212. *see also under* Ochoa Gautier,
    Ana María
aesthetics 1, 2, 8, 9, 23, 29, 37, 38, 41, 42,
    49, 113, 121, 132, 140, 151, 154,
    155, 159*fn*, 160, 166, 182, 185, 194,
    195, 202, 203, 206
affect 9, 31, 47, 70, 72, 117*fn*, 138, 159*fn*,
    161, 183
African National Congress (ANC) 115,
    117, 119
Afrikaans/Afrikaners 11, 34, 43, 59, 78,
    87, 115, 172. *see also boeremusiek*;
    Boers
Agawu, Kofi 8, 22, 23, 206
  quoted 9, 110
Agnew, Vanessa 2, 212
Ahmed, Sara and Claudia Castañeda,
    Anne-Marie Fortier, Mimi Shellery
    16, 19, 36, 201, 209, 210, 211
  quoted 17, 42, 49, 72, 77, 138, 139, 154,
    183
Allingham, Rob 16, 37, 38–9, 43
  quoted 37*fn*
Anglican church 9, 38
amadlozi/idlozi 6, 33, 45, 47, 69, 71,
    72–3, 115, 116, 123, 143, 152, 165,
    176, 188, 209

amahubo/ihubo 6, 9, 15, 39, 41, 44,
    45*fn*, 47, 56–7, 57*fn*, 61, 83, 107,
    111, 112, 130, 138, 139, 143, 144,
    146, 147, 149, 152, 154, 155, 156,
    159, 160, 164 + *fn*, 167, 171, 172,
    177, 182*fn*, 183, 185, 187, 188,
    201
amakhosi 34, 45, 141*fn*, 177
amandla 47
ambitus 41, 147, 148, 149, 150, 155, 158
ambivalence. *see under* Bhabha, Homi
ancestors. *see amadlozi*
Anglo-Zulu war 94
Anku, Willie 110
antiphony 27, 39, 147
apartheid era 16, 17, 22, 28, 33, 71, 75, 76,
    118, 141, 154, 205
  anti-apartheid action 78, 125
  censorship 24, 40, 77, 101, 117, 161
  cultural boycott 28*fn*, 33–4, 72, 92,
    120, 123, 173
  cultural policies 20, 70, 97–8, 105, 117,
    138–9, 209
  described 19, 36–7, 42, 43
  curfew laws 43
  governments 16, 77, 94, 115
  ideology 36
  legacy 86, 105, 115, 126
  pass laws 78
  post-apartheid era 15–16, 23, 33, 74,
    77–8, 94, 98–9, 108, 120, 122, 172,
    176*fn*
  repressive impact 13, 36, 51, 74, 92,
    115, 120, 172, 181, 208–9
  segregation 11, 18 + *fn*, 22, 27, 33, 36,
    92, 99, 154, 176
  'separate development' 12, 16, 19, 86,
    89, 104, 106, 193

Index

appropriation 4, 5, 14, 22, 28, 29, 31, 32, 54, 65, 78, 81, 87, 94, 101, 105–7, 120, 131, 139, 160, 165, 181, 188, 206, 209, 211
Arom, Simha 110
aural space 48, 154, 181, 185–202, 205
authenticity 14, 16, 43, 58, 126, 184
   authentication 104, 187

B
Bafana isiColenso (band) 61
Ballantine, Christopher 10, 23, 36, 39, 71, 74, 154
Bambatha Rebellion 27, 32, 43
Bantu 172, 209
Barz, Gregory E. 2, 5
BAT Centre. *see under* Durban (eThekwini)
Battle of Isandlwana 27
Battle of the Blood River 27, 32
'Bayethe'. *see under* Majozi, Mxolisi; Mnyandu, Zibakwakhe
Belgium 69, 121, 122, 123, 126
Bergin, Sean 125–7, 125*ill*, 128, 132, 133
Berglund, Axel-Ivar 47, 70, 116
   quoted 6, 47
Bhabha, Homi K. 12–17, 20, 65, 72, 139, 209, 210, 211
   'ambivalence' 13, 14, 64, 177, 178, 209, 210
   'double-and-split' 13, 138, 206, 208, 210
   'event and enunciation' 15, 48, 51, 113, 127, 159*fn*, 184, 208
   'hybridity' 15, 17, 71, 126, 139, 154, 184
   'location of culture' 14–15, 48, 159*fn*
   'mimicry' 14–16, 17, 32, 42, 43, 45, 133, 138, 154, 165, 198, 201, 208
   'mother cultures' 138, 139
   quoted 14, 16, 154, 183–4
   'stereotypes as fetishes' 13, 22, 86, 106–7, 109, 113, 133, 205, 209, 211
   'Third Space' 14–16, 19, 22, 48, 184, 208, 211
   'unhomely' 200, 201
Bhaca 27, 59 + *fn*, 101*fn*3, 120

Bhengu, John (a.k.a. Phuzushukela) 36, 37 + *fn*, 69, 182, 193
bhinca 12–13, 48
Bhunu. *see* Boers
Black Atlantic. *see under* Gilroy, Paul
Bloechl, Olivia A. 2, 8, 20, 105, 127, 138, 210–12
   'nearly agential pressure' 45, 86, 133, 205
   quoted 5, 20, 24, 64, 108
blues 38–9, 173, 178–81
   'Zulu blues' 11–12
   blue note 64, 180
body 7, 10, 13, 32, 42, 43, 108, 110, 138, 147, 205, 209, 211
   embodied knowledge 7, 8, 109, 203
boereliedjies 9, 44, 60
boeremusiek 38–9, 60–1
boereorkes 59
Boers 14, 31 + *fn*, 43, 44, 60, 143, 186, 189
Botswana 11
Britain/British/UK 11, 31 + *fn*, 85, 94, 121–2, 172–3
Brown, James 173, 175, 214, 215
bull (symbolic). *see ubukunzi*
Buthelezi, Chief Mangosuthu 4–5, 94, 207, 210

C
Canada 120, 121
Cape Town (iKapa) 160
Carter, Paul 19, 209
   quoted 18, 36
Carton, Benedict and Malcolm Draper 106
   quoted 28*fn*
Castro-Gómez, Santiago 18, 20, 65
   quoted 206
Catholic church 9, 64
Celtic 44
Cetshwayo 94
Childs, Peter and Patrick Williams 13–14
Chiliza, Joseph Bhekizizwe 124*ill*
Chiyi, Wiseman 108*ill*
chorus
   backing 11, 27, 33, 39, 41, 80, 84*ill*, 107, 109–10, 111, 141, 147–9, 151, 155, 156, 158, 159, 188, 189, 191, 193, 195, 201

response 80, 130, 143, 152
simulated/imagined 147, 149, 150, 152, 159
summoned 157
'tapestry' 149, 155, 159
chromaticism 63, 179, 192 + *ill*, 193, 195
Chunu 32, 59. *see also under* maskanda styles
Clegg, Johnny (a.k.a. Sikeyi) 6, 16, 21, 23, 27–35, 31*fn*3+4, 33*fn*, 35*fn*, 38, 39, 41*fn*, 42, 45, 49, 51, 54, 57, 59, 60, 61, 87, 111, 116, 117, 142–3, 144–5, 168, 171, 185
quoted 6–7, 12–13, 17, 27, 34, 36, 44, 48, 50, 52 + *fn*, 53–4, 56*fn*, 58, 59, 64, 70, 128, 143, 166, 168, 182, 186
My Favourite Zulu Street Guitar Songs DVD 29, 33 + *fn*, 38
Clifford, James 10
and George E. Marcus 3
quoted 50–1, 207
Collins, Tom 34, 37, 55–6, 144–5
'oriflammes' 55, 56, 145
quoted 38, 49, 55, 56
colonial/colonialism 5, 12, 13–14, 20, 22, 33, 41, 42, 57*fn*, 65, 108, 109, 205, 209–10
administrations/governments 77, 106, 171
authority 10, 28, 32, 113, 127, 138–9, 141
colonizer and colonized 12, 13, 14, 32, 193
encounters 41, 43, 60, 139
environment 15–16, 18
guilt 75
imported/imposed knowledge 4, 7, 42, 172–3, 209
modes of hearing 2
postcolonialism 12, 15–16, 126, 204
precolonialism 4, 14, 22, 34, 36, 42, 78, 83, 139, 140, 154
heritage of 41, 57 + *fn*, 146–7
Commodores, The 173, 174
composition
compositional device 144, 149–50, 211.
see ubugaku

Coplan, David B. 10, 17, 23, 34, 39, 71, 74, 77, 139, 189
quoted 37, 91, 97, 109, 112
Coullie, Judith: quoted 165, 176

D
dance
indlamu 81, 112
ingoma 7, 9, 19, 27, 34, 41–2, 57 + *fn*, 101, 105, 107, 112, 134, 139, 141, 171, 176, 188
isicathulo 57
izigiyo 165
ukugiya 6, 9, 15, 33, 34, 38, 41, 47, 112, 165
umqonqo 112, 128
umgqashiyo 112
umzansi 27, 57 + *fn*, 58, 62, 64, 112, 128, 204 (*see also* Umzansi Zulu Dancers *and under* maskanda styles)
Davies, James: quoted 43
Davies, Nollene 23, 34, 35*fn*, 139, 147, 171
quoted 168, 177
De Jong, Nanette & King Madzikane II 72, 101*fn*3, 139
Democratic Alliance (DA) 115
Derrida, Jacques 3, 15, 64, 134, 210, 211
Dingane ka Senzangakhona 167*fn*
disavowal 13, 64, 154, 184, 209
displacement. *see under* place
djembe 124, 126–7, 131, 173
Dlamini, Sazi 6, 41*fn*, 44, 47, 51, 55, 56, 57 + *fn*, 60, 61, 63, 127, 132–3, 134, 147, 204
quoted 6, 41, 43, 44, 56, 128, 131, 132, 193–4, 204, 208
'double-and-split'. *see under* Bhabha, Homi
'double consciousness' 201
'double hearing' 15, 17
Douglas, Mary: quoted 7, 32
Dublin 29, 32
Du Bois, W. E. B. 201
Durban (eThekwini) 1, 12, 21, 35, 49*fn*, 52, 57, 58, 70, 71, 73, 74, 75, 94, 96, 97, 118
BAT Centre 77, 79, 85, 190

Centre for Jazz and Popular Music 73
Daily News 78
Ekhaya Arts Centre 85 + *fn*
KwaMashu 78, 85, 86, 122, 211
Stable Theatre 73, 74, 76*ill,* 84, 110*ill,* 188, 190, 199, 201
Vibe FM (radio station) 78, 84-6, 87 + *ill,* 122, 211
white community 17-8
dwelling 12, 16, 18, 48, 51, 139, 188*fn,* 208

E
Ebony. *see* Khama, Linah
Ekhaya Arts Centre KwaMashu. *see under* Durban (eThekwini)
eloquence 14, 139, 141, 147, 183, 188-90, 202, 211
Erlmann, Veit 2, 4, 10, 13, 38-9, 54, 55, 57, 60, 64, 139, 144-5
quoted 5, 9, 18, 22, 41, 42, 54, 137, 209
equivocality 1, 65, 144
ethnography 3, 5, 10, 206, 207
Eurocentrism 19*fn,* 65, 111
eurogenic 8-10, 18, 20-1, 31, 38, 43-4, 55-6, 65, 116, 128, 133, 144, 189, 203, 207, 209-10

F
falsetto 57, 130, 148, 149, 159, 187
Feld, Steven 2, 3, 92, 182, 183, 192, 195, 205, 210
quoted 2, 7
'schizophonic mimesis' 182-4, 192, 195. *see also* Keil, Charles
festivals 76, 91, 92, 98, 122, 164
Kushikisha Imbokodo 22, 77-83, 79*ill,* 82*ill,* 83*ill,* 84*ill,* 86-7, 88*ill,* 95, 107, 126, 167, 168, 190, 195, 198
MTN Onkweni Royal Cultural (MORC) 22, 93-101, 98-9*ill,* 118, 126
fetish. *see under* Bhabha, Homi
flute. *see umtsingo*
fundamentals 49, 50, 54, 130 + *ill,* 144, 145, 148, 149, 155, 156, 158, 191, 192, 199
funk 154, 155, 160, 173, 200

G
Gallo (record company) 37, 69, 92, 118
Gates Jr., Henry Louis: 'signifying' 7, 8, 9, 154, 166, 167, 201
Gauteng 94, 120
Gaye, Marvin 15
'Sexual Healing' 10, 163, 171
score 164*ill*
geography. *see* place
ghoema 160
Gilroy, Paul: *The Black Atlantic* 154, 165, 177, 201
gospel 9, 42, 71-2, 92, 117, 119, 154, 155, 185, 188, 199, 201
afro 80, 164
global 139
and maskanda 69, 81, 164, 183-4, 190, 198
voice 81, 107
gourd bow 9, 49, 54, 56, 130, 131, 139, 144-5, 148, 183, 192-3, 209 (*see ugubhu; umakhweyana*)
Graeber, David 2, 138, 207
groove 10, 39, 41, 64, 81, 141, 148, 150-2, 158, 159, 193, 195, 199
gumboot. *see under* dance: *isicathulo*
Gumbrecht, Hans Ulrich 128
quote 207
Gunner, Liz 77, 105, 167
and Mafika Gwala 165, 168
quoted 131*fn*
gxagxa 12-4, 48

H
Hadebe, Mqapheli 108*ill*
Hahn, Tomie 2, 7, 18, 139-40, 203
quoted 8-9, 137, 139, 154, 161
harmony
bi-tonal 130, 145, 191, 193
blues 178-81 + *ill*
cadence 38, 60, 155, 179, 181, 209
cyclic 38, 80, 81, 107, 150, 181
functional 181
progression 38, 39*ill,* 80, 81, 107, 151, 156, 163, 181, 199

tonal 38, 44, 55, 56, 155, 191–2, 193, 198*ill*
triadic 54, 55, 60, 145, 155, 164. *see also under* scales
Hegel, G. W. F. 65
hegemony 4–5, 9–10, 14, 17, 20, 32, 34, 50, 61, 133–4, 144, 171, 207, 211
heterophony 54, 60, 130, 148, 155, 180–1, 182
score 40*ill*, 197*ill*
hip-hop 9, 92, 119, 140, 171–3, 176–7, 178, 180*fn*, 181, 182, 183–4, 185
global 15, 139, 155, 165
HIV/AIDS 45, 123, 171
historiography 8, 10, 29*fn*, 34, 35, 128, 131, 133
Hlope, Makhulu 80
'homing' 16, 42, 139, 154, 201
homophony 54, 164, 180, 194, 199
hubo a song 160, 189, 203, 209
hybridity. *see under* Bhabha, Homi

I
ibhodlo. see under voice
idlozi. see amadlozi
igama 5–9, 10, 16, 22, 28–9, 32, 41, 47–8, 64, 116, 128, 131–2, 134, 140–1, 143, 147–50, 152, 154, 157, 168, 176, 189, 190–1, 199, 203, 209
igogogo 63
iHashi Elimhlophe (White Horse). *see* Ngcobo, Bheki
iHashi namamPoni (record company) 119
ihubo. see amahubo
ilado. see under maskanda: *isihlabo*
imbongi 165, 168, 177
Imithente (band) 21, 107, 164
imfilitshi 9, 54, 55, 59, 201
Impey, Angela 2, 35*fn*, 48, 139, 145, 147, 148, 149
quoted 48–9, 86, 149*fn*, 186*fn*
Indian community in Africa 78, 87
indlela 48–9, 186*fn*, 187
Inkatha Freedom Party (IFP) 94, 104, 109, 115, 117
isangoma 69
isicathamiya 10, 44, 60, 61, 94, 101, 107, 172, 181, 199

isihlabo. see under maskanda
isitorotoro 9, 22, 139, 144, 148, 150–1, 159, 160, 167, 171, 183, 201
isitweletwele 148
score 150*ill*, 151*ill*, 152*ill*
izibongo. see under maskanda
izigiyo. see under dance
Izingane Zoma (band) 35
Izintombi (band) 35, 119, 164
Izintombi zika Shwii (album) 119

J
James, Deborah 10, 17*fn*, 75
jazz 9, 38–9, 42, 60*fn*, 91, 107, 112, 139, 140, 171, 181
composition 56
global 22, 139, 154, 155, 160, 173
harmony 44
improvisation 2
performers 1, 43, 52, 80, 119, 120, 154, 155
South African 101, 126, 154, 156, 158, 159, 160, 181, 190, 200, 201, 209
Jenkins, David (a.k.a. Qadasi) 21, 27–8, 28*ill*, 29–34, 29*fn*, 38, 39, 42, 44, 45 + *fn*, 59, 87, 118, 187, 188
Child of Africa (album) 29, 38
live performances 29, 32–3, 33*fn*, 41
jive 80, 200
Johannesburg (eGoli) 11, 35, 36, 70, 71, 73, 74, 91, 111, 118, 122, 190
City Council 115
Downtown Studios 117, 118
Jeppe Hostel 111
Mai Mai Market 29, 33
Juluka (band) 45
J. Mofokeng & Associates (JMA) 91

K
Kant, Immanuel 65
Keil, Charles and Steven Feld 49*fn*
Khama, Linah (a.k.a. Ebony) 33, 71, 75, 92–3, 118, 119
quoted 119, 121
kholwa 12–13, 48
Khombisile Band. *see Abagqugquzeli*

Khoza, Bheki 21, 37, 38–9, 40, 55, 57, 119–20, 154–5, 156, 160, 203
  quoted 38, 43, 44, 52, 59, 60, 61, 117, 181–2, 182*fn*, 186, 187
Khoza, Sipho (a.k.a. Thwalofu) 181–2
Khumalo, Mphatheni (a.k.a. Mfaz' Omnyama) 45, 103*ill*, 117–18, 119, 181, 182
  'Lolo sizi olungaka' 189*fn*
  'Sxaxa Mbij' 119
Khumalo, Nandi 159 + *fn*, 204
kiba 10, 17*fn*
Kidjo Angélique 126
kings of Zulu nation. *see amakhosi*
Kirby, Percival R. 23, 44, 139, 183
  quoted 35*fn*
Kora Records (record company) 115, 154
Krims, Adam 180
  quoted 177
Kunene, Madala 21, 33, 94, 120
  quoted 185
kwaito 18*fn*, 107, 173
kwela 60*fn*, 200
KwaZulu 52, 60, 94, 141*fn*
KwaZulu-Natal 11, 43, 52, 57, 59, 60, 87, 94, 120
  map 53*ill*
  Bergville 53*ill*, 58
  Colenso 53*ill*, 57, 59
  Department of Arts and Culture (DAC) 86–7, 88*ill*
  KwaBhidla 74, 86*fn*
  KwaMakhutha 122
  Mandeni 69
  Mapumulo 53*ill*, 57, 58
  Midlands 57, 58
  Msinga 53*ill*, 54, 57, 58, 59
  Ndwedwe 52–3 + *ill*, 54, 57, 58
  Ulundi 22, 93, 94, 95, 96, 97, 118
  Umkomazi 53*ill*, 59, 111
  University (UKZN) 49, 73, 96, 122, 127

L

Ladysmith Black Mambazo (band) 94, 95, 107, 121
Langa, Thokozani 21, 94, 107, 118, 164

Lebhaca, Ichwane
  Ubuyile Imaqondana Egoli (album) 120
Lebombo (band) 125 + *ill*
Limpopo 75
Linda, Salomon Popoli
  'Mbube'/'Wimoweh'/'The Lion Sleeps Tonight' 92, 199
lobola 45, 78
'location of culture'. *see under* Bhabha, Homi
Luthuli, Bhekumuzi 94, 164, 172

M

Mabaso, Pinky 83*ill*
Madalane, Ignatia 33, 34, 78*fn*, 80, 141–2, 143, 173–6, 204
  quoted 31, 32, 141
  translations of lyrics 30, 129, 142, 169, 174–5, 213–20, 221–6
magic 207–8
'magical negro' 32
Magogo kaDinuzulu, Constance [Princess] 146–7
  'Kwabase sabulawa nguDingane' 167*fn*
Magubane, Rodgers (a.k.a. Mtekhala) 36, 108, 164, 189*fn*
Mahlatini and the Mohatella Queens. *see* Nkabinde, Simon
Mahlobo, Thabani Albert 188
Majozi, Mxolisi (a.k.a. Zuluboy) 21, 22, 165, 171–83, 207
  'Bayethe' 45, 177, 189*fn*
  'DJ Gogo' 22, 165, 173–81
  lyrics 174–5, 214–15
  score 178*ill*, 179*ill*
  Inqolobane (album) 172, 173
  quoted 59*fn*, 172, 173, 176*fn*, 177, 178, 180*fn*, 181, 187, 209
Makeba, Zenzile Miriam 80 + *fn*, 81
Makhoba, Sithembiso 33
Mamba, Phola 125 + *ill*
Mandela, Nelson Rolihlahla 104
mandolin 60
Maniglier, Patrice 210
marabi 10, 60*fn*, 80, 155, 181, 199, 200
  score 200*ill*

Marre, Jeremy: *Rhythm of Resistance* 45
Martens, Jeremy 36, 106
Masekela, Hugh Ramapolo 154
maskanda/umaskandi
   composition. *see ubugaku*
   isihlabo 38, 41, 45, 55, 121, 155, 178, 179*ill*, 180, 181, 182
   izibongo 9, 15, 19, 22, 33, 34, 37, 41 + *fn*, 47, 76, 77, 80, 81, 86, 107, 124, 132, 134, 165–71, 172, 176–8, 190, 203, 208–9
   lead/front singers 33, 39, 41, 61, 64, 73, 75, 77, 79–80, 97, 108, 130, 147, 148, 149–50, 152, 155, 156, 157, 159, 167, 187, 191, 195
   lyrics 31, 32, 40, 41, 75, 76, 77, 80, 81, 116, 123, 127, 128–30, 131, 132, 134, 141–4, 165, 166, 168, 171, 172, 177
   origins 10–11, 29, 34–5, 36, 43–4
   overseas aspiration 74–5, 95, 120–4, 165, 206
   rural nostalgia 35–7
   rural-urban divide 13 + *fn*, 14–15, 48, 55, 69, 91, 107, 138, 141, 159–61, 159*fn*, 176, 186, 189, 204
   walking songs 16, 37–8, 44, 48–9
   white 27–34, 42
   women 34–8, 72–81, 83, 165, 167–8, 170–1
   working conditions 73–4, 91–2
maskandafication 9–10, 15, 19–20, 22–3, 93, 113, 120, 132, 137–41, 155, 159*fn*, 160, 171, 183, 185, 198, 200–3, 205–8
maskanda genres
   gospelmaskandi 81, 164, 183–4, 190
   maskandiR&B 22, 163, 164, 183–4, 199, 208
   (ma)skandihop 22, 172, 183–4, 208
maskanda instruments/instrumentation 11, 38, 80, 81, 83, 98, 99–100, 118, 121, 126, 148, 149, 155, 159–60, 180, 194
   bass 10, 38, 60, 112, 130, 156, 158, 159, 178, 180, 191, 193, 195, 199, 200
   melodic 81, 121, 155, 163–4, 190, 195
   concertina 11, 35, 38, 39, 41, 42, 43–4, 52 + *fn*, 54, 57, 59, 60, 63, 149, 155, 183, 201
   drums/drumkit 38, 39, 81, 99, 111–12, 193, 195, 199, 201
   guitar 14, 34, 36–9, 42, 43–4, 45, 49*fn*, 50, 54, 69, 81, 83, 144, 145, 147, 148–9, 151–2, 155, 156, 173, 176, 180, 181, 183, 192, 193, 198, 199, 201, 209. *see also* Zulu: street guitar
      as accompaniment 57
      acoustic 37, 70, 122, 131, 140–1, 155
      backstage/backing 117–18, 185
      capo 56
      jazz 43, 52, 119, 154
      lead 39, 199
      learning to play 28, 33, 62, 116, 122
      second 112, 195
      solo 101, 140–1
      tuning 49, 52, 55, 60, 151
      ukupika 19, 27, 37, 41, 55, 64, 180, 190, 195, 199
      ukuvamba 37
   percussion 80, 112, 126, 166, 177, 193, 200–1
   synthesizers 38, 98, 155, 159–60, 180, 181, 193, 195, 201
(maskanda) styles 34, 47–67
   isiBergville 58
   isiBhaca 51 + *fn*, 59, 188
   isiCece 50
   isiChunu 51 + *fn*, 54, 55, 59, 60, 61
   isiKhunzi 60
   isiMandolino 55, 60
   isiManjemanje 60
   isiNdwedwe 52–3, 52*fn*, 54, 55, 60, 61
   isiShameni 27, 52–3, 55, 57 + *fn*, 59, 60–1, 112, 124, 163–4, 171, 182
   isiZulu 49, 51 + *fn*, 55, 56, 57, 59, 60, 61, 63, 112, 124, 131, 144, 145, 191, 192, 199, 208
   isiZulu *esikhulu* 62, 63, 64, 204
   umzansi 27, 53, 57*fn*, 58, 62, 63, 64, 204
Masuka, Dorothy 80
   'Into Yam' 80 +*fn*

Masuku, Bongani 33
mbaqanga 10, 44, 60 +*fn*, 99, 101, 107, 120, 155, 182 +*fn*, 185, 190, 194, 199
Mbeki, Thabo: 'African Renaissance' 104
mbube 121, 199
  score 199*ill* (*see also* Linda, Salomon)
Mchunu, Moses 181–2
Mchunu, Sipho 38, 45, 50, 86, 133, 205
  quoted 31
  'Sab' Inganono' 21, 27, 29–32, 38, 39, 42–5, 51, 86, 133, 143, 147, 205, 208
  lyrics 30, 41, 213
  score 39–40*ill*
Meintjes, Louise 7, 10, 13, 57, 60*fn*, 71, 78, 81, 92, 121, 134, 142–3, 180, 183, 191
  quoted 72, 82, 99–100, 104–5, 117*fn*, 120, 159*fn*, 182, 188
Meredith, Martin 12, 74
  quoted 11, 12
metre (music) 38, 39, 57 +*fn*, 64, 109, 111–13 +*ill*, 141, 144, 156, 158–9, 164, 166, 176–8, 180, 193, 199, 204
Mfaz' Omnyama (Black Woman). *see* Khumalo, Mphatheni
Mhlongo, Busi 21, 69, 70, 76, 94, 120, 172
  Urban Zulu (album) 120
migrant 12–14, 17 +*fn*, 34–6, 41–2, 48, 75, 107, 117 +*fn*, 118, 139, 147, 159*fn*, 160. *see also qhafi*
  labour migration 10–12, 13, 27, 35, 36, 38–9, 41, 44, 48, 52, 53–5, 57, 58, 70, 74, 78, 83, 107, 146–7, 160
Mija, Abraham 21, 92
  quoted 118–19, 187
'mimicry'. *see under* Bhabha, Homi
Miya, Khoni 21, 36, 71, 72–5, 76, 77–8, 79*ill*, 80, 83, 92, 93, 107, 120, 133, 167–8, 171, 208–9
  quoted 35, 51–2, 72, 73, 74, 91, 94, 117, 134, 185, 187, 190, 202
Miya, S'kho (Khombisile Phylis) 21, 22, 70, 73, 74–6, 76*ill*, 78, 80, 82–3, 82*ill*, 84–6, 87*ill*, 91, 92–3, 94, 95, 96–8, 96*ill*, 98–9*ill*, 100*ill*, 106*fn*, 107, 108*ill*, 109–10, 110*ill*, 111, 112, 117, 120, 122, 133, 134, 165, 167,

168–71, 187, 188, 190 +*fn*, 200, 201, 205, 206, 207, 208–9, 211–12.
  see also Abagqugquzeli
'Ibhoxongwana' 76
  lyrics 220
'Ingculazi Iyabulala' 45, 98
'Ngilobole' 85, 187, 198, 200
  lyrics 216–17
'Nith' Angiqome Bani' 76, 109
  lyrics 217–19
'Sithi Khuzani' 22–3, 98, 112, 187–8, 189–97, 199, 202, 205
  lyrics 216
  score 111*ill*, 191*ill*, 192*ill*, 194*ill*, 195*ill*, 196–7*ill*
Ungcayi Lweqhikiza (album) 22–3, 74, 168, 171, 190, 191, 193, 195
'Wayibulal' Inhliziyo Yami' 76.
Mkhize, Khayalethu 108*ill*
Mkhonza, Bongani 141–2, 204
  translation of lyrics 142, 223–4
Mlu(ngisi) DJ 85
Mnguni, Zwelakhe (a.k.a. Khetelo) 124*ill*
Mnyandu, Khethani 102*ill*, 117
Mnyandu, Zibakwakhe Johnston (a.k.a. Phuzekhemisi) 21, 28, 45, 81, 94, 102–3*ill*, 109, 117, 118, 119, 120, 164, 185, 192, 203
'Bayethe' 81
'Emapalamende' 117
'Imbizo' 102*ill*, 117, 189*fn*, 192
  quoted 194
'Sxaxa Mbij' 119
Sesihlangene (album) 120
Mobile Telephone Networks Group (MTN) 94, 95, 97
mode (music) 38, 42, 44, 47, 81, 116, 120, 131, 149, 155, 190–3, 198, 199
Monson, Ingrid T. 7, 8, 10, 47, 93, 137, 140, 154, 167, 201, 210
  quoted 2–4, 23, 42, 166, 189, 200
Moribo (television programme) 91, 93, 101, 118, 163
'mother cultures'
  see under Bhabha, Homi
mouth organ/harmonica. *see imfilitshi*
Mozambique 11, 69, 107
Mpande 95

Mpondo 59
Mtshare, Nontobeko 83*ill*
Muller, Carol Ann 23, 34, 154
multivocality. *see under* voice
Mundy, Rachel 2, 207, 212
Mziwoxolo (House of Peace). *see* Josefa Nkwanyana

N
Naidoo, Mageshen 106, 125
Namibia 11
Natal 43, 52, 57, 58, 59
Ndabandaba, Somnyama 108*ill*
Ndebele 101*fn*3
Ndladla, Zweli 165
Ndlovu, Dolly 83*ill*
the Netherlands/Dutch 56, 94, 121–4, 131, 132
New National Party (NNP) 115
Ngcobo, Bheki (a.k.a. iHashi Elimhlophe) 21, 45, 92, 94, 102*ill*, 116, 119, 120, 121, 122, 164, 172
   'Sxaxa Mbij' 119
Ngcobo, Bheki (a.k.a. Khetuwise) 63
   'Sevelina' 63, 64
      lyrics 221
      score 62*ill*
Ngcobo, Selby 95, 96, 98, 100*ill*
   quoted 109
Ngcobo, Shiyani 21, 49*fn*, 55, 60, 62–3, 64, 65, 91–2, 109, 130*fn*, 141, 147, 148, 173, 194, 204, 208
   'Angikholwa' 123
   'Asinankomo' 22, 127–8, 130 + *fn*, 133, 134, 141, 187, 204
      lyrics 129, 222–3
      score 130*ill*
   'Ingonyama' 123
   'Inhliziyoyami' 123–4
   Introducing Shiyani Ngcobo (album) 121–2
   'Isithembu' 109, 116–17
      lyrics 220–1
   'Isphiwosami' 123
   'Izangoma' 116
   'Izinyembezi' 63–4
      lyrics 221–2
      score 63*ill*
   quoted 49, 116, 185

'Sevelina' 63, 64
   lyrics 221
   score 62*ill*
'Siyafunda' 148, 187–8
'Thongo lami' 123
   tour to the Netherlands 56, 121–34, 123*ill*, 124*ill*, 195, 205, 209
Ngema, Nomcebo 91, 92, 94
   quoted 117
Ngobese, Bongekile and Tholakele Ngobese 35, 119
Nguni 42, 44, 56
Ngwabe, Maureen Bongekile 56, 124*ill*, 128–30
Ngwane, Melody 80
Ngwane, Sfiso 107
Ngwekazi, Nhlanhla 21, 27, 91, 92, 94, 165, 182, 207
   quoted 118, 163, 172, 178
Nkabinde, Concord 1, 3, 24, 27, 28, 71, 75, 85, 92, 106, 125–6, 204–5, 211
   quoted 1, 3, 106*fn*, 205
Nkabinde, Simon (a.k.a. Mahlatini) 69, 81, 82, 121, 132, 191, 209
Nkwanyana, Bongani 6, 21, 38, 39, 40, 47, 55, 57, 60, 64, 71, 77, 92, 115–16, 117, 119–20, 141 + *fn*, 143–4, 145, 148–50, 151–2, 154–8, 159–61, 171, 181, 182 + *fn*, 186, 187, 188, 203
   'Iiyabhubha' 155
   'Inkunzi Emnyama' 22, 140–4, 140*fn*, 141*fn*, 145, 147, 149, 150, 151–3, 154–5, 156–8, 159, 163, 187, 188, 199, 204, 208
      lyrics 142, 223–4
      score 146*ill*, 147*ill*, 153*ill*, 156*ill*, 157*ill*, 158*ill*
   'Intambo' 155
   'Ishumi Lompondo' 155
   quoted 37, 54, 55, 58, 60, 61, 115, 116, 138, 142, 160, 167, 182, 189, 194
   'Umahangula' 155
   'Umona' 155
   Yash'inkani (album) 22, 119–20, 140, 154–5, 160–1, 163, 188
Nkwanyana, Josefa (a.k.a. Mziwoxolo) 21, 69–70, 74, 88, 116, 120, 144–5, 159 + *fn*, 206
   'Kanti Ielungelo libavala' 116–17

Ngihamba Nomngani (album) 69
  quoted 69, 149, 159, 187, 194
  'Wentandane Zobaba' 159
    score 160*ill*
Nkwanyana, 'Mrs' (mother of Josefa) 144, 145, 148, 149, 150-1, 191
  'Molomolo Mama' 145, 148, 149, 150
    lyrics 224
    score 145*ill*
  'Mthembu kaMthele' 150-1
    score 150*ill*, 151*ill*, 152*ill*
Nokwe, Tu 6, 21, 47, 69
Nozuko 81
  quoted 80
Nthethe, Lichaba 21, 91, 92, 93, 94, 97, 101 + *fn*4, 104, 118
  quoted 194
Ntuli, D. B. 23, 41, 168, 171
  quoted 168
Ntuli, Nothi 21, 28, 75, 117-18, 117*fn*, 159*fn*, 165, 172, 182, 185-6, 206
  quoted 118, 185, 186, 186-7, 187, 201
  Sanibonani (album) 118
Nxumalo, Elias 204
  translations of lyrics 30, 129, 169, 213, 216-20, 222-3, 224
Nxumalo, Sipho 33
Nyezwa, Mxolisi 5, 72, 101*fn*3, 139
Nzewi, Meki 110
Nzimande, Hamilton 37, 69
Nzimande, Tshepo 21, 35-6, 38, 47, 59, 92, 165, 167-8, 182, 187, 207
  quoted 35, 47, 101*fn*3, 120, 163-4, 186 + *fn*, 199
  'road of growing' 186 + *fn*, 187. *see also indlela*

O
Ochoa Gautier, Ana María 2, 18, 20, 42, 45, 51, 64, 65, 72, 113, 127, 138, 140, 184, 188-9, 206, 210, 211
  acoustic assemblage 19, 36, 45, 51, 72, 127, 138, 144, 184, 211
  quoted 5, 19, 23, 36, 144, 189, 190, 193, 211
ocularcentrism 18, 20, 65
O'Jays, The 173
Olsen, Kathryn 10, 17-18, 23, 34, 35 + *fn*, 36, 37*fn*, 42, 47, 49, 63, 70, 71, 75, 77, 101*fn*3, 106, 120, 122, 123, 139, 164*fn*, 168, 182, 185, 193
  quoted 16, 17, 37, 109
'oriflammes'. *see under* Collins, Tom
ostinato 38, 60, 147, 155, 181, 198, 200
Otherness 13, 23, 71, 85, 127
  Othering 17, 18, 20, 83, 111, 209
overseas. *see pesheya olwandle*
overtone 107, 145, 147, 151-3, 160, 188, 192

P
Pan-African 104, 127
partial (music) 49, 56, 150 + *ill*, 151 + *ill*, 152 + *ill*
patriarchy 36, 109, 115
Pedi 52
Peirce, Charles Sanders 42
pesheya olwandle 74-5, 87, 95, 120, 122, 165, 201, 205, 206. *see also under* maskanda: overseas aspiration
'phantom districts'. *see under* place
Phungula, Bonisiwe 83*ill*
Phuzekhemisi (Drinker at the Chemist). *see* Mnyandu, Zibakwakhe Johnston
Phuzushukela (Sugar Drinker). *see* Bhengu, John
Pietermaritzburg (umGungundlovu) 94
Pieters, Marieke 124 + *ill*, 125, 126, 128
pitch (music) 55, 56, 82, 148-51, 159, 166, 177, 180, 187, 188
place 16, 48-9, 52, 94, 120, 139, 167, 209
  constructed/imaginary 16, 48, 58, 72, 75, 105, 131*fn*, 209
  displacement 11, 12, 13*fn*, 27, 44, 52, 71, 78, 201
  'phantom districts' 48, 53, 143, 211
polygamy 76, 78, 97, 105, 108-9, 113, 117, 171
polyphony 180-1,
polymetre 109-13
Pooley, Thomas M. 168, 170, 171, 177
  quoted 165, 166
pop music/popular music 11, 21, 22, 27, 80, 91, 92, 93, 99, 107, 126, 164, 178, 199, 200
  afropop 35, 73, 92, 101, 107, 126, 190 +*fn*
  global 124, 138. *see also* South African popular musics

postcolonialism. *see under* colonial
praise 9, 71, 80, 123, 165–8, 167*fn*, 170, 172, 173, 176–8, 203
  praise name 6, 168
  praise poet. *see imbongi*
  self-praise (*izibongo*). *see under* maskanda
Pretoria (Tshwane) 78
Protestant church 44, 60, 61, 64, 181–2 + *fn*
Pyper, Brett: quoted 77, 93, 105

Q
Qadasi (White Person). *see* Jenkins, David
qhafi 12, 48
Qoma, Bafazana 'Buff' 111

R
Radano, Ronald and Tejumola Olaniyan 2, 212
Radebe, Maqhinga 28*ill*, 33
Radebe, Noxolo 154
Ramanna, Nishlyn 23, 154, 160*fn*, 200, 201
  quoted 200–1
rap music 22, 71–2, 83, 165, 172, 173, 176–8, 180
  global 71–2
RASA Utrecht 122–3, 124, 125, 126, 195
R&B 9, 15, 42, 101, 107, 117, 140, 163–4, 173, 181, 183–4, 185, 188, 199, 200, 209
  global 15, 71–2, 139, 154, 155. *see also under* maskanda genres: maskandiR&B
reggae 39, 42, 101, 119
register (music) 82, 130, 145, 148, 149, 151, 170, 187, 199
resonance (music) 44, 56, 64, 82, 144, 145, 148, 150–1 + *ill*, 158, 180, 182, 188–9, 209
rhythm (music) 6, 38–9, 43, 56, 59 + *fn*, 64, 110–12, 144, 148–51, 155, 158–9, 168, 177–8, 181, 187–8, 193, 201
Rhythm of Resistance (documentary film) 45
Rice, Timothy 8, 10, 50–1, 207
riff 22, 38, 47, 64, 81, 83, 149 +*fn*, 151, 163, 164*ill*, 181, 191 + *ill*, 199 + *ill*, 200*ill*
Rogosin, Lionel: *Come Back Africa* 80*fn*
Rycroft, David K. 23, 44, 144–5, 146–7, 168, 170–1, 177, 183
  quoted 12, 13*fn*, 41*fn*, 56, 139

S
Sagiya (record company) 190
sangoma. see isangoma
saxophone 38, 125 + *ill*, 180
scales. *see also under* harmony
  blues scale 179 + *ill*, 180, 181
  heptatonic 155, 178, 200
  hexatonic 42, 54, 55, 145, 155, 190, 191, 199
  pentatonic 19, 42, 44, 50, 52*fn*, 54, 55, 57, 63 + *ill*, 124, 130 + *ill*, 131, 145, 155, 156, 178, 181, 199
  octatonic 44
scat 83, 159, 167
Scherzinger, Martin 3, 8, 9, 23, 51, 134, 137, 139–40
  quoted 61, 137, 154, 161, 204
'schizophonic mimesis'. *see under* Feld, Steven
Scotland 43–4
Second Lining 160
sefela 10
Sgqebhezana (Talker) 80, 81, 167
Shabalala, Bhekizizwe Joseph 98
  quoted 95–6
Shabalala, Njabulo 33, 120, 124*ill*, 126
Shaka kaSenzagakhona 59 + *fn*, 78
Shaka Zulu
  feature film 28*fn*
  television series 27–8
Shameni river 52–3
Shandu, Senzywsky Musho 93
Shingana 95
Shwi noMtekhala 21, 119, 163, 164, 171, 181
  'Imali' 36, 189*fn*
  'Ngafa' 10, 15, 108, 163, 164, 171, 189*fn*, 192
  lyrics 224–6
  score 164*ill*. *see also* Xaba, Mandla; Magubane, Rodgers
Sikeyi (Peg for Oxen Yoke). *see* Clegg, Johnny
Simon, Paul: *Graceland* 33, 92, 94, 121
Small, Christopher 8, 12, 210
  quoted 3, 14
Smith, Bruce R. 132
  quoted 18
'soils of significance' (Eva Hoffman) 16, 45, 72, 77, 139, 154, 209, 211

Sotho 139
Soul Brothers (band) 163
soul (music genre) 71-2, 92, 154-5, 173, 185, 200, 201
    (musical quality) 163-4
South Africa
    audiences 124
    Constitution 78, 108
    Parliament 117
South African Broadcasting Corporation (SABC) 91, 115
South African popular musics 10, 181, 200
sponsors/sponsorship 94, 95, 104
Stable Theatre. see under Durban (eThekwini)
Steingo, Gavin 2, 5, 173
    quoted 18*fn*
'stereotype'. see under Bhabha, Homi
stick fighting. see umgangela
subaltern 4, 8, 10, 12, 17, 133-4, 165, 201, 211
sub-Saharan Africa 11, 41, 123, 176
Swazi 139, 148
swing (music genre) 124, 200
    (musical quality) 112-3, 155-6, 158, 159, 178, 193
Szendy, Peter 18, 19, 36, 209, 210, 211
    quoted 9, 18, 137, 183

T
Tembu 32, 59
texture (music) 40*ill*, 42, 55, 60-2, 64, 131, 144-8, 151-2, 155-6, 158, 177-8, 180, 195, 197*ill*, 204
'Third Space'. see under Bhabha, Homi
timbre 56, 57, 60-1, 64, 81-2, 130-1, 144, 148-50, 153, 159-60, 188, 190-1, 200
'transubstantiation' 206-8
Tropentheater Amsterdam 22, 122, 123, 127, 132, 205
Tsonga 139, 146-9
Tugela river 52, 54, 55, 69
tune/tuning 36, 38, 49-50, 52, 55-6, 57, 60, 131, 151, 185, 199
Turino, Thomas 2, 42, 43, 100, 154, 183
    quoted 7, 192, 206

U
ubeshu 19, 101, 105, 107, 124 + *ill*, 125-6, 128-30, 132, 172, 189
ubugaku 9, 32, 35*fn*, 38, 45, 55, 56, 73, 116, 120, 144, 149-50, 153, 155-6, 185, 205
ubukhosi 141*fn*
ubukunzi 34, 140, 142-3, 144, 150, 152, 154, 158, 224
ubuntu 104
ugubhu 9, 54, 56, 57, 139, 144, 145 (see also gourd bow)
Ukhozi FM (radio station) 115
ukugiya. see under dance
ukupika. see under maskanda instruments: guitar
ukuvamba. see under maskanda instruments: guitar
ululation 107
umakhweyana 15, 22, 34, 35*fn*, 39, 54, 55, 56, 139, 144-5, 146-7, 148, 149, 150, 159, 160, 167, 171, 183, 191, 201 (see also gourd bow)
    calabash 145
    score 145*ill*
umaskandi. see maskanda
umbaqanga. see mbaqanga
umbaselwa 33, 83, 101, 107, 108*ill*, 126, 189
umculo 6, 30
umgangela 34, 38, 59, 182
umgqashiyo. see under dance
Umkomazi Dance Group 111, 112 + *ill*
    'Ya khulum' ingoma' 111-12
    score 112*ill*
umlungu 86
umtsingo 57, 131, 139, 167
umuntu 86
umuthi 69-70, 142, 143, 152
umqonqo. see under dance
umzansi (south coast) 57 + *fn*. see also under dance; maskanda styles
Umzansi Zulu Dancers 117*fn*, 159*fn*
The Undercover Princes (television programme) 95
University of KwaZulu-Natal (UKZN). see under KwaZulu-Natal
US/North American culture 32, 165, 172-3, 176-7, 178, 180*fn*, 188
    African-American 163, 173, 200-1

V

vaudeville 38–9, 60
Venda 101, 139
Vibe FM (radio station). *see under* Durban (eThekwini)
Vilakazi, B. W. 168
    quoted 41*fn*
violin 11, 38, 180
Viveiros de Castro, Eduardo 2, 207
voice
    bending 150, 152*ill*, 159, 164
    blending 147, 148, 150,
    cry 57, 159, 163–4, 187–8, 189, 191, 203
    humming 59, 143, 151, 152, 188
    ibhodlo 22, 77, 81–3, 121, 134, 208–9
    inflections 38, 57, 80, 107, 148, 151, 159, 191
    multivocality 144, 147–8, 150
    war cry 31, 33, 83, 101, 121
volksliedjies
    'Sarie Marais' 43

W

Withers, Bill 173
West Africa 123, 126, 177
white appropriations 28–32, 75, 83–9, 205, 206, 211
World Music Network 91–2

X

Xaba, Mandla (a.k.a. Shwi) 119, 163
    on polygamy 108–9
    and Rodgers Magubane (a.k.a. Mtekhala) 36, 108, 164. *see also* Shwi noMtekhala
Xhosa 52, 87, 101*fn*3, 139, 191

Y

'Ya Khulum' Ingoma'
    see Umkomazi Dance Group
Youssou N'Dour 126
YouTube 29–31, 33*fn*, 137, 140

Z

Zambia 11, 107
Zimba, Kennedy 120
Zimbabwe 11, 120, 107
Zuiderpershuis, Antwerp 122, 123, 126
Zuluboy. *see* Majozi, Mxolisi
Zulu royal house 94, 95, 97, 104, 105, 106
    Onkweni branch 94. *see also* kings of Zulu nation
Zulu 77, 83, 87, 101*fn*3
    culture 13, 14, 27–8, 36, 61, 65, 71, 78, 95, 104, 105, 126, 128, 138–9, 141, 165, 172, 177
    deep Zulu 14, 15, 138–9, 141, 154, 177, 186, 202, 205
    dress 28 + *ill*, 32, 83*ill*
    heritage/tradition 39, 47, 57, 64, 71, 77, 78, 81, 91, 95, 104, 108, 130, 131, 138, 139, 154, 171–2, 173, 176 + *fn*, 178, 181, 188, 203, 207, 208
    identity/'Zuluness' 16, 19, 81, 82, 86, 91, 98–101, 104, 105, 121, 131, 132, 133, 138, 140, 185–6, 188
    Kingdom 33, 41
    language 28, 31, 32, 52, 74, 79, 81, 97, 99, 112, 166, 172
    nationalism/nationalists 71, 109, 115
    poetry 32
    speech 57, 148, 168, 171, 172, 177
    street guitar/wandering guitarist 11, 13, 14, 17–18, 27, 37, 40, 41, 42, 43, 50, 57, 70, 140–1, 180, 182 (*see also* Clegg, Johnny: *My Favourite Street Guitar Songs*)
    urban Zulu 14, 138–9, 186
    women's role 75, 77–8
    'Zulu Trad' 43, 139
Zuma, Jacob Gedleyihlekisa 119
Zuz'Muzi (record company) 92, 118
Zwelithini, Goodwill kaBhekuzulu 27, 123

www.ingramcontent.com/pod-product-compliance
Lightning Source LLC
Chambersburg PA
CBHW062123300426
44115CB00012BA/1783